Earth Wise

Earth Wise

A Guide to Today's Environmental Issues

THOMAS G. SPIRO *and*
HELEN H. SPIRO
with ALEXANDRA SOLDATOVA

McFarland & Company, Inc., Publishers
Jefferson, North Carolina

ISBN (print) 978-1-4766-9808-3
ISBN (ebook) 978-1-4766-5587-1

LIBRARY OF CONGRESS CATALOGING DATA ARE AVAILABLE

Library of Congress Control Number 2025032242

Front cover image: © Sergey Nivens/Shutterstock

Printed in the United States of America

*McFarland & Company, Inc., Publishers
Box 611, Jefferson, North Carolina 28640
www.mcfarlandpub.com*

*To Aaron, Benji, Jordan, and Nate
and the generations to come*

Acknowledgments

We thank Larry Smith for inspiring us to write this book and providing important advice along the way.

And we thank Jen Fox, Larry Hubbell, Ron Kaufman, Jeremy Nobel, Gordan Orians, Gini Stimpson, and Mary Margaret Welch for stimulating discussions and encouragement.

Table of Contents

Preface

Earth Wise is a comprehensive guide to today's critical environmental issues. It goes behind the headlines to explain underlying causes simply and clearly and to consider proposed solutions. Concise yet also wide-ranging, *Earth Wise* explores the many environmental systems of our planet. It deals with the impacts of human activity and presents both the harms caused and the positive measures needed to address them. In 11 chapters, the topics range from climate change and energy, through air pollution and access to clean water, to food production, biodiversity, and, finally, sustainability.

Thomas and Helen Spiro wrote *Earth Wise* collaboratively. They were joined by Alexandra Soldatova, an environmental research scientist, who produced instructive illustrations, checked facts and references, and offered editorial suggestions. We view *Earth Wise* as a legacy to the next generation, who inevitably must deal with the environmental issues we describe.

Helen Spiro has a professional background in law, writing, and education and served as executive director of the Rutgers University Environmental and Occupational Health Sciences Institute. She took on the vital task of making sure the *Earth Wise* narrative is both lively and accessible to non-scientists.

Tom Spiro, a chemistry professor, taught for many years at Princeton University, where in 1970, at the height of student unrest over the war in Vietnam, he was asked to teach something of societal relevance. He responded by developing and launching one of the first courses in environmental chemistry. At that time, people around the world were becoming aware of the need to protect the environment, spurred by the beautiful images of the planet beamed back to Earth in 1968 by the first astronauts. Nineteen seventy also saw the celebration of the first Earth Day and the creation of the U.S. Environmental Protection Agency. The United States and many other countries adopted laws regulating air and water quality, the release of toxic substances, and the protection of endangered species.

Teaching and developing that environmental course led Thomas Spiro to write a college text, *Chemistry of the Environment* (University Science Books), now in its third edition. *Earth Wise* grew out of this textbook writing experience. But the material is entirely new, synthesized from a wide range of sources, from research reports to news articles and websites.

The concluding chapter of *Earth Wise* grapples with what it will take to leave our planet at least as well off as we found it. In this chapter we encounter individuals and organizations that are working creatively to improve the environment. They take the long view and are committed to future generations—a view that we also share.

Introduction

When astronauts first orbited the moon on the *Apollo 8* mission in 1968, one of them, Bill Anders, turned his camera to the moon's horizon, where planet Earth was rising. The resulting photo electrified the world and set it on a new course.

Seeing our beautiful blue planet against the barren moonscape, suspended in the blackness of space, the astronauts were awestruck. They felt love and tenderness for our unique and fragile globe. After maneuvering outside the International Space Station in 2008, astronaut Ron Garon expressed his feelings in the *Orbital Perspective*:

> It was as if time stood still, and I was flooded with both emotion and awareness. But as I looked down at the Earth—this stunning, fragile oasis, this island that has been given to us, and that has protected all life from the harshness of space—a sadness came over me.... In spite of the overwhelming beauty of this scene, serious inequity exists on the apparent paradise we have been given.... Seeing Earth from this vantage point gave me a unique perspective.... We are all traveling together on the planet and ... if we all looked at the world from that perspective we would see that nothing is impossible.[1]

These feelings were shared by many on Earth, creating a visceral urge to unite and protect it. It is no accident that the first Earth Day was celebrated around the world in 1970. Of course, admiration of the earth's beauty has always existed in us. In 1854, Henry David Thoreau wrote movingly of his love and respect for nature in *Walden* and advocated for preservation of wild spaces in his home state of Massachusetts. In 1872, spurred by the inspirational writings of naturalist John Muir,[2] the United States established Yellowstone National Park, the world's first large-scale wilderness preservation. The idea spread to other countries around the world. In the 1960s the focus shifted to the preservation of the environment more broadly. Two biologists were especially influential: Rachel Carson wrote *Silent Spring*,[3] alerting a wide public to the environmental damage from massive application of pesticides, and Paul Ehrlich wrote *The Population Bomb*,[4] questioning how many people the planet could support. At the end

3

FIGURE 1. Taken aboard *Apollo 8* by Bill Anders on December 24, 1968, this iconic picture shows Earth peeking out from beyond the lunar surface as the first crewed spacecraft circumnavigated the Moon, with astronauts Anders, Frank Borman, and Jim Lovell aboard. Image credit: NASA.

of the decade, the astronauts' view from space brought home the realization that our planet is unique and limited and that it needs our protection to sustain life.

Since 1970, this need has become more urgent. In 1970 the world's population stood at 3.6 billion, having increased by a billion just since 1951 and by two billion since 1900. Today there are eight billion of us sharing the planet, and the number is projected to grow to nine to 10 billion by 2050. The surge in population over the last two centuries was mainly the result of continuing high birth rates but lower death rates, thanks to improved sanitation and nutrition. Recently birth rates have been falling around the world, as decreasing child mortality and better education have improved economic prospects for families. It is likely that the population will stabilize during this century. But that still leaves a huge population to share the earth's resources. Whether this can be done sustainably and equitability is a critical issue for humanity.

Meanwhile, another critical issue is whether the earth can sustain the waste that we generate. As the population increases, and with it the desire for a better life, consumption of food and goods increases faster, placing stresses on the environment. Pollution is one facet of the problem, and global warming is the other. Rising standards of living have been driven by the Industrial Revolution and burning of fossil fuels to generate energy. The worldwide combustion of coal, oil, and gas is raising the level of carbon dioxide and other heat-trapping (*greenhouse*) gases. In turn, the steadily rising temperatures at Earth's surface are increasing the intensity of heat waves, melting glaciers and the polar ice sheets, and raising the ocean level. They are intensifying droughts, storms, and floods. Habitat destruction, economic losses, and human misery are all increasing with the changing climate. Global warming has become the overarching challenge of our time.

But humans are capable of solving problems as well as creating them. In addition to Earth Day, 1970 saw the creation of the U.S. Environmental Protection Agency, and the United Nations Environment Programme (UNEP) was established in 1972. Laws regulating air and water quality, the release of toxic substances, and the protection of endangered species were enacted in the United States and around the world. In many regions the regulations worked well. The air became cleaner in many cities, and polluted rivers were cleaned up. The harnessing of renewable energy by solar cells and modern windmills brought promise for the replacement of fossil fuels, while energy-efficiency technology slowed the increase in power plants. But growing populations and economic development overwhelm these gradual improvements. The rapidly growing cities of the developing world have become severely polluted, and the demand for more energy rises inexorably.

Yet consciousness of the dangers is spreading widely. Public interest in the environment is heightening, putting pressure on governments and businesses. *Sustainability* has become a watchword for cities and corporations, as measures are put in place to promote clean energy and less waste. Being worldwide, the problems need international cooperation. In 1992, the UN convened an Earth Summit in Rio de Janeiro, its first Conference on Environment and Development. The meeting focused on climate change, the loss of biological diversity, and the destruction of forests and soils. This was followed in 1997 by a meeting in Kyoto, Japan, which produced a protocol, signed by 192 countries, that set definite targets for greenhouse gas reductions. Then, in 2015, the Paris Agreement committed countries to strengthen these targets in order to limit global warming to 1.5°C (2.7°F) above pre-industrial levels. The global temperature elevation is already 1°C, and we are feeling the effects of climate change. The 1.5°C target was chosen to avoid more disastrous effects.

The required reductions in greenhouse gas emissions are very large, and it is unclear whether they will be achieved. But there is widespread determination to do so. Scientists have known since the late 19th century that greenhouse gases warm the earth[5] and have been warning about the dangers of global warming for a long time.[6] For much of that time governments paid little heed despite the accumulating evidence of climate change. More than 30 years passed between the Rio and Paris meetings, and the warming continues. Many people still don't believe that human activity is responsible or that we can do anything about it. Or they think the price of trying would be too high. Powerful economic interests, particularly the fossil fuel companies, have fueled climate skepticism and outright denial. But the tide of opinion has shifted. Increasingly, people believe that we have to do something if the earth is to remain habitable for our children and their children. Meanwhile, there is heightened concern about air and water pollution and its inequitable burden on low-income communities, especially those of color.

This book is intended for those concerned, and sometimes confused, by the recurring headlines about environmental issues. It aims to provide background on how environmental forces work and their effects on us and on the habitat we share with one another and with the other creatures living on the earth.

The chapters deal with climate change, with air and water pollution, with land use and food production, with health and toxic substances, and with energy. How we generate and use energy undergirds all of our environmental issues. The book deals with problems, of course, but also points to promising solutions. It aims to provide readers with the grounding needed to evaluate the warnings and advice coming at us from all sides and to form their own opinions and plans for action.

1

Is Our Planet Warming,
and If So, Why?

1. Is the Climate Changing?

On June 30, 2019, a storm dumped three feet of hail on Mexico's Jalisco State. "I witnessed scenes that I had never seen before: hail more than a meter high," tweeted Enrique Alfaro, the governor of Jalisco, "and then we ask ourselves if climate change exists."[1]

There is no proof that this freakish weather event is directly tied to climate change. Still, people experience stronger hurricanes and more torrential rain than they can remember. Flooding extends farther than it did, especially along coasts. Lakes and rivers no longer freeze over the way they used to. Droughts last longer. Wildfires burn unprecedented amounts of forest as well as people's homes. Climate scientists warn that these effects come from warming of the planet. They are confident that the warming is caused by our releasing gases into the atmosphere, especially carbon dioxide, CO_2. CO_2 comes from burning fossil fuels: coal, oil, and gas. It also comes from burning and cutting down trees.

But some people are skeptical about all this. The argument about global warming and climate change is very emotional. After all, so much is at stake. Deforestation and fossil fuel use are tied to enormous industries and economic activity. Curbing them would cut profits, dislocate workers, and alter personal habits. If it is not true that humans drive climate change, if the variability in climate is natural, then we could avoid these painful and costly changes. So climate skeptics have great appeal, and their voices are amplified by intense lobbying, funded mainly by the industries whose profits are threatened.

2. Yes, the Planet Is Warming

Here is the evidence. Figure 2 shows temperatures from measurements taken around the globe and averaged over the year. The underlying upward trend is clear. For the past 50 years, the temperature has risen steadily. It increases more on land than in the oceans because water absorbs more heat than land does. The earth is now about 1.1°C (2°F) warmer than it was a century ago. A temperature rise of 1.1°C may seem pretty small, but it has big effects, as we'll see.

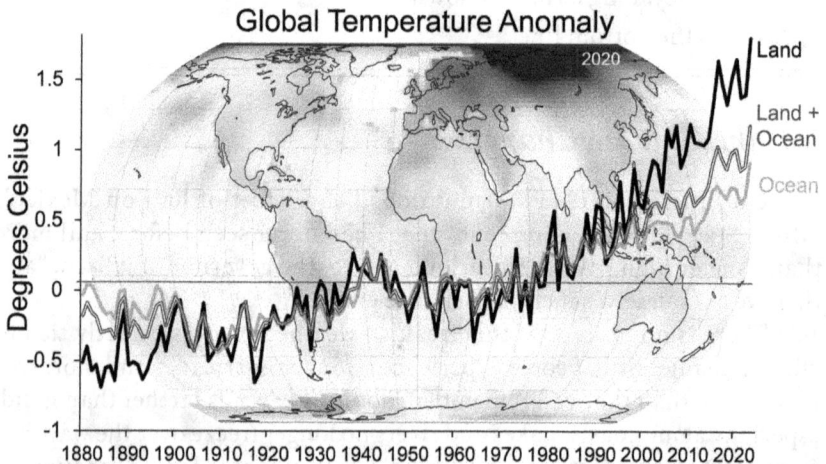

FIGURE 2. Global temperature differences from the 1901–2000 average on land and ocean surfaces (data from NOAA National Centers for Environmental information, Climate at a Glance: Global Time Series, August 2024). Background image is a heat map showing the increase in temperature (dark zones are the hottest) in 2020, relative to what they were 50 years earlier, from NASA Earth Observatory. Map credit: Joshua Stevens, based on data from the NASA Goddard Institute for Space Studies.

Some people brush off this temperature trend as just natural variability. "The earth has always gone through cycles of ice ages and warming; it is no different now," they say. And yes, long ago there *were* ice ages, many of them. Scientists plotted the zigzag temperature pattern in Figure 3, which extends back nearly a million years.[2] They measured deuterium/hydrogen ratios in annual layers of deep ice cores from Antarctica. This ratio tracks the temperature because water evaporates at different rates when it contains the two forms of hydrogen.

The glacial cycles coincide with changes in Earth's orbit around the sun, which bring the planet closer or farther from the sun.[3] Scientists are still figuring out exactly why the temperature swings occurred. One reason is that when Earth is closer to the sun, the ice sheets start to melt. The melting exposes darker water below. The darker water absorbs more

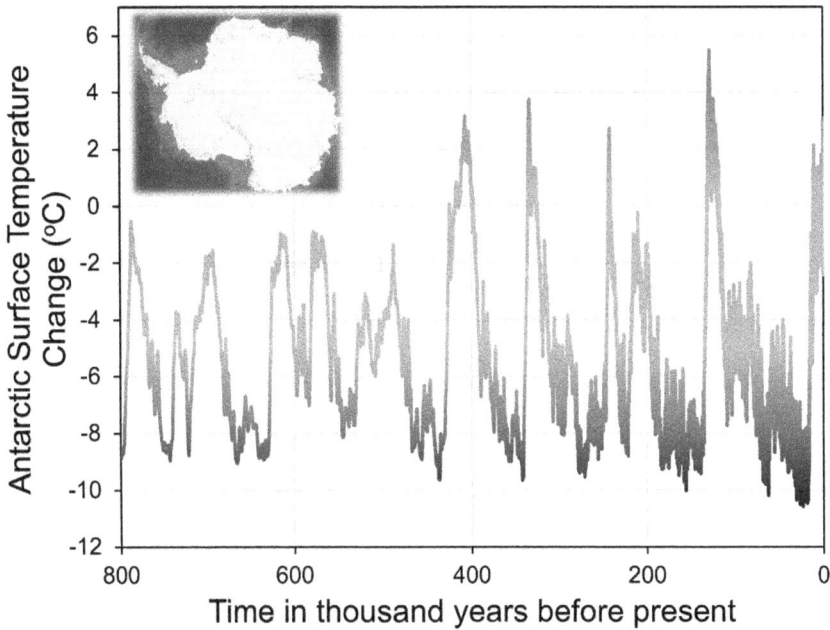

FIGURE 3. Surface temperature changes in Antarctica, showing eight consecutive glacial cycles, plotted using data from Jean Jouzel and Valerie Masson-Delmotte, "EPICA Dome C Ice Core 800KYr Deuterium Data and Temperature Estimates," *PANGAEA* (2007), https://doi.org/10.1594/PANGAEA.683655, a supplement to Jean Jouzel et al., "Orbital and Millennial Antarctic Climate Variability Over the Past 800,000 Years," *Science* 317, no. 5839 (August 10, 2007): 793–96. Inset image of Antarctica generated from NASA Worldview application (https://worldview.earthdata.nasa.gov/), part of the NASA Earth Observing System Data and Information System (EOSDIS).

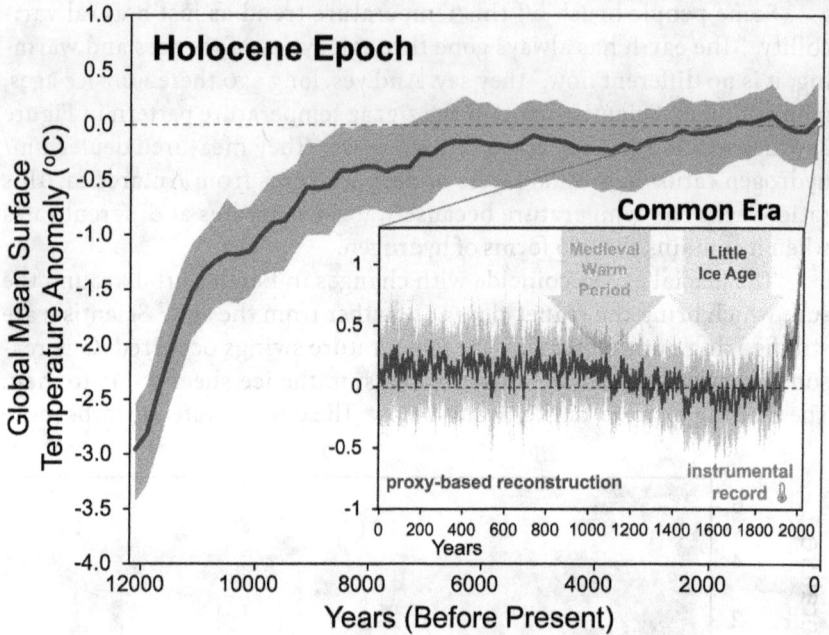

FIGURE 4. Global surface temperatures over the last 12,000 years. Data from the supplementary information file available from Matthew B. Osman et al., "Globally Resolved Surface Temperatures Since the Last Glacial Maximum," *Nature* 599, no. 7884 (November 10, 2021): 239–44. The inset gives an expanded view of the last 2,000 years from PAGES 2k Consortium (PAGES2k Consortium: Raphael Neukom et al., "Consistent Multidecadal Variability in Global Temperature Reconstructions and Simulations over the Common Era," *Nature Geoscience* 12, no. 8 (July 24, 2019): 643–49; plotted using data from Raphael Neukom et al., "NOAA/WDS Paleoclimatology-PAGES2k Common Era Surface Temperature Reconstructions," NOAA National Centers for Environmental Information (July 24, 2019), https://doi.org/10.25921/tkxp-vn12. The gray areas represent the range of uncertainty in the data. From 1850 onward, global near-surface temperature from direct measurements (Colin P. Morice et al., "An Updated Assessment of Near-Surface Temperature Change from 1850: The HadCRUT5 Data Set," *Journal of Geophysical Research: Atmospheres* 126, no. 3 (February 16, 2021): e2019JD032361, the HadCRUT5 data set, downloaded from HadCRUT.5.0.1.0 data, downloaded from http://www.metoffice.gov.uk/hadobs/hadcrut5 on October 8, 2023 © British Crown Copyright, Met Office 2021, provided under an Open Government License, http://www.nationalarchives.gov.uk/doc/open-government-licence/version/3/.

sunlight, so Earth heats up more. As Earth moves farther from the sun, this effect runs in reverse, cooling the planet. There were eight glacial cycles, or ice ages. The last ice age ended about 12,000 years ago, and we are now enjoying the warm, interglacial period.

Would that explain the current warming trend? If we zoom in and look more closely at the last 12,000 years (Figure 4),[4] the recent temperature increase is really striking. To reconstruct the temperature on the shorter timescales, scientists measure the width of annual tree rings[5] and the different isotopes of the element oxygen in seashells.[6]

After a quick post-glacial warm-up about 7,000 years ago, the earth's temperature was relatively stable till the middle of the 20th century, when it suddenly rose rapidly. And the rising temperature is global, no matter where on Earth the measurements are taken. This dramatic rise is clearly not part of the natural variability seen in the ice age temperature pattern.

3. Why Is It Warming?

The recent temperature rise closely tracks the level of CO_2 in the atmosphere (Figure 5).[7] The rise of CO_2 started with the Industrial Revolution, powered by burning coal, oil, and natural gas, called fossil fuels. The name derives from these fuels having been formed in the earth from the remains of prehistoric plants and animals that were buried before they had a chance to decompose. CO_2 also comes from deforestation, much of it tied to clearing land for industrial farming, particularly in the tropics.

The amount of carbon burned annually throughout the industrial era (Figure 6)[8] resembles the graph of CO_2 concentration in the atmosphere (Figure 5).

Human beings, with their home heating and cooling, their cars and planes, their industries and their commercial farms have steadily pumped CO_2 into the air. But that doesn't prove that humans caused the warming, or does it? How can CO_2 heat up the earth? The answer is the "greenhouse effect."

4. What Is the Greenhouse Effect?

A greenhouse works by allowing the sun to shine through the glass roof to heat the plants and earth below. The heat can't easily pass back through the glass, so it stays trapped there (Figure 7). Also, the walls and roof prevent the heated air from mixing with the surrounding air.

Similarly, when the sun heats up the earth, the heat stays trapped in the earth's atmosphere (Figure 7). The sun is so hot that it produces white light, like an iron rod when it is heated to very high temperatures in a

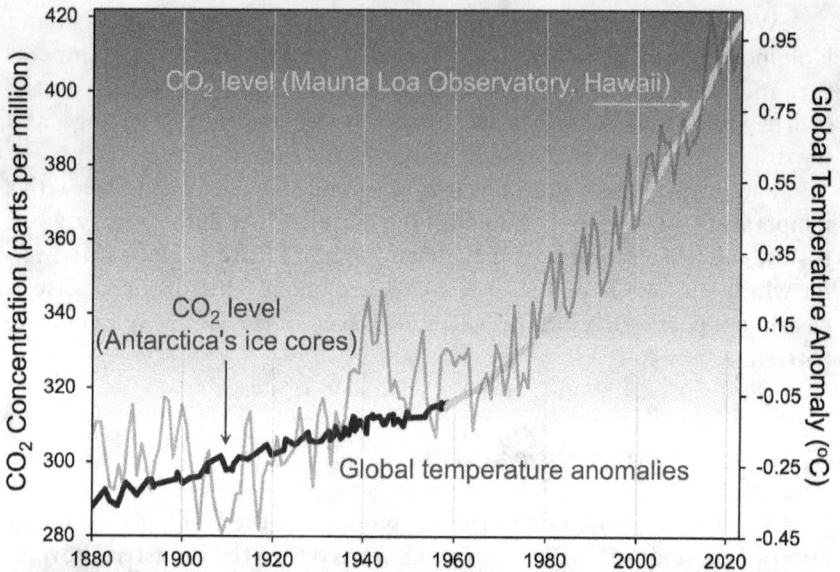

FIGURE 5. Atmospheric CO_2 level, determined in Antarctica's ice core bubbles (from Mauro Rubino et al., "A Revised 1000 Year Atmospheric $\delta 13C\text{-}C_{O2}$ Record from Law Dome and South Pole, Antarctica," *Journal of Geophysical Research: Atmospheres* 118, no. 15 (August 16, 2013): 8482–99); data downloaded from Bernhard Bereiter et al., "Antarctic Ice Cores Revised 800KYr CO_2 Data," NOAA National Centers for Environmental Information dataset (2015) on October 5, 2023, from http://ncdc.noaa.gov/paleo/study/17975, which is a supplement to Bernhard Bereiter et al., "Revision of the EPICA Dome C CO_2 Record from 800 to 600 Kyr Before Present," *Geophysical Research Letters* 42, no. 2 (January 28, 2015): 542–49). CO_2 level after 1958 is from air samples at the Mauna Loa, Hawai'i, observatory measured by NOAA from the mid-troposphere-8 to 12 kilometers (~5 to 7 miles)-above the ground; data from NOAA Global Monitoring Laboratory, "Global Climate Change. Vital Signs of the Planet," https://climate.nasa.gov/vital-signs/carbon-dioxide, accessed on August 27, 2024. Due to the eruption of the Mauna Loa volcano, measurements from Mauna Loa Observatory were suspended as of November 29, 2022. Observations starting in December 2022 are from a site at the Maunakea Observatories, approximately 21 miles north of the Mauna Loa Observatory. The CO_2 measurements track the global temperature record.

furnace. When the rod is removed and cooled, it turns red and then stops glowing. But if you put your hand a few inches away, you will still feel the heat. The radiation is no longer visible because our eyes are not sensitive to it. It is called "infrared" because it is redder than our eyes can see. The glass panes of the greenhouse, and the earth's atmosphere, are transparent to the sun's white light, but they absorb and re-radiate infrared

Global CO_2 Emissions from Fossil Fuel Use and Industry

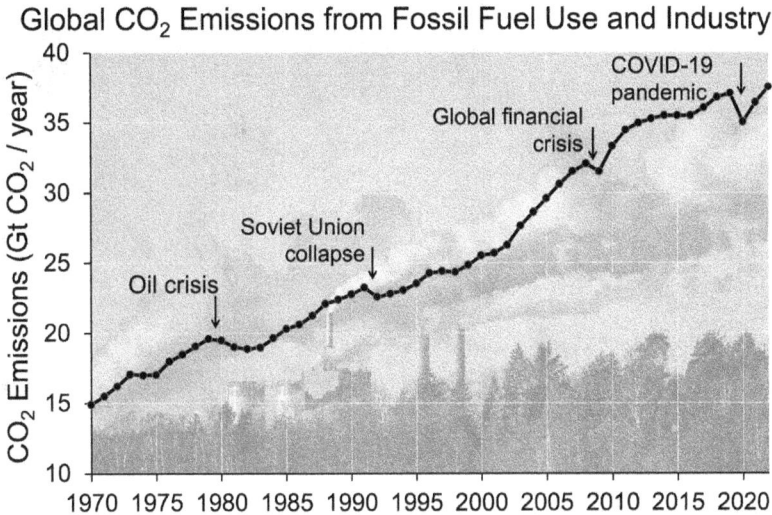

FIGURE 6. Global CO_2 emissions from fossil fuel use and cement production (1Gt = 1 billion tons). Data downloaded from Global Carbon Project (2023): Pierre Friedlingstein et al., "Global Carbon Budget 2023," *Earth System Science Data* 15, no. 12 (December 5, 2023): 5301–69. Supplemental data of Global Carbon Budget 2023 (Version 1.1) [Data set], downloaded from https://doi.org/10.18160/gcp-2023 on August 23, 2024. Background photo by Daniel Moqvist on Unsplash, downloaded from https://unsplash.com/photos/white-clouds-over-city-buildings-during-daytime-WZw6zs0kKzo. The indicated historical crises produced dips in the steady upward trend.

light emitted by the heated earth. This is what keeps the air warm in the greenhouse and at Earth's surface. (The glass greenhouse is further heated because the air inside cannot mix with the outside air.)

We are lucky to have the greenhouse effect. Without it, Earth's surface would be 33°C (59°F) colder than it is, and everything would be frozen. But we are now getting too much of a good thing. The increasing CO_2 is amplifying the greenhouse effect, leading to global warming.

5. How Do CO_2, and a Few Other Gases, Produce Earth's Greenhouse Effect?

Here is a puzzle. CO_2 is only 0.04 percent of all the atmospheric gases[9] (Figure 8; the concentration is often given as 400 ppm [parts per million], which is the same thing).

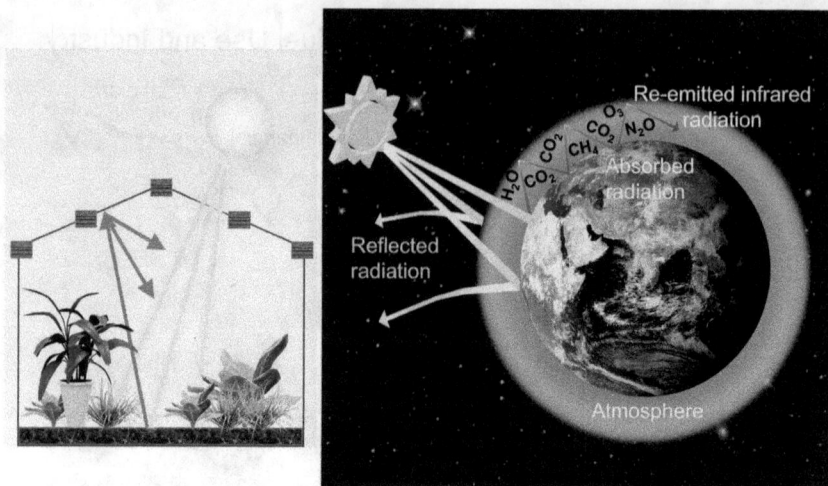

FIGURE 7. *Left*: In a greenhouse, the glass is transparent to sunlight but traps the earth's heat. *Right*: Earth's atmosphere is likewise transparent to sunlight, but CO_2 and other greenhouse gases absorb and re-radiate Earth's infrared radiation, which heats up the surface. Earth image in the center is from the collection Blue Marble, NASA Goddard Space Flight Center Image by Reto Stöckli, downloaded from https://visibleearth.nasa.gov/images/57723/the-blue-marble. The starfield image by NASA's Near-Earth Object Wide-Field Infrared Survey Explorer (NEOWISE). Credit: NASA/JPL-Caltech/IPAC/UCLA, downloaded from https://www.jpl.nasa.gov/images/pia26385-nasas-neowise-captures-final-image-moments-before-end-of-mission.

How can such a minor amount drive climate change? The answer is that most of the air molecules cannot absorb infrared radiation and so cannot trap heat. In order of abundance, they are nitrogen, N_2 (78 percent), oxygen, O_2 (21 percent), and argon, Ar (0.93 percent). So 99.9 percent of air molecules have only one or two atoms. But three or more atoms are needed to absorb infrared radiation. That's why CO_2 comes to the fore, even though its abundance is only 0.04 percent. Other molecules with three or more atoms are even less abundant. (This accounting is for dry air. The important but separate role of water molecules, H_2O, is discussed below.)

Many polyatomic molecules enter the atmosphere all the time, but most of them react with light and O_2 fast enough that they do not build up significantly. However, CO_2 is stable and lasts for decades until it is absorbed by the oceans or taken up by green plants through photosynthesis. It is the most important "greenhouse gas."

Methane, CH_4, is the second most important greenhouse gas. It is the main component of natural gas that is used for heating buildings or for gas

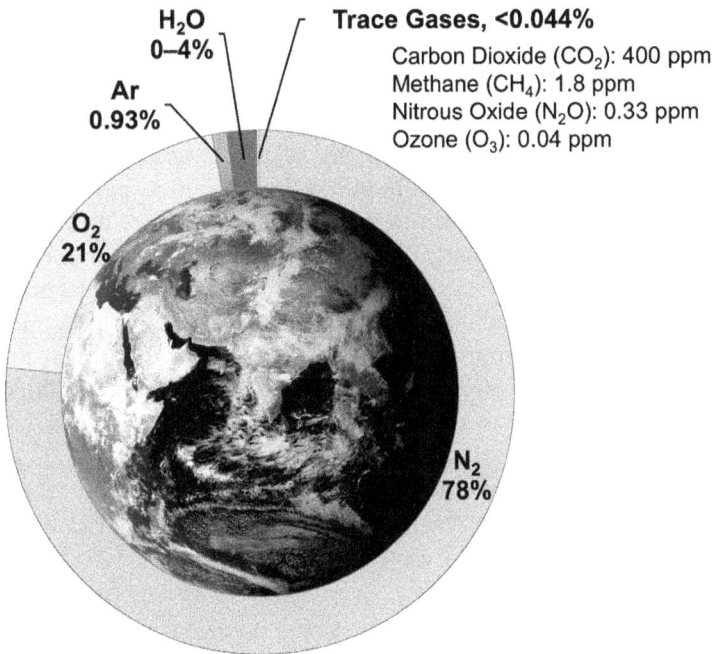

H_2O
0–4%

Ar
0.93%

O_2
21%

Trace Gases, <0.044%

Carbon Dioxide (CO_2): 400 ppm
Methane (CH_4): 1.8 ppm
Nitrous Oxide (N_2O): 0.33 ppm
Ozone (O_3): 0.04 ppm

N_2
78%

FIGURE 8. Diagram of the atmosphere's composition. The greenhouse gas concentrations are too small to be seen. They are listed in the figure. Earth image in the center is from the collection Blue Marble, *NASA Goddard Space Flight Center Image by Reto Stöckli*, downloaded from https://visibleearth.nasa.gov/images/57723/the-blue-marble.

stoves. It leaks into the atmosphere from production wells and pipelines. Gas production soared recently, after "fracking" was introduced. Fracking gets at gas trapped in rock layers by fracturing the rock with high-pressure water to release the gas.[10] Methane also comes from bacteria living in wetlands, landfills, rice paddies, manure ponds, and the stomachs of cows. Methane in the atmosphere is rising even faster than CO_2.

Molecule for molecule, methane is a much more powerful greenhouse gas than CO_2 (30 times more powerful on a 100-year timescale), but it disappears in about 12 years through reactions in the atmosphere.[11] Because it is so powerful, reducing methane emissions benefits the climate even more than curbing CO_2 emissions. Methane escape can be slowed by plugging leaks, capping landfills, and improving agricultural practices.

The third most important greenhouse gas is nitrous oxide, N_2O, which is 300 times more powerful on a 100-year timescale than CO_2.[12] N_2O is produced by bacteria acting on nitrogen compounds. N_2O stays in the atmosphere for a long time, and its concentration has also been rising faster than CO_2. The main culprit is nitrogen fertilizer, used in great amounts to increase crop yields.

Some industrial chemicals will also become important greenhouse gases if their production is not controlled. Chlorofluorocarbons, CFCs,[13] which contain chlorine and fluorine atoms, bonded to carbon atoms, are exceptionally strong and long-lived greenhouse gases. They don't get destroyed till they drift into the stratosphere. Once used extensively as foaming agents for plastics (e.g., Styrofoam) and as refrigerator fluids (the "freons"), they are now regulated and are going out of production (see Chapter 2, "What about the Ozone Hole?"). Despite this, atmospheric CFCs are still rising from discarded products that contain them and from industrial side products. Another industrial gas, sulfur hexafluoride, SF_6, is even more stable than the chlorofluorocarbons.[14] Used as an insulator in high-voltage transformers and wind power generators, SF_6 is accumulating in the atmosphere and is already responsible for 0.2 percent of the extra warming by greenhouse gases. SF_6 is included in international agreements on curbing greenhouse gases (see Chapter 2, "Curbing Emissions").

6. Water Vapor Is a Big Player

Actually, the most important greenhouse gas of all is water, H_2O. Water vapor is a potent absorber of infrared radiation[15] and is much more abundant than CO_2. Averaged over the globe, water vapor is about 4 percent of the atmosphere, 100-fold higher than CO_2. So why worry about CO_2?

The answer is that temperature controls water vapor rather than the other way around. Humidity increases with temperature, as water molecules escape from rivers, lakes, and oceans. When the earth warms, water vapor goes up, and being a greenhouse gas, it increases, warming further. This is called a positive feedback. The warming effect of additional CO_2, or of the other greenhouse gases, becomes larger because of water.

7. How Long Have We Known?

The greenhouse effect is very old news.

- It was proposed as early as 1824 by the renowned French scientist and mathematician Joseph Fourier.[16]
- In 1856, the American scientist Eunice Newton Foote (also an inventor and women's rights campaigner) first discovered that certain gases warmed when exposed to sunlight and predicted that

rising CO_2 levels would increase atmospheric temperature.[17] Sadly, her scientific contributions went unnoticed until rediscovered by 20th-century women scientists. In 2022, the American Geophysical Union instituted the Eunice Newton Foote Medal for Earth-Life Science in her honor.

- In 1861, the Irish physicist John Tyndal discovered that trace gases, especially H_2O and CO_2, were responsible for warming the atmosphere.[18]
- In 1886, the Swedish chemist Svante Arrhenius calculated the expected warming of the planet from a doubling of the CO_2 concentration.[19]

So the basic science of the greenhouse effect has been known for a very long time. As more and more CO_2 poured into the atmosphere from fossil fuel burning, 20th-century scientists looked more closely at the likely effect on the climate. Computers made possible increasingly sophisticated studies of climate. Some of the best studies were carried out by scientists who worked for fossil fuel companies. These companies needed to know whether their assets, the coal, oil, and gas deposits, were at risk. And they were. Their scientists' climate analyses agreed with those of independent scientists. They concluded that increasing emissions from fossil fuels would indeed lead to global warming. Since at least 1977, Exxon scientists warned their executives of "potentially catastrophic" human-caused global warming.[20] But the companies chose not to publicize these warnings. Instead, they launched a decades-long public relations campaign to sow doubt on climate science.

In 1988, in the midst of a record heat wave, NASA scientist Jim Hansen warned the U.S. Congress that "the greenhouse effect has been detected and is changing our climate now."[21] In response, many energy and fossil fuel companies formed the Global Climate Coalition to lobby U.S. politicians and media to dismiss climate science. Legal proceedings revealed the companies' internal scientific work and their subsequent public relations and lobbying campaign. Suits against the companies were brought for the damages incurred through climate change.[22] Climate change litigation started in the United States in the 1980s and then spread globally. In 2021, a Dutch court made headlines by ruling that by 2030, Shell oil must reduce emissions by 45 percent. By 2022, there were 1,550 cases in 38 countries holding corporations accountable for impacts of climate change,[23] and the number continues to grow. How many cases succeed and how judgments will be enforced remains to be seen. But the litigation is impacting public perception of climate change and the role of fossil fuels.

Energy companies supported and publicized skeptical scientists.

These individuals doubted the climate science, without actually having participated in the research. An able communicator for climate skeptics, Jerry Taylor appeared regularly on TV and radio to insist that the climate change science was uncertain and there was no need to act. He changed his mind in 2014 after realizing that his arguments were based on a misinterpretation of the science. He expressed regret about his role in the debate: "For 25 years, climate skeptics like me made it a core matter of ideological identity that if you believe in climate change, then you are by definition a socialist. That is what climate skeptics have done."[24]

8. *The Bottom Line*

Yes, the globe is warming and at a rate exceeding anything for thousands of years. And yes, the warming is because of carbon dioxide as well as methane and nitrous oxide, all of which are increasing fast because of us humans. In the next chapter we will look at the consequences of this warming.

2

So Why Does
Warming Matter?

Topics:

1. What are the consequences of global warming?
   A. Heat waves
   B. Wildfires
   C. Ocean heating and acidification
   D. Sea level rise
   E. Melting ice
   F. Ocean current slowing
   G. Crop failure
   H. Ecosystem destruction
   I. Disease spread
   J. Climate anxiety
   K. Loss of insurance
2. How does warming lead to extreme weather?
   A. Storm intensity
   B. Floods
   C. Even cold snaps
   D. Droughts
   E. Climate refugees
3. How warm will it get? Climate modeling
4. What can we do?
   A. Curbing emissions
   B. Maintaining forests
   C. Adaptation
   D. Geoengineering
5. Where do we stand?

---

1. What Are the Consequences of Global Warming?

(A) Heat Waves

Heat waves already produce more casualties than any other natural disaster, and the toll will likely steadily rise with increasing global temperatures. In the United States, 1,600 people died of heat-related causes in 2021, 60 percent more than the number four years earlier.[1] Europe saw about 60,000 heat-related deaths in the record-breaking heat wave of summer 2022.[2] As the average global temperature increases, heat waves become hotter and last longer, and Europe is already experiencing this effect, summer after summer (Figure 9).[3]

High extreme temperatures can be deadly for older people and people

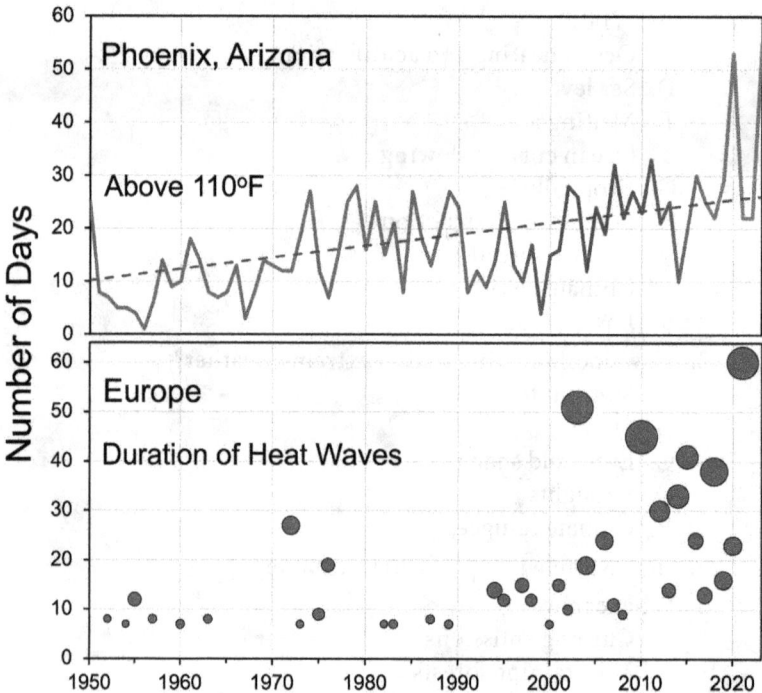

FIGURE 9. *Top*: Number of days above 110°F (43°C) in Phoenix, Arizona, tripled in the last six decades. Data are from SC ACIS Version 2, NOAA Northeast Regional Climate Center, http://scacis.rcc-acis.org. *Bottom*: Duration of heat waves in Europe and their magnitude (area and severity), expressed by circle sizes, plotted using data from Table 1 in Ondřej Lhotka and Jan Kyselý, "The 2021 European Heat Wave in the Context of Past Major Heat Waves," *Earth and Space Science* 9, no. 11 (November 4, 2022): e2022EA002567.

with cardiovascular or respiratory conditions. People without access to air-conditioning or who work outside are especially vulnerable. People are less productive during heat waves and become irritable; violent incidents increase.

Heat waves particularly affect cities because buildings and pavement absorb heat; the resulting higher temperature is called the "urban heat island" effect. Phoenix, one of the fastest growing cities in the United States, is a prime example of this effect; the number of days with temperature above 110°F (43°C) tripled since the 1950s (Figure 9). Trees can provide shade, and buildings with "cool roofs" that reflect sunlight decrease heat exposure, but they are sparse in cities. Since trees are scarcest in the impoverished parts of cities, poor people are particularly affected by the heat island effect.

People retreat to air-conditioned buildings if they can. Phoenix grew to be the fifth largest city in the United States because of air-conditioning, which enabled it to endure 55 days with temperatures over 110°F in 2023 (Figure 9). But most of the world doesn't have air-conditioning because it is expensive. And if there is a power failure, air conditioners are useless. When all the air conditioners turn on at once, they strain the energy system. During heat waves power failures are more likely, worsening negative health outcomes.

Some places around the globe will become too hot to live in. According to a recent study,[4] nearly half the world's population will face heat that is beyond human tolerance: 2.2 billion people in Pakistan and India's Indus River Valley, one billion in eastern China, and 800 million in sub–Saharan Africa. These populations are mainly low income, illustrating how heat waves are a major source of climate injustice.

(B) Wildfires

Rising temperatures dry the land, so vegetation burns easily. Wildfires erupt suddenly, threatening people, buildings, and wildlife. On August 11, 2023, a fire burst onto the historic Hawaiian town of Lahaina, with almost no warning. About 100 people died and 2,200 buildings were destroyed.[5] The flames were fueled by thick grasses that spread above the town during the wet spring and dried out during the hot summer. Large-scale ranching and sugarcane and pineapple plantations spread over much of Hawai'i during the 1800s but declined in recent decades due to high production costs. The abandoned plantations were taken over by invasive African grasses that had evolved to burn and regrow quickly.[6] Hawai'i is now at high risk from annual wildfires.

Wildfires spread polluting smoke over wide regions and release vast quantities of CO_2. This is an example of *positive feedback*: the hotter the climate, the more the forests burn, and the more CO_2 the fires release, the hotter the climate.

Forest fires are natural, of course. Some trees even require periodic fires to open their seeds and renew growth. But even those trees cannot survive the intense fires brought on by stronger heat waves. Fires are also more intense when the trees are stressed by destructive insects that spread further during hot weather. Intense fires also destroy ground cover, causing mudslides when the rains come. Most U.S. wildfires start with highly combustible dry grass and shrubs. Fires in the United States burned over five times as many acres in 2020 as in 1983 (Figure 10).[7]

In 2019–2020, unprecedentedly large fires ravaged Australia because of a severe drought and intense heat wave. On the hottest day, the average maximum temperature across the entire continent was 41.9°C (107°F). Over 24 million acres burned across the country.[8] It was the costliest natural disaster in Australian history.

In 2023, wildfires burned across the forests of Canada, over an area the size of North Dakota, comprising about 5 percent of Canada's total forest.[9] Tens of thousands of people fled their homes, including the residents

FIGURE 10. Annual acreage of U.S. wildland fires increased fivefold from 1983 to 2022. Data from the U.S. National Interagency Fire Center, "Wildfire and Acres. Total Wildland Fires and Acres (1983–2023)," https://www.nifc.gov/fire-information/statistics/wildfires, accessed August 25, 2024. Background photo by Kyle Miller, Wyoming Hotshots, U.S. Forest Service, taken on August 3, 2020, during the Pine Gulch Fire in Colorado, downloaded from https://www.flickr.com/photos/nifc/50320947931/in/gallery-189503663@N07c-72157716656992987.

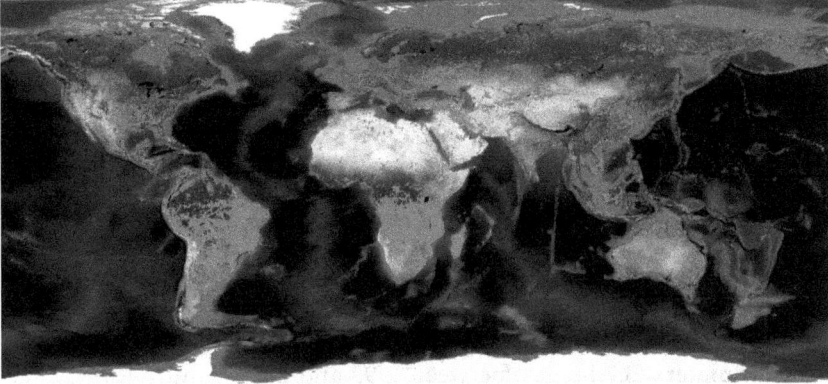

FIGURE 11. Forest fires around the world during September 2020, seen through overlays of satellite photographs. The map is generated from NASA Fire Information for Resource Management System satellite observations (NASA FIRMS), part of NASA's Earth Observing System Data and Information System (EOSDIS).

of Yellowknife, the capital of the Northwest Territories. Smoke from the fires drifted over much of the country and south across the U.S. border, fouling the air of Midwest and Northeastern states, eventually reaching Europe. The fires emitted some 1.5 billion tons of CO_2, triple the annual amount released directly from fossil fuel use in Canada.[10]

Vast swaths of the world's tropical forests have burned, often from fires deliberately set to clear land. The NASA photo in Figure 11 captures the dramatic worldwide extent of fires seen from space during September 2020. The tropical forests have been absorbing huge amounts of CO_2, offsetting some of the rising emissions from fossil fuels. But now they are on the verge of emitting more CO_2 from logging and wildfires than they are absorbing.[11]

(C) Ocean Heating and Acidification

The oceans absorb 90 percent of the increased greenhouse warming. Rising water temperatures stress sea creatures because the oxygen they need is less soluble in warm water. Aquatic species are disappearing at double the rate of land-based species.[12] Locally caught fish are an important source of protein for about half the world's population. As the fish migrate to colder water, they disrupt historical fishing rights and promote conflicts among fishing fleets (see Chapter 9).

Not only are oceans getting warmer; they are becoming more acidic because CO_2 dissolved in water becomes an acid. As the acidity goes up, sea creatures have greater difficulty forming shells. Some oyster farms already feel this effect, producing fewer and smaller oysters. Coral reefs, which harbor innumerable sea animals, are in trouble. When heated, coral polyps "bleach," expelling their colorful life-giving algae. The acidity hampers their reef-building ability (see Chapter 8).

(D) Sea Level Rise

When water is heated, its volume increases. As oceans expand because of the heat, the sea level rises. Warming also melts glaciers and ice caps, and the meltwater raises the sea level further. The sea level rose 9.5 centimeters (3.7 inches) between 1993 and 2023 (Figure 12).[13] About half the rise was from the water expanding and half from meltwater. Four inches may not sound like much, but every inch rise increases the flooding of coastlines during high tides and storm surges. By 2100, the sea level is likely to rise at least one foot (30 centimeters) above 2000 levels, even if greenhouse gas emissions decrease.[14]

Sea level rise may be the greatest threat of global warming. Millions of people live in areas prone to inundation and will have to move, usually

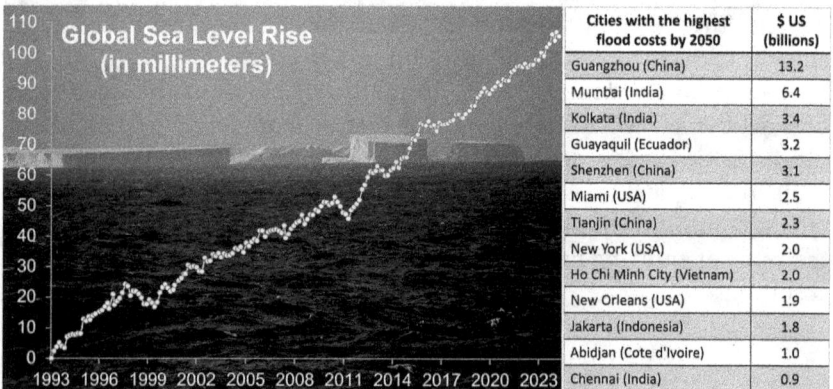

Cities with the highest flood costs by 2050	$ US (billions)
Guangzhou (China)	13.2
Mumbai (India)	6.4
Kolkata (India)	3.4
Guayaquil (Ecuador)	3.2
Shenzhen (China)	3.1
Miami (USA)	2.5
Tianjin (China)	2.3
New York (USA)	2.0
Ho Chi Minh City (Vietnam)	2.0
New Orleans (USA)	1.9
Jakarta (Indonesia)	1.8
Abidjan (Cote d'Ivoire)	1.0
Chennai (India)	0.9

FIGURE 12. *Left*: Global sea level since the start of the satellite altimeter record; data from NOAA Laboratory for Satellite Altimetry, "Global Sea Level Time Series," downloaded on August 26, 2024, via https://www.star.nesdis.noaa.gov/socd/lsa/SeaLevelRise/LSA_SLR_timeseries.php. Background photograph of an iceberg in Southern Ocean from NOAA Photo Library, taken by Lieutenant Elizabeth Crapo, NOAA Corps, https://www.noaa.gov/media/digital-library-photo/pl23anta0013jpg. *Right*: Estimate of flood costs (in billions U.S. $) for the world's highest risk cities, Stéphane Hallegatte, Colin Green, Robert J. Nicholls, and Jan Corfee-Morlot, "Future Flood Losses in Major Coastal Cities," *Nature Climate Change* 3 (August 18, 2013): 802–6.

to places that are already overcrowded. Many will swell the ranks of the world's refugees. Some of the world's largest cities are threatened. The table in Figure 12 gives an estimate of the likely flood costs for the most vulnerable cities.[15]

(E) Melting Ice

The earth's polar regions are particularly sensitive to global warming. The tropics absorb most of the sun's heat, which then flows and converges toward the poles. That is where the temperature rises most rapidly. Figure 13 shows the dramatic decrease in Arctic ice cover between 1979 and 2020.[16]

In the Arctic, most of the ice floats on water, and melting the ice exposes the water below. The white ice reflects sunlight, but the dark water absorbs sunlight and converts it to heat. That accelerates the warming (another example of a positive feedback; the warmer it gets, the faster the warming). Native communities depend on the sea ice for hunting, as

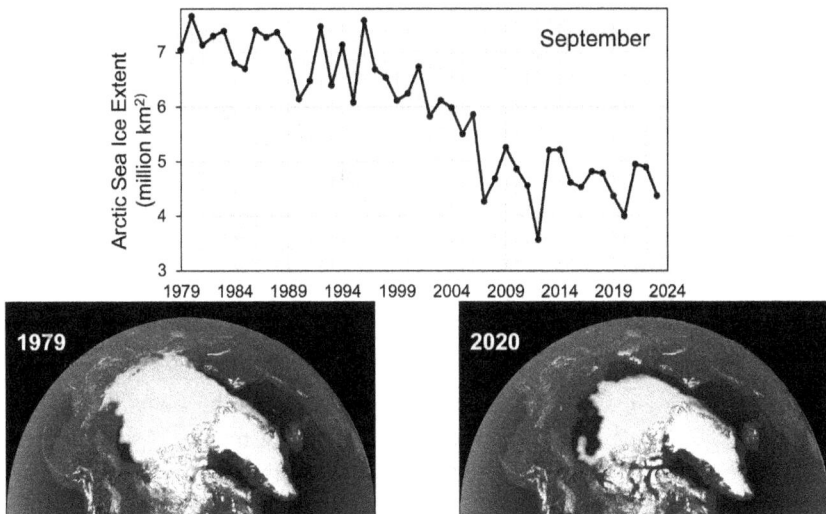

FIGURE 13. Arctic sea ice extent annual minimum (September average) shows ice shrinking by half from 1979 to 2023 as observed from space by satellites; data from National Snow and Ice Data Center, "Sea Ice Index," downloaded on October 11, 2023, from https://nsidc.org/arcticseaicenews/sea-ice-tools/. Map images show the minimum Arctic Sea ice in 1979 and 2020 as derived from satellites' passive microwave data. Image credit: NASA/Goddard Space Flight Center Scientific Visualization Studio. The Blue Marble data are courtesy of Reto Stockli (NASA/GSFC).

do polar bears; both are endangered by the Arctic melting. The diminishing sea ice even impacts gray whales, massive creatures that migrate over 12,000 miles from their winter breeding grounds in the lagoons of Mexico's Baja Peninsula to their foraging grounds in the Arctic. The whales eat crustaceans that feed on algae that grow on the underside of sea ice. Malnourished gray whales have been washing up on Pacific shores since 2019. The gray whale population declined from about 27,000 to 14,500 between 2016 and 2023.[17]

On Arctic land, the frozen ground (permafrost) softens and releases methane, the product of decaying plant matter from previous warm periods. Methane's greenhouse contribution is 30 times that of CO_2. The greater the melting of permafrost, the greater the greenhouse effect, another positive feedback.

Melting ice sheets do not directly raise the ocean level since the ice and meltwater have the same mass. But ice melting on land does raise the ocean level when the meltwater flows into the sea. Mountain glaciers are retreating everywhere since rising temperatures mean less snowfall and more rain. The ice caps of Greenland and Antarctica hold a huge amount of solid water. They are unlikely to melt completely unless greenhouse gas emissions continue at the current rate till the year 3000. If they did, the oceans would rise nearly seven meters (23 feet)![18]

It was long thought that massive winter snows would keep the ice caps stable. But ice shelves are melting because of warmer air above and warmer water below. They buttress the ice on land, and as they melt, the flow of glaciers from the land accelerates. North Greenland has lost 35 percent of the ice shelves that fringe its ice cap.[19] Similarly, 40 percent of Antarctica's ice shelves have dwindled over the past 25 years.[20]

(F) Ocean Current Slowing

Ocean currents carry heat and nutrients around the world like a conveyor belt. The sun heats tropical waters, which flow toward the poles. As it travels, the surface water evaporates and loses heat to the atmosphere. Salt is left behind when water evaporates or freezes, so the current becomes saltier as well as colder. Salt and cold make the water denser. It sinks near the poles, driving the deep water back toward the tropics, where it rises again, completing the conveyor belt, known as thermohaline circulation.[21]

But as global warming melts more polar ice, the surface water becomes less dense and sinking diminishes, slowing the conveyor belt. Less heat is carried in the surface currents despite the overall warming. One of these currents is the Gulf Stream, which heats much of Europe and tempers its climate. This is why Madrid is warmer than New York despite being just as far from the equator. If the Gulf current slows and even stops altogether, European winters will be colder. If greenhouse emissions continue on the present course, the Gulf Stream is expected to stop by the middle of the 21st century.[22]

The 2004 film *The Day After Tomorrow* was based on the premise that an abrupt shutdown of the Gulf Stream plunges the entire northern hemisphere into a new ice age overnight. Although this scenario is impossible, the consequences of shutting down or major slowing of the ocean current conveyor belt would nevertheless be disastrous. Aside from cooling Europe, there would be shifts in the world's rain belts, bringing more drought to tropical regions. Important fisheries that are supported by the upwelling of deep nutrient-rich waters, especially along the South American and African coasts, could collapse. And since the sinking polar currents carry CO_2 to the deep ocean, less CO_2 would be taken up by the ocean. Global warming would accelerate even more.

(G) Crop Failure

Higher temperatures spell trouble for agriculture. Crops wilt at excessive temperatures and fail to produce seed. They lose water and shut down photosynthesis. The yield for corn, one of the world's biggest crops, will drop by 7 percent for each degree of warming.[23]

The climate zones best for particular crops will shift away from the equator. Some regions may actually benefit from milder climates (e.g., Canada and Russia). In general, farms will be distressed. Agricultural productivity is likely to decline, especially in tropical areas where food security is already precarious. Important tropical crops, like coffee, chocolate, and mangoes, are at risk because their insect pollinators, already stressed by loss of habitat, die off at higher temperatures.[24] The problems will worsen as drought and flooding increase with global warming (see below). Closely spaced extreme weather events, such as flooding and excessive heat, can create serious global food shortages.

(H) Ecosystem Destruction

Rising temperatures put whole ecosystems at risk. For example, mountains accommodate plants and animals that are adapted for the temperature ranges of specific altitudes. As temperatures rise, these ecosystems migrate to higher altitudes. But they run out of room at the mountain top; these "sky island" communities may disappear. The sky islands of the American Southwest and northern Mexico, where the Chihuahuan and Sonoran deserts converge, house a remarkable diversity of species.[25]

Many ecosystems are affected by the rapid Arctic warming. Polar bears, who live on sea ice, are losing their habitat. Migrating birds, many of which nest in the Arctic, may be at risk if they miss crucial feeding times for their chicks because the growing season starts earlier as temperature rises. The birds are further stressed by diminished feeding opportunities at stopover points along migration routes. Habitat loss at these stops is mostly due to human activity, but rising sea levels at coastal stops and increasing drought at inland stops add to the stress. And coral reefs, which are very sensitive to temperature, are threatened with extinction as the ocean heats up. This topic is discussed in detail in Chapter 10 on biodiversity.

(I) Disease Spread

Rising temperatures increase bacterial growth rates and the virulence of waterborne bacterial diseases, like cholera, especially in areas with poor sanitation. Increased flooding spreads contaminated water and aggravates the problem. Fungal diseases are also spreading. Most fungi are adapted to cool weather and do not survive at body temperature. But the fungus causing valley fever, found in Central and South America and the U.S. Southwest, lives in hot, dry soil. Its range is expanding as hot, dry climates expand; the range now extends into Washington State.[26] And as fungi evolve in a hotter world, new diseases may emerge. A likely example is the recently discovered *Candida auris*,[27] which causes illness that is difficult to treat. There are only a few antifungal medicines, and fungi can evolve resistance to them, especially when they are used widely in agriculture to control fungal-induced plant diseases.

Insect-borne diseases can spread to regions that were previously too cool for the insects to survive. Malaria infects up to a quarter of a billion people worldwide and kills over half a million, most of them children in sub–Saharan Africa.[28] It could threaten many more as malaria-bearing mosquitoes move into newly warm areas where people lack natural immunity to the disease. Dengue fever, another major mosquito-borne tropical disease, is likely to spread as well.

Some effects of warming are indirect. Warming oceans increase the growth of algae that sometimes contain toxins. When small fish eat the algae, the toxins pass up the food chain. On the U.S. Pacific Coast, sea lions and sea otters suffer brain damage and epilepsy from the algal toxin domoic acid.[29] Crab fisheries sometimes have to close to protect people from eating domoic acid–laden crab meat that causes "amnesic shellfish poisoning."[30]

(J) Climate Anxiety

Even psychotherapists are seeing the effects of climate change. Patients increasingly complain of losing sleep and feeling depressed by thinking about climate change and its consequences.[31] The Climate Psychology Alliance North America now maintains a list of nearly 300 psychotherapists around the country who are "climate aware." In 2017, the American Psychological Association defined "ecoanxiety" as "a chronic fear of environmental doom."[32] Ecoanxiety arises from fears that are rational, although they are also fanned by alarmist news and media posts. Dealing with ecoanxiety is difficult for therapists trained to address personal problems and irrational fears. Support groups for therapists are being established to share experiences and best practices.

(K) Loss of Insurance

Homeowners in the United States face more than climate anxiety. In many areas house insurance is becoming hard to obtain because of greater risks of fires or floods.[33] Insurance losses from climate disasters have made insurance companies more cautious about the risks they are willing to take, leading some of them to withdraw from whole areas of the country. Major insurers have stopped writing policies in California because of wildfire risks. Without insurance, homeowners are vulnerable to catastrophic losses, and the market value of their homes will likely decline.

2. How Does Warming Lead to Extreme Weather?

(A) Storm Intensity

The warmer it gets, the faster water evaporates, and the water vapor sweeps upward with the warmer air. As the air rises, it cools, and the water vapor condenses and forms clouds. Rain or snow fall from the clouds back to the surface, completing what is called the hydrological cycle. Heat is absorbed when liquid water vaporizes and is released again when it condenses back to liquid. The released energy drives winds and creates storms.

A lot of energy is absorbed and released when air moves across large stretches of warm water, as in the tropical oceans. Vast rotating storms form, called hurricanes in the Atlantic and the Caribbean, typhoons in the Pacific, and cyclones in the Indian Ocean. Residents of coastal areas know the destructive force of the winds and rain of these giant storms and of storm surges, the massive ocean waves that flow far inland. Rising sea

FIGURE 14. Hurricane Otis at its Category 5 peak intensity while encroaching on Acapulco, Guerrero, Mexico, on October 25, 2023. Image credit: EOSDIS Worldview, NASA, from NASA's Terra Satellite. The image downloaded from Wikimedia Commons, https://commons.wikimedia.org/wiki/File:Otis_2023-10-25_0431Z.png.

levels strengthen the surges. The most devastating storms are more frequent in a warming world.

Storms also strengthen faster, leaving less time to prepare or evacuate.[34] In 2023, Hurricane Otis slammed into Acapulco, Mexico, with

165 mph winds (Figure 14). This tourist and boating city of 1 million had almost no warning as the storm had intensified by 115 mph in just 24 hours.[35] About 100 people died or were missing, including crew members on yachts in the harbor. There was extensive damage to homes, hotels, hospitals, and airports. More than 10,000 utility poles blew over, knocking out power and internet connections. Flooding and mudslides added to the devastation.

(B) Floods

Catastrophic flooding will happen regularly. As rising temperatures drive the hydrological cycle harder, rainfall increases, not just in hurricanes but in rainy areas everywhere. Downpours produce floods when the surface water accumulates faster than it can drain away. Floods have always been with us, but they increase with rising temperatures because the atmosphere holds more water vapor. Most of the water vapor is produced by tropical oceans, where it forms "atmospheric rivers" that flow with the wind and produce rain or snow as they rise and cool over land. These "rivers" are responsible for the biggest floods. In the Western United States, floods caused $51 billion in damage over the last 40 years, half of which was caused by 10 big atmospheric river storms.[36] In 2019, spring flooding in the U.S. Mississippi River basin menaced nearly 14 million people.[37] Around the world, more people live in floodplains than ever.[38] Bangladesh, located on the Ganges River Delta, is particularly prone to flooding, which affects up to two-thirds of the country.

Snowstorms will get bigger since there is more water vapor to condense into snow, and accumulated snow will melt earlier in the spring, contributing to more severe flooding. Earlier melting of mountain snowpack has dual effects: stronger spring floods but also summer and fall water shortages because the diminished snowpack no longer fills reservoirs.

(C) Even Cold Snaps

But winter cold snaps are also increasing in unexpected places. In February 2021, Texas had a days-long deep freeze that shut down equipment, leaving millions without electricity.[39] How does that square with global warming? The answer lies in the jet stream winds that circle the Arctic, high in the atmosphere.[40] They are the result of the temperature difference between the North Pole and the equator that interacts with the rotation of the earth. The jet stream keeps the frigid Arctic air from spreading south. But sometimes the jet stream weakens and forms large kinks that bring Arctic air far south and tropical air far north. Figure 15

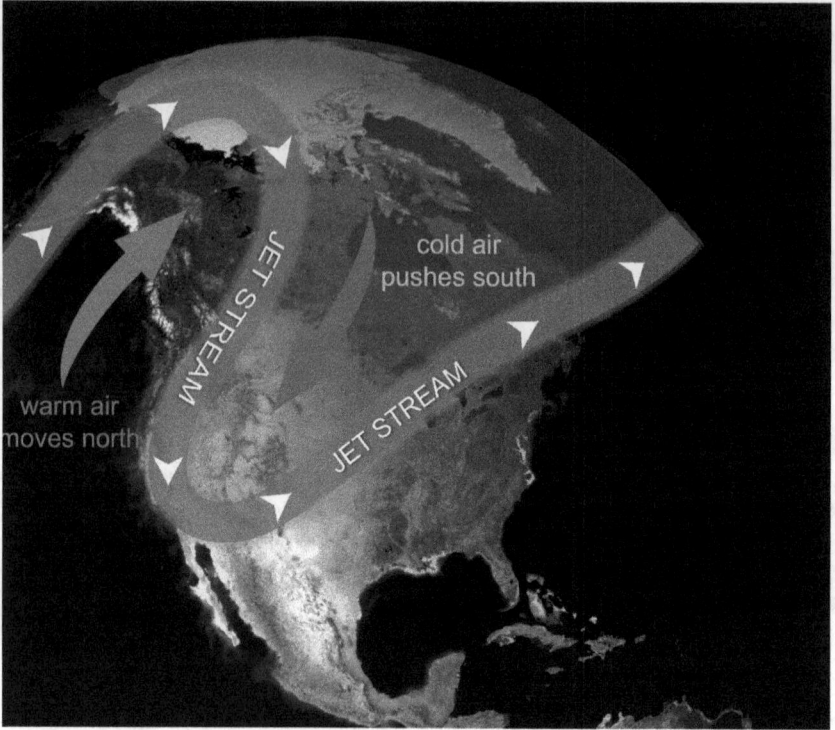

FIGURE 15. Illustration of a jet stream that warmed up Alaska and cooled down Las Vegas at the end of 2014. Adapted from Wallace Witkowski, "Las Vegas Colder than Anchorage as 2014 Draws to End," *MarketWatch*, December 31, 2014.

illustrates one of those kinks that brought unusual cold to the Southwest of the United States and unusual warmth to Alaska at the end of 2014. That made Las Vegas colder than Anchorage!

Since the Arctic warms faster than the tropics, the temperature difference between them decreases and weakens the jet stream. So we have more frequent cold snaps and heat waves.

(D) Droughts

Warming also causes longer droughts in dry areas.[41] Soil moisture decreases and the air becomes drier. When the soil dries, the cooling effect of evaporating water disappears, reinforcing the general warming. Stream flow and aquifers diminish. Water for irrigation is harder to obtain, impacting agriculture. As the global temperature rises, droughts will last longer and spread farther. Droughts depress agricultural production and raise food prices. Because the food market is international, droughts have serious consequences far beyond a locally affected region.

In 2009, a severe drought in Australia, a major wheat exporter, sharply reduced the winter wheat harvest. In 2010, a major drought in China forced it to import wheat from the depleted world market. At the same time, a severe heat wave withered crops in Russia, another major wheat exporter. This combination of droughts created a world shortage of wheat, sharply raising prices. In Egypt, the world's largest wheat importer, the price of bread tripled in 2011, leading to food riots. The food riots preceded mass protests in Cairo that brought down the government, ushering in the "Arab Spring."[42] Food prices were not the only cause of the protests, but they certainly contributed. In 2011, severe drought in Syria, combined with poor water management, forced thousands of farmers to abandon the countryside and move to cities, already crowded with Iraqi refugees. Mass protests were met by force, and that led to the civil war that eventually produced millions of refugees. One million immigrants flooded Europe in 2015 and 2016. Drought was not the only cause of all this upheaval, but it played an important role.[43]

(E) Climate Refugees

Like the Syrian refugees, desperate migrants around the world want to enter better-off countries to escape violence and/or poverty. Drought or flooding is often a cause of their desperation. In North America the would-be immigrants crowding the U.S.-Mexico border are escaping poor living conditions in Mexico and Central America. A large swath of Guatemala, Honduras, and El Salvador has sparse, irregular rainfall. In recent years this area has experienced severe drought, interspersed with drenching rain that floods the land. Crops are devastated, impelling farmers to abandon their homes. Although these countries are also plagued by corruption and violence, crop failure is a major factor that drives migrants to the U.S. border.

Coastal flooding from sea level rise also creates climate refugees. Half of the population in Bangladesh lives less than 15 feet above sea level. If sea level rises by 20 inches, as is projected by 2050, the country would lose about 17 percent of its land and 30 percent of its food production.[44] Nearly one-third of its population would be displaced.[45] Many who are displaced by the floodwaters crowd into the nation's capital, Dhaka. But some leave the country for neighboring India and elsewhere. In May 2017, Bangladesh was the largest single origin of migrants arriving in Europe.

3. How Warm Will It Get? Climate Modeling

Effects of global warming are already being felt. How much bigger will they get? To answer this critical question, scientists build computer models of the climate. These models simulate the atmosphere, oceans, and land surface and apply the laws of physics and chemistry to the flows of energy over time.

An international organization of scientists, the Intergovernmental Panel on Climate Change, collects and compares calculations from around the world. Figure 16 compares the collected results, as of 2021, for global temperatures since 1850.[46] The various models all fall within the gray band of temperatures; they track the actual temperature record very well. The calculations reveal the importance of the rising greenhouse gas levels by showing what would have happened in the absence of the human-caused increase.

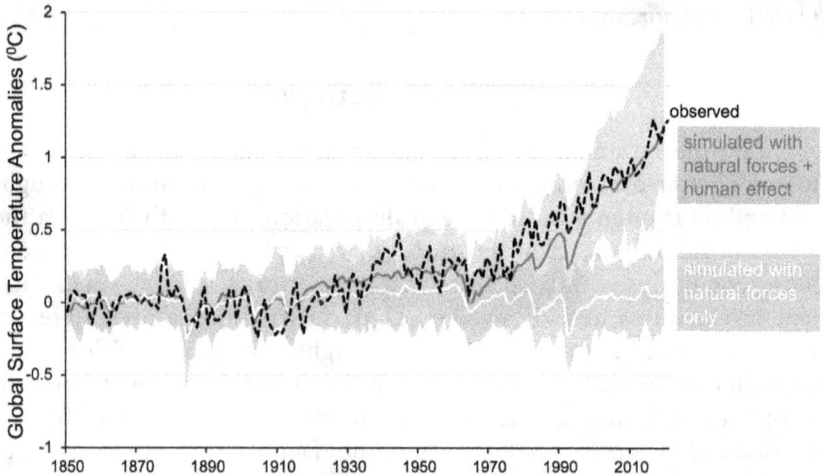

FIGURE 16. Global surface temperature annual averages, relative to 1850–1900, as observed (dashed line) and simulated using both human and natural forces, or only natural forces (solar and volcanic activities); shaded areas are range of the simulations. Plotted using data from the Intergovernmental Panel on Climate Change (IPCC). Data downloaded on October 12, 2023, from https://catalogue.ceda.ac.uk/uuid/0b2759059ad6474098e40dad73e0a8ec, part of Nathan P. Gillett, Elizaveta Malinina, Darrell Kaufman, and Raphael Neukom, "Summary for Policymakers of the Working Group I Contribution to the IPCC Sixth Assessment Report-Data for Figure SPM.1 (v20221116)," NERC EDS Centre for Environmental Data Analysis, July 3, 2023.

4. What Can We Do?

(A) Curbing Emissions

The most obvious way to stop warming is to stop emitting greenhouse gases, but that's very difficult. Modern civilization runs on energy from fossil fuels. As developing countries increase their economic activity and raise their standard of living, they will need more energy. Alternative energy sources, particularly wind and solar energy, though developing rapidly, lag behind fossil fuels. More ways to use energy efficiently are coming. The next two chapters cover these topics.

Economic policies play a big role in curbing greenhouse gas emissions. Some countries provide subsidies to encourage fuel-saving technologies. Others have set a target "cap" on total emissions and allow emitters to buy tradable permits, or they put a tax on emissions (a "carbon tax").

Since emissions are a global problem, international agreement and cooperation is essential. Countries have been negotiating on climate measures under UN auspices since 1979 (see Figure 17 timeline[47]). The world is already 1.1°C hotter than it was before the Industrial Revolution. The 2015 Paris Agreement aimed for a temperature rise of no more than 1.5°C to avoid unacceptable damages.

Emissions have leveled off and started to decline in developed countries (Figure 17) but have ballooned in developing countries, especially India and China. Many countries have pledged to reach "net-zero" carbon emissions (net zero means that any emissions must be balanced by uptake measures, such as planting trees and capturing carbon) by 2050, and China has pledged to do so by 2060. How these targets are to be achieved remains unclear. A 2023 UN report takes stock of progress since the 2015 Paris Agreement.[48] Trends are in the right direction and the growth of atmospheric CO_2 is slowing but not by enough to limit increased global temperature to the target 1.5°C increase. Greater efforts to reduce emissions are urgently needed.

(B) Maintaining Forests

Maintaining forests is vital for controlling atmospheric CO_2. Sustainable forestry practices, like selective logging and controlled burning, keep forests healthy and minimize destructive wildfires. Controlled burns can reduce the risk of intense fires by 60 percent for at least six years, according to a study of California forests.[49] Native American tribes had managed forests with controlled burns for centuries before Europeans appropriated the land. Thereafter, fires were suppressed whenever they occurred. As a

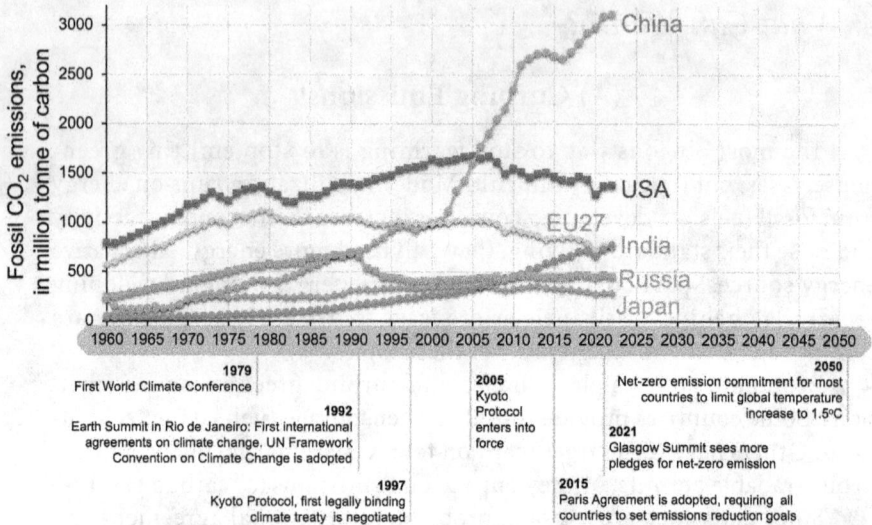

FIGURE 17. Over the last 40 years, CO_2 emissions from fossil fuels leveled off and began to decline for Japan, the European Union, and the United States but ballooned for India and China as their economies grew rapidly. Sharp drops will be needed to achieve net-zero emissions by 2050. The timeline of international climate negotiations is shown. Data from Global Carbon Project (2023): Pierre Friedlingstein et al., "Global Carbon Budget 2023," *Earth System Science Data* 15, no. 12 (December 5, 2023): 5301-69. Supplemental data of Global Carbon Budget 2023 (Version 1.1) [Data set], downloaded from https://doi.org/10.18160/gcp-2023.

result, new shrubs and saplings fueled the intense fires that subsequently broke out. Policy has now returned to using controlled burns and selective clearing of saplings and undergrowth to reduce the risk of fire disasters. But the policy is limited by the risk of controlled burns getting out of control as the temperature increases and the forests dry out. Also, people are building houses in forested areas, creating pressure to fight any fires that threaten the houses.

Tropical forests in the Amazon, Africa, and Indonesia are particularly threatened by fires, many deliberately set to clear the land for cattle production and plantations. At the Glasgow climate conference, 110 countries, containing 85 percent of the world's forests, agreed to stop and reverse deforestation by 2030. Low-income countries were promised significant funding to help lower their emissions and adapt to climate change.

Replanting trees can draw down a lot of CO_2. Timber companies routinely replant forests that were harvested but usually with a single species in rows to facilitate logging when they mature. Tree plantation monocultures absorb only about half as much CO_2 as do natural forests with a diversity of trees.[50] Restoring natural forests is the best way to store carbon.[51] If this were done globally, the forests could potentially store a huge amount of carbon, about 20 times the global annual emissions.[52]

Planting "tiny forests" on small plots of degraded urban land is a promising development. Japanese botanist Akira Miyawaki found that protected areas around temples and shrines had resilient ecosystems with a large variety of native vegetation.[53] He advocated dense planting of varied species of native trees on degraded land. After intensive soil restoration, planting, and three years of gardening care, the trees grow rapidly, and the ecosystem can mature in only 20 years. It supports diverse wildlife, including local pollinators which help it thrive.[54] Miyawaki forests on urban plots provide greenery for city dwellers, help clean the air, clean and store runoff water, and reduce the urban heat island effect. Tiny forest initiatives are spreading around the world, across Europe, Russia, Africa, the Middle East, Asia, and South America. India has hundreds of them and Japan has thousands.[55] The projects bring locals together to reclaim wasteland and plant Miyawaki forests. Miyawaki won the 2006 Blue Planet Prize, considered the environmental equivalent of a Nobel Prize.

(C) Adaptation

Communities can minimize the damage from climate change. Coastal cities around the world are strengthening defenses against rising sea levels and stronger storms. The Netherlands, the lowest lying country of Europe, has a history of digging canals and building dikes to keep out the sea. Cities like Rotterdam are converting ponds, garages, parks, and plazas into part-time reservoirs. Amsterdam is developing floating communities, interconnected houseboats that can rise with the sea level. And a Dutch firm is planning a floating housing complex for the Maldives capital, which sits three feet above sea level. China suffers from flooding and now has a "sponge city" initiative to ensure that urban lands can absorb and reuse stormwater. The idea is to minimize flooding by storing as much water as possible with a combination of storage tunnels, permeable pavements, rain gardens, constructed ponds, and wetlands.

In Florida, builders are putting homes on pillars to prevent flooding, using metal roofs and tying them down to resist hurricane winds, and installing close-fitting solar panels that don't lift off in the wind. They preserve nearby wetlands and native vegetation that absorb floodwaters. Whole neighborhoods are being built to be resilient in storms.

Communities need help to respond to their particular adaptation needs. When local communities are included in the preparation of adaptation plans, the measures taken are much likelier to be effective. Some areas may have to be abandoned altogether. Small nations on low-lying islands are already making contingency plans to transfer residents before the land is completely submerged.

An important aspect of climate adaptation is the development of new crop varieties that have better heat and drought tolerance. These new varieties are especially important for small farmers in tropical areas that feed much of the world's population. Better crops and animals for the developing world is the focus of an international network of agricultural research laboratories organized by CGIAR (Consultative Group for International Agricultural Research).[56]

Individuals can also take measures to adapt. To keep vegetables from heat-induced wilting, U.S. farmers are harvesting crops at night. Several companies also sell personal cooling gear for outdoor work.[57] Construction workers in Qatar, where outdoor temperatures often exceed 120°F (48.9°C), put on water-soaked work clothes that are designed to remove heat through evaporation, cooling the wearer for up to seven hours.

A major adaptation issue is how to absorb climate refugees, as they abandon drought- and flood-ravaged farms and towns. Many move to nearby cities, which are already poorly equipped to handle swelling populations. Others move across borders to other countries, with varying immigration policies and capacities. Countries and cities will need to prepare to respond to the influx of climate refugees.

When civil war in Syria triggered the European refugee crisis of 2015/16, German chancellor Angela Merkel welcomed 1 million refugees, with the much-quoted slogan "Wir schaffen das" (We can do it). Although there was serious political fallout, integration of the refugees is largely succeeding. But to avoid even larger political shocks, international agreements on the treatment of refugees are urgently needed.

(D) Geoengineering

Other measures to curb warming involve large-scale global technologies. One method is to capture CO_2 and sequester it from the atmosphere (discussed further in Chapter 3). A variety of chemical absorbents are available to capture CO_2 and then release it in concentrated form for storage. The likeliest place to store it is deep in the earth, in rock strata. It would eventually react with the rock and form a stable mineral. The largest direct air carbon capture and storage (CCS) facility, named Orca, was launched recently in Iceland.[58] Similar facilities are being developed around the world.[59]

But CCS is costly. Each stage requires substantial energy and material. Worldwide emissions of CO_2 currently amount to 40 billion tons a year, representing a formidable target for CCS. Switching to renewable energy (see next chapter) is currently a much lower cost option. But if the 40-billion-ton reduction can't be met by mid-century, then CCS will also be needed.

A more radical idea is to reduce the amount of sunlight that reaches the earth, an approach called solar radiation management.[60] The fraction reflected back into space is mostly determined by cloud cover. Clouds form when water vapor condenses to droplets, and this condensation happens around small particles floating in the air. These particles are plentiful over land areas but are scarcer over the oceans. Cloud "whitening" to reduce the absorption of sunlight could be achieved by spraying a mist of salt from seawater into the marine cloud layer to increase the density of cloud droplets. This could be done from a fleet of specially equipped ships.

For more global cooling, sunlight could be reflected back into space from reflective materials spread widely around the earth. The most plausible proposal would inject white sulfate particles into the stratosphere with fleets of aircraft. The particles would circulate for a long time before settling back to Earth. Volcanic eruptions do the same thing. The eruption of Mount Pinatubo in 1991 injected 10–20 million tons of sulfur into the stratosphere and cooled the climate by 0.5°C for a year.[61] Sulfate particles are a natural part of the atmosphere. But the amounts needed are large, and the sky would be continually hazy. And crop productivity would be lowered by diminishing the sunlight, affecting the food supply in many regions. Also, diminishing the solar heating would do nothing to curb ocean acidification from the rising CO_2 that threatens shell-forming sea creatures. Still, solar management would be the quickest method to cool the earth and could provide time to implement the needed emission reduction and energy conservation steps. But getting international agreement to implement such a strategy would be a huge obstacle.

5. Where Do We Stand?

Putting it all together, we know that the earth is warming, caused by rising levels of heat-trapping greenhouse gases. They rise mainly because we burn up the earth's stores of fossil fuels and cut down its forests. The warming produces increasingly deadly heat waves, melts the Arctic, raises sea level, threatens aquatic life, disrupts ecosystems and agriculture, and spreads insect-borne diseases. The rising temperature also intensifies storms and floods and extends droughts.

What to do? Strong measures to reduce fossil fuel burning and deforestation and to trap and store CO_2 would curb the rise of greenhouse gases. That is the main task. Till that happens, communities will need to adapt as best they can. Planting more trees and creating wetlands or other "sponges" to absorb floodwaters will help. Cooling of the earth with sun-reflective particles in the stratosphere might provide extra time but is unlikely to be implemented anytime soon and should not distract from the more urgent measures of adaptation and reducing greenhouse emissions.

3

Energy Sources

Will There Be Enough? Will It Be Clean Enough?

Topics:

1. Why worry about energy?
2. Can we do without fossil fuels?
   A. Coal: Plentiful, cheap, and dirty?
   B. Oil: King of transport?
   C. Gas: An intermediate step?
3. Can we take back the CO_2?
4. Should emitters pay?
5. Can solar and wind save us?
   A. Storing energy when the sun hides and the wind dies down
   B. Getting the energy to where it is needed
   C. Decentralization: Sun and wind are everywhere
   D. A race against time
6. What about hydropower?
7. How big a role can geothermal and ocean energy play?
8. Is nuclear energy the elephant in the room?
   A. Are nuclear reactors safe?
   B. What about nuclear waste?
   C. Are reactors connected with bombs?
   D. What is the future of nuclear energy?
9. Will we get to fusion energy?
10. Are fuel crops emission-free energy?
11. Summary

Primary Energy Consumption in Terawatt-hours (TWh) by Regions

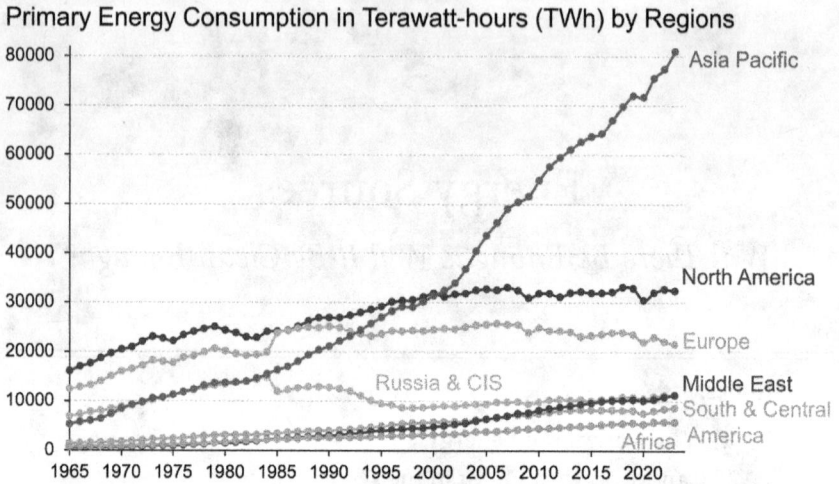

FIGURE 18. Energy consumption in the world's regions; a terawatt-hour is the energy flowing at one trillion watts for an hour. Note how Asia's consumption has grown sevenfold since 1970 and shows little sign of slowing. Data from Energy Institute, "Statistical Review of World Energy 2024, 73rd Edition," accessed August 25, 2024, https://www.energyinst.org/statistical-review.

1. Why Worry About Energy?

Energy is vital to us, but the way we produce it is driving climate change. Modern life depends entirely on energy. Energy runs factories; it heats and air-conditions buildings; it cooks and refrigerates our food; it powers cars, trucks, trains, ships, and airplanes. The world uses a huge amount of energy and will need much more as the population increases and as developing countries improve their standard of living. Energy consumption has leveled off in Europe and North America, but is exploding in Asia, driven by rapid economic development in China, India, and Southeast Asia (Figure 18).[1] The rest of the world uses relatively little energy now, but will need much more as more countries grow economically.

But here's the thing. Most of our energy comes from coal, oil, and gas. We hear a lot about renewables: wind, solar, biomass. But right now, they are far behind fossil fuels as energy sources.

Figure 19 shows how much energy is consumed annually from each source.[2] At the top are the big three: coal, oil, and gas. Oil and gas continue to rise. Coal consumption recently leveled off, but still remains at a very high level. The other sources, though rising, are still relatively small. All of this fossil fuel consumption pumps out huge amounts of CO_2 and methane. Agriculture and deforestation also contribute to the staggering amount of greenhouse gases we release every year. The total is 40 billion

Primary Energy Consumption in Terawatt-hours (TWh) by Source

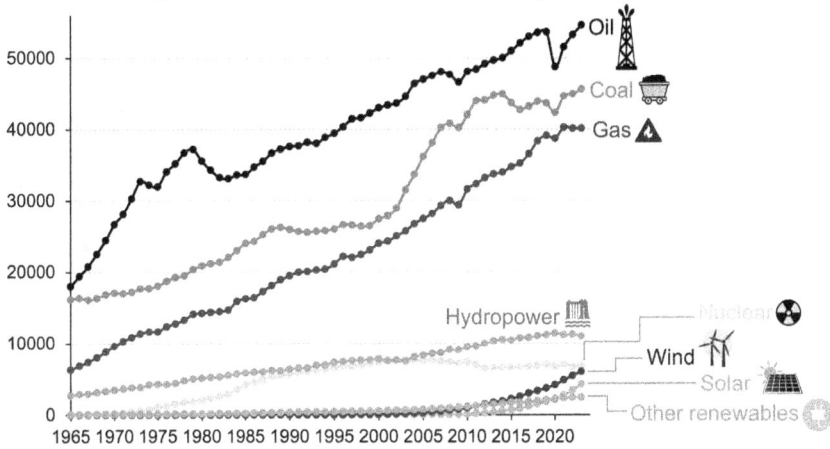

FIGURE 19. Sources of the world's energy supply. Data from Energy Institute, "Statistical Review of World Energy 2024, 73rd Edition," accessed August 25, 2024, https://www.energyinst.org/statistical-review.

tons and rising. We are already experiencing global warming, with stronger heat waves, droughts, disastrous storms and floods, than ever before. And climate scientists warn that these will become truly catastrophic unless we reduce those emissions to zero by mid-century. The term they use is net zero, meaning any emissions would have to be balanced by taking greenhouse gases out of the atmosphere. This can be done by planting trees and deep-rooted plants or by sucking CO_2 out of smokestacks or out of the air itself and storing it somewhere (see Chapter 2). Neither measure comes anywhere close to matching the 40 billion tons of emissions annually. So fossil fuels will have to go, replaced by non-emitting energy sources. That is an enormous challenge, but it is not impossible. Let's look at how the challenge might be met.

2. Can We Do Without Fossil Fuels?

Coal, oil, and gas are called fossil fuels because they are the remains of plants and sea creatures that were buried in the earth many millions of years ago. They were transformed by movements in the earth's crust that subjected them to high pressures and temperatures. These fossil deposits are stores of energy produced long ago. We are living off this solar inheritance.

(A) Coal: Plentiful, Cheap, and Dirty?

After coal-fired steam engines and locomotives were invented, coal powered the Industrial Revolution. Coal was also used widely for heating buildings and still is in parts of the world. In high-income countries, it has been largely displaced by cleaner-burning oil and gas. Now coal is used mainly to run the large steam-powered generators that produce our electricity. Coal's share of electricity production is large, but is declining. In the United States, coal produced half of the electricity in 2010 but only 20 percent in 2020;[3] no new coal plants are being built and old ones are shutting down.

Coal is abundant and widely spread around the world. But as the cost of other energy sources has come down, they compete effectively with coal. And there's lots of harm in coal. It releases twice as much CO_2 per unit of energy than natural gas and about 1.5 times as much as diesel or gasoline.[4] It also pollutes the air. Burning it releases unhealthy small particles copiously. Natural gas is replacing most of the coal and is abundant and cheap. It is also cleaner burning than oil or coal. Solar and wind energy are now also cheaper than coal in most places.

Coal mining is also unhealthy for those working in the mines, and it damages the environment. Deep coal mines are dangerous; fires and collapses have cost many miners their lives. And breathing coal dust causes "black lung" disease.[5] Near-surface coal is "strip" mined, a process that scrapes away overlying soil so that the coal can be shoveled out mechanically. Whole mountaintops are removed in this way, with great damage to the local ecology.[6] Although mineowners cover and replant the scarred land, forests are very slow to recover, and the original ecosystem is lost.[7] And local communities are impacted by air pollution in and near the mines (Chapter 6). Nevertheless, they are dependent on the mines for jobs and are devastated when the mines close. Despite coal's problems, coal plants continue to be built, especially in China and India. These are huge and rapidly developing countries that need all the electricity they can produce.

(B) Oil: King of Transport?

Oil is the basis of our transportation system. Cars, trucks, buses, trains, ships, and airplanes all run on oil. Its big advantage is that as a liquid, it can easily be carried in portable tanks. It can be refined into fractions appropriate for different kinds of engines. Although cleaner burning than coal, it also emits unhealthy fine particles, plus volatile organic compounds (VOCs) and nitrogen oxides (NO_x) gases that cause smog and toxic ozone. These emissions are released close to where people live and work.

Unlike coal, crude oil reserves accumulate in pools in a few regions of the globe. The biggest pools lie under the Middle East, particularly Saudi Arabia, Iraq, and Iran, giving this region outsized geopolitical significance and warfare. In other oil-rich nations like Nigeria and Venezuela, the hunt for oil has led to violence and suffering.

Because so many regions depend on oil imports, shipping lanes are crowded with oil tankers. Shipping accidents produce oil spills, fouling coastlines and estuaries. Perhaps the most infamous spill was the grounding of the supertanker *Exxon Valdez* in Alaska's pristine Prince William Sound in 1989.[8] Two hundred and sixty thousand barrels of crude oil spilled into the water. The oil contaminated 1,300 miles of coastline, killing 22 killer whales, 250 bald eagles, thousands of otters and seals, hundreds of thousands of seabirds, and billions of salmon and herring eggs. The remote location, accessible only by plane, helicopter, or boat, made containment and remediation of the spill especially difficult. Heavily contaminated beaches were eventually cleansed by dousing them with specially formulated fertilizer that would enhance the growth of naturally occurring microbes that consume oil. Exxon spent about $2 billion on cleanup costs and another $1 billion to settle civil claims and criminal charges.[9] Marine habitat and animal recovery programs are still ongoing.

But the *Exxon Valdez* spill was dwarfed by the 4.9 million barrels of oil that gushed from the bottom of the Gulf of Mexico when a deep-water oil rig operated by BP blew out.[10] It killed 11 workers on the platform. The leak continued for nearly three months before it was finally plugged. The oil fouled beaches and ecologically sensitive wetlands from Florida to Louisiana and closed several fishing grounds. Some of the oil was skimmed up at the surface, and much of it was burned, producing copious black clouds (Figure 20).[11]

But much of it remained in the water column. The lighter oil eventually evaporated or was consumed by microorganisms, while heavier oil sank to the Gulf floor, damaging coral and deep-water organisms.[12] Dolphins and other marine life died in record numbers afterward. BP was fined $20.8 billion, the largest environmental damage settlement in U.S. history. As of 2018, cleanup costs, charges, and penalties had cost the company more than $65 billion.[13] Work to restore the Gulf's ecosystems will likely continue to 2030.

On land, pipelines can leak and contaminate groundwater. In 2022 about 12,000 barrels of oil spilled from a burst pipe onto farmland in Kansas.[14] Fearing the likely contamination, indigenous people throughout North America resist pipeline construction under tribal lands. Tanker

FIGURE 20. Black smoke from a controlled burn of surface oil during the 2010 Deepwater Horizon oil spill. Photo credit: U.S. Coast Guard, downloaded from https://csl.noaa.gov/news/2011/105_0920.html.

trains often derail, spilling oil and catching fire. In 2013, an oil train from North Dakota, the heart of an oil fracking boom, derailed in the town of Lac-Mégantic in Quebec, Canada. The accident killed 47 people, burned 30 buildings, and spilled 40,000 barrels of oil.[15] The world's largest land-based oil spill occurred in Uzbekistan in 1992. An oil well blew out and spewed over two million barrels of oil, which caught fire and burned for two months.[16]

Oil has become more available through high-volume hydraulic fracturing, or fracking.[17] Wells extend horizontally through oil-bearing rock whose pores are too small to permit the oil to flow. Water, mixed with sand and chemicals, is forced into the wells at high enough pressure to fracture the rock, freeing the oil to flow through the cracks and into the wells. Because of fracking, oil production has surged in the United States. Fracking has opponents in some areas because it can cause earthquakes, and poorly constructed wells can contaminate the underground water supply.[18]

Oil also comes from Canadian tar sands, vast stretches of which lie below the northern forests. The forest is cleared and the sands are dug up and heated to release the oil in the tar. This practice destroys the local environment. The tar sands produce much more CO_2 than conventional oil. All that digging and heating produces three to four times as much CO_2

as conventional crude oil extraction.[19] Much of the tar sands oil is sent through the Keystone pipeline from Alberta through the United States to refineries on the Texas Gulf Coast for overseas export. Tar sands oil is more corrosive than conventional crude. The pipeline has leaked more than 20 times since it started in 2010, much more than other pipelines carrying conventional crude.[20] A planned extension of the pipeline, Keystone XL, would have greatly increased the pipeline capacity, but it was strongly opposed by environmental groups, Native American tribes, and farmers, ranchers, and business owners along its proposed route. Because tar sands oil threatens the climate, world leaders, like the Dalai Lama, Archbishop Desmond Tutu, and many Nobel prize–winning scientists, expressed their opposition to Keystone XL. The political battle lasted through three U.S. administrations until the project was finally canceled in 2020. By then, major oil companies had scaled back their tar sands holdings and major new tar sands projects were halted.[21]

(C) Gas: An Intermediate Step?

Natural gas (which is mostly methane, CH_4) is the cleanest burning fossil fuel. It releases the least CO_2 per unit of energy. Because it reduces CO_2 emissions relative to coal and oil, natural gas has been considered a "transition fuel" on the road to decarbonization. It is the favored fuel for heating buildings and producing electricity. Natural gas now eclipses coal in U.S. power plants, accounting for over 40 percent of electricity production versus coal's 17 percent.[22] And like oil, gas has become more available through fracking. But gas leaks, from both gas and oil wells and pipelines, release a lot of methane. These leaks are a serious matter since methane is a greenhouse gas 20 times more potent than CO_2.

The leaks from production and transportation of natural gas and oil account for about 40 percent of methane emissions, and methane is responsible for about 30 percent of greenhouse warming.[23] The 2021 United Nations Climate Conference launched the Global Methane Pledge, which now encompasses 155 countries committed to a 30 percent cut in methane emissions by 2030.[24] And 50 oil and gas companies, representing nearly half of global production, pledged to reach near-zero methane emissions by stopping leaks.[25]

3. Can We Take Back the CO_2?

If the main problem with fossil fuels is the production of CO_2, why not capture the CO_2 and get it out of the way? It can be captured from the exhaust stream of existing power plants by using chemical adsorbents. It can even be sucked out of the air with absorption towers. After separation, the CO_2 can be stored by pumping it into deep aquifers or porous rock layers underground. The combination is called CCS (carbon capture and storage—see Chapter 2). But CCS takes a lot of energy and is costly. The energy is needed because the CO_2 concentration is only about 20 percent in power plant exhaust and only 0.04 percent in air. Very large volumes of exhaust gas or air must be pumped through the absorbent to capture the CO_2, which must then be released (usually by heating), then concentrated to send it to where it is stored. The amount currently being captured is less than a thousandth of the CO_2 being emitted. Instead of burial, the captured CO_2 could be used to make products, like plastics, or new hydrocarbon fuels. But these processes are expensive, and industrial products could store only a small fraction of the CO_2 that we emit.

Another option is to plant trees and deep-rooted plants that capture and store CO_2 in their tissues. China plants billions of trees—the Great Green Wall—to stop soil loss and the spread of deserts.[26] Restoring wetlands also helps because marshes store a lot of CO_2; water covers the plants when they die and slows their decomposition. Well-tended crops can also store significant amounts of carbon in the soil, especially if the soil is not plowed ("no-till agriculture"; see Chapter 10).

Biochar is another promising storage method. Biochar, or charcoal, is made by heating plant matter under low oxygen conditions. Mixing biochar into soils improves soil quality and raises crop yields. The buried biochar is long lasting and stores carbon in the ground.[27] Biochar used by ancient farmers in the Amazon River basin has lasted thousands of years. If it were used widely by farmers today, biochar could help reduce the amount of CO_2 in the atmosphere.

One other possibility is to spread alkaline minerals in the ocean. Alkali reacts and neutralizes acids, and CO_2 is acidic in water. So adding alkali induces more CO_2 to be taken up. Because of its natural alkalinity, the ocean already absorbs about 30 percent of global CO_2 emissions. Adding more alkalinity would increase this fraction. Over geological time, CO_2 is drawn out of the atmosphere through weathering, when rainwater washes over alkaline minerals in the earth's crust and transports their dissolved fraction to the oceans. Purposely adding alkaline minerals would amount to enhanced weathering. But the amounts needed to make an impact are very large. Experiments are underway to evaluate which minerals would work best, how they would be spread, and where they would come from.[28] Scientists will also evaluate possible ecological harm from the added minerals, such as altering the plankton composition.

Another ocean-based approach enables the growth of CO_2-absorbing phytoplankton and kelp by bringing nutrient-rich deep water to the ocean surface. When the phytoplankton and kelp, or the organisms that feed on them, die, they sink to the bottom, carrying their carbon with them and enrich the deep water with nutrients. Along many coastlines, winds carry the warm surface water away from the shore, replacing it with cold water from below. This is called upwelling. The nutrients from below feed some of the world's most productive kelp forests and fisheries. But large stretches of ocean remain stratified with warm lighter water overlying cold heavier water. In the absence of mixing, the warm surface lacks nutrients and cannot support life.

The Climate Foundation proposes to bring deep water to the surface with simple wave-action pumps: long, light-weight tubes with one-way valves at each end, attached to buoys.[29] As the waves move the buoys up and down, the valves open and close to admit cold water and move it up to the surface, promoting phytoplankton growth. Attaching light-weight net arrays to the pumps would allow kelp to grow. When nutrients are available, kelp grow rapidly. Kelp forests (see Chapter 9) draw down more CO_2 per acre than tropical rainforests. Absorbing ocean CO_2 also reduces acidity and supports shellfish growth. So enhanced deep-water upwelling could both reduce atmospheric CO_2 and enhance marine biological productivity. Some of the kelp could be harvested for use in food, fertilizer, and biofuels.

All of these carbon storage strategies are important. But reducing emissions by eliminating fossil fuels is by far the most effective and cheapest way to stop the rise in atmospheric CO_2.

4. Should Emitters Pay?

Since burning fossil fuels imposes enormous costs on society and the environment, why shouldn't the producers of these fuels pay the cost? We could make emitters pay for the damage they do by putting a price on the carbon released. Carbon pricing is a market-based approach to reducing CO_2 emissions. It makes alternative energy sources more competitive and encourages investments in energy conservation and carbon storage. Without a price on carbon, corporations have little incentive to make such investments.

Carbon taxes, the most direct way to price carbon, are already imposed in countries like Canada, Finland, Sweden, the United Kingdom, Ireland, and Chile. The results are mixed; they depend on how large the tax is and to whom it is applied. Taxes are universally unpopular, so taxpayer resistance has thwarted many proposals.

A more palatable method is called "cap and trade." A cap is placed on the level of emissions allowed in any given year. Allowances to emit carbon up to this cap are given out or auctioned off. A market in which these allowances are bought and sold sets the carbon price and encourages investment in emissions reduction. Cap and trade has the advantage of fixing a definite target for emissions reduction.[30] The European Union has the largest greenhouse gas cap and trade system.[31] It includes all 27 member countries and four neighboring ones. China has set up a cap and trade system. So have several states in the United States. These are all fairly new, and it remains to be seen how effectively they curb greenhouse gas emissions.

Since fossil fuels are burned everywhere, the emissions cap should really be worldwide. International emissions trading arrangements are now under discussion.

5. Can Solar and Wind Save Us?

Electricity production accounts for the largest share of greenhouse gas emissions (Chapter 4). But the sun and wind could produce all the energy we need. Wind power uses windmills to turn rotors that generate electricity, while solar panels, made of silicon, absorb the sun's rays and converts them to electric current. Solar thermal stations also provide solar electricity. They have large arrays of mirrors, all focused on a single spot, that makes a fluid hot enough to drive a steam electric generator. The fluid itself stores enough energy for nighttime electricity. These "solar tower" plants are built in areas with perennial sunshine (Figure 21).

Offshore wind power is expanding rapidly because offshore winds are stronger and more reliable than wind over land. And solar farms can even be floated on protected sunny waters (Figure 22).

Solar and wind power generation has no emissions at all. If solar and wind could replace all fossil fuels for electricity production, that would reduce greenhouse gas emissions a lot. And since electricity could replace fossil fuels for heating and transportation, clean electricity could eliminate most greenhouse gas emissions. But there are challenges to replacing all fossil fuel power plants.

(A) Storing Energy When the Sun Hides
and the Wind Dies Down

A big problem is that windmills work only when the wind blows, and solar power works only when the sun shines. But people and industry need

FIGURE 21. Solar tower power plants near Seville, Spain. Photo by Koza1983 via Wikimedia Commons, https://upload.wikimedia.org/wikipedia/com mons/2/22/PS20andPS10.jpg; https://creativecommons.org/licenses/by/3.0/ legalcode.

FIGURE 22. Floating photovoltaic plant in Changbin, Taiwan. Photo credit: Ciel & Terre International.

electricity to be continuous. Since electricity demand is lower at night, the daily rhythm of electricity use matches the available sunlight to some extent. Winds die down at night too. But the wind can die for a long spell, and cloudy conditions can obscure the sun for a long time. Demand could easily exceed supply if solar and wind become major suppliers to the grid.

What's needed is some way to store solar and wind energy to even things out. Electric utilities sometimes use "pump storage," pumping water uphill to a reservoir, then running it back down through electric turbines to recover the stored energy. But reservoirs need to be regularly drained and refilled; they are unpopular and difficult to site. Many power companies are betting on batteries for storage. Big enough batteries are very expensive. The race is on to develop really cheap massive batteries, but there is no winner yet.[32]

Other storage methods are being developed. One is thermal storage, when a heat-storing substance releases the heat to operate a power plant. An example is the high-temperature fluid in solar thermal plants mentioned above. One company is using large, inexpensive carbon blocks to store electricity from renewable sources for industrial power and heating.[33] Other methods that may prove useful are compressing air in caverns, spinning massive flywheels, and lifting and lowering heavy weights.[34]

A promising alternative is hydrogen gas. Electricity from wind and solar power plants can produce hydrogen from water by electrolysis. The hydrogen can be stored and converted back to electricity as needed in a fuel cell (Chapter 4) or burned directly in a power plant. The first U.S. hydrogen storage project is in a Utah coal town, where caverns are being hollowed out in underground salt domes. The town's coal power plant, which had been scheduled to close, will be modified to burn hydrogen instead of coal.[35]

(B) Getting the Energy to Where It Is Needed

Another problem is that the best sites for solar and wind power may be far from where the electricity is most needed. In the United States, the southwestern desert is optimal for solar generation, while the midwestern plains have the steadiest winds. Farmers in Iowa can profit as much from renting land for windmills as they do from crops (Figure 23). But much of the population lives along the Atlantic and Pacific coasts. It takes time and money to establish rights of way and construct new transmission lines to send electricity over hundreds of miles.

These projects are often opposed by communities that are already established along proposed rights of way. A variety of regulatory hurdles also stand in the way. Europe, China, and India are developing

FIGURE 23. Wind towers on an Iowa farm. Photograph by Carol M. Highsmith. Retrieved from the Library of Congress, Prints & Photographs Division [reproduction number LC-DIG-highsm-39653], www.loc.gov/item/2016630471/.

high-voltage transmission grids to carry electricity over long distances. They are using direct-current technology,[36] which is more efficient than the usual alternating current for long-distance transmission. In the United States a proposal to build a "macro-grid" of high-voltage transmission lines along the existing interstate highways[37] would break the logjam of local barriers and get the most effective renewable power to where it is needed.

(C) Decentralization: Sun and Wind Are Everywhere

Sun and wind are everywhere. Decentralization is a key advantage of solar and wind power. Solar panels can be set up anywhere the sun is plentiful. The wind is harder to harness for small generators because windmill efficiency decreases rapidly with smaller size. But efficient small wind turbines are being developed to use in windy locations.

Nearly 800 million people in low-income countries have no electricity.[38] Most of them live in areas remote from the grid. Reaching them with new transmission lines may be impractical or cost too much. Installing solar panels sufficient to provide critical needs—lighting, water pumping, TV reception, cell phone charging—is much less expensive than expanding the grid. The panels can be installed on rooftops, for individual households or small businesses, or at small central stations, with a micro-grid to connect villagers. The panels use batteries for storage and backup. There are programs that help villagers obtain and install solar panels. For example, the nonprofit Indian company Selco has installed 300,000 solar units in remote Indian villages; Selco also trains local entrepreneurs to set up their own solar businesses.[39] In Bangladesh, where 17 million households are off the grid, SOLshare company sells a low-cost electronic box that allows users to sell and buy solar electricity.[40] Those without solar panels can buy electricity from solar homeowners, who earn extra income on their solar investment. Local interconnections in a village form a solar micro-grid, allowing local electricity trading and efficient allocation of the collective solar energy. SOLshare expects to operate 20,000 micro-grids by 2030, serving over a million users, eventually interconnecting them with the national grid.[41]

In grid-connected communities, people can save on electricity bills by using rooftop solar power. The savings pay off the equipment cost in a relatively short time, 10 years on average in the United States.[42] Electricity generated beyond household needs is fed back to the grid, providing credits to the household and adding to the grid's storage capacity. Electric cars can be equipped with two-way connections, allowing them to be charged but feeding electricity back to the grid when the cars are not in use.[43] With enough rooftop solar panels and electric cars, the electric utility could avoid having to build excess generating capacity needed when electricity demand is high, during a heat wave or cold snap, for example.

There are now affordable house batteries that store a few days' worth of household use and provide for essential needs during extended power outages (storms, wildfires, earthquakes). Rooftop solar power can make a community more resilient when stronger storms bring down transmission lines, knocking out power and igniting wildfires.

This decentralized form of electricity generation is expanding rapidly around the world. In California, all new houses must include rooftop solar systems. Nationwide, 3 percent of U.S. homes have rooftop solar, while Germany has 11 percent and Australia has 30 percent of homes with rooftop solar power.[44]

(D) A Race Against Time

Solar panels and windmills are spreading everywhere, and their cost has come down dramatically as production scales up and methods improve. In most places they are now the cheapest option for electricity generation. In Texas, historically the United States' major oil- and gas-producing state, solar and wind energy provided less than 1 percent of the state's electricity in 2001 but about 25–30 percent in 2022.[45] By 2025, solar and wind power are expected to overtake coal power worldwide.

Some people question the greenhouse advantage of wind and solar because it takes a lot of energy to build, install, and maintain wind towers and solar plants. This energy currently depends mostly on fossil fuels. But the amounts required are way less than the amounts of fossil fuels that are burned to produce electricity directly. There is, however, a problem with the special metals needed to manufacture solar panels, wind towers, and batteries. Expanding wind and solar requires expanded mining, often in low-income countries with few environmental and labor protections.

Wind and solar power are growing rapidly but have a long way to go. As of 2022 they still accounted for only 12 percent of world electricity, while fossil fuels provided two-thirds.[46] And the demand for electricity is expected to double by 2050. Building enough wind and solar power, as well as sufficient energy storage and transmission capacity is a race against time.

6. What About Hydropower?

Dams to control flooding and hold back water in reservoirs have been around for a long time. High dams can house turbines, which convert the energy of the water falling through them into emission-free electricity. Dams now generate 16 percent of the world's electricity.[47] China has the largest share of hydropower. Its Three Gorges Dam is the largest hydroelectricity generator in the world.

Developing countries often see dam construction as vital to economic growth. But the dams can also produce conflict with downstream countries that view upstream dams as a threat to their water supply. Having constructed the Aswan Dam, Egypt and upstream Sudan now worry about a huge dam that Ethiopia has constructed on the Blue Nile, even farther upstream. Ethiopia considers the dam as critical to supplying sorely needed electricity to its 125 million people (slightly more than Egypt's 112 million) and supporting its rapidly developing economy. Despite years of negotiations, the three countries have yet to implement a water-sharing agreement.[48]

Although hydropower doesn't emit CO_2, dams create other problems. They displace people who live behind the dams, and archaeologic treasures get buried under reservoirs. If the reservoir overfills from flooding, the dam can collapse with devastating effects downstream. This danger will increase as floods intensify because of global warming. Dams block fish from migrating upstream to spawn, a blockage only partially offset by fish ladders. The many dams on the Columbia River system in the Northwest of the United States have greatly reduced the Pacific salmon population, causing losses to commercial fisheries and to Native American tribes that depend on the salmon for food.

Dams also retain silt that must eventually be flushed out before it engulfs the turbine intakes. In the tropics, the still water behind a dam can harbor disease-causing organisms. And new reservoirs can release methane as the newly buried vegetation decays without oxygen.

There are harmful effects downstream as well. Egypt's Aswan Dam stopped the annual flooding of the Nile valley that used to fertilize the crops. The crops now require chemical fertilizers. Also, the Nile delta is subsiding and being invaded by saltwater.

Problems like these have galvanized public opposition, significantly limiting the number of possible dam sites. It is unlikely that hydropower will expand fast enough to further lower CO_2 emissions significantly.

7. How Big a Role Can Geothermal and Ocean Energy Play?

The earth's crust insulates us from its molten core. But weak spots in the crust allow molten rock to flow near the surface, producing hot springs and volcanic eruptions. Wells at these hot spots produce steam that can be used to generate carbon-free electricity and hot water that can be used for heating houses. Iceland, a land of many volcanoes and geysers, gets 30 percent of its electricity from geothermal plants and heats 90 percent of its homes with geothermal water. Geothermal sources supply 25 percent of electricity for El Salvador and 38 percent for Kenya. Kenya's geothermal percentage is the highest of any country, thanks to the volcanic region of East Africa's Great Rift Valley.[49] Elsewhere geothermal power is a minor part of the energy mix; in the United States, it accounts for 0.4 percent of electricity.

But there is much greater potential than the readily accessible hot spring regions provide. Not far beneath the surface of the continents lie rocks that are hot enough to produce usable steam. The advanced drilling technology that enabled fracking can access hot rocks for steam. Instead of fracking to release trapped oil and gas, fracking can crack hot rocks through which water can be pumped to produce steam, which can be captured in separately drilled wells. "Enhanced geothermal" processes are currently being tested at a number of sites. The U.S. Department of Energy estimates that 12 percent of the country's electricity could be supplied by enhanced geothermal energy.[50] Globally, the potential is very large.[51]

The oceans' tides and waves carry a lot of energy, but capturing it is hard. Experiments are underway with wave action devices to produce electricity. But seawater corrosion limits their effectiveness. Plus, the effects of such technologies on marine life are unknown. The oldest commercial tidal power station, opened in 1966, is along the Brittany coast in France, where unusually high tides funnel into estuaries.[52] Several other tidal plants operate in Canada, South Korea, China, and Russia.

Another energy source is the temperature difference between the surface and the deeper ocean, which is as much as 20°C in the tropics. Siphoning the cold water to the surface can power a low-efficiency heat engine. The technology is called ocean thermal energy conversion.[53] Also the cold, nutrient-rich ocean water is useful for air-conditioning and for fertilizing crops. Hawai'i has an experimental station that provides power, cooling, and irrigation to greenhouses on shore,[54] so ocean energy sources can be useful locally but will likely remain a small part of the global energy mix.

8. Is Nuclear Energy the Elephant in the Room?

The splitting of uranium atoms, a nuclear fission process, powers atom bombs; it also powers nuclear reactors for electricity. Ten percent of the world's electricity comes from these reactors.[55] They operate day in and day out, regardless of weather, with no greenhouse gas emissions. They would seem to be the perfect way to replace fossil fuels for electricity. They have many advocates. So what's the problem?

(A) Are Nuclear Reactors Safe?

Well, yes and no. Nuclear reactors can't explode, like atom bombs, because they have control rods that drop down among the uranium fuel rods and prevent a runaway nuclear reaction. But if they lose the coolant that carries away the heat to the steam generator (Figure 24), then the fuel rods get hot and melt. The molten rods react with residual water to produce hydrogen, which can cause a conventional (non-nuclear) explosion. Since uranium fission builds up radioactive elements in the fuel rods, an explosion can release a lot of radioactivity.

That is what happened in 1986 to a nuclear plant at the town of Chernobyl,[56] in Ukraine, then part of the Soviet Union. A combination of malfunctioning controls and operator misjudgments caused loss of cooling water. Then a disastrous explosion blew off the roof of the plant and released a cloud of radioactive debris. Two workers were killed by the explosion and 28 more died of radiation effects. Chernobyl's 120,000 residents

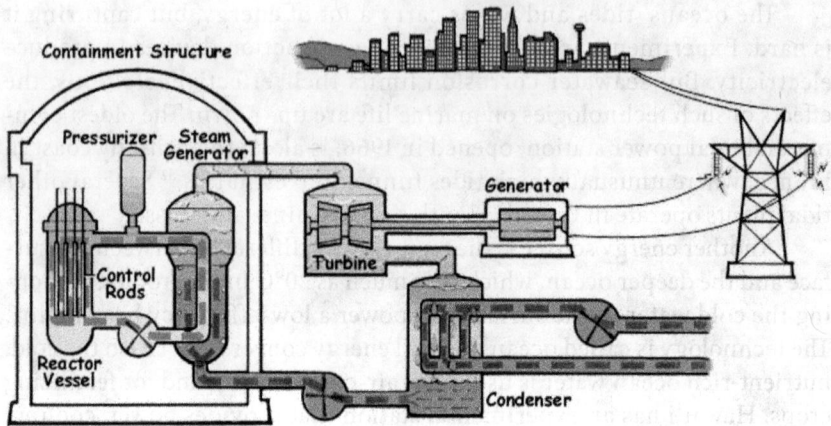

FIGURE 24. In a nuclear reactor, control rods in the nuclear fuel are adjusted to keep the reaction from running out of control. Water under pressure circulates through the reactor vessel and heats a steam generator that runs the electricity-generating turbine. Graphic is "Pressurized Water Reactors," U.S. Nuclear Regulatory Commission, accessed February 9, 2024, https://www.nrc.gov/reactors/power/pwrs.html.

were evacuated from a radioactive zone extending 30 kilometers around the reactor. The explosion lofted a radioactive cloud that drifted over Europe. Radioactive particles rained out on downwind countries. They contaminated milk from cows that ate fallout-contaminated grass; the milk had to be thrown away.

In 2011, a magnitude 9 offshore earthquake sent a huge tsunami crashing into the Japanese coast. It resulted in widespread destruction and 20,000 deaths. The wave engulfed an oceanside nuclear power facility at Fukushima, knocked out the power grid, flooded the plant's backup diesel generators, and halted the emergency cooling water system.[57] Fuel rods melted, and a series of explosions followed. Fortunately, the containment building stayed in place. But some radioactive material escaped into the atmosphere and the seawater. As a precaution, over 150,000 people were evacuated from surrounding communities. No health effects from the radioactivity have yet been detected, although several hundred eventual cancer deaths are expected. A decontamination program for the area will take 30–40 years. The main result is a huge psychological toll on the displaced residents, like that at Chernobyl 25 years earlier.

Taken as a whole, the safety record of the nuclear industry is quite good. The hundreds of nuclear plants worldwide had a number of accidents. But there have only been two real disasters. Many non-nuclear industrial accidents have taken more lives, and non-nuclear pollution contributes to many more deaths. Nevertheless, the possibility of another Chernobyl or Fukushima casts a pall over the industry. Precautions to prevent conceivable accidents and to reassure the public make construction and maintenance of nuclear plants hugely expensive.

(B) What About Nuclear Waste?

The uranium fuel rods in a reactor have to be replaced each year. The spent rods are placed in pools of water to dissipate the heat and let the most intense radioactivity decay away. In the United States, the rods are then stored in concrete casks, which have an estimated lifetime to 100 years. Eventually they are to be buried deep underground. But the U.S. site, under Yucca Mountain in Nevada, is embroiled in controversy, and its future is uncertain.[58] The problem is that the radioactive elements in the spent rods include some that last for hundreds of thousands of years. Ensuring that they do not escape to the environment over such a long time is a huge challenge. Finland is the first country to open a geological storage site for its nuclear waste.[59] It is almost 1,500 feet deep, located close to Finland's nuclear power plants, which supply one-third of the country's electricity.

(C) Are Reactors Connected with Bombs?

Yes, they are. Naturally occurring uranium has only 0.7 percent of uranium-235 (U-235), the form that undergoes nuclear fission. High-tech methods are needed to concentrate U-235 to the 4 percent needed to maintain the fission reaction in the fuel rods. Once acquired, these same methods can concentrate U-235 further to the level required by bombs, about 20 percent. This connection is the focus of international concern about proliferation of nuclear weapons in countries that develop U-235 concentration technology for nuclear power development. The controversy about Iran's nuclear weapons capability is a case in point.

Another weapons connection involves the element plutonium, which builds up in fuel rods over time. One form of the element, Pu-239, can undergo nuclear fission, like U-235. This is not a problem while plutonium stays in the fuel rod. But some countries want to reprocess fuel rods, to extract the Pu-239 as well as the remaining U-235 for more reactor fuel. Pu-239 can itself be fashioned into a bomb.

However, spent fuel rods must be handled remotely, making reprocessing hazardous and expensive. The cost is currently greater than the cost of the nuclear fuel it can provide.

(D) What Is the Future for Nuclear Energy?

Nuclear power began as a spin-off of nuclear weapons development during and after World War II. It expanded rapidly through the 1970s and 1980s, then leveled off. Fossil fuel prices fell, and public worries about nuclear safety rose, especially in the aftermath of the Chernobyl disaster. Nuclear plants around the world are aging, and few new ones have been built. Several European countries are phasing out nuclear power. But China and India have ambitious plans for new plant construction to meet rapidly growing electricity demand. The United States still has the largest number of nuclear power reactors, 93, which supply 18 percent of its electricity supply.[60] Their future is uncertain.

On the other hand, nuclear power can help limit greenhouse gas emissions. And new designs for safer and cheaper nuclear plants are being developed. The main problem is time and money and the unsolved problem of nuclear waste disposal. The new designs will take several years to authorize and build, while climate urgency grows each year. And the costs are unlikely to match the dropping costs of solar and wind energy.

9. Will We Get to Fusion Energy?

Energy can also come from nuclear fusion, specifically from fusing nuclei of hydrogen into heavier nuclei of helium (Figure 25). Nuclear fusion powers the sun's outpouring of light. But harnessing it to generate electricity is very hard because it requires extremely high temperatures, millions of degrees, to initiate the reaction. No reactor could withstand such temperatures for long. Scientists hope to solve this problem by using magnetic fields to keep hot plasma away from the walls of a reactor.

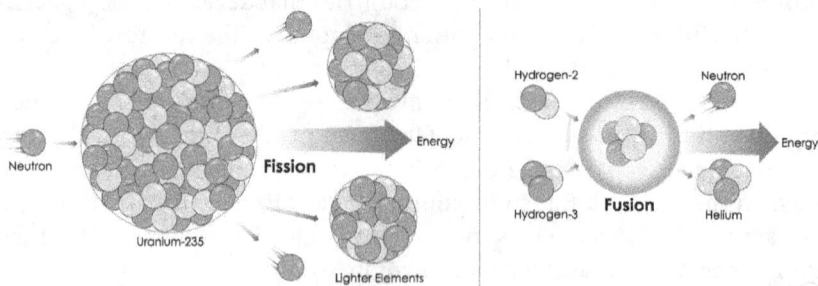

FIGURE 25. Nuclear fission versus nuclear fusion processes to generate energy. Illustration by Alexandra Soldatova.

Alternatively, they might be able to use powerful lasers focused on frozen pellets of hydrogen, forcing them to implode and fuse.

An international consortium is building a large, expensive demonstration plant to generate fusion energy by 2035.[61] But there are around 30 privately funded fusion energy companies that hope to build smaller fusion energy machines to power an electrical grid within the next decade.[62] If it succeeds, fusion could be a source of almost limitless energy. One kilogram of fusion fuel could yield as much energy as 10 million kilograms of fossil fuels.[63] But the goal remains years away.[64]

10. Are Fuel Crops Emission-Free Energy?

Fuels can be made from harvested plants (Figure 26). This "biomass energy" counts as renewable because the CO_2 released by burning the fuel is taken up again when the vegetation grows back. But biomass fuels are decidedly not free of emissions. Energy is needed to plant and tend crops, harvest the vegetation, and convert it to fuel, usually with machines that burn fossil fuels. When these inputs are taken into account, the net saving of CO_2 emissions is just a fraction of the CO_2 released.[65]

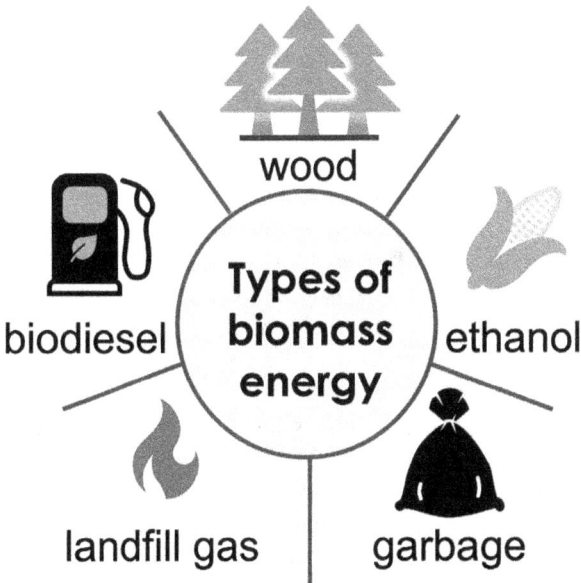

FIGURE 26. Types of biomass-derived energy sources. Adapted from U.S. Energy Information Administration, https://www.eia.gov/energyexplained/biomass/.

The most widely used biomass transportation fuels are ethanol and biodiesel. Brazil is a leader in fuel ethanol production. In the United States, gasoline is blended with about 10 percent ethanol because a federal mandate requires oxygen-containing additives to reduce emissions of smog-forming pollutants. Ethanol is made by fermenting starch from corn in the United States and sugar from sugarcane in Brazil.

The reduction in CO_2 emissions from ethanol fuel, relative to gasoline, is about 40 percent in the United States, when land clearing, growing corn, and converting it to ethanol are taken into account.[66] Brazilian ethanol from sugarcane does much better, about 60 percent,[67] because of abundant sunshine and high yields. Ethanol is much harder to make from cellulose, which is more abundant in plants than starch or sugar. Cellulose-based ethanol plants are not a commercial success.

Biodiesel is made from vegetable oils, mostly soy or palm oil. It is blended into ordinary petroleum diesel as fuel for cars and trucks. When made from soy oil, biodiesel reduces CO_2 emissions by about 60 percent relative to gasoline.[68] It does even better if made from waste vegetable oil or waste animal fat, turning the waste into a resource.[69] But the demand for biodiesel is much larger than waste oil and fat can supply. Palm oil is also an efficient source; tropical palm plantations are highly productive. But palm plantations threaten tropical forest, especially in Indonesia and Malaysia (see Chapter 9). They destroy rich forest ecosystems and displace many local communities that rely on the forests. The massive fires set to clear the forest emit huge amounts of CO_2 and smoke and contaminate the air over large regions.

Ethanol and biodiesel could drive up food prices by competing with food crops for agricultural land. As populations expand and climate-related crop failures become more common, growing enough food is an increasing challenge. Biofuels could be made from hardier plants grown on marginal land but would then cost more. An attractive option may be to make biodiesel from algae, which grows in ocean water and has high oil content.[70] But currently the cost and energy requirement of extracting the oil is prohibitive.

Wood is the traditional biomass fuel, and it is still widely used for heating and cooking, especially in the developing world. But woodsmoke is unhealthy to breathe because of all its tiny particles. Many cities prohibit the installation of wood fireplaces in new housing.

But power plants can be fueled by wood pellets instead of coal. The European Union counts wood energy as renewable and has subsidized it as part of its green energy strategy. So wood is now Europe's largest renewable energy source, far ahead of wind and solar. Initially the idea was to use sawdust and waste wood to make compressed wood pellets to fuel power plants. But whole trees have increasingly been logged in central Europe to feed the growing demand.[71] When the trees grow back, the emitted CO_2 is taken back from the atmosphere. But regrowing trees takes a long time. And the CO_2 initially emitted from burning the wood can actually exceed that from burning coal. That's because wood contains water and burns less efficiently than coal. Wood proponents argue that meeting the fuel demand will motivate the planting of more trees on marginal lands, thereby absorbing more CO_2. But opponents fear that the demand will instead encourage logging of mature forest, making the problem worse.

Drawn by the European subsidies, large quantities of wood pellets are imported from the U.S. East Coast. The southeastern states are filled with fast-growing pines and hardwood trees and can be logged more sustainably than the mature forests of Europe.[72] Also, downed and diseased trees can be used for the wood pellets. They should in any case be thinned out to reduce the danger of wildfires. But again, opponents of wood fuel argue that counting wood as a renewable fuel will encourage mass deforestation.[73]

Methane, another biomass fuel, is formed naturally in landfills and manure piles. Methane that escapes to the atmosphere is a powerful greenhouse gas. But it can be collected and burned as a fuel. Farms use anaerobic digesters to make methane from manure and other organic wastes; the residue left behind can be high-grade fertilizer. These digesters are especially prevalent in China and India and are spreading in Europe as part of the push to more renewable energy.[74] Finally, garbage can be burned in "waste-to-energy" incinerators to generate electricity, as described in Chapter 4.

11. Summary

The Industrial Revolution came about by harnessing fossil fuels: coal, oil, and gas. As economic development spread around the world, the burning of fossil fuels increased dramatically. The resulting CO_2 and other greenhouse gases are raising temperatures at the earth's surface. The effects of global warming are already clear. They will continue to increase unless we curb fossil fuels. Most countries are committed to eventually replacing fossil fuels with alternate energy sources. Some will use more nuclear power, which produces no greenhouse gases, but safety concerns about reactors, nuclear waste, and nuclear weapons raise costs and public opposition. Hydropower is also free of emissions, but dams bring their own environmental and political problems that make suitable new sites hard to find. Meanwhile, solar and wind power have become price competitive with fossil fuels, but we need ways to store their energy economically to deal with their intermittent character. Biomass and geothermal power can also contribute to low emissions energy.

In sum, our urgent problem is how to produce enough energy without raising the planet's temperature to disastrous levels. The answer is to slow and stop fossil fuel burning very soon. Many ways to do this are available, and they all need to be pursued. But it will take enormous effort and political will to do so.

4

Using Energy

Can Less Mean More?

1. How Can We Use Less Energy and Still Have a Better Life?

The world produces more and more energy, and that releases more and more greenhouse gases. But do we actually need so much energy? That's an important question because any energy that is not needed reduces the amount that must be produced. If our goal is to reduce fossil fuel burning, we can switch to clean energy. But that means building new clean energy plants, which takes a lot of time. Or we can reduce the amount of energy we use, which has an immediate effect. We are running out of time. So conserving energy is very important.

Saving energy doesn't mean we have to go back to living in caves. A lot can be done without diminishing the quality of life. As a matter of fact, our lives will be enhanced. That's because in addition to slowing global warming, reducing fossil fuel use improves the quality of the air we breathe (Chapter 6). Energy production and use account for three-quarters of global greenhouse gas emissions (Figure 27). This includes power plants that provide heat and electricity for homes and factories, manufacturing and construction, farm equipment, fertilizer production, and transportation: all those cars, trucks, buses, trains, ships, and planes. Let's look at some of the ways we can be more efficient in key stages of this vast energy system by saving fossil fuels *before* they are burned.

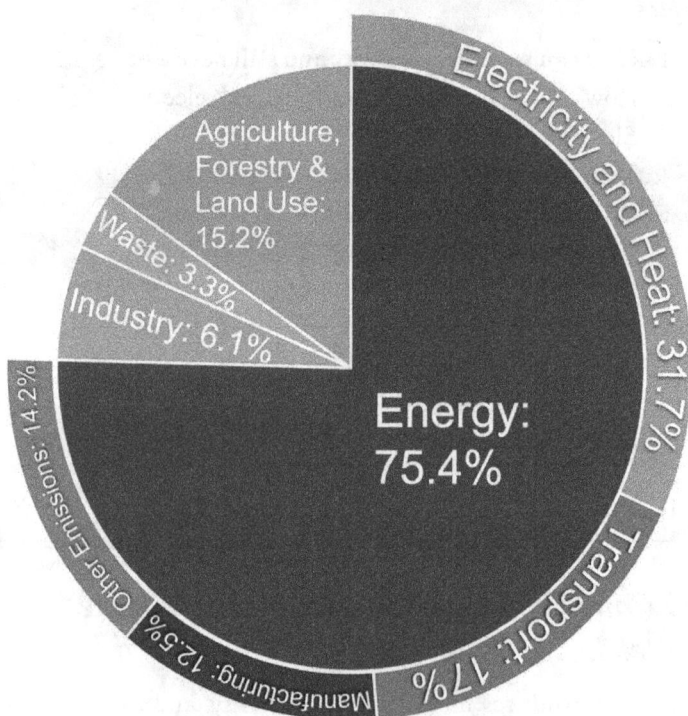

FIGURE 27. Global greenhouse gas emission by sector in 2019. The energy sector includes contributions from electricity and heat (for residential, commercial, and industrial buildings), transport, and manufacturing and construction. Data from Climate Watch. 2022. Washington, D.C.: World Resources Institute. Accessed online at https://www.climatewatchdata.org/ghg-emissions on October 27, 2023. Climate Watch Historical GHG Emissions are derived from several sources, including FAO 2021, FAOSTAT Emissions Database (Land-Use Change, Forestry, and Agriculture data), and OECD/IEA, 2021 (CO_2 Emissions from Fuel Combustion data).

2. How Can We Use Less Fuel and Get More Electricity?

When we burn fuels to make electricity via steam-driven turbines, a lot of the energy is wasted as escaped heat. Coal power plant thermal efficiency is only about 32 percent, meaning that two-thirds of the coal energy is wasted. Nuclear plant efficiencies are currently in the same range, 32–34 percent. Gas power plants do better, at about 44 percent efficiency.[1] Gas, heated in a stream of compressed air, can also drive a gas turbine generator, which is basically a jet aircraft engine with a spinning turbine that generates electricity. The exhaust gas from the turbine is hot enough to make steam for a conventional steam generator. This combination of gas turbine and steam generator, a combined-cycle gas turbine, has an overall efficiency of 60 percent.[2] Although gas is a fossil fuel, it produces less CO_2 than coal or oil, and its higher efficiency means less CO_2 is emitted per unit of energy.

Fuel can also be used more efficiently by heating buildings with the waste heat instead of throwing it away. Hot water from the steam generator can be piped to buildings, replacing furnaces and saving the fuel they would have burned. Producing two useful forms of energy, heat as well as electricity, is "cogeneration." District heating systems, in which the hot water is recovered from a power plant and piped to all the buildings in a district, are widely used in Europe, Japan, and northern China. In the United States, cogeneration plants operate on smaller scales, providing both heat and electricity to individual factories and groups of buildings at universities and individual businesses.[3] Small-scale cogeneration facilities are especially beneficial in remote areas with limited grid infrastructures.

3. Electrify Everything?

Electricity runs all our appliances. But it could also replace fossil fuels for heating buildings and for transportation. This would save a lot of energy because electric motors are very efficient. For example, cars' internal combustion engines waste up to 80 percent of the fossil fuel energy, while only 20 percent energy is lost in electric cars motors.[4] And if the electricity to charge the cars comes from emission-free sources—hydro, solar, wind, or nuclear—that eliminates fossil fuels altogether.

For heating houses, electrical heat pumps use less energy than fossil fuel furnaces or boilers.[5] A heat pump is essentially an air conditioner operating in reverse, pumping heat into a building rather than out of it. On hot days, the same device can run forward as an air conditioner. The heat pump and air conditioner efficiencies go down as the weather gets colder or hotter outside. They work best in temperate climates. But as the technology improves, even cold-climate places like Alaska, Sweden, and Norway adapt heat pumps to help keep well-insulated homes warm.

The low efficiency of ordinary heat pumps in either cold or hot climates can be overcome with a geothermal heat pump. Its working fluid circulates through pipes buried underground, where the temperature is fairly constant year-round regardless of the weather.

4. Transportation: Can We Kick the Oil Habit?

Transportation uses half of the world's oil and a quarter of total energy production. Cars, buses, trucks, trains, ships, and planes run on liquid fuels extracted from oil. Production of all these vehicles is increasing, especially in China, India, and other developing countries. If their operating efficiencies were improved, there would be a huge reduction of CO_2.

Regulations can help. For example, mileage standards for internal combustion engines compel automakers to improve the fuel mileage of their cars. In the United States, average car mileage has increased since 1975, while real-world CO_2 emission from the engines decreased (Figure 28).[6] But some of this improvement was offset by drivers switching to larger vehicles as gasoline prices dropped. Sports utility vehicles, which comprise around 45 percent of all car sales globally,[7] are classified as light trucks, which have lower mileage standards than cars.

Air pollution complicates efficiency measures. To combat smog and ozone (Chapter 6), municipalities, states, and countries impose limits on the emission of unburned hydrocarbons and nitrogen oxides. Catalytic converters are used to achieve these limits, but they lower fuel efficiency. Better mileage is possible with higher compression engines, which burn gasoline more completely and get higher power. But their higher temperatures boost nitrogen oxide production and worsen smog substantially (Chapter 6). Diesel engines naturally have high compression, making nitrogen oxide control difficult. In a 2015 scandal, Volkswagen paid hefty fines and had to recall millions of diesel cars. It had circumvented nitrogen oxide limits by programming diesel car engines to operate less efficiently while being tested.[8]

Diesel engines emit soot and are a major source of small particles (PM2.5—see Chapter 6), the major health hazard in polluted air. Even though diesel trucks are equipped with particle traps in their exhaust pipes, the trucks are major contributors to the PM2.5 load in cities.

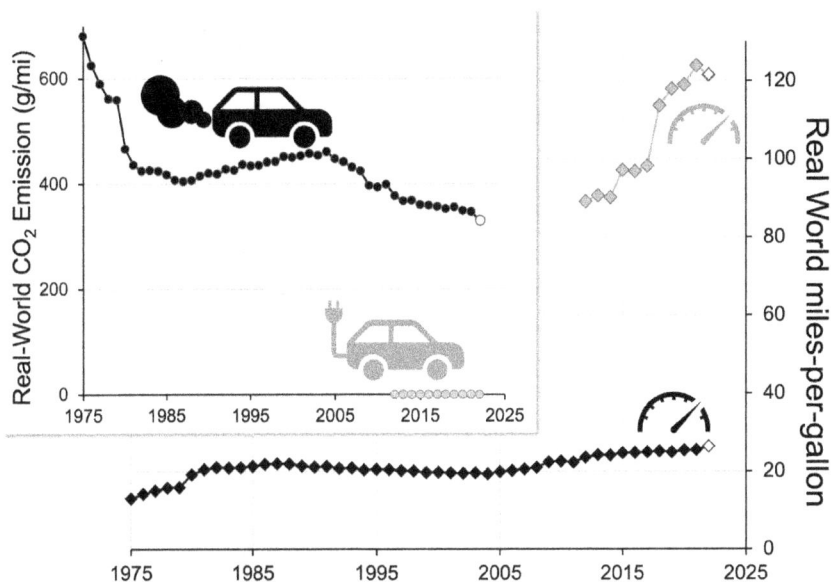

FIGURE 28. Car mileage and CO_2 emissions estimates, averaged for all light-duty vehicle models (black dots) sold in the United States and compared to electric vehicles (gray dots). (Real-world miles per gallon for electric vehicles are for Tesla models, calculated as miles driven using the same energy content as a gallon of gas.) Fuel economy (miles per gallon) is improving only slowly because of increasing consumer demand for lower mileage trucks, pick-ups, and SUVs. Data are from U.S. Environmental Protection Agency, "2022 EPA Automotive Trends Report," www.epa.gov/automotive-trends/explore-automotive-trends-data, accessed October 26, 2023.

Electric cars, on the other hand, have no emissions. And even if the electricity is generated with fossil fuels, electric cars use about one-third less fossil fuel than gasoline-fueled cars because the motors are so efficient (Figure 28). If the electricity is generated by renewable sources, then of course no fossil fuel is used. Electric vehicles now comprise 14 percent of all vehicles sold globally, and their numbers are increasing rapidly.[9] Norway, in which 27 percent of vehicles currently in use are already electric or plug-in hybrid, will ban new cars with internal combustion engines by 2025. Many other countries have enacted or are considering such bans by 2030 or 2040. By 2050, almost all internal combustion engines are expected to have disappeared, along with their tailpipe emissions.

Electric vehicles need batteries to store their electricity supply. The traditional lead-acid battery is far too heavy to be scaled up to the power needed to run an electric vehicle, so much lighter lithium-ion batteries are used instead. They are relatively new batteries and are being further developed to improve storage capacity. The environmental costs of mining lithium and other metals used in the batteries need to be addressed.[10]

Battery capacity limits a vehicle's driving range. That and cost are obstacles to wider adoption of electric vehicles. Also, recharging the battery from an ordinary electrical outlet takes several hours. Stations for fast recharges are few and far between except in urban centers. But costs and driving range are improving rapidly, and charging stations are proliferating. China leads in installation of public charging points, and Europe follows. An alternative to charging stations is "battery swapping," emerging in Asia. A fully charged battery replaces the depleted one, which can be charged during off-peak hours from the grid.

For long-range transport, by airplanes, trucks, trains, and ships, batteries of sufficient size will likely remain too heavy. Hydrogen storage (see Chapter 3) might be an emission-free solution for long-range transport. Hydrogen has the highest energy content per gram of any fuel. A pound of H_2 carries 236 times as much energy as a pound of lithium battery. However, hydrogen occupies a much larger volume than liquid fuels; liquid fuels made from hydrogen may turn out to be more practical for long-range transport.[11]

5. Fuel Cells: Will Hydrogen Become Our Main Fuel?

Fuel cells generate electricity directly from a fuel without burning it. They don't work with fossil fuels because the reactions are too slow, but they do work with hydrogen gas. The fuel cell reacts hydrogen with oxygen in the air, producing electricity and water. There are no emissions. Special tanks, made of strong composite material, can store the hydrogen at high pressure. Fuel cell plus hydrogen tank weigh less than batteries storing the same amount of energy. So airplanes, trucks, trains, and ships could run on fuel-cell electricity from hydrogen. Or they can burn the hydrogen to drive a motor, like any other fuel. However, burning does produce polluting nitrogen oxides.

Fuel cell cars can also drive longer distances on a tank of hydrogen than on a battery charge, and filling the hydrogen tank takes only minutes like gasoline. Hydrogen filling stations, however, would need to be built on a massive scale to service cars.

The two methods, electricity from batteries or from hydrogen, are alternative routes to saving fossil fuels. Battery technology is further advanced now, but hydrogen and fuel cell technology may catch up.

But where can we get the hydrogen?

(A) Hydrogen: Gray, Blue, Green, and White

Today, hydrogen is mostly made from natural gas by reacting it with water at high temperature and pressure. This hydrogen is mostly used in oil refining and to produce ammonia for fertilizer. Lots of CO_2 is emitted because the reaction produces CO_2 along with the hydrogen and because extra gas is burned to achieve the high temperature needed to run the reaction. Also, some methane, the main component of natural gas, leaks out into the atmosphere. Methane is a far more potent greenhouse gas than CO_2. So hydrogen from natural gas, called "gray hydrogen," is definitely not a "clean" fuel.[12]

Gas producers are proposing to capture and bury the CO_2 as a step toward limiting global warming. The hydrogen produced from natural gas with carbon capture is called "blue hydrogen" (Figure 29), distinguishing it from gray hydrogen, which is produced with release of the CO_2 to the air. But it is not clear who would pay for the carbon capture, an energy-intensive process itself that, for now, requires burning of more fossil fuels. And it does not solve the problem of methane leakage. Because so much gas is used, even a small leak rate would cancel any greenhouse advantage.[13]

But hydrogen can come from water instead of natural gas. In water electrolysis, a 200-year-old technique, electricity can split H_2O into its elemental constituents, H_2 and O_2. That's just the reverse of the fuel cell, which combines hydrogen and oxygen to make electricity and water. Even if the electricity comes from fossil fuel power plants, greenhouse emissions are lower than for hydrogen made from gas. And if the electricity is from renewable sources, then the hydrogen has no associated greenhouse emissions. It is "green hydrogen." Today, green hydrogen is more expensive than blue or gray hydrogen, but improvements in electrolyzer technology will bring the cost down in time. It is also possible to use chemical catalysts and even algae to harness solar electricity more effectively in green hydrogen production.

Not many geologists believed that there is hydrogen to be found in the earth's crust in significant quantities. But in 1987, drillers detected copious hydrogen in a water well at the village of Bourakebougou in Mali.[14] Enough hydrogen was coming from the well to fuel a power plant that now provides the village with electricity. The hydrogen flow has not decreased since the plant started up in 2012, indicating a continuous natural source of the gas. Natural ("white," or sometimes called "gold") hydrogen has been detected in many places around the globe. But we don't yet know whether and where there might be commercially significant reservoirs. Deep drilling has always been directed at layers of sedimentary rock,

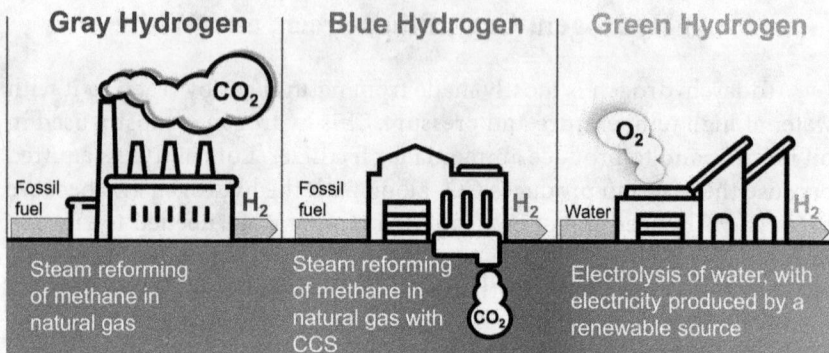

FIGURE 29. Hydrogen gas can be produced from natural gas, with high greenhouse gas emission (gray hydrogen), or from natural gas with carbon capture and storage (CCS; blue hydrogen), or from electrolysis of water, with essentially zero emission if renewable electricity is used (green hydrogen). Adapted from Hellonext, https://www.hellonext.world/green-blue-and-grey-hydrogen-the-main-differences/.

which were once ocean bottoms. There, buried organisms would have been transformed into oil and gas, but no one thought to look for hydrogen.[15]

The natural hydrogen found at Bourakebougou likely results from the reaction of water with hot, iron-containing rock. The iron can extract the oxygen atom of H_2O, leaving H_2, hydrogen gas. If water continues to flow through the rock, hydrogen production would also be continuous. That makes natural hydrogen a potentially renewable source of energy, but we don't know how significant a source it could become. Exploration is underway, with many start-ups popping up.

(B) The Path Ahead for Hydrogen

Hydrogen has a public relations problem. It stems from the 1937 tragedy of the Hindenburg, a hydrogen-filled dirigible.[16] It was a competitor to airplanes for transporting cargo and people. Hydrogen was used to fill the balloon because it is much lighter than air. As the Hindenburg carried passengers across the Atlantic, it caught fire and burned while landing in New Jersey in a lightning storm. Thirty-six people were killed, and dozens more were injured. Hydrogen was blamed, but it was actually the canvas walls of the dirigible and the diesel fuel for the craft's engine that burned. Hydrogen is certainly flammable, and it may have sparked the fire. But it escapes into the air too fast to continue burning. In a car, it is actually less dangerous than gasoline, whose heavier-than-air vapors can pool on the ground and catch fire.

Hydrogen could also be a storage medium for the electric grid if storing solar and wind energy becomes critical (Chapter 3). Like natural gas, hydrogen could be stored in underground caverns. From there, it could be shipped in retrofitted gas pipelines and carried to fuel cells anywhere that electricity is needed. There would then be a "hydrogen economy" in which hydrogen is a major energy currency. Whether provided by fuel cells or power generators, electricity is key to an emissions-free future.

6. Do Materials Matter?

They certainly do. It takes lots of energy to process raw materials and fashion them into the structures and products we use. Figure 30 illustrates how much raw stuff we produce every year.

Making products lighter or more durable can save energy. Replacing steel with much lighter aluminum and plastics has allowed carmakers to lighten cars and increase mileage. The development of specialty steels that can withstand high temperatures allowed development of the gas turbine that drives jet aircraft and higher efficiency power stations (discussed above).

Reducing the amount of material can also save energy. Computers have become increasingly powerful but also much smaller over the years. Many other products have become smaller and lighter, saving energy in transporting and using them.

Industry directly emits greenhouse gases as by-

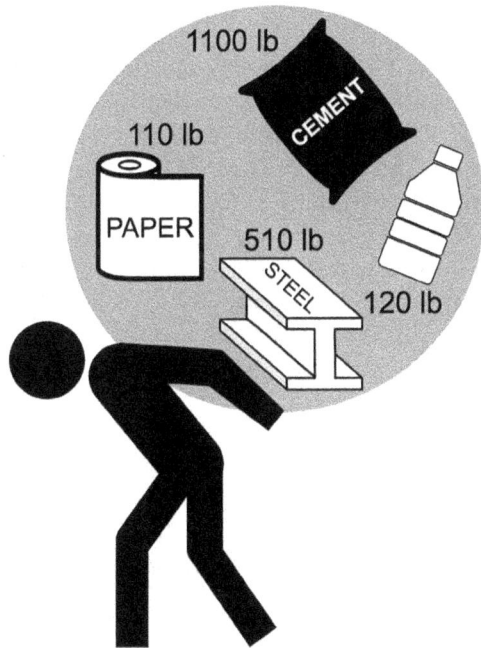

FIGURE 30. Every year, over 1,000 pounds of cement, over 500 pounds of steel, and over 100 pounds of plastic and paper products are manufactured per person. Data are from Global Cement and Concrete Association (2023), World Steel Association (2023), Global Plastics Outlook Database (2019), and Statista (2022).

products of manufacturing processes. But it releases even more from burning fossil fuels to get energy to drive these processes that often occur at high temperatures. Improving these processes could cut a lot of emissions.

Steel is a huge contributor to global warming, accounting for about 8 percent of global greenhouse emissions.[17] To make steel, iron ore is dumped into a coal-fired blast furnace. Several high-temperature steps convert the ore to iron and then to steel, which is iron alloyed with a small amount of carbon to give it strength. The process emits CO_2 copiously: 1.83 tons of it for every ton of steel.[18] And every year we produce about a quarter of a ton of steel per person on the planet. Steelmakers could eliminate these emissions by (1) using an electric arc furnace to provide the needed heat and (2) using hydrogen made from renewable electricity to reduce the oxide ore to iron. Several companies plan to make "green steel" this way.

Mining and shipping of the iron ore add a lot to steel's emission cost. About 40 percent of the world's iron ore is dug up in the Western Australian desert. Huge diesel-powered machines dig the ore in dozens of mines and haul it to waiting freight ships at Port Hedland, more than 100 miles away. Energy companies are planning a major solar and wind farm, eight times the area of New York City,[19] to take advantage of the abundant sunshine and wind near the mines. Green hydrogen will be made with the electricity from the farm and used to power the mines and trucks, replacing diesel.

As a result of these kinds of energy savings, energy consumption hardly changed in Europe and North America over the last 40 years (Figure 18 in Chapter 3) despite several-fold growth in their economies. Worldwide energy growth is instead driven by the developing economies of Asia.

7. Can We Survive Concrete?

Concrete is second only to water as the most used material in the world. Nearly 30 billion tons of it are produced each year. That's about four tons for every person on the planet.[20] China accounts for about half the world's total, reflecting its rapid economic development. Concrete has been used for thousands of years: the Great Wall of China, the Roman Coliseum, and the Greek Parthenon are examples of concrete that withstood centuries of weathering and human turbulence. Modern concrete, in contrast, must be repaired after about a hundred years. Key to the Great Wall's longevity was the Ming dynasty's innovation of adding sticky rice–lime mortar to impart mechanical stability.[21] In the case of Roman concrete, the key addition was volcanic ash and tiny chunks of lime with self-healing properties.[22]

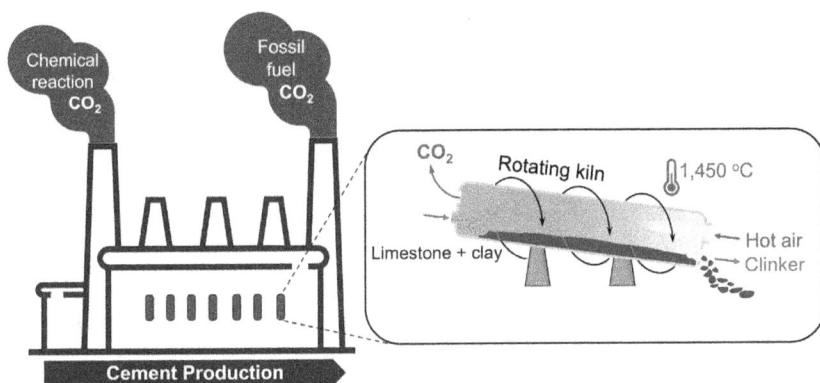

FIGURE 31. Roasting limestone, CaCO3, to make cement, drives off CO_2, leaving CaO, the active ingredient in the "clinker." CO_2 is also released from the fossil fuel burned to achieve the needed high temperature. Adapted from Carbon Brief Infographics, https://www.carbonbrief.org/qa-why-cement-emissions-matter-for-climate-change/.

Concrete is made by mixing crushed stone, gravel, and sand with cement, which holds the aggregate particles together and hardens in place. The cement is made by roasting a mixture of clay and limestone in a kiln (Figure 31), grinding up the resulting "clinker" and combining it with other minerals in water. Limestone is calcium carbonate, $CaCO_3$, and roasting it drives off CO_2, leaving calcium oxide, CaO, or lime. Lime is a reactive substance that is responsible for cement's binding properties. Burning fossil fuel for the roasting adds to the CO_2 released by the $CaCO_3$. Like steel, cement production accounts for 8 percent of global greenhouse gases. Each ton of cement produces about a ton of CO_2.

Concrete has other environmental impacts. An estimated 1.7 percent of all water used globally goes into cement production.[23] The very high temperature of the roasting flame produces copious nitrogen oxides. And construction projects raise dust, including the fine particles that are the main health hazard of air pollution (Chapter 6). Globally, an estimated 7.8 percent of nitrogen oxides and 6.4 percent of fine particles are attributed to the use of concrete.[24]

Engineers are working on reducing emissions from cement production or finding alternative materials for cement, often using artificial intelligence to aid in the search.[25] Methods include:

- Adding back CO_2, which reacts with the lime to form $CaCO_3$ and hardening the cement while it is setting.[26]
- Replacing limestone with fly ash from coal plant wastes or slag from steel production.[27]

- Use an electrolyzer, to convert limestone to lime, leaving bicarbonate behind instead of CO_2.[28]
- Use magnesium silicates, abundant in the earth's crust, instead of limestone.[29] The silicates do not produce CO_2.

Many companies are working on these alternatives, hoping to scale up to the challenge of making a dent in cement's climate footprint.[30] Because cement is so cheap and widely used, cement companies are reluctant to change how they operate. Altering the way concrete is made is a huge opportunity for reducing greenhouse emissions but also a huge challenge.

Unfortunately, concrete also attracts corruption, especially in developing countries.[31] Large construction projects—bridges, dams, stadiums—lend prestige to those in power and offer opportunities for bribes that inflate costs and saddle the country with debt. In Brazil, a scandal involving huge construction companies that built the facilities for the 2014 World Cup and the 2016 Olympics ensnared many politicians and led to the fall of the government and the imprisonment of a former president.[32]

8. Can Waste Be Turned Into Energy?

Materials and energy are also connected at the end of the life of consumer products when they are discarded as waste. Since municipal trash contains much combustible material, why not burn it and recover the energy as electricity and heat? Municipalities around the world are doing this in "waste-to-energy" projects, not only to recover energy but also to minimize the need for landfills. There are over 2,000 such projects worldwide, many of them in Japan and European countries. Japan, having little space for landfills, burns 75 percent of its municipal waste with energy recovery.[33] But globally, waste-to-energy plants treat just around 11 percent of the world's municipal solid waste; 5 percent of it is composted and the rest is landfilled or just dumped.[34]

The trash is burned in an incinerator, whose heat generates steam and drives an electricity generator, just as in power plants. Trash also contains non-combustible material; metals and glass shards are recovered from the residue for recycling, and the remaining waste, reduced up to 90 percent by volume, is sent to a landfill. This remaining waste is mostly ash and could be used as a limestone replacement in concrete production, as described above. The waste heat from the incinerator can be used to heat homes and factories in the municipality.

People fear that incinerators emit pollutants; proposals for municipal incinerators attract local opposition. But modern incinerators have effective emission control systems and meet stringent air pollution standards.[35] To ensure public acceptance, the Toshima incineration plant in Tokyo was constructed with a tall stack to clear nearby skyscrapers and with a sport center and a heated swimming pool next to it.[36]

9. Does Recycling Work?

Recycling products can save energy because less raw material needs to be extracted from the earth and processed (Figure 32). Using recycled steel saves over 70 percent of the energy required to mine iron oxide ore and transform it into steel. Recycling copper, used widely in electronics, saves 85 percent of the energy required for primary production. For aluminum, the energy saving is even greater, 95 percent, because the ore, aluminum oxide, is very stable and requires a great deal of energy to extract aluminum metal from it.[37] Recycling paper saves 68 percent of the energy that goes into cutting trees, making wood pulp, extracting the cellulose, and making it into paper.[38] According to the U.S. Energy Information Agency, recycling a ton of paper also saves 7,000 gallons (26,500 liters) of water, 3.3 cubic yards (2.5 cubic meter) of landfill space, and a ton of CO_2 emissions.[39] Recycling plastics saves 88 percent of the energy that goes into pumping oil from the ground and transforming it into petrochemicals from which plastics are currently made.[40]

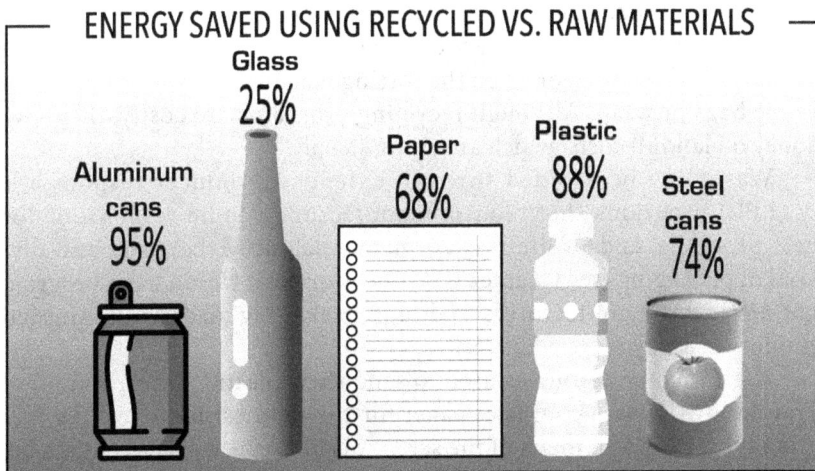

ENERGY SAVED USING RECYCLED VS. RAW MATERIALS

Glass
25%

Aluminum cans
95%

Paper
68%

Plastic
88%

Steel cans
74%

FIGURE 32. Energy saved using recycled versus raw materials. Icons made by Freepik from www.flaticon.com.

Recycling rates depend greatly on the nature of the products. Steel, the most widely used metal in the world, has a high recycling rate, 60 percent, partly because so much of it is used in construction.[41] It can be recovered when buildings are demolished. Sixty percent of copper, which is mostly used in wiring, is recycled in the United States[42] and 40 percent on average globally.[43] The recycling rate of aluminum, most of which is used in construction and transportation, is even higher at 76 percent.[44] So is the recycling rate of lead, used mostly in batteries; in the United States, 99 percent of lead-acid batteries are recycled.[45]

Recycling is harder to do for consumer products because they are widely dispersed. In the United States, only half of aluminum soda and beer cans are recycled.[46] In Europe, the recycling rate is much higher, 73 percent.[47]

Recycling of consumer products is also a way for cities to deal with trash, most of which is dumped in landfills. As these fill up in urban areas, the trash has to be hauled to more distant locations, raising costs and increasing fuel consumption. Also, landfills generate methane, a powerful greenhouse gas, because bacterial decomposition of organic matter uses up the available oxygen. That allows methane-producing anaerobic bacteria to take over. The methane can, however, be collected from the landfill to be used as fuel.[48] Until capped, landfills can also emit fumes that are offensive to nearby residents and may be harmful to their health.

Recycling and composting programs reduce the volume of trash. But their success depends on the diligence of households in sorting the trash and on the industrial demand for recycled material. Problems arise when the contents of recycling bins are contaminated with food or other waste and must be discarded, or when the sorting machines become fouled with plastic bags or wrap. Although recycling programs are costly, they save money on landfill costs, which are rising steeply.

Waste can be avoided through extended producer responsibility (EPR) programs that require manufacturers to be responsible for their products' end-of-life management, including recycling and disposal of packaging (see Chapter 11).[49] The European Union has a program that motivates manufacturers to design packaging made with minimal amounts of easily recycled materials.

High-income countries used to send their plastic, paper, and other scrap to low-income countries eager for the monies that recycling fees brought in. However, much of the scrap was not recycled at all but simply dumped, polluting the receiving countries. In 2017, China banned importation of scrap material; before that, China imported nearly half of the world's scrap plastic and paper.[50] Malaysia, Thailand, and Vietnam also stopped accepting trash. U.S. plastic scrap exports to all countries fell by half, from 750,000 to 375,000 tons, between 2017 and 2019.[51] In 2019, 187 countries agreed to dramatically restrict international trade in scrap plastic under the Basel Convention Treaty.[52] The problem of plastics recycling is taken up in the next chapter.

10. Can New Technology Help?

Technology offers many opportunities for energy savings. Lighting is a clear example. Inefficient incandescent bulbs were replaced, first by compact fluorescent bulbs and then by light-emitting diode (LED) bulbs, now in standard use (Figure 33). Compact fluorescents use four times less[53] and LEDs 10 times less energy than incandescent bulbs[54] for the same amount of light. The bulbs' lifetimes also increase in about the same proportion. LEDs provide huge savings in energy and costs. Lighting consumes about 15 percent of the world's electricity production. Meanwhile, as many as

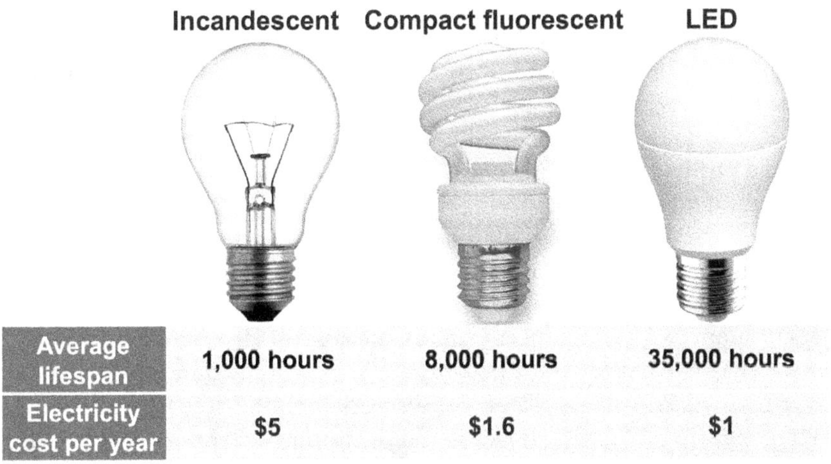

	Incandescent	Compact fluorescent	LED
Average lifespan	1,000 hours	8,000 hours	35,000 hours
Electricity cost per year	$5	$1.6	$1

FIGURE 33. Electricity cost per year for the three kinds of light bulbs (2017 estimates from the Consumer Federation of America). Light bulb photographs are from WikiCommons. Incandescent light bulb photo by Haider, https://commons.wikimedia.org/wiki/File:Light-bulb-1.jpg; https://creative commons.org/licenses/by-sa/4.0/legalcode; CFL light bulb photo by Sun Ladder, https://commons.wikimedia.org/wiki/File:06_Spiral_CFL_Bulb_2010-03-08_(white_back).jpg; https://creativecommons.org/licenses/by-sa/3.0/legalcode; LED light bulb photo by Kingled, https://commons.wikimedia.org/wiki/File:?arówka_led_E27_10W_bulb_kingled_krakow.jpg; https://creative commons.org/licenses/by-sa/4.0/legalcode.

750 million people lack electricity and have no lighting at all; 80 percent of them live in sub–Saharan Africa.[55]

The efficiency of both industrial and household appliances—refrigerators, washers and dryers, air conditioners, and so forth—has greatly improved through technological advances. Government programs help too. The United States has an Energy Star program that rates and publicizes appliance efficiencies. The European Union has a similar program. Since Europeans typically pay twice as much for electricity as Americans do, their appliances were developed to be more efficient. In 2014, the UNEP launched a public-private partnership, United for Efficiency, to encourage adoption of high-efficiency appliances and energy-efficient lighting around the world.[56]

Buildings can save energy too, beyond better insulation and more efficient heating and cooling systems. "Smart buildings" use sensors and microchips to adjust temperature and lighting only as needed by the building occupants. "Smart windows" can adjust the optical quality of the glass to increase or decrease the amount of light allowed into the building.[57]

Online working and learning can have a big energy impact by reducing transportation to and from work. The 2020 worldwide Covid-19 pandemic forced millions of people to work and learn online. It also accelerated new information technologies and new modes of using them. And online shopping ballooned. Delivery vehicles use less energy per purchase than driving to the store. If you drive to the store, you'd have to buy 24 items to make the trip equal to the carbon footprint of just one item ordered online, according to one study.[58] If you take the bus, you'd have to buy eight items.

However, technology also has environmental costs. The massive development of artificial intelligence (AI) is straining electricity, water, and material resources.[59] There has been a huge expansion of data centers to support AI, drawing enormous amounts of electricity. A great deal of water is needed to cool the computers, and many data centers are in dry areas where water is scarce (see also Chapter 8). These large computer farms require rare earth elements and lithium, which are also needed for electric vehicles and in wind generators. On the other hand, many environmental innovators are hopeful that AI will open better avenues to energy and resource conservation and perhaps to more resource-efficient AI computers as well.

11. Summary

Saving energy is even more important than producing it. Saving electricity is especially important because it can provide heat, light, and motion much more efficiently than burning fuels can. Renewable sources can replace fossil fuels for electricity production but require better battery and hydrogen technology for electricity storage. Batteries and hydrogen are also crucial for electrifying transportation. Replacing fossil fuels would combat global warming and make the air much cleaner.

Changing how materials are made and used can save a lot of energy. Steel and cement manufacturing together account for over 10 percent of greenhouse gas emissions. So new methods of production and use of these materials are especially important. New technologies can save energy by improving efficiencies. And they save transportation costs and energy when people work, learn, and shop online. The advent of AI has brought a massive drain on energy, water, and material resources but also the promise of accelerating steps toward energy and resource conservation.

5

Plastics

Love Them or Hate Them?

Topics:

1. Better living through plastics
2. Plastics are essential
3. Plastics save energy
4. Drowning in plastic waste
5. Plastics break up: micro- and nanoplastics
6. What about bioplastics?
7. Does recycling work?
8. Extended producer responsibility
9. Innovation could save plastics
10. Summary

"I just want to say one word to you. Just one word. Are you listening? Plastics." This famous line from the iconic 1967 film *The Graduate*[1] was advice from a family friend to the new college graduate, clueless Benjamin, that plastics were the business opportunity of the future. The counterculture audience of the 1960s loved the film but ridiculed the advice. It was, however, prophetic.

Between 1950 and 2019, production of plastics increased from two million to over 400 million tons a year (Figure 34).[2] For better and for worse, we live in a material world made largely of plastics. All manner of products are made from plastics: clothes, appliances, furniture, vehicles, machines, piping, containers, and wrapping of all kinds. About 100 pounds of plastics are produced annually for every person on the planet, and demand continues to increase.

Asia accounts for about half of plastics production, 32 percent in

Global Plastics Production / million tons

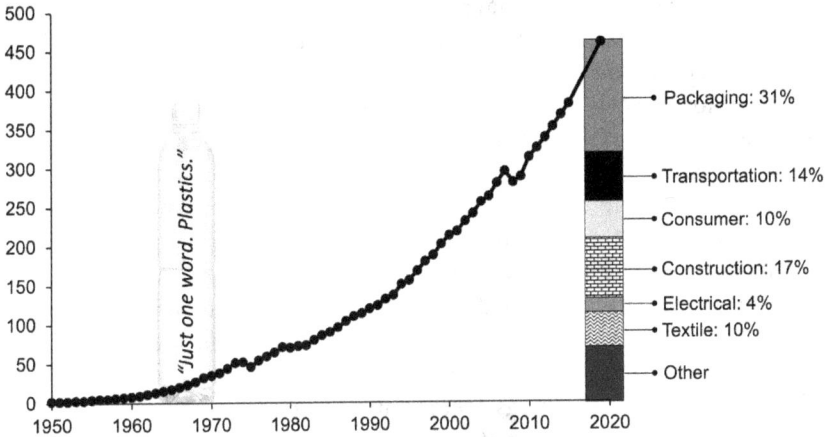

FIGURE 34. Global plastics production has increased exponentially since 1950s with no sign of slowing down. Data from Roland Geyer, Jenna R. Jambeck, and Kara Lavender Law, "Production, Use, and Fate of All Plastics Ever Made," *Science Advances* 3, no. 7 (July 19, 2017), https://doi.org/10.1126/sciadv. 1700782. The data point for 2019 and plastic waste contribution from different sectors are from Global Plastics Outlook Database, Organisation for Economic Co-operation and Development, OECD (2022), https://stats.oecd.org/view html.aspx?datasetcode=PLASTIC_USE_10&lang=en, accessed on March 13, 2024. Nearly one-third of all plastics produced goes into packaging material.

China alone.[3] Plastics create nearly 4.5 percent of global greenhouse gas emissions, more than all the world's airplanes combined.[4]

Plastics are an integral part of modern life, but waste plastics increasingly pollute the planet, and plastic fragments are accumulating in our bodies. What can we do about that?

1. Better Living Through Plastics

In 1862, Alexander Parkes, an English artisan/chemist, patented cellulose nitrate, made by treating cotton fibers with nitric acid and dissolving them in vegetable oil.[5] He called it Parkesine. It was the first commercial plastic. Parkes was hoping to make billiard balls out of Parkesine instead of ivory. Billiards became very popular in the mid–19th century, and the demand for balls was threatening elephants with extinction because their tusks were the source of ivory. Parkes' business failed, but his invention was taken up and developed further by John Hyatt, an American, who called it celluloid. His Celluloid Manufacturing Company succeeded and produced celluloid billiard balls, thereby saving many elephants. So the first commercial plastic was a boon for the environment.

Celluloid was cheap. So it was soon made into many more articles that had been made more expensively from natural materials. Perhaps the most notable celluloid product was photographic film. Celluloid film became the basis of the movie industry, which became hugely successful in the 1920s.

In 1907, Belgian chemist Leo Baekeland introduced Bakelite. The first fully synthetic plastic, Bakelite was made under heat and pressure from two simple chemicals, formaldehyde and phenol, both obtained from petroleum. Bakelite was initially developed as a substitute for shellac, which was being used to insulate electrical wire at a time of rapid electrification. Shellac is a resin secreted by the lac bug in trees in the forests of India and Thailand. It takes many thousands of bugs over six months to make a pound of shellac.[6] So Bakelite freed the making of insulation from the need to collect and kill lac bugs. Light, hard, and durable, Bakelite was also made into many other products, like cases for newly available radios and telephones.

Subsequently, petroleum producers formed alliances with chemical companies to make new plastics, using waste products from petroleum refineries. The best known of these plastics are:

1. *Polyethylene*, a light, flexible, and strong, heat-resistant material, used as an insulator on radar cabling in World War II.[7] Later it was made into a range of products, from shopping bags to food containers to artificial hip and knee joints. Polypropylene is a similar plastic.

2. *Nylon* was developed as artificial silk. Parachutes, ropes, body armor, and helmet liners were made of nylon during World War II. After the war, women's nylon stockings became an international sensation.

3. *Acrylic* (polymethylmethacrylate), formed into transparent and shatter-resistant plastic sheets, was made into aircraft windshields, gun turrets, and submarine periscopes during World War II.

4. *PET* (polyethylene terephthalate), developed during World War II and adopted by Coca-Cola Company in the 1970s to bottle its beverages, is now everywhere in plastic drink bottles and synthetic polyester fiber.

5. *PTFE* (polytetrafluoroethylene), created by accident in the late 1930s and known commercially as *Teflon*,[8] is the coating on non-stick cookware and catheters and is widely used as a lubricant.

6. The very strong plastic poly-paraphenylene terephthalamide was also an unexpected discovery of the 1960s.[9] Commercialized

as *Kevlar*, it is now used in spacecraft, bulletproof vests, and in gloves and other articles of clothing that protect users from cuts, abrasions, and heat.

7. *Polystyrene*, developed in the 1930s, is used in rigid objects like bottles, trays, and disposable cutlery. When foamed (trade name *Styrofoam*), it is used for insulation, packaging, and disposable food containers.

8. *PVC* (polyvinylchloride), also developed in the 1930s as an alternative to natural rubber, became widely used to make a variety of products: pipes, flooring, siding, inflatable products, and packaging. Its properties derive from its additives. PVC is the third most widely produced plastic, after polyethylene and polypropylene, and one of the most concerning from environmental and health safety perspectives.

The raw material for plastics mostly comes from oil refineries. Petrochemicals are shipped to chemical plants for conversion to polymers, long chains of linked molecules, which are the raw materials of plastics. Plastics are generally stronger, lighter, and more durable than traditional materials. They can also have entirely unique properties. For example, plastic fabric can be breathable yet water repellent, a property not available in traditional fabrics.

2. Plastics Are Essential

Plastics have become essential to our way of life. We are surrounded by plastics. In clothes, appliances, cars, containers, electronics, our homes, everywhere we turn there are plastics.

Modern medicine would be impossible without plastics. Single-use items like tubes, needles, syringes, catheters, bandages, and gloves ensure that each use is germ-free. Reused catheters, for example, frequently cause infections. Medical-grade plastics are used for heart valves, hip and knee replacements, and other implants. And polypropylene plastic makes for lightweight artificial limbs that allow a wide range of motion.

Another important use of plastic film is reducing food waste by protecting food from contamination by microbes and extending storage times in markets and homes. Plastic film and vacuum packing can reduce meat waste by 75 percent.[10] Since meat production contributes a large share of greenhouse gas emissions (Chapter 10), waste reduction has a huge environmental benefit.

Plastic water bottles, a bane of plastic waste (see below), are essential during emergencies. Bottled water is the most important commodity during and in the aftermath of pandemics, hurricanes, floods, earthquakes, warfare, and terrorist attacks. These disasters can impair municipal water systems or cross-contaminate them with sewage lines. People may have to be self-sufficient for weeks or more. During the crisis of lead-contaminated water in Flint, Michigan (see Chapter 7), residents used bottled water for nearly four and a half years. Social agencies distribute bottled water to underserved communities and homeless people.

3. *Plastics Save Energy*

In addition to being extremely useful, plastics save energy because they are lighter and often better suited to their function than traditional materials. For example, substituting glass with PET in beverage bottles saves an estimated 52 percent of the energy needed to transport the bottles.[11] Modern cars are about 15 percent plastic, making them lighter and more fuel efficient than all-metal cars.

Pipes made of the plastic PVC (polyvinylchloride) are lighter than those made of iron or copper, and they take much less energy to produce. In addition, no soldering is needed at its joints. Many municipalities are plagued by lead contamination of drinking water because of corroded lead-containing solder at iron pipe joints, especially where feeder lines connect buildings to the water main. Replacement of the feeder lines with PVC piping alleviates lead contamination. PVC is used in many consumer products other than underground piping, but there are toxicity concerns (see Chapter 8).

Styrofoam, the white material made of blown polystyrene polymer, makes cups useful for hot beverages. The polystyrene is impervious to water, and the foam provides insulation. But discarded Styrofoam containers are seen on beaches worldwide. Styrofoam cups have mostly been replaced by paper cups because people object to unsightly plastic litter and because many municipalities have banned or limited the use of Styrofoam cups. But paper is weakened by water. So the cups have to be coated inside with a thin layer of waterproof plastic; as a consequence, they can't be recycled.[12] Paper cups are typically heavier than Styrofoam cups. Because producing paper takes about three times more energy, pound for pound, than producing Styrofoam, a paper cup takes up to 36 times more energy to make than a Styrofoam cup.[13] Plastic bags are similarly energy saving compared to paper bags, but the energy advantages are outweighed by concern about litter.

And what about reusable cups and bags? They reduce the litter created by single-use cups and bags, but they are not necessarily better for the environment. For example, growing and milling cotton takes so much energy and water that a cotton shopping bag would have to be used hundreds of times to beat single-use plastic bags.[14] Heavier, reusable plastic bags are a better bet for the environment. On the other hand, people often accumulate too many reusable bags and have to dispose of them, eliminating their environmental advantage.

4. Drowning in Plastic Waste

Discarded plastic is accumulating in the environment. Landscapes and beaches are littered with plastic bottles and bags (Figure 35), especially in low-income countries that have limited trash collection. And plastic debris ends up in the oceans, where it circulates in rotating currents called "gyres."[15] The biggest gyre is in the north Pacific Ocean, between Hawai'i and California. The plastic floating in this gyre has been called the "Great Pacific Garbage Patch." Much of this plastic can't be seen because it is too small or far beneath the surface.

FIGURE 35. Marine debris on a beach on the island of Kaho'olawe in Hawai'i. Photo credit: NOAA Marine Debris Program, https://marinedebris.noaa.gov/images/marine-debris-hawaii.

In an effort to clean up at least the larger pieces of floating garbage, a nonprofit project, Ocean Cleanup,[16] employs a large collection line towed by boats at each end. In 2022, Ocean Cleanup collected over 150 tons of plastic in the Pacific Ocean, which it compacts and recycles. It also intercepts garbage in rivers before it gets to the oceans. Using similar towline technology, it has collected 840 tons from polluted river systems.[17] Many similar organizations are working on a mission to collect plastic and other debris from the oceans, beaches, and river systems around the globe.[18]

While cleanup is helpful, it would be much more effective to prevent the discarding of plastics by improving garbage collection systems, which are poorly resourced or absent altogether in much of the world. Plastic litter has environmental impacts other than being unsightly. When mistakenly eaten by animals and birds, discarded plastics clog their digestive system. Marine animals are often ensnared by plastic and drown (Figure 36).

The World Wildlife Fund estimates that over 100,000 whales, seals, and turtles die every year from eating or being trapped by plastics.[19] Recent studies also found plastic in the guts of 90 percent of the seabirds tested[20] and 100 percent of the turtles.[21] Land-based animals, including cows, elephants, camels, and zebras, die from eating plastic bags.[22] In Africa, drains and sewers are often clogged by plastic bags, leading to flooded drains that support large populations of mosquitoes that spread

FIGURE 36. Green sea turtle ensnared by fishing net. Photo credit: NOAA Marine Debris Program, https://marinedebris.noaa.gov/multimedia/photos/impacts.

malaria. And when plastic bags are tossed in the recycling bin with other plastics, they clog the sorting machines, necessitating expensive repairs.

Discarded plastic bottles are everywhere. An astonishing 600 billion plastic drink bottles per year are produced globally.[23] Packaging is a major source of plastic waste. Ninety-five percent of plastic packaging is disposed of after one use.[24] To combat the flood of plastic waste, many countries, regions, and municipalities have banned single-use plastic bags or charge fees for them, leading to substantial reductions. Germany, for example, reduced plastic bag use by 70 percent just between 2015 and 2018; it banned lightweight plastic bags altogether in 2022.[25] Likewise, California saw a 70 percent reduction after it banned single-use plastic bags in 2014.[26] Plastic drinking straws and eating utensils have also come under scrutiny.[27] Disney is eliminating plastic straws and stirrers at all its theme parks and resorts. And McDonald's restaurants are swapping plastic straws for paper, as is Starbucks, which used an estimated 1 billion plastic straws per year.

5. Plastics Break Up: Micro- and Nanoplastics

Although discarded plastics do not biodegrade, they do eventually break up into smaller pieces from exposure to sun, heat, and reactive gases in the environment. The time it takes to break down varies with the material.[28] A plastic bottle can take up to 300 years to degrade completely in the ocean.[29] Fishing line, which is especially dangerous to marine animals, can last for an estimated 600 years. The fragments continue to break up over time, eventually reaching microscopic dimensions. Microplastics break up further into nanoplastics, particles smaller than one micrometer (1/70th the diameter of a human hair). Micro- and nanoplastics have been found everywhere, from the tops of mountains as high as Mount Everest[30] to the bottom of the ocean, down to the Mariana Trench.[31] The flood level of rivers can even be measured from the layer of plastic fragments deposited on the riverbanks.[32] Layers of plastic deposits are so widespread that they define our geologic era as the "Plasticene."[33]

Our food and water contain micro- and nanoplastics. Humans ingest about five grams (the weight of a credit card) of plastics each week.[34] Most of it is in our water, especially bottled water. A recent study using high-power laser detection found about 240,000 nanoplastic particles in a one-liter (33 oz) plastic bottle of water, many more than in tap water.[35] The air we breathe has plastic particles as well. What are all these particles doing to us? We don't know.

As discussed in Chapter 6, air particles smaller than 2.5 micrometers

(PM2.5) aggravate respiratory and heart disease in humans and wildlife. They are small enough to penetrate lung cells and enter the bloodstream. Micro- and nanoplastics have been found in most human organs. Ominously, they have been found in human placenta and so could affect fetal development.[36] Nanoplastics add to the load of PM2.5 particles in the air. Their numbers are small, relative to all the other particles in the air, but the numbers are growing.[37] And nanoplastics have special properties. Typically, their surfaces repel water and attract organic molecules. So nanoplastics could carry toxic chemicals with them. Also, plastics contain additives, substances that increase toughness or flexibility or add color. As the plastics break up in the environment, some of these additives could accumulate at the particle surfaces, thereby increasing the particles' toxicity when ingested.[38] Of particular concern are plasticizers, substances that increase the flexibility of plastics. Some of these plasticizers, like bisphenol A (BPA) and phthalate esters, are endocrine disrupters (Chapter 7). At high enough doses they can interfere with the body's hormones. They have been linked to obesity, reproductive problems, and even cancer. Could nanoplastics increase exposure to these chemicals? Hard to tell since our understanding of human exposure risks is still limited.[39] The health concern about nanoplastics is yet another reason to curb plastic waste.

6. What About Bioplastics?

Companies are turning to plastics made from plant material instead of petroleum products.[40] By avoiding fossil fuels, these bioplastics help slow climate change. They also hold out the promise of biodegradation since bacteria can attack plant material.

The most widely used bioplastic is starch itself, modified by heating with plasticizers, like glycerol (derived from vegetable oils). The result is "thermoplastic" starch which can be molded or made into film. The second most widely used is polylactide (PLA), based on lactic acid produced by fermentation of sugars or starches. Both are used mainly on film for food packaging. Often the two are blended since PLA is stronger but also more expensive. Many other starch- or cellulose-based plastics are in development.[41] In 2022, bioplastics made up only 0.4 percent of global plastics production,[42] but demand is increasing rapidly.

Bioplastics like PLA retain some of the chemical groups from plant material. They can potentially be attacked and consumed by bacteria in the environment. However, this process is generally slow, sometimes taking years, depending on how the bioplastics are formulated. During that time the bioplastic breaks up into smaller fragments just as petroleum-based plastics do.

Bioplastics that biodegrade are used for "compostable" food containers and utensils. However, the label "compostable" does not mean that you can toss the item on your backyard compost pile. Instead, industrial compost facilities are required in which the temperature rises sufficiently to allow biodegradation to take place. These facilities are limited in number and accessibility. As of 2023, the United States had 200 food-waste composting plants, only 60 percent of which accepted compostable plastics.[43] And only a few cities have compost pickup programs. But compostable containers can play a useful role in reducing waste. The city of Milan tripled its collection of food waste after introducing compostable bags for the waste.[44]

Bioplastics can't be mechanically recycled the way synthetic plastics can. They contaminate the recycling stream and have to be separated and trashed. Because of these limitations, most bioplastics end up in landfills (as do most plastics; see below). So biodegradation is not currently a win for the environment. But it would be if more plastics, especially in packaging, were truly biodegradable on their own or in backyard compost. See the innovative examples that are discussed below.

7. Does Recycling Work for Plastics?

Not very well, currently. Recycling and composting programs reduce the volume of trash, but their success depends on the diligence of households in sorting the trash and on the industrial demand for recycled material. Often, "recycling" is actually "downcycling" in which the waste is processed into products of lower value than the collected items. Park benches from recycled plastics is an example. In addition, the triangular "chasing arrows" recycling logos on plastic goods are confusing.[45] The emblem doesn't mean that the item can be recycled, only that it *could* be recycled if appropriate technology were available. The number enclosed by the arrows identifies the types of plastic. Only "1," standing for PET (polyethylene terephthalate), used in polyester fabrics and in plastic water and drink bottles, and "2," standing for HDPE (high-density polyethylene), used in milk containers, plastic bags, trash cans, and plastic wood, are currently recycled at all. Plastics labeled with "3" (PVC, polyvinylchloride) and higher are not accepted in most curbside recycling programs. The logo is so widely misunderstood that the EPA has recommended not using it. California has banned its use unless the product is actually collected and recycled.

Problems also arise when the contents of recycling bins are contaminated with food or other waste or when the sorting machines become fouled with plastic bags or wrap. Recycling programs are costly. But well-managed programs generally save money on landfill costs, which are rising steeply.

When trash is collected, most of the plastic in it ends up in landfills, and little is recycled. That's because different kinds of plastic need different recycling processes and are difficult to separate from one another in the waste stream. In the United States, only 9 percent of plastic is recycled.[46] Europe does better, at 38 percent,[47] but the global average is less than 10 percent.[48]

A small portion of plastic is burned in waste-to-energy incinerators, but most goes to landfills. The landfill fraction in the United States is actually increasing as the total tonnage of plastic waste continues to increase.

It is possible to "de-polymerize" some plastics using heat and chemical or enzymatic reactions to convert the polymer molecules in plastic back to the simple chemicals from which they were made.[49] These chemicals can then be "re-polymerized" to remanufacture the plastic and put it back in production. This process of chemical recycling saves chemicals and energy relative to making new plastic. But the amount of savings depends on details of the process. It is only practical if the waste streams contain only the kind of plastic that is to be recycled. It is not an answer to the plastic waste problem.

8. Making Producers Take Care of Plastic Waste

Waste can be reduced through extended producer responsibility (EPR) programs. EPR requires manufacturers to be responsible for end-of-life management of their products, including recycling and disposing packaging. On the principle that polluters should pay, EPR shifts responsibility from consumers to producers of plastic items. That pushes producers to incorporate the environment into planning for their products' manufacture, distribution, and disposal. Member countries of the European Union have EPR programs,[50] as have a growing number of states in the United States.[51] In these programs, producers pay for collection, sorting, and recycling of plastics. Often, the programs are accompanied by mandatory bottle deposit and return systems that have been shown to increase plastic bottle recycling rates.[52] The European Organisation for Packaging and the Environment estimates that producers in Europe pay over €3 billion in responsibility fees each year.[53]

EPR works by having producers and distributors join a producer responsibility organization (PRO) to implement and oversee collection and recycling of plastics. Several U.S. states have designated the nonprofit Circular Action Alliance[54] as the PRO for their industries. In Germany, companies pay an annual fee to obtain a green dot label, identifying their product as recyclable.[55] The annual fee is lowest for highly recyclable material, incentivizing companies to shift away from hard-to-recycle products. The system was started in 1991 and turned the previous 3 percent annual increase of packaging into a 3 percent annual decrease,[56] with over 94 percent of it collected for recycling. British EPR regulations, in force since 1998, increased the packaging recovery rate by 68 percent.[57]

9. Innovation Could Save Plastics

Innovative new materials could make a big impact on plastic waste. The company Ecovative makes a packaging material out of mushroom mycelium grown on hemp "hurd," a by-product of the hemp fiber industry.[58] After use, this mushroom-based packaging can be broken down and composted, even in home gardens. Molded mushroom packaging can replace Styrofoam. Many companies, including Dell and IKEA, are now "growing" mushroom packaging to fit their products.[59] And biodegradable food film can be made from fibers extracted from banana peels.[60] Another company, Monosol, makes water-soluble packaging films from polyvinyl alcohol.[61] The film can be made into dishwasher and laundry detergent packets, litter bags, and agricultural packaging, all of which dissolve away after use.

Chitosan, made from the shells of crustaceans, is an edible coating that can be applied to vegetables to retard spoilage.[62] Edible plastics can also be used for disposable food wrappers, dishware, and cutlery in hospitals and fast food restaurants.[63] Edible, biodegradable alternatives to single-use plastic containers are being developed from seaweed feedstock.[64] The Tom Ford Plastic Innovation Prize[65] went to three companies that all use seaweed to make plastic alternatives.[66] One of the finalists, London-based Notpla company has developed Ohoo!,[67] a low-cost edible water pouch made from seaweed and calcium chloride–based alginate. It was used in the London Marathon to replace thousands of plastic water bottles and cups.[68]

Some innovations eliminate packaging entirely. For example, instead of wrapping pallets of goods in plastic film, distributors can secure the goods with ratchet straps or reusable pallet wraps. Consumers can get lower prices for using reusable containers when buying products. Retailers can eliminate unnecessary plastic film for products like stacks of tuna cans or yogurt containers, greeting cards, and bed linens. For example, Carlsberg has replaced the plastic rings that once had strangled wildlife when discarded. Now six-packs of beer are held with dots of recyclable glue that keep the cans together.[69]

10. Summary

Plastics are an integral part of modern life, offering lightweight strength and durability for innumerable articles in household and industrial use. Medical care is entirely dependent on plastics for testing, surgery, dispensing medicines, and preventing infection. Plastics save energy by reducing weight and resisting wear. But discarded plastic has become an unsightly global menace that harms wildlife and threatens human health, especially as it breaks up into ever smaller long-lived particles. Current recycling and incineration practices are woefully inadequate. Plastic waste fills up landfills and is building up in the environment, especially as low-income countries decline to be dumping grounds for waste from high-income countries.

Improvements will come as producers are persuaded, voluntarily or through ordinances, to be responsible for their products' end of life. They can redesign products and delivery systems that use less packaging. The packaging can be made easy to reuse or recycle, or it can be made rapidly biodegradable. New kinds of plastics that readily dissolve or biodegrade after use also offer promise for reducing the burden of plastic waste.

6

How Unhealthy Is Our Air?

1. Bad Air Kills

Unhealthy air is a scourge in cities around the world, from New Delhi to Beijing to Mexico City to Los Angeles. This photo shows the dramatic difference between rare good days and frequent bad ones (Figure 37).

Air pollution is one of the leading causes of death. The World Health Organization estimates that about seven million people around the globe die each year prematurely of air pollution.[1] An estimated 3.2 million are victims of indoor air pollution. They are among the 2.3 billion people who cook using open fire or inefficient stoves. The rest are victims of outdoor air pollution.

Although people don't lie gasping in the streets, there is a strong association between air pollution levels and hospitalization and death rates.[2] Air pollution kills mainly by aggravating heart disease and lung diseases like asthma. Control measures have cut air pollution a lot in high-income countries but not much in low-income countries. Half the deaths from air pollution are in China and South Asia, while only one-fifth of the deaths are in Europe and North America.[3]

FIGURE 37. Shanghai skyline on a clear day (left; photo by Ralf Leineweber via Unsplash, https://unsplash.com/photos/oriental-pearl-tower-shanghai-china-sRMzAdjWK_E) and on a smoggy day (right; photo by Mike Soldatov).

2. What's in the Polluted Air?

A lot of stuff gets spewed into air. Figure 38 shows the stuff that produces air pollution.

The directly emitted "primary pollutants" (left side of Figure 38) react with one another in the air and produce "secondary pollutants" (right side of Figure 38): ozone, droplets of nitric and sulfuric acids (HNO_3 and H_2SO_4), and particles of ammonium nitrate and sulfate (NH_4NO_3 and $[NH_4]_2SO_4$). These droplets and particles are small, making them particularly hazardous (see why below). Here are the main sources:

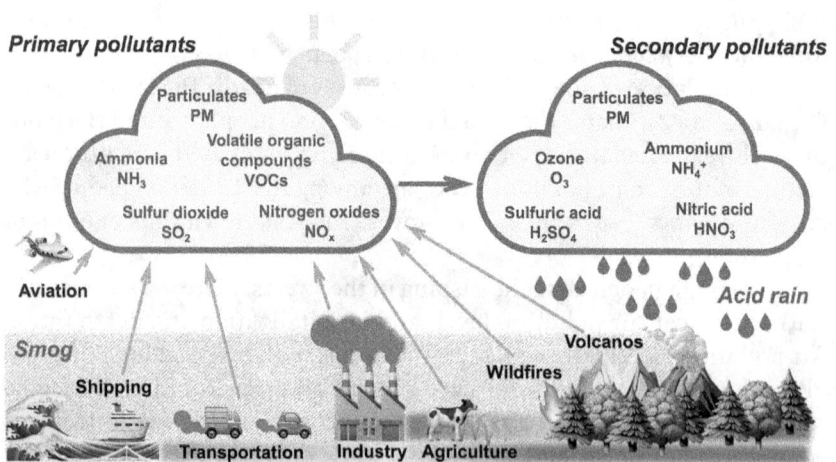

FIGURE 38. Major air pollutants and their sources. Illustration by Alexandra Soldatova.

Transportation and industry emit most of the pollutants in cities. Nitrogen oxides (NO_x, which represents nitric oxide, NO, and nitrogen dioxide, NO_2) come from burning fuels. NO_x forms when the atmosphere's nitrogen and oxygen combine at the high flame temperatures in the engines of cars, trucks, buses, and trains. In urban areas, vehicle engines are the major emitters of NO_x, along with power plants and some high-temperature industrial processes. Volatile organic compounds (VOCs) also come from engines when fuel escapes being burned up and gets emitted. There are many other VOC sources, including paints and solvents in homes and industry; even trees and other plants produce VOCs. Sulfur dioxide (SO_2) comes from burning sulfur, which occurs in fossil fuels, especially coal and also oil. NO_2 and SO_2 react with oxygen to produce sulfuric and nitric acid droplets, which wash out as acid rain.

Burning coal and oil releases soot particulate matter (referred to as black carbon). Soot from diesel engines is prevalent along roadways.

Agriculture releases ammonia from manure and fertilizer on farms. The ammonia reacts with sulfuric and nitric acid droplets in the air to form ammonium sulfate and nitrate particles. These newly formed particles are very small and contribute to the pool of small particles (PM in Figure 38) that are the major air pollution health hazard (see below). Ammonia accounts for 30 percent of fine particles in the air over the United States and 50 percent over Europe.[4]

Wildfires release copious smoke, with fine particles making up 90 percent of the total mass.[5] The fires have become larger and more intense as global temperatures rise and the smoke travels far, polluting the air in distant places. New York City does not normally suffer from wildfire smoke, but smoke drifting from huge fires in Canada turned the skies orange and gave NYC the worst air quality of any major city in the world on June 7, 2023.[6]

3. Smog, Old and New: Ground-Level Ozone and Nitrogen Dioxide

The word "smog" is a contraction of "smoke" and "fog." It was applied to the foul air of early 20th-century London and other industrial cities, where smoke from coal fires mixed with fog to produce deadly clouds. The "Great Smog" that enveloped London for five days in 1952 killed 4,000 people and sickened 100,000 more. The eventual death toll is estimated to have been 12,000.[7] In many parts of the world, coal for heating buildings has been largely replaced by cleaner-burning oil and gas or electricity. But coal heating is still common in low-income countries and is a major contributor to air pollution.

The increase in automotive traffic everywhere in the world after World War II brought a different kind of smog, exemplified by Los Angeles, the first major city to rely entirely on cars and trucks. Sunny Los Angeles is rimmed by mountains and by the Pacific Ocean from which cool breezes blow inland, trapping the air against the mountains. The city's air became increasingly acrid and hazy, with a brownish tint. This type of smog is called *photochemical smog*. It results when sunlight shines on a mixture of NO_x and VOCs. NO_2 gives smog its brown color. The colored gas absorbs sunlight, and the sun's rays kick off chemical reactions that produce ozone, O_3, a high-energy form of oxygen.

High in the stratosphere, naturally produced ozone protects life on Earth by screening out the sun's harmful ultraviolet rays (next section). But at ground level, ozone is harmful. It attacks the membranes of the lung, leading to respiratory distress and contributing to cardiovascular disease. People with asthma or other breathing difficulties are particularly affected. Ozone causes harm at quite low levels. As part of the National Ambient Air Quality Standards, the U.S. Environmental Protection Agency has set an air quality standard of 70 ppb (parts per billion, i.e., 70 molecules of ozone in 1 billion air molecules), above which ozone is likely to do harm.[8] This standard may not be protective enough, especially for children.[9] The World Health Organization guideline for ozone is stricter, at 50 ppb.[10] Ozone decomposes inside buildings, reacting with chemicals on the walls and other surfaces. So on days with high ozone, health authorities alert people, especially those who already have lung or heart issues, to stay indoors.

While generated mainly in urban centers, ozone can drift long distances from urban to rural areas to become a regional pollutant. Besides affecting health, ozone inhibits plant growth and lowers crop yields.

Ozone formation increases as ground temperatures increase. There is more ozone in summer than in winter. Summer is also when plants are growing and people spend more time outdoors, making ozone more dangerous. NO_2, the gas that forms ozone in urban air, is itself harmful, attacking the lining of the lung.[11] NO_2 and O_3 have similar health effects, and NO_2 can also drift downwind, although it breaks down faster than O_3.

Ground-level ozone has been increasing around the world due to increasing traffic and higher temperatures. However, high-income countries have seen a decreasing trend thanks to control measures like catalytic converters on cars. But ozone continues to increase in low-income countries which lack regulatory and enforcement capabilities.

4. What's the Effect of the Ozone Hole?

Air is warmest at the earth's surface and gets steadily colder with increasing height above the earth. But the temperature rises again above about 60,000 ft (18 km) up. That point marks the boundary between two regions of the atmosphere, the troposphere below and the stratosphere above. Just above this boundary is the stratospheric ozone layer.

Stratosphere ozone acts as a sunscreen. It absorbs the sun's ultraviolet rays, which would otherwise reach the earth's surface and destroy organic molecules, harming all life forms. The few ultraviolet rays that do get through the ozone layer can cause skin cancer. If the global sunscreen were to thin out, cancer incidence would increase, as would damage to sensitive plants.

This danger was dramatized in 1985 by the discovery of the "ozone hole" over Antarctica[12] (Figure 39). From the 1970s onward, the ozone concentration decreased dramatically during the Antarctic spring.

The culprit turned out to be chlorofluorocarbons, or CFC's (trade name Freons). These gaseous molecules were used in aerosol sprays, as foaming agents for plastics, and as refrigerants. Their appeal was that they are nontoxic and nonflammable and therefore safe for human use. But when they drift up to the stratosphere, the sun's ultraviolet rays break them down, releasing chlorine atoms. Likewise, bromine-containing fire extinguishing chemicals, called halons, release bromine atoms when hit by the ultraviolet rays. Each chlorine or bromine atom breaks down many ozone molecules in a chain reaction.

Scientists long ago warned about the danger to the ozone layer of chlorine and bromine.[13] But little was done until the dramatic discovery of the ozone hole kicked off international negotiations that led to agreements to end the production of CFCs and halons.[14] As a result, the concentrations of chlorine and bromine in the stratosphere are declining, and the ozone hole is beginning to heal (Figure 39).[15] This successful example of international cooperation to counter a global environmental threat spurred subsequent campaigns to gain international agreement on greenhouse gas emissions. But global warming has proved to be a far thornier political problem than stratospheric ozone depletion.

Stratospheric and ground-level ozone are not the same issue. We want to maintain ozone levels in the stratosphere to protect us from the sun's harmful ultraviolet rays but minimize it at ground level to avoid ozone damage to plants and animals, including us.

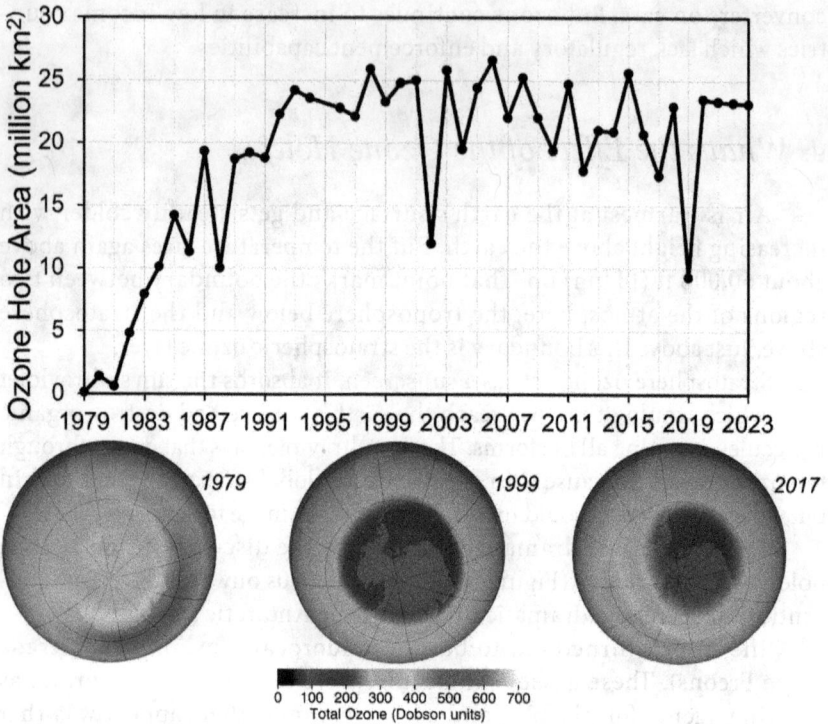

FIGURE 39. Ozone hole area above Antarctica, in the Antarctic spring, when the hole is largest. The maps are satellite images of ozone concentrations over Antarctica during October. Data and image source: NASA Goddard Space Flight Center (2024), "NASA Ozone Watch: Images, Data, and Information for Atmospheric Ozone," https://ozonewatch.gsfc.nasa.gov, accessed April 22, 2024.

5. Tiny Particles Are the Worst

Surprisingly, particles in the air are the greatest danger to our health. Of the estimated seven million deaths annually from air pollution, 4.3 million are from exposure to particles and 0.4 million are from ozone.[16] Many kinds of particles float around, so it might seem odd to lump them together. But a strong association between mortality and the air concentration of small particles was discovered in 1993 and has been confirmed many times since.[17] Particle-related excess deaths are mainly from lung and heart diseases.

The size of the particles is critical. Inhaling large particles, such as dust or pollen, produces little harm (except for allergic reactions) because they settle out on the surfaces of the nose and throat. But the smallest

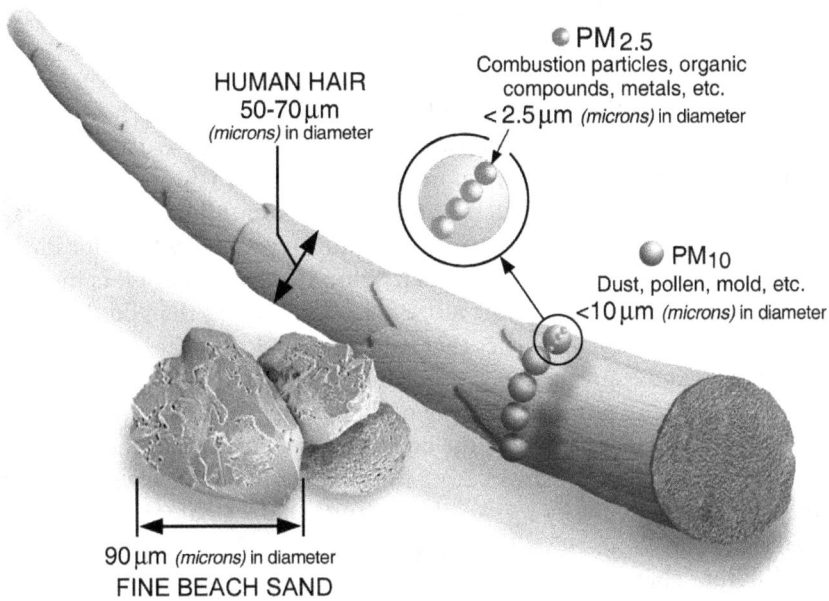

HUMAN HAIR
50-70 μm
(microns) in diameter

🌑 PM$_{2.5}$
Combustion particles, organic
compounds, metals, etc.
< 2.5 μm *(microns)* in diameter

● PM$_{10}$
Dust, pollen, mold, etc.
<10 μm *(microns)* in diameter

90 μm *(microns)* in diameter
FINE BEACH SAND

FIGURE 40. PM particle sizes. Source: U.S. Environmental Protection Agency, "Particulate Matter (PM) Basics," https://www.epa.gov/pm-pollution/particu late-matter-pm-basics.

particles reach the lung, damaging the airways and penetrating the lung's membranes. Small particles also penetrate blood vessels and get carried around in the blood. The particles of concern have diameters less than 10 microns across. A micron, or micrometer, is one-millionth of a meter. For comparison, a human hair is 50–70 microns wide (Figure 40).[18]

The lung-penetrating particles have diameters of 2.5 microns or less. They are labeled PM$_{2.5}$. The small particles are especially bad for people with asthma or other breathing difficulties. They also aggravate heart disease. A study of cars in urban traffic showed that equipping them with air filters lowered the blood pressure of the passengers.[19]

In addition to penetrating lung cells, these particles are small enough to enter the olfactory nerve connecting the nose to the brain. They can then travel to brain cells, where they can cause neurological damage. PM$_{2.5}$ particles have been linked to mental illness,[20] dementia,[21] and even autism.[22] Normal memory and attention suffer as well, as measured by cognitive tests.[23] In a recent study, installing air filters in classrooms improved student test score performance.[24]

PM$_{2.5}$ particles come from various sources and are usually lumped together because size is the easiest thing to monitor. But there is increasing evidence that not all $PM_{2.5}$ are the same. A study of mortality downwind from coal plants found that $PM_{2.5}$ from coal burning had about twice the average $PM_{2.5}$ effect.[25] The decline of coal for power generation in the United States over the past 20 years has had a significant public health benefit. The coal plant $PM_{2.5}$ particles are mainly sulfate particles from the sulfur in coal. The reason they are more lethal might be that they carry other toxic coal combustion products. Another study found that the association with Alzheimer's disease was greater for soot particles than for $PM_{2.5}$ in general.[26] Soot is carbon matter left behind when coal or oil is incompletely burned. It likely harbors more toxic compounds than do the inorganic sulfate or nitrate particles that come from SO_2 and NO_2 emissions.

Miners and construction workers often breathe in high levels of mineral dust. That can produce scarring of their lungs and lead to pulmonary failure or lung cancer. Usually, the dust is from silicate rock, and the lung condition is called silicosis. In 2019, there were 140,000 newly diagnosed silicosis cases globally, up by two-thirds from 1990.[27] Coal miners develop "black lung" disease from breathing coal dust. Although rock and coal are different chemically, lung damage from rock and coal dust are similar. They produce inflammation, and the resultant scars become fibrous, eventually destroying lung function. Safety regulations usually require the use of masks and breathing apparatus for workers exposed to rock and coal dust. After passage of the Federal Coal Mine Health and Safety Act in 1969, the prevalence of black lung disease among U.S. miners decreased by about 90 percent.[28] But cases have again gone up, likely because high-grade coal deposits have been used up and mining lower-grade coal requires more rock drilling. Coal mining communities are also impacted by the coal and rock dust.[29] They suffer more heart and lung problems and also birth defects. In fact, mothers living in a mining area have a six-times higher risk of birth defects than mothers elsewhere who smoke.[30]

In the special case of dust from asbestos, the lung condition is asbestosis. Asbestos is a naturally occurring fibrous silicate that has been useful in roofing, flooring, insulation, and brake linings. Asbestos sheds long thin fibers that are particularly dangerous when they lodge in lung tissue. Cancer of the abdominal lining, called mesothelioma, is strongly linked to asbestos.[31] For these reasons, asbestos has been banned in many countries but not in China, the United States, Russia, Canada, or India.[32] Disposal of asbestos from preexisting structures requires special handling with hazard suits and equipment.

Cities often have unhealthy levels of particles in the air. Pollution controls have lowered the levels in many places, but they are often difficult to implement because of poverty and weak administrative structures. There is no evidence of a safe level below which there is no health effect.

6. Pollution Mitigation: Success Stories

An important step in reducing emission of VOCs and NO_x was the development of the catalytic converter for cars and trucks. This tailpipe device uses platinum and rhodium chemistry to burn up the VOCs and to convert NO_x back to nitrogen and oxygen. It reduced smog significantly, first and foremost in the Los Angeles area. Stringent controls on emissions from cars, trucks, factories, and power plants led to substantially cleaner air, even though population and traffic density increased. Despite improvement, Los Angeles still has the highest ozone levels in the United States, with over 150 days per year exceeding the standard.[33] Los Angeles is not the only hot spot. Large cities all over the world experience high ozone levels[34] (Figure 41).

Cleaning the air has real health benefits. Children in Los Angeles had 20 percent less asthma in 2006 than in 1993 despite increased population and traffic density.[35] Over 500 childhood asthma cases and about 100 preterm births are estimated to have been avoided in several Northeastern U.S. states because of lower power plant emissions.[36] The avoided

Measurements of ozone concentration above 70 ppb around the world

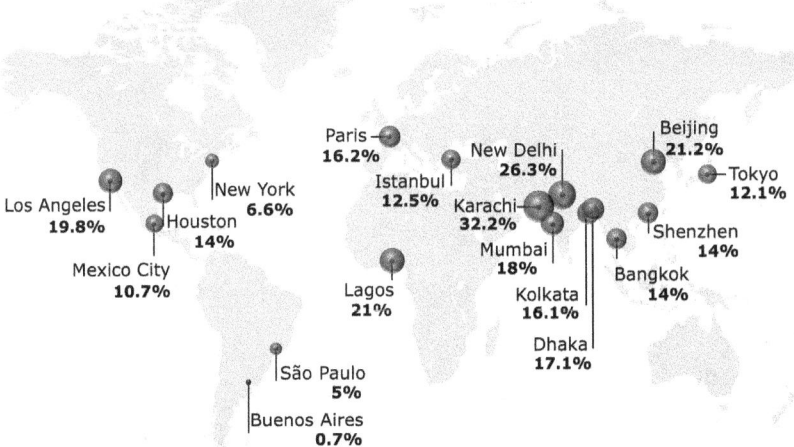

FIGURE 41. High ozone: Percent of measurements when ozone concentration was above 70 ppb, from one year of satellite data. Data from Jet Propulsion Laboratory, Tropospheric Emission Spectrometer Mission Science Team; Karen E. Cady-Pereira et al., "Seasonal and Spatial Changes in Trace Gases over Megacities from Aura TES Observations: Two Case Studies," *Atmospheric Chemistry and Physics* 17, no. 15 (August 7, 2017): 9379–98. Figure adapted from NASA/JPL-Caltech, "Revealing Air Quality over Megacities," https://tes.jpl.nasa.gov/tes/science/highlights/revealing-air-quality-over-megacities.

health costs alone were estimated to save roughly $200 million. Globally, nearly two million children get asthma from traffic-related air pollution every year.[37]

Another air pollution success story involves combating acid rain in the 1970s. Coal-fired power plants produce SO_2 copiously because of coal's high sulfur content, and the SO_2 turns into sulfuric acid in the air. To avoid polluting the local area, these power plants have tall chimneys to loft their smoke high in the air, where it is carried off by the wind. But this practice transfers the pollution to areas downwind, where rain washes out the acid. Acid rain harms forests because it leaches nutrients from the soils. It also harms fish and other aquatic life in lakes. In the middle of the 20th century, forests and lakes in the U.S. Northeast and Canadian Southeast downwind from power plants in the U.S. Midwest and western Ontario were hit by acid rain. Fish disappeared from mountain lakes. Acid rain also fell on Scandinavia and eastern Europe downwind from the industrial areas of western and central Europe, damaging forest and lake ecosystems. The glaring consequences gained public attention, and acid rain became an international political issue.[38]

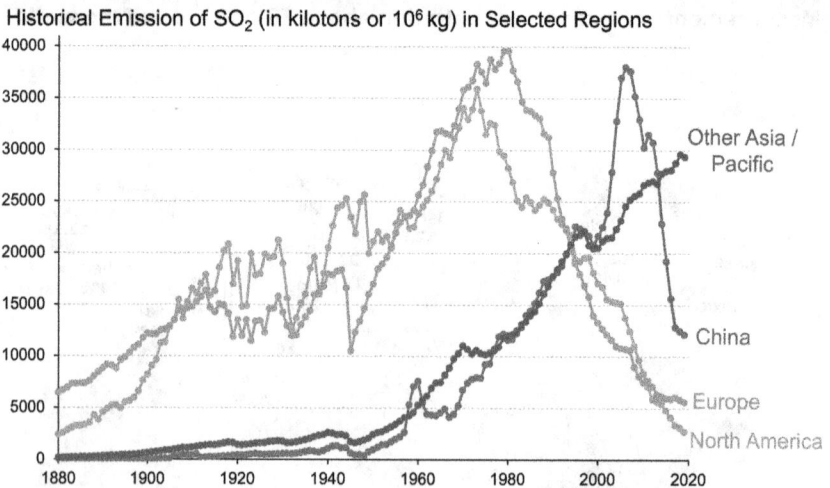

Historical Emission of SO_2 (in kilotons or 10^6 kg) in Selected Regions

FIGURE 42. SO_2 emission estimates in different regions, from the Community Emissions Data System (CEDS): Rachel Hoesly et al., "Historical (1750-2014) Anthropogenic Emissions of Reactive Gases and Aerosols from the Community Emissions Data System (CEDS)," *Geoscientific Model Development* 11 (January 29, 2018): 369–408, plotted using data downloaded from Patrick R. O'Rourke et al., "CEDS V_2021_02_05 Release Emission Data," data set, Zenodo (CERN European Organization for Nuclear Research), February 5, 2021, https://doi.org/10.5281/zenodo.4509372.

In the 1970s, government regulations, and international negotiations tackled these problems successfully. Installing exhaust gas SO_2 scrubbers and switching to coal with lower sulfur content dropped SO_2 emissions by 85 percent in both the United States and Europe[39] (Figure 42). NO_2 emissions, another contributor to acidic air, also decreased considerably, thanks to auto and truck exhaust catalysts. The areas formerly affected by acid rain are now slowly recovering.

Acid rain is still a significant problem in some parts of the world, especially India, where growing economies are fueled by coal-fired power plants. In the last decade, China implemented strict controls that stopped the growth of its emissions, slashing emission of major pollutants (Figure 42), improving air quality, and extending the country's life expectancy.[40]

7. Toxic Organic Molecules in the Air

The air we breathe often contains organic molecules that might harm us. Many of these occur in petroleum or are side products of fossil fuel combustion. For example, benzene is released from gasoline or diesel engines. Over time, breathing in benzene can lead to cancer. Soot from incomplete combustion is released from diesel engines and coal fires. The soot contains many toxic organic molecules, like poly-aromatic hydrocarbons, PAH (molecules containing multiple benzene units). PAH can also lead to cancer.[41] Catalytic converters on cars and trucks get rid of benzene and other combustion side products, and particle traps filter out soot from truck exhaust. But in many places, these pollution-control devices are not required or they are not maintained and monitored. Standards for maximum air concentrations of toxic molecules are set by the U.S. Environmental Protection Agency and similar agencies in other countries, but the standards are not always enforced.

Toxic organic molecules are also released from industrial plants. These releases are regulated, but ineffective enforcement as well as industrial accidents expose people living nearby to these pollutants. Childhood leukemia cases are rising, especially in low-income countries, likely from rising exposure to benzene and similar molecules.[42] Mexico saw about a 10 percent increase in childhood leukemia in just five years, from 2007 to 2012.[43]

The people living near industrial facilities are usually among the poorest in both low- and high-income countries. The 85-mile stretch of the Mississippi River between New Orleans and Baton Rouge is nicknamed "Cancer Alley" because 200 refineries and petrochemical plants are concentrated there.[44] The communities in the area were historically poor and largely Black. In 2000, half the population was African American. Residents complain of foul odors and of neighbors dying of cancer. Community activists have fought further expansion of the petrochemical industry with some success.

In Louisiana, permits issued for industrial plants specify limits on pollutant releases, but compliance relies on self-reporting of violations, and enforcement actions against violators can take years. Overall, air quality has improved substantially in recent years. But according to the Environmental Protection Agency, Louisiana still has the highest toxic air emissions per square mile of any state.[45] The Louisiana Tumor Registry does not show excessive cancer rates in the New Orleans–Baton Rouge area relative to the rest of the state.[46] So the "Cancer Alley" designation is not backed up by the available data. But the causes of cancer, including personal factors like smoking and obesity, are so varied that it is difficult to connect cases with environmental agents. There is little doubt that people living near petroleum operations breathe in elevated levels of toxic molecules.

8. Bad Air Indoors Too

Buildings can pollute indoor air. Poorly finished walls and carpets can give off harmful chemicals. When Hurricane Katrina devastated New Orleans in 2005, 100,000 families were housed in emergency trailers.[47] But many soon moved out because of bad air from formaldehyde, which was released by resins used in the plywood construction. Formaldehyde irritates the eyes and lungs. A particularly dangerous indoor pollutant is carbon monoxide, a product of incomplete combustion. It can accumulate to deadly levels from malfunctioning stoves and space heaters or idling cars.

Disease-causing microorganisms can also spread indoors. Poorly cleaned air-conditioning systems of large buildings can foster the growth of pathogens (like the Legionnaire's disease bacterium that causes a severe pneumonia[48]) that are then circulated through the air.

More deaths are caused by indoor than outdoor air pollution. The worst indoor pollution occurs in low-income countries, where poor people cook over wood, dung, or coal fires, often in unvented spaces. Inefficient cookstoves produce high levels of pollutants, especially particles (Figure 43). The risk of pneumonia doubles in children under five who are exposed to smoke from solid fuel cookstoves.[49]

The Global Alliance for Clean Cookstoves,[50] a partnership of government agencies and private groups, is working to spread efficient stoves and cleaner fuels (kerosene, natural gas, solar). Despite progress, around

FIGURE 43. Indoor air pollution in Guatemala. Photo credit: ©Nigel G. Bruce.

one-third of the world's population, 2.3 billion people, still breathe bad air from inefficient cookstoves.

9. The Bottom Line

Lots of things are spewed into the air that are unhealthy to breathe. Some of the worst effects result from how these pollutants, especially those from traffic, mix and react chemically. These reactions produce ozone and fine particles, both of which are particularly harmful. Fine particles are by far the worst offenders, accounting for the vast majority of the estimated seven million worldwide premature deaths from air pollution. Deaths and disease would be greatly reduced by replacing the unvented fires, used by billions of poor people, with clean-burning or solar stoves. Poor people often live in industrial areas and are exposed to toxic chemicals released from petroleum operations. They also live close to heavily trafficked roads.

Fortunately, air pollution is declining around the world, as people improve the efficiency of stoves and furnaces, often because of public health regulations. In more advanced communities, electrification of stoves, replacement of furnaces with electric heat pumps, adoption of electric cars, and improved public transit are leaving the air much cleaner. Ending fossil fuel combustion will enormously benefit human health in addition to staving off extreme climate change.

7

Clean Water
for a Thirsty World

1. Are We Running Out of Water?

No, but usable water is running low. We live in a watery world. Almost three-quarters of Earth's surface is covered with water, giving our planet its beautiful blue color when viewed from space. But almost all of it, 96.5 percent, is in the oceans and seas and is too salty for land plants and animals. Around 1.7 percent of Earth's water is locked in glaciers and the polar ice caps, and another 1.7 percent is in aquifers, deep underground.[1] That leaves only 0.1 percent in freshwater lakes and rivers (Figure 44).

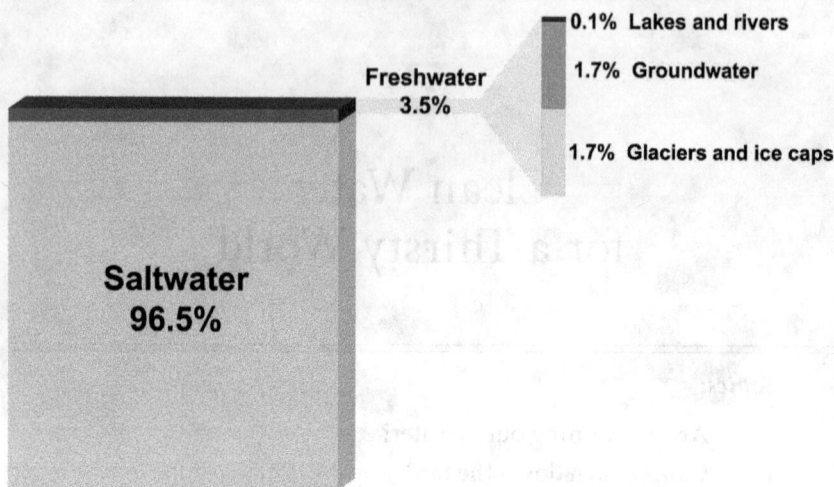

0.1% Lakes and rivers

Freshwater
3.5%

1.7% Groundwater

1.7% Glaciers and ice caps

Saltwater
96.5%

FIGURE 44. Earth's water resources. Adapted from "Vital Water Graphics. An Overview of the State of the World's Fresh and Marine Waters," United Nations Environment Programme, 2002, with values from Peter H. Gleick, "Water Resources," in *Encyclopedia of Climate and Weather*, vol. 2, ed. Stephen H. Schneider (New York: Oxford University Press, 1996), 817-23.

However, the sun renews the fresh water continuously by heating all the surface waters, fresh and salt, which evaporate and rain back as fresh water. The runoff from the rain feeds the rivers and seeps into the ground. Humans use half the accessible runoff for agriculture and for industry and domestic use,[2] but the amounts vary widely in different regions. Americans use 10–20 times as much water per person as Africans.[3] And water use is increasing everywhere as populations and economies grow. People need more water to grow food, to run power plants and industry, and to use in homes and farms (Figure 45).

But the increasing withdrawal from freshwater sources is unsustainable. Already, water supplies are drying up worldwide, particularly in drought-prone areas. Reservoirs are drawn down and rivers run low. Water is pumped out of underground aquifers—layers of porous rock or clay and sand into which the runoff infiltrates. As the aquifers empty, the water table drops, requiring ever deeper and more expensive wells and pumps. And the land above subsides. Areas of Mexico City are sinking an inch per month from groundwater depletion and compaction of the ancient lake bed on which the city is built.[4] Near the ocean, aquifers become infiltrated with salt water, and wells become unusable. And sinking of the land near the shore adds to the dangers of sea level rise. Satellite radar measurements show sinking along the entire eastern seaboard of the

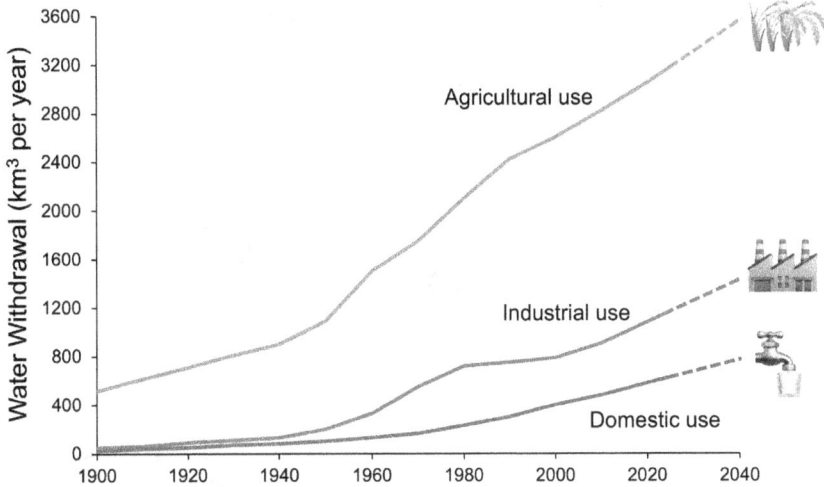

FIGURE 45. Water use increases worldwide (values to 2040 are obtained by linear extrapolations). Adapted from Igor A. Shiklomanov, "Global Water Use Withdrawal and Consumption by Sector," in Philippe Rekacewicz and Delphine Digout, "Vital Water Graphics: Evolution of Global Water Use," United Nations Environment Programme/GRID-Arendal (2005), https://www.grida.no/resources/5786.

United States: in Boston, Atlantic City, Norfolk, Charleston, and Savannah, dams and stressed aquifers increase the sinking rate up to four inches per decade.[5]

Withdrawals from rivers affect habitats downstream and the people who live nearby. The Colorado River is used by seven western U.S. states, all of which face water stress from drought and increasing demand. By the time it empties into the Gulf of California, the mighty Colorado is a mere trickle. Dams on the river provide hydroelectric power to millions of people. But drought and increasing withdrawals lower the levels of the reservoirs behind the dams and thereby lower the available power. Between 1999 and 2014, Lake Mead, the reservoir behind Hoover Dam, dropped by about 120 feet (37 meters), reducing power generation by 23 percent (Figure 46).[6] By 2021, the lake was at 34 percent capacity, and the U.S. government declared a water shortage, forcing large cuts in water supplied to Arizona and smaller cuts to Nevada and Mexico.[7]

Global warming makes water problems worse. Droughts become longer and increase the demand for water. Storms also intensify, dumping more rain. The extra rain, together with earlier melting of winter snow, increases flooding. In addition to the direct damage they cause, floods frequently pollute water supplies. And because snow melts earlier in the

Lake Mead monthly elevation at Hoover Dam (feet)

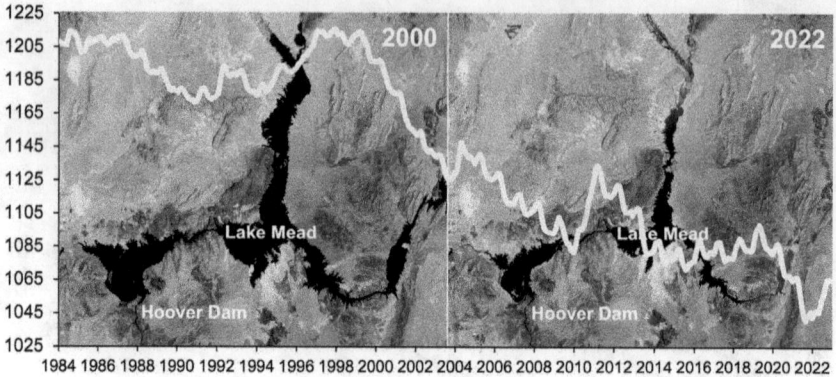

FIGURE 46. Water level in Lake Mead, formed by the Hoover Dam, has been continuously dropping for the last 20 years, after holding steadily in the past. NASA satellite images from July 2000 and 2022 document shrinkage of the Colorado River watershed. Height of the lake from the U.S. Bureau of Reclamation, Lower Colorado Region/Lower Colorado River Operations, "Lake Mead at Hoover Dam, End of Month Elevation (Feet)," accessed November 14, 2023, https://www.usbr.gov/lc/region/g4000/hourly/mead-elv.html. NASA Earth Observatory images by Lauren Dauphin, using Landsat data from the U.S. Geological Survey, https://earthobservatory.nasa.gov/images/150111/lake-mead-keeps-dropping.

spring, less water is available later in the summer. The high mountains of the world feed the major rivers on which vast populations depend. Shrinking glaciers amplify water shortages because the rivers they feed diminish.

Water shortage leads to political "water wars." Agricultural interests vie with cities to get more of the available water. Constructing more dams can help control floods and create reservoirs to capture runoff, but dam projects run into opposition. The land under the potential reservoir is already being used by people and may house valuable cultural artifacts. And reducing river flow below the dam affects downstream populations. As of this writing, tension is increasing between Ethiopia, which is building a dam on the upper reaches of the Nile River, and Egypt, which depends on the power from its downriver Aswan Dam.[8]

There are also ecological impacts. When the Aswan Dam was built, the Nile stopped carrying sediment to its fertile delta, which is subsiding and becoming salty, reducing crop yields.[9] In some rivers, migratory fish can't reach their spawning grounds. In the U.S. Pacific Northwest, dwindling salmon populations, historically a critical food source for Native American tribes, are motivating calls to remove dams.[10]

Water scarcity falls hardest on low-income countries which lack the resources for large-scale waterworks. Rural communities have no running water. Family members, usually the women, must carry water over increasing distances from streams or communal wells. To support their family's subsistence, farmers may need to leave their farms and seek work in urban areas, where aging water systems are overburdened by the swelling populations.

2. Can We Turn Down the Tap?

We can't control the hydrological cycle that supplies fresh water, but we can do lots to save water. Households can use water-saving toilets, showers, and washing machines. Yards can be planted with drought-tolerant plants instead of water-hungry lawns. Rainwater, sometimes called "green water," can be collected for household use and for watering gardens. In larger buildings, "gray water," water drained from sinks, showers, washing machines, and dishwashers, can be used to flush toilets and for irrigation. Water-stressed cities encourage such measures with public appeals to save water, high water bills, and occasional rationing (e.g., yard watering limitations) during droughts. With measures like these, San Diego cut its per capita use in half over three decades.[11] Nevertheless, severe drought forced the Southern California water district to reduce water use by an additional 35 percent in 2022.[12] New rules include a limit on lawn watering in Los Angeles to eight minutes on two days per week.

Water use by industry exceeds that of households (Figure 45), but much of that is power plant cooling water,[13] which is discharged back to the body of water from which it is taken or is reused in a closed-cycle cooling system. Manufacturing accounts for 10–25 percent of the industrial water. Factories can conserve water by recycling it. L'Oréal, the French cosmetic company, has committed to making its factories "dry" by cleaning and reusing all its wastewater.[14]

3. Thirsty Agriculture

Agriculture is the biggest water user by far (Figure 45). It takes 70 percent of the water that humans withdraw from runoff. Crops require large amounts of water. Water delivers nutrients from the soil to the plant and then escapes as vapor through the leaves in a process called "transpiration." The transpiration rate is different for different plants, so the water requirements vary from crop to crop (Figure 47). Legumes and nuts are particularly thirsty, requiring up to 5,000 liters of water per kilogram of harvested crop. In contrast, vegetables like potatoes, tomatoes, or onions

Water Requirements (in L per kg of crop)

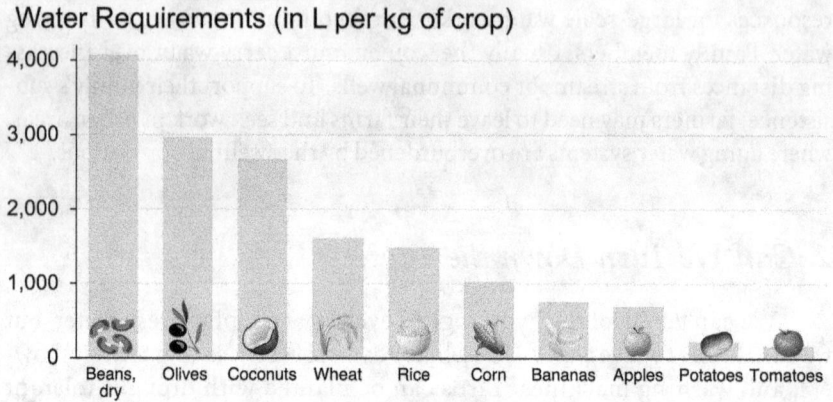

FIGURE 47. Global average water requirements, in liters, for a 1-kilogram yield of the indicated crops. Data from M.M. Mekonnen and A.Y. Hoekstra, "The Green, Blue and Grey Water Footprint of Crops and Derived Crop Products," *Hydrology and Earth System Sciences* 15, no. 5 (May 25, 2011): 1577–1600.

need only 100–200 liters per kilogram. The major cereal crops, wheat, rice, and corn, together account for about 40 percent of global water consumption.[15]

In some areas farmers can rely on rainfall alone. But irrigation improves crop yields and is essential in dry areas. About 40 percent of world food production relies on irrigation. So improved irrigation offers big opportunities for saving water. Traditional pumping and diversion of water into furrows next to crops, known as "flood irrigation," gets only about half the water into the plants; the rest is lost to evaporation or runoff.

FIGURE 48. Surface, sprinkle, and drop irrigation of crop fields. *Left*: Surface irrigation on a lettuce field in Arizona (photo by Jeff Vanuga, USDA Natural Resources Conservation Service, via Wiki Commons, https://commons.wikimedia.org/wiki/File:NRCSAZ02006_-_Arizona_(295)(NRCS_Photo_Gallery).tif). *Middle*: Sprinkler irrigation (photo by philip junior mail, via Unsplash, https://unsplash.com/@oongjr). *Right*: Drip irrigation of a California vineyard (photo by Jessica Griffiths, U.S. Department of Agriculture, Agricultural Research Service, https://www.ars.usda.gov/oc/images/photos/dec17/d3882-1/).

Sprinklers are more efficient, getting three-fourths of the water into the plants. Best of all is drip irrigation, with hoses that deliver water directly adjacent to the plant stalks. This method gets almost all (85–95 percent) of the water into the plants[16] (Figure 48).

Increased irrigation efficiency also reduces *salinization*, a condition in which salts build up in the soil and eventually stop plants from growing. Salts are left behind when irrigation water evaporates and when there is poor drainage. Salinization impacts about one-fifth of irrigated lands and occurs especially in dry regions.

4. Who Waters Industrial Farms?

Industrial farms often use center pivot irrigation in which a long pipe with spray heads revolves around a tube that taps into an aquifer below. Such systems generate perfectly circular irrigated fields, as seen from space (Figure 49). They carpet much of the U.S. Midwest.

After pivot irrigation was introduced in the 1950s, the amount of irrigated farmland expanded enormously. With pivot irrigation, the Midwest region now grows nearly one-third of the world's corn and soybeans.[17] The water is pumped from the huge Ogallala aquifer that underlies most of the Midwest. But with all that pumping, the water table is dropping, in some places up to two feet a year.[18] Rain and snowmelt recharge the aquifer at an

FIGURE 49. *Left*: Center pivot irrigation on a cornfield in Arizona (photo credit: United States Geological Survey Agency, https://www.usgs.gov/media/images/center-pivot-irrigation-system-watering-a-cornfield-arizona). *Right*: A satellite image of circular fields characteristic of center pivot irrigation (southwestern Kansas in late June) (image credit: NASA/GSFC/METI/ERS-DAC/JAROS, and U.S./Japan ASTER Science Team, https://earthobservatory.nasa.gov/images/5772/crop-circles-in-kansas).

average rate of only three inches a year. Pumping costs increase as wells go deeper. Streams in the area run low, endangering habitats for fish and animals. The present pumping rate will deplete parts of the aquifer completely within this century.[19] Farmland is already turning to dust in some areas as wells run dry. Saving what is left of the aquifer will require changing farming practices (see Chapter 10).

Pivot irrigation is also used on large swaths of land in Australia, New Zealand, and Brazil. Global companies buy fertile lands internationally and use the local groundwater to irrigate crops for sale on the international market or to sponsoring governments. When the aquifers dry up, the companies move elsewhere. An example is Saudi Arabia, which used its oil drilling technology to drill down up to one kilometer into deep aquifers.[20] Pivot irrigation turned parts of the desert green.[21] For a time, Saudi Arabia was a major exporter of produce, and the world's fifth largest producer of wheat.[22] But the aquifer became depleted, wells dried up, and Saudi Arabia had to end wheat production in 2016.

The kingdom now offers low-interest loans to companies in other countries that grow crops and send at least half of the output back to Saudi Arabia. It also bought up major farms in other countries. A favorite place is the state of Arizona, where anyone can buy land and pump unlimited amounts of water. Although it is illegal to ship water out of the state, there is no restriction on shipping "virtual water" in the form of agricultural products. Saudi Arabia's largest dairy company bought 15 square miles of Arizona farmland, with 15 water wells, to grow alfalfa, a particularly thirsty crop, as food for Saudi cows.[23] But in 2023, the governor of Arizona announced termination of the Saudi company's land leases, calling it unacceptable "to pump unchecked amounts of groundwater out of our state."[24] The state is under pressure to curb its many industrial farms as it faces cuts in its share of water from the Colorado River.

5. What About Low-Income Countries?

A billion subsistence farmers in low-income countries rely on rains or on channeling gravity flow of water from springs or streams. As these sources become unreliable due to climate change, the farmers may have to abandon their farms. Many countries provide farm subsidies for wells and the electricity needed to pump irrigation water. But often these subsidies lead to environmentally harmful practices, including overpumping of aquifers. For example, the aquifer under Punjab, a major agricultural state in northwest India, is declining unsustainably. Formerly able to irrigate with canal water, farmers now pump water from tube wells that were once 50 feet deep but are now reaching down 500 feet.[25] Farmers take on increasing debt to dig the wells. Inability to repay debts contributes to the high rate of suicide among Indian farmers.

Electricity for the pumps is a drain on the already overloaded power system. But the government provides farmers with free electricity, limiting their incentive to save water. Power cuts are frequent, so farmers use diesel generators to run the pumps, adding to greenhouse gas emissions. And the government subsidizes the price of diesel. It also subsidizes the fertilizer and pesticides used on the farms.[26] The Punjab was once the leading edge of the Green Revolution (see Chapter 10), which dramatically improved agricultural yields in much of the developing world. But reliance on major inputs of fertilizer, pesticides, and especially irrigation water wastes energy as well as water. Farm subsidies have also been a political hot potato for successive Indian governments.

Major food companies can play an important role by helping their suppliers to save water. The Mars food corporation found that rice was the major water guzzler in its supply chain. It teamed up with the International Rice Research Institute to reduce water usage among 2,000 basmati rice farmers in the Punjab.[27] In place of the traditional continuous flooding of rice fields, the farmers alternately drained and flooded the fields to keep optimum water levels. Not only was water usage reduced by 30 percent, but rice yields increased,[28] greatly improving the farmers' income. These practices could save water and energy in rice-growing regions throughout the world.

6. A Thirst for Meat?

Twenty percent of irrigation water goes to crops that feed domestic animals.[29] Meat production represents an extravagant expenditure of water. A kilogram (2.2 pounds) of beef requires an astonishing 15,400 liters (nearly 4,000 gallons) of water,[30] when the water to grow the feed is taken into account (Figure 50). Cattle grazing on rain-fed grassland do not compete with humans for water use. But during much of their growth, most beef cattle are fed on irrigated hay or corn. Sheep uses two-thirds, and pork uses less than half as much water as beef. Chicken is the least water-thirsty meat but still requires 4,300 liters of water per kilogram.

In the United States, beef production has fallen by one-third since 1980 (Figure 51), while chicken has soared in popularity. Substitution of chicken for beef saves water, but total meat production—chicken, beef, and pork—rose 15 percent between 1980 and 2020.

While the changes largely reflect the U.S. diet, export of chicken and

Water Requirements (in L per kg of meat)

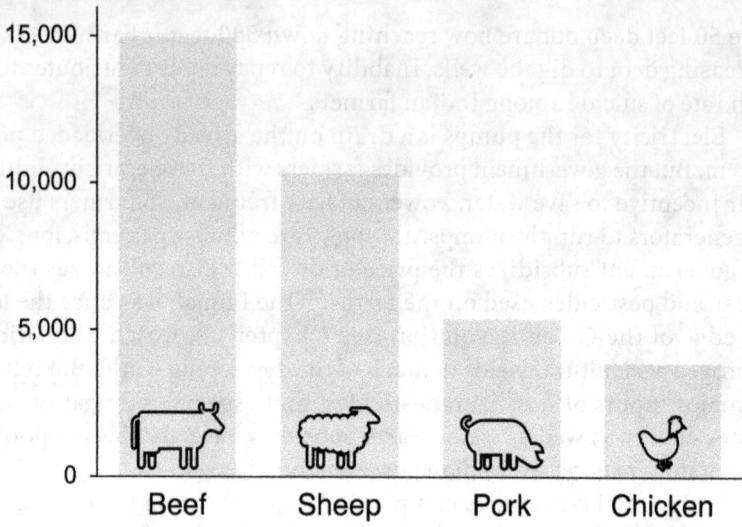

FIGURE 50. Global average water requirements for producing meat from cows, sheep, pigs, and chickens. Data from Mesfin M. Mekonnen and Arjen Y. Hoekstra, "A Global Assessment of the Water Footprint of Farm Animal Products," *Ecosystems* 15 (January 24, 2012): 401–15.

Food Production in the U.S.

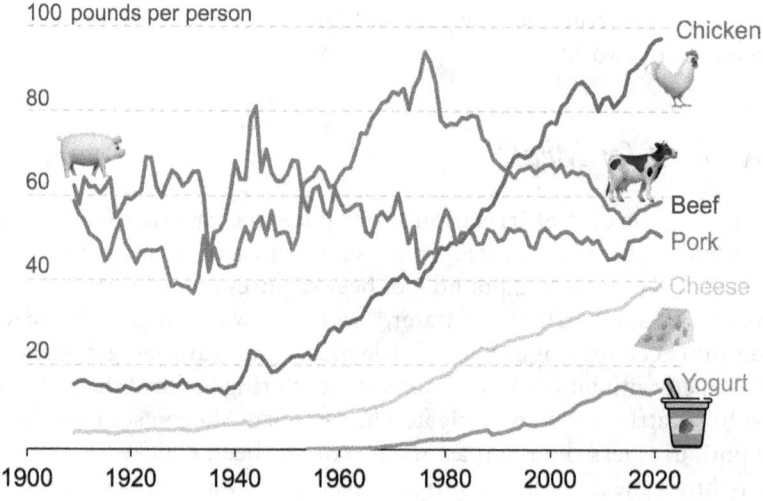

FIGURE 51. U.S. per capita food production. Data from U.S. Department of Agriculture: "Food Availability (per Capita) Data System," Economic Research Service, accessed May 20, 2024, https://www.ers.usda.gov/data-prod ucts/food-availability-per-capita-data-system/food-availability-per-capita-data-system/#Food%20Availability.

dairy have also risen, reflecting farming efficiency, government subsidies, and foreign demand. The state of Arkansas, once covered in cotton, is now devoted to soybean crops, which feed enormous chicken operations. The crops are irrigated by groundwater from a shallow aquifer, whose water level is steadily decreasing.

Meanwhile across the country, the state of Idaho, long known for its potatoes, has become a major dairy producer to feed a fast-growing appetite for cheese and yogurt.[31] Much of the state is high desert, normally supporting only sagebrush. But when irrigated from the aquifer below, the moderate climate and ample sunshine support fields of alfalfa. Alfalfa needs much more water than potatoes. In Idaho, the alfalfa feeds 700,000 dairy cattle, second only to California and Wisconsin.[32] Water levels in the aquifer are steadily falling. The rise of cheese in the diet reflects the popularity of pizza, one of America's favorite fast foods. The pizza habit supports Idaho's dairy farmers at the expense of their aquifer.

High-income countries consume a lot of meat, although Europe consumes one-third less than the United States.[33] But as people elsewhere raise their standard of living, they eat more meat. Reducing the amount of meat people eat would free up land and water for vegetable production, stretching the food supply considerably.

In addition to consuming water, livestock can also pollute it. When they roam on pastureland, livestock fertilize the grass with their excrement. But when they are confined in large industrial feedlots, their excrement is collected in huge holding ponds that produce foul odors, release the greenhouse gas methane and the air pollutant ammonia. Outflow from the holding ponds overfertilizes rivers and lakes downstream.

7. Artificial Intelligence Is Thirsty Too

Big technology companies—Amazon, Google, Microsoft, Meta—store enormous amounts of data in "the cloud." The cloud sounds insubstantial, but it actually consists of server farms: huge buildings with thousands of computers. The computers run on electricity, and they require water to carry away the heat they generate. These data centers are so massive that they can strain regional water supplies. There has been pushback from affected communities. Meta ran into opposition to its planned $1.1 billion data center in Talavera de la Reina, a small city in Spain's drought-stricken central plain. The data center would need 176 million gallons a year of cooling water. A group fighting the project calls itself Tu Nube Seca Mi Río ("Your Cloud Dries Up My River" in Spanish).[34] Artificial intelligence (AI) companies generally keep their water consumption secret.[35] But a yearlong legal battle revealed that Google's three data centers in The Dalles, Oregon, use more than one-quarter of the municipal water supply.[36]

Data center expansion is accelerating because of the huge computer requirements of AI. Technology companies are racing to develop AI products, which require huge amounts of data. More and more cooling water is needed. To get a dozen responses from the popular ChatGPT application requires about a pint of cooling water.[37] Researchers suggest that current trends in AI development could drive up global cooling water withdrawals from streams and aquifers to up to 6.6 billion cubic meters by 2027. This would amount to about half the water consumed by the United Kingdom each year.[38]

Technology companies have pledged to conserve water as much as possible through reuse and efficiency measures. They also propose to put more water back into aquifers than they consume. For example, they would fund improvements in leaky irrigation infrastructure or to restore wetland systems.

8. Can We Use Seawater?

Why not remove salt from ocean water (*desalination*) to get usable water? Desalination is happening, but it is costly in money and energy. The simplest method, distillation, is also the costliest. A desalination still boils the water off, leaving the salt behind. The vapor is then cooled in a condenser to produce pure liquid water. Solar distillation is how nature provides us with fresh rainwater. Distillation is straightforward, but it takes considerable energy to convert water to its vapor. Instead of distillation, modern desalination plants use *reverse osmosis*, a process that squeezes salts out by forcing water through a membrane whose pores reject the salt. The energy required to apply the needed pressure is much less than that required to vaporize water. Chemists have been able to make membranes that admit water molecules but not the salt ions. As of 2022, more than 21,000 desalination plants operate around the world, about half of them in the Middle East and North Africa.[39] They supply about 1 percent of the fresh water used by humans, mostly in arid regions by the sea, like Israel and Saudi Arabia. Kuwait obtains nearly all of its fresh water by desalination. As costs go down, fresh water from the ocean will become increasingly important in coastal areas, where much of the human population lives. Farther inland, however, the cost and energy required to lift and transport the water becomes prohibitive.

Reverse osmosis can also be used to purify brackish groundwater (water that is saltier than fresh water but not as much as seawater) or

FIGURE 52. Solar-powered reverse osmosis water kiosk in rural Kenya to turn raw water with a high salt content into potable water. Photo credit: Konsta Punkka (photographer)/Solar Water Solutions.

salty runoff from irrigated fields. In sunny areas, small reverse osmosis units powered with solar panels can provide village water (Figure 52). For example, one such unit supplies the village of Burani, Kenya, 30 kilometers southwest of Mombasa, with 20,000 liters a day of fresh water from a well with high salt content.[40] The solar panels can also charge up to 10 cell phones at a time in this off-the-grid village.

9. Salt Is a Problem Too

When desalination plants remove salt from seawater, where does the salt go? Back to the sea. There are two outputs: fresh water to the land and saltier water, called brine, to the sea. The seas contain so much water that the effect of desalination plants on their overall saltiness is miniscule. But the effect on the shallow waters at the coastline can be substantial. Since salt makes water denser, the brine discharge from desalination plants sinks to the bottom, where it can affect the growth of seagrass and the life it supports. The brine from older distillation plants is hot as well as salty. So their discharge heats the local seawater, adding to the environmental stress. In addition, if the power plants that provide electricity to run desalination plants burn fossil fuels, they discharge heated cooling water, further heating the seawater near the shore.

Dubai, the most populous city in the United Arab Emirates, is a major transit, shopping, and tourist hub. Sitting on the Arabian coast, Dubai uses an extravagant amount of fresh water, 164 billion gallons a year (620 billion liters), all supplied by numerous desalination plants.[41] They provide domestic water to 3.6 million residents, plus up to 1 million visitors at a time. To enhance tourism, the city built spectacular water features, including the world's deepest scuba diving pool and a ski run inside a megamall with freshly made snow. Dubai has the world's tallest building, with a peak cooling capacity equivalent to 10,000 tons of melted ice. To extend its developable shoreline, the city is building a series of artificial islands, further impacting the water (Figure 53). The temperature of the water surrounding one of these islands increased 13 degrees over 19 years.[42]

There have been red tides from algal blooms large enough to shut down the desalination plants, which have been attributed to land reclamation as well as the brine and industrial discharges.[43] But the ecological effects of the brine discharges are hard to gauge because so much else is disturbing the seawater from all the development on the shoreline.

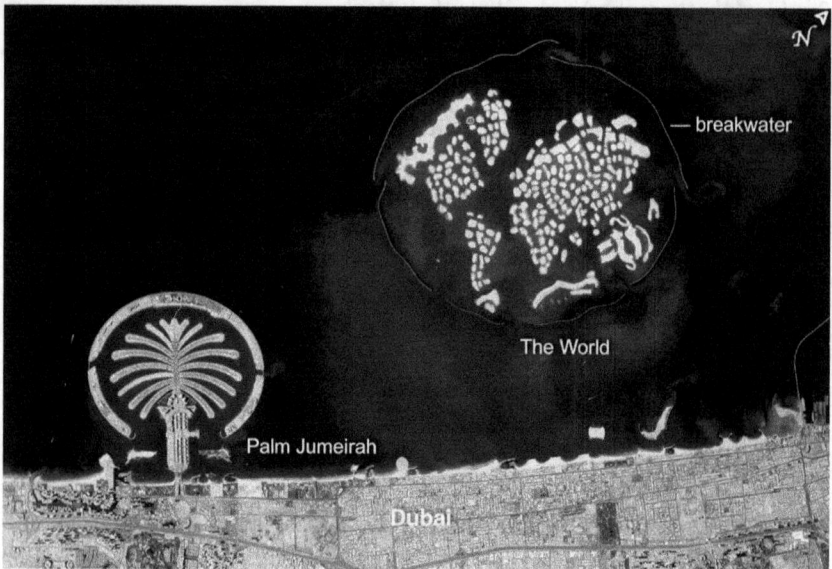

FIGURE 53. Dubai's human-made archipelagos: the Palm Island (Palm Jumeirah) and the World Islands. Photographs taken by the International Space Station crew, January 13, 2010. Credit: NASA/JSC Gateway to Astronaut Photography of Earth. Downloaded from "Artificial Archipelagos, Dubai, United Arab Emirates," NASA Earth Observatory, https://earthobservatory.nasa.gov/images/42477/artificial-archipelagos-dubai-united-arab-emirates.

The United Arab Emirates' neighbors, Bahrain, Kuwait, Saudi Arabia, and Qatar, also rely on desalination and are all developing rapidly. Development around the shores of the relatively shallow Persian Gulf has destroyed salt marshes and mangrove swamps. About 70 percent of the coral reefs that once flourished in the area are gone, along with their associated fisheries.[44]

Extra salt is also a problem for freshwater streams and lakes. Road runoff of deicing salt is a major source in areas of cold winters. But salt ions also leach out of rocks and dirt disturbed by land clearing and construction and out of irrigated fields. Rainwater carries the leached salts into groundwater and into streams. In coastal areas the groundwater can be contaminated by saltwater intrusion, especially if the aquifer is being pumped out.

When salts contaminate drinking water, they can elevate hypertension in those who drink it. They can also mobilize other pollutants from the soil or cause pipes to corrode. This is how lead got into the tap water in Flint, Michigan (see below), when the city switched to a water source with high salt and acid content. Salts and associated contaminants can also harm aquatic plants and animals that have evolved in a low-salt environment.

10. How Safe Is Drinking Water?

(A) The Burden of Waterborne Disease

Lakes and rivers harbor pathogens (disease-causing microorganisms) from animal or human waste. Even wilderness areas contain pathogens from wild animal wastes. Towns treat water from nearby lakes or rivers or from municipal wells to remove or kill harmful microorganisms. Chlorination to disinfect water supplies was widely introduced in the United States and Europe around the turn of the 20th century. It dramatically reduced waterborne diseases.[45]

Sewage treatment plants are also critical. Untreated sewage contaminates the water supply of anyone living downstream or by the near-shore ocean waters. The treatment plants use friendly bacteria to decompose the organic material in sewage, including any pathogens. Some treatment plants have extra stages to remove excess ammonium, nitrate, and phosphate, which can act as nutrients for blooms of algae downstream. In the United States, many sewage plants were constructed or upgraded in the wake of the 1972 Clean Water Act, which regulates what can be discharged into the water.[46]

Waterborne diseases, like cholera, typhoid fever, and dysentery, remain a major health problem worldwide, particularly in low-income countries. Their overpopulated cities have old, inadequate water treatment and sewage treatment plants. The water from taps is unsafe to drink until boiled. In rural areas, wells are contaminated by animal and human wastes. More than 2 billion people lack access to safe drinking water.[47] One million deaths a year—nearly 2.5 percent of all deaths—are attributable to unsafe drinking water.[48]

Safe water is the goal of many projects in underserved communities. The Planet Water Foundation installs "AquaTowers," special water filtration systems, in rural communities of Asia and Latin America.[49] An "AquaTower" is a gravity-fed tank with three filtration stages based on membrane technology and activated carbon that remove particles as small as bacteria and viruses. Often installed near school communities, the towers not only provide access to safe drinking water but also promote good hygiene practices with their special built-in handwashing stations.[50] And UNICEF supports water, sanitation, and hygiene construction projects in several areas impoverished by political turmoil, including South Sudan, the Central African Republic, Iraq, and Venezuela.[51]

(B) And Pollutants

Viruses, bacteria, and amoeba that cause disease are the biggest danger in human water supplies. In addition, harmful molecules are discharged into waterways from industrial and domestic sewage as well as runoff from roadways and farms. The Cuyahoga River in Cleveland was so polluted that in 1969 it caught fire.[52] Publicity about the fire spurred the modern environmental movement and led to the passage of the U.S. Clean Water and Safe Drinking Water Acts. Billions of dollars were spent to clean up effluents and restore rivers and lakes. Not only was the Cuyahoga cleaned up, but Lake Erie, into which the Cuyahoga flows, returned to health.[53] Many other waterways were similarly restored, both in the United States and around the world. But low-income countries have greater difficulties because of limited budgets and weak enforcement. So they still face major pollution problems.

A recent concern is the discovery of polyfluorinated alkyl substances (PFAS) in many water supplies.[54] They are called "forever chemicals" because they take a long time to break down in the environment. They repel both water and oil and are useful as ingredients of nonstick cookware, fabric, food packaging, and firefighting foam. But they leach out of these products and find their way into waterways. The most exposed communities are near PFAS manufacturing plants and near airports and military bases where PFAS-containing firefighting foam is heavily used. But PFAS are also found at low concentrations in surface- and ground-waters and in municipal water supplies throughout the United States and around the world.[55] What levels are harmful? Extensive research is underway to answer this question (see Chapter 8 on toxicity). Meanwhile, industry is shifting away from the PFAS molecules found to be most toxic and substituting others, whose full effects have yet to be determined. Municipalities are left wondering what to do about PFAS since removing them from water requires expensive filtration through activated charcoal.

Lead in drinking water is another serious problem.[56] Lead affects nerve cells and, at even low levels, can slow mental development in children (see Chapter 9). Lead gets into drinking water from pipes that connect the water mains to houses. Older pipes were made of lead (in fact, "plumbing" is derived from *plumbum*, Latin for "lead"), and the solder that connects pipes and fittings contained lead. Lead pipes and solder were banned in the United States in 1986 (an amendment to the Safe Water Act). But older pipes remain in use. Usually, a surface layer of insoluble lead carbonate prevents the lead from leaching into the water. But if the water is acidic, this protective layer dissolves. Water districts add lime to reduce acidity. Many also add phosphate to form an additional protective layer of lead phosphate.

The lead problem is highlighted by the drinking water crisis in Flint, Michigan, which ignored these precautions. In April 2014, in the midst of a financial crisis, the city stopped buying treated water from the Detroit water authority and drew water instead from the Flint River.[57] But no measures were taken to counter the river's acidity, nor was protective phosphate added. A year and a half later, the city switched back to the Detroit water authority after elevated lead levels were found in many homes' tap water. By then, 5 percent of Flint children had elevated lead levels in their blood, double the rate before the water switch. A community group played a key role in bringing attention to the problem, working with university scientists to carry out a lead testing program. They pressured state government to declare an emergency and to dig up and replace the lead service pipes. The episode called attention to the danger of lead in water, leading to protective measures nationwide.

Test kits to measure lead in tap water are readily available, as are filters that can trap the lead. But people with low incomes may not be aware of the problem or can't afford the filters. So they are likely to bear the burden of undetected lead because they often live in areas with old lead plumbing.

(C) Unsafe for Fish Too

Streams and lakes are often clogged with algae because of over-fertilization from insufficiently treated sewage outflows and farm run-off. When the algae die off, all the oxygen in the water is used up by bacteria feeding on the dead algae. Fish and other animals then suffocate. *Anaerobic* bacteria, bacteria that don't need oxygen, take over, producing hydrogen sulfide and other toxic chemicals. The same process occurs at the mouths of rivers that drain agricultural areas, producing "dead zones" devoid of fish and marine animals. A major example is the dead zone in the Gulf of Mexico at the mouth of the Mississippi River.[58]

Algae growing along the oceanfront (often seen as "red tide") can themselves produce toxic molecules that poison sea creatures, making them unsafe for human consumption. And sewage outflows, even from properly run sewage treatment plants, can contain chemicals that harm fish. These chemicals include pharmaceuticals, such as antibiotics, which people flush down the drain.[59] Antibiotics are particularly concerning. Antibiotic resistance can spread among the bacteria, producing resistant strains that harm not only fish but also humans. People are urged not to flush their unused drugs but to dispose of them safely. Drugstores now have bins for dropping off unused pharmaceuticals.

(D) Can Bad Actors Be Natural?

Naturally occurring but harmful inorganic chemicals, especially arsenic and fluoride, can also contaminate wells. At low concentrations, fluoride strengthens teeth and bones. It is often added to toothpaste and to municipal water supplies in some countries to protect teeth from cavities. But at higher concentrations, fluoride weakens bones instead. Ingestion over a long time can lead to skeletal fluorosis: bone deformities and fractures.[60] Arsenic in drinking water produces skin disorders and even cancers.

Both arsenic and fluoride occur naturally in rocks and are gradually released as the rocks weather. They wash into aquifers and settle into the lower clay layers. If the aquifer is pumped from many wells faster than rainwater can recharge it, water seeps out of the clay layers, carrying along some of the accumulated arsenic and fluoride. The faster the aquifer is pumped, the greater the arsenic and fluoride concentration in the well water.

Arsenic and fluoride contamination particularly affects poor villagers who rely on local wells for their drinking water. About 150 million people, mostly in Asia, are at risk of drinking arsenic-laden well water.[61] In Bangladesh, about 45 million people drank arsenic-laced water for many years before the danger was discovered.[62] Ironically, the problem grew out of a UN-sponsored effort, starting in the 1960s, to provide safe drinking water by sinking tube wells into the shallow aquifer below. The program did in fact greatly improve health by curbing waterborne diseases, but the arsenic in the water went undetected for years.

Rocks with high fluoride levels underlie parts of India. Approximately 25 million people there are affected by fluorosis, and 66 million are at risk from excessive groundwater fluoride.[63] In many other areas of the world, including California, China, Mexico, and regions of South America, overpumping of aquifers is accompanied by rising levels of arsenic and fluoride. Fortunately, arsenic and fluoride can be filtered out of the water using inexpensive material like alumina or iron hydroxide.[64] Locally made bone char ("natural carbon" made from the bones of cattle) is also effective at filtering out both fluoride and arsenic from the water.[65]

11. What Is Acidification All About?

In addition to being a heat-trapping gas (Chapter 1), carbon dioxide dissolves in water and forms carbonic acid. The hydrogen ions it

FIGURE 54. Pteropod shells dissolve in acidified water. *Left:* a pteropod that has lived for six days in normal waters in laboratory conditions. *Right:* a pteropod showing the effects of living in acidified water for the same time period. The white lines indicate shell dissolution. Photo credit: NOAA, downloaded from "Ocean Acidification: A Wake-Up Call in Our Waters," National Oceanic and Atmospheric Administration, April 1, 2016, https://www.noaa.gov/ocean-acidification-high-co2-world-dangerous-waters-ahead.

releases can inhibit seashells from forming. Sea life is well adapted to the pre-industrial level of CO_2, 280 ppm, but it runs into trouble as the CO_2 level rises. This is the problem of ocean acidification. Since the Industrial Revolution, ocean acidity has increased by about 30 percent.[66]

There are naturally occurring upwellings of acidic water along the U.S. West Coast, during which oysters can't form larvae and oyster farms fail.[67] Higher CO_2 levels will worsen these episodes. Shells of pteropods ("sea butterflies"), tiny creatures that provide food to sea animals from krill to whales, have been shown to dissolve at 700 ppm CO_2,[68] a level predicted for the year 2100 at current CO_2 emission rates (Figure 54).

Acidification of seawater also reduces the ability of reef-building corals to produce their skeletons. Corals are already in trouble from rising temperatures, and acidification adds further stress. It threatens reefs that provide habitat for an estimated 1 million species of sea creatures. Acidification can also affect the behavior of non-shell organisms. The ability of some fish, like clownfish, to detect predators and locate suitable habitat decreases in more acidic waters. Polluted air contains stronger acids than CO_2, particularly nitric and sulfuric acids (HNO_3 and H_2SO_4), that create "acid rain" (Chapter 6).

12. Summary

Water is abundant on our planet, but fresh water is a precious resource. It is scarce in much of the world because of growing population and food production. Global warming worsens the problem because dry areas get drier and wet areas get more floods. Mountain snowpack melts earlier, increasing spring flooding and fall drought. Faster runoff reduces the amount of rainwater available for filling aquifers.

Agriculture uses most of the fresh water for irrigation, and aquifers are being pumped unsustainably. The problem is compounded by industrial farms that sink shafts deep into aquifers to water giant pivot-irrigated fields. Corporations buy land internationally for such farms because the water underneath is considered a free resource. Meat, especially beef production, consumes water extravagantly. Crops for animal feed use 20 percent of irrigation water. Irrigation water presents the greatest opportunity for conservation. But cities also need to implement conservation practices and protect and expand reservoirs. Low-income countries need help to improve agricultural practices and conserve water.

Removing salt from seawater expands the water supply but requires a lot of money and energy. Reverse osmosis is the most efficient way to do this. Now more than 16,000 desalination plants operate along ocean shores. But discharge of the removed salt can harm the ecology of the near-shore seawater. Freshwater streams and lakes also get contaminated by salts in runoff from the land.

The most acute problem is providing water that is safe to drink. Waterborne diseases take a terrible human toll, especially in low-income countries. But even in high-income countries, which have made much progress in cleaning up their waters, keeping water free from harmful contaminants is a major concern.

Earth's water is subject to acidification. The rising levels of CO_2 in the air mean elevated carbonic acid levels in water. Sea creatures have a harder time making calcium carbonate shells. That threatens ocean food chains, coral reefs, and shellfish farms.

8

Toxic Substances

Are We Being Poisoned?

Topics:

1. What substances can harm us?
2. What are endocrine disrupters?
3. Does everything cause cancer?
4. How dangerous is radioactivity?
5. What are POPs?
6. What minerals are toxic?
    A. Lead
    B. Mercury
    C. Arsenic and fluoride
7. Ecotoxicity
    A. Tires versus coho salmon
    B. Sunscreens versus corals
8. What's the solution to pollution?
9. Summary

---

1. What Substances Can Harm Us?

Just about everything, if we take in too much. Even water, if we drink an excessive amount, can make us sick. The idea that "the dose makes the poison" has been around since the Middle Ages. "Toxic" and poisonous are the same thing. The toxic dose is very different for different substances. At the most dangerous end of the toxicity scale is botulinum toxin, from a lethal bacterium that can grow in improperly canned foods and in wounds. In laboratory rat-feeding studies of acute toxicity, half the rats die at the tiny dose (called LD_{50}) of 0.000001 milligrams[1] (less than one-billionth of an ounce) per kilogram of body weight (Figure 55). At the

Substance	LD$_{50}$, mg/kg (oral, rat)	Toxicity category
Water	90,000	IV: Very low
Table sugar	30,000	IV: Very low
Ethanol	7,000	IV: Very low
Malathion	5,400	IV: Very low
Table salt	3,000	III: Low
Methanol	2,000	III: Low
Vanillin	1,600	III: Low
Formaldehyde	500	II: Moderate
Caffeine	367	II: Moderate
Aspirin	200	II: Moderate
DDT	135	II: Moderate
Sodium fluoride	52	I: High
Methylmercury	30	I: High
Arsenic	15	I: High
Parathion	14	I: High
Tetraethyllead	14	I: High
Botulinum toxin	0.000001	I: High

FIGURE 55. Acute toxicities, according to the EPA's four toxicity categories: very low, low, moderate, and high. Values are from "Explore Chemistry," NIH, National Library of Medicine, National Center for Biotechnology Information, https://pubchem.ncbi.nlm.nih.gov and "SDS: Safety Data Sheet," https://www.fishersci.com/us/en/catalog/search/sdshome.html.

other end of the scale is sugar, for which LD$_{50}$ for rats is 30,000 milligrams per kilogram, roughly half a cup of sugar per pound of animal. Although people respond differently than rats, we can expect that a 200-pound person might keel over on eating 100 cups of sugar at a sitting! (We don't really know the human LD$_{50}$ since it is unethical to use people to find out.) Manufactured compounds also have a wide range of toxicity. The insecticide parathion is as toxic as arsenic,[2] but a related insecticide, malathion, is less toxic than aspirin[3] (Figure 55).

How people are exposed matters too. For example, to remove wrinkles, the lethal botulinum toxin is actually injected into people's faces (as "Botox"). If injected properly, the toxin does not migrate to the rest of the body. Some toxins are dangerous when breathed in. For example, mercury metal ("quicksilver") is harmless if swallowed; it passes right through the digestive system. But mercury vapor is dangerous. When inhaled, it goes through lung tissues and is then highly toxic. That is why spilled mercury should never be swept up or vacuumed. To avoid breathing it in, before cleaning it up one should spread an immobilizing agent like sulfur on the mercury.

Ingestion is how we are exposed to most toxins. Both naturally occurring and synthetic toxins get in our food and water in many ways. They may be part of our food (green potatoes, for example, contain plant toxins),[4] or they can accompany invaders, like molds. Or they may be airborne and land on plants that livestock eat. The disastrous 1986 explosion of the Chernobyl nuclear power plant in the former Soviet Union spread a cloud over Europe that rained radioactive elements down onto the grass that cows ate. Their contaminated milk had to be discarded. Closer to Chernobyl itself, more than three decades after the accident, cow's milk still has elevated radiation levels in villages as far as 140 miles from the reactor site.[5]

Most of the time we don't need to worry about a deadly dose as much as we do about repeated low doses of potentially toxic substances (Figure 56). We want to avoid getting sick or suffering damage from chronic exposures. But how do we know what to avoid?

Agencies like the World Health Organization and the U.S. Environmental Protection Agency keep track of harmful substances that people might breathe, drink, or eat and set recommended maximum doses in air, water, and food. These doses are determined from exposure studies with lab animals, mostly rats or mice, and from epidemiological studies with people. The maximum safe dose for lab animals is adjusted to account for possible differences between animals and people. Let's look at the things to worry about.

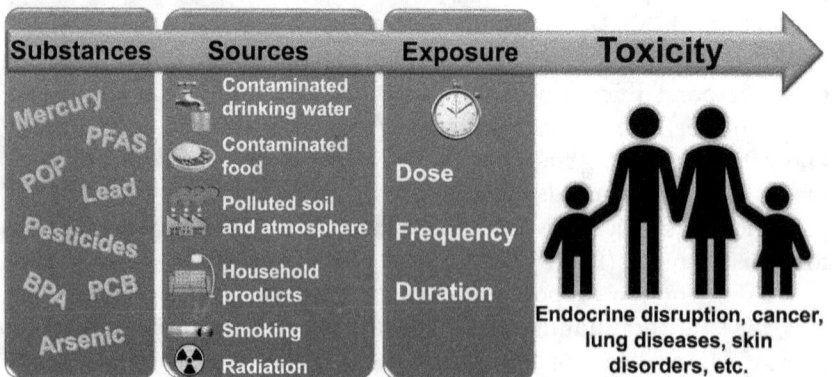

Substances	Sources	Exposure	Toxicity
Mercury PFAS POP Lead Pesticides BPA PCB Arsenic	Contaminated drinking water; Contaminated food; Polluted soil and atmosphere; Household products; Smoking; Radiation	Dose; Frequency; Duration	Endocrine disruption, cancer, lung diseases, skin disorders, etc.

FIGURE 56. Diagram of pollutants and their sources, and the factors that determine our exposure to them. Illustration by Alexandra Soldatova.

2. What Are Endocrine Disrupters?

Both natural and man-made chemicals can interfere with the body's hormones, known as the endocrine system. Hormones control vital biological processes, such as growth and development, reproduction, sleep, energy balance, and metabolism, by turning key genes on and off. Endocrine disrupters mimic or block hormones, affecting the process that the hormone controls.[6] For example, the sex hormones, androgen and estrogen, maintain the male and female sexual systems. Both are inhibited by the pesticide DDT and its breakdown products in the environment. High levels of DDT were found in a Florida lake's alligators, after heavy rains in 1980 flooded the waste pond of a pesticide factory, sending contaminated wastes into the lake.[7] The number of alligators declined drastically, and surviving juvenile alligators failed to develop functioning sex organs.

Effects on prenatal and childhood development are of particular concern since hormones control developmental stages. In the 1950s when DDT was sprayed everywhere to kill insects, the daughters of women who had high blood concentrations of DDT were found to have elevated levels of breast cancer, hypertension, and obesity.[8] Even the next generation (granddaughters) had indications of health problems, showing that DDT's effects can persist over three generations. So curbing DDT use had important benefits for both human and wild animal health.

Another endocrine-disrupting chemical, bisphenol A (BPA), a plasticizer used widely in food packaging, toys, and personal care products, has been the subject of many studies and heated debates.[9] BPA is a component of polycarbonate plastic, a tough, clear plastic used to make beverage bottles. Although BPA is an integral part of the plastic, traces of it can leach out at high temperature or if the liquid it holds contains acid. The studies connected the chemical not only to hormone function disruption but also to fertility, lung function, and metabolic disorders and to cancer.[10] Canada was the first country to ban the use of BPA in the making of baby bottles,[11] followed by a similar ban by the European Union in 2011[12] and the U.S. Food and Drug Administration in 2012.[13] The European Food Safety Authority set a very low recommended limit for BPA ingestion, less than one nanogram per kilogram of body weight a day (one nanogram is one-thousandth of a microgram).[14] Some countries are moving toward a complete ban of BPA in food packaging materials.

People are exposed to a wide range of potentially endocrine-disruptive chemicals. Their levels are mostly very low, but simultaneous exposure to different chemicals might have enhanced effects.

3. Does Everything Cause Cancer?

Well, not everything, but many chemicals could cause cancer if people are exposed enough. As with toxicity in general, "the dose makes the poison." Cancer-causing chemicals produce mutations in our DNA, the molecule from which our genes are made. To do that, the chemical must gain access to the DNA inside our cells. By reacting with the DNA, they can alter the genetic code. These changes in the code are called mutations. The body has several ways to keep this from happening, but mistakes can slip through. Occasionally mutations that alter genes controlling cell growth allow the cells to proliferate and invade the surrounding tissue, becoming cancerous. Several mutations must accumulate in a set of genes to generate cancer. The longer we live, the likelier that becomes. Six percent of cancer patients are 65 and older.[15] Another factor is the rate at which normal cells proliferate in different parts of our body. The greater this rate, the greater the chances for mutations to accumulate. This is why tissues with rapidly growing cells (breast in females, prostate in males) are prone to cancer.[16] And drugs or alcohol, which are processed by the liver, stimulate it to make more cells. Alcohol consumption is one of the biggest factors for liver cancers.[17]

Cancer is what many people fear most when it comes to chemicals in the environment. But connecting cancer to any particular exposure is really hard. Cancer is fairly common. Approximately one in five men and women develop cancer at some time in their lives, usually as they grow older.[18] Mutations occur all the time. They can be caused by radiation (including X-rays and cosmic rays, ultraviolet radiation, and radioactivity) and by chemicals that react with DNA. The body itself produces "reactive oxygen species," forms of oxygen that can cause mutations.

So with all this going on in the body, how do we evaluate the extra influence of chemicals in the environment? Toxicologists feed suspect chemicals to lab mice and rats and look for cancers. They measure how cancer incidence in the rodents depends on the dose. Then they calculate the dose at which cancers first appear. To apply this finding to humans, regulators divide this minimum dose by a safety factor, generally one million, to establish a safe dose.[19] Sounds simple, but there are lots of complications.

For one thing, the biochemistry of mice and rats is different from humans. For years the sweetener saccharin was branded a carcinogen because it was found to produce bladder cancer in male rats. But it turned out to be a biochemical reaction of male rats not shared by humans (or female rats for that matter).[20] For another thing, the measurements require using high doses of the chemical being tested. There is a lot of uncertainty about the effect of low doses.

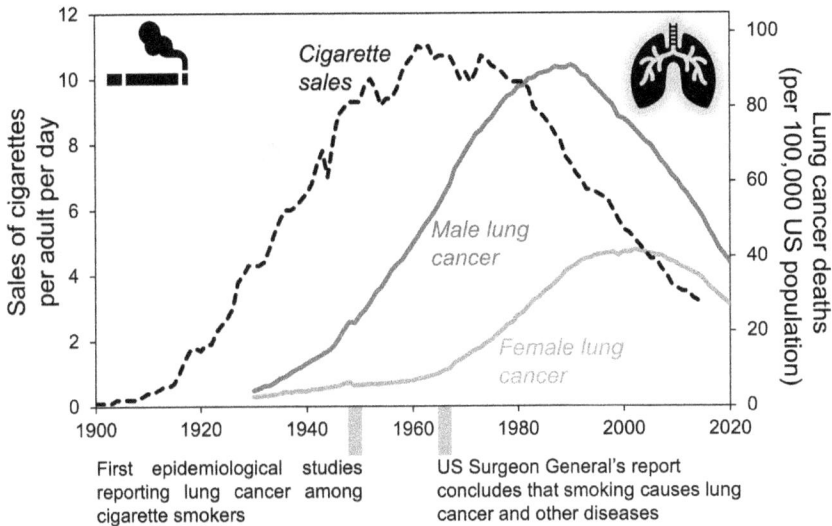

FIGURE 57. Cigarette smoking and lung cancer in the United States. Death rates are averages for all ages; data from American Cancer Society, Cancer Facts & Figures 2017, National Center for Health Statistics, and Centers for Disease Control and Prevention, 2022, https://www.cancer.org/research/cancer-facts-statistics/all-cancer-facts-figures/cancer-facts-figures-2017.html. Sales of cigarettes data are from Hannah Ritchie and Max Roser, "Smoking," OurWorldInData.org (2023), https://ourworldindata.org/smoking, based on Barbara Forey, Jan Hamling, John Hamling, Alison Thornton, and Peter Lee, "International Smoking Statistics," (2017), http://www.pnlee.co.uk/ISS.htm.

So regulators look at other evidence as well, like how often cancers show up in people exposed to a carcinogen. For example, workplace exposure studies have shown that vinyl chloride, from which polyvinyl chloride (PVC) plastic is made, causes liver and other cancers.[21] Benzene, produced in oil refining, causes leukemia.[22] And asbestos, used for insulation, causes mesothelioma, cancer of the lung's lining.[23]

But exposure in the general population is difficult to evaluate. Smoking and lung cancer have the clearest relationship.[24] Figure 57 shows that lung cancers in the United States tracked the rise in smoking but with a time lag of about 50 years. That's how long it takes, on average, for the smoke damage to produce enough mutations in lung cells to cause a cancer. Women took up smoking later than men and developed lung cancer later. Smoking leads to 90 percent of lung cancers.[25] It is harder to get convincing human data for environmental carcinogens because so many other factors can contribute to cancer.

4. How Dangerous Is Radioactivity?

Radioactive elements, occurring naturally or produced from human activities, can cause cancer. As with toxic chemicals, it is the accumulated dose that determines the outcome. Radioactive elements spit out nuclear fragments, which we call radioactivity. These fragments have a lot of energy. They can knock apart molecules in their path, including molecules that have critical biological roles, like DNA. Enough damage to DNA can produce cancer-causing mutations. This is the great worry about radioactivity.

But this worry needs to be put in context. We all live with a natural background of radioactivity. There are many radioactive elements in the earth's crust and even in food.[26] For example, bananas contain small amounts of naturally occurring radioactive potassium. But the dose is so small that you would have to eat a billion bananas for the radioactivity to be lethal.[27]

Another common example is the element radon, a naturally occurring radioactive gas. It seeps from uranium-containing rocks in various locations. It can accumulate to dangerous levels in the basements of houses and needs to be vented to the outdoors. Radon disintegrates in a few days to a stable element, lead. So the radon disappears from the air quickly when vented. Most of the background radioactivity we live with comes from radon.

Exposure to radioactivity should be a worry only if it significantly exceeds the background level.[28] Nuclear reactors have protective structures that limit any escaped radioactivity to levels much lower than the background.[29]

Although radioactivity damages biological tissues, the nuclear fragments are mostly stopped after traveling a short distance. Many materials, including clothing and our own skin, protect us from most radioactivity. The main danger is radioactivity that reaches internal organs from radioactive elements that are ingested or inhaled (like radon, which is the second leading cause of lung cancer after tobacco smoking) (Figure 58). Three radioactive elements produced in nuclear reactions are particularly hazardous because the elements actually have important roles in our physiology. One is iodine-131. Iodine is a naturally occurring part of thyroxine, a hormone made in the thyroid gland. So radioactive iodine-131 accumulates in the thyroid gland. There, it can cause thyroid cancer, especially in children because their growing thyroids need more iodine. This was the only cancer that was found at elevated levels in the aftermath of the Chernobyl nuclear disaster in the former Soviet Union.[30] Fortunately, thyroid cancer can be treated and is rarely fatal.

Another fission product is cesium-137, which is chemically like

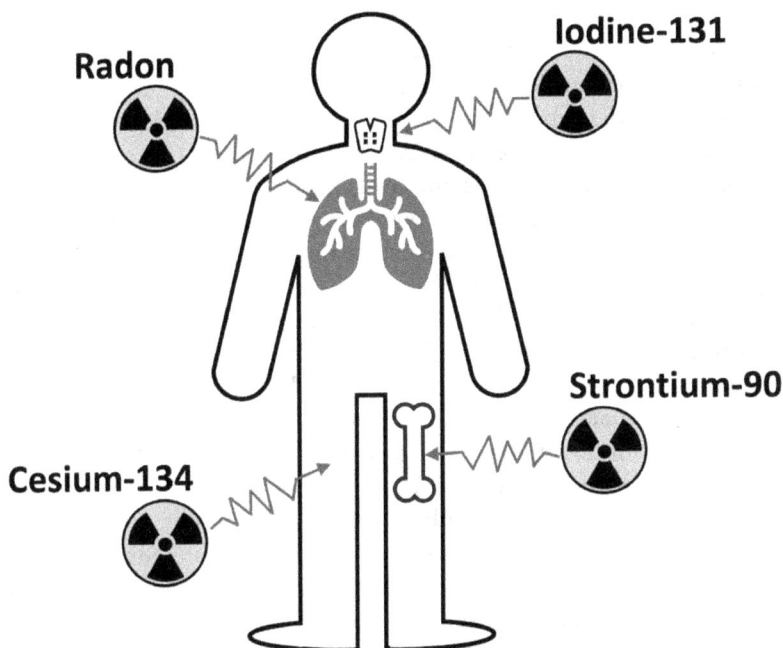

FIGURE 58. Radioactive elements affect different parts of the body. Illustration by Alexandra Soldatova.

potassium and can substitute for the body's potassium. A third dangerous fission product is strontium-90. Strontium-90 can substitute for calcium in bones and teeth, where it can lodge for a long time (its half-life is 29 years),[31] emitting its damaging nuclear fragments. When strontium-90 falls on grass that cows eat, it can contaminate the milk supply. "The Baby Tooth Survey,"[32] a study started in 1958, showed an increase in radioactive strontium in babies born close to nuclear bomb testing sites.[33] Early results from this study became a big factor in public pressure for the adoption in 1963 of an international treaty banning the testing of nuclear bombs in the air or under water.[34]

5. What Are Pops?

Persistent organic pollutants (POPs) are organic molecules (molecules based on carbon) that break down only very slowly in the environment. They are escaped industrial chemicals or else pesticides that were sprayed on fields in years past. The most infamous pesticide, DDT, developed on the eve of World War II, was used to limit the insect-borne diseases malaria and typhus among troops and civilians. At that time, it saved many lives. Its discoverer, Paul Müller, won the 1948 Nobel Prize in medicine.[35] In the decades after the war, DDT and similar chemicals were widely sprayed on crops to kill insect pests, but they killed many beneficial insects along with the pests. And being persistent, they built up in food chains, affecting animals and birds as well. Rachel Carson's classic book from 1962, *Silent Spring*,[36] drew attention to the ecosystem destruction that these pesticides caused. Birds at the top of the food chain, especially bald eagles, laid eggs with thin shells that cracked before they could hatch. DDT and its relatives interfered with hormones controlling eggshell formation. Sharply declining bird numbers led to the insecticides being banned nationally (in 1972) and internationally (although DDT can still be used against malaria mosquitoes in tropical areas).[37] Since then, eagles have become common again. DDT also had human health effects, spanning several generations (see above).

Another set of POPs are polychlorinated-biphenyls (PCBs), industrial oils that were used in heavy-duty electrical transformers and other equipment. They were also used as plasticizers, flame retardants, and additives in paints, building sealants, and carbonless copy paper. PCBs are no longer manufactured but still contaminate sites where they were dumped.[38] Another group of POPs are dioxins,[39] which were side products from manufacturing certain chemicals. The most notorious of these was "Agent Orange," a dioxin-containing mix of herbicides used by the United States during the Vietnam War to denude forests that hid guerrilla soldiers. Dioxins are also emitted by fires, particularly trash fires. The smoke carries these chemicals far away and deposits them on pastures where they accumulate in the meat and milk of grazing livestock. Because the smoke is diluted by the time it reaches pastures, dioxin concentrations fortunately remain very low in the food supply.[40]

POPs mostly don't dissolve in water, but they do dissolve in oils or fats. They concentrate in animal fat tissues, and when bigger animals eat smaller animals, the POPs concentrate further. This process, called biomagnification, accounts for the strong effect of DDT on eagles, which are top predators. POPs slowly evaporate and can travel far on the wind before getting rained out. They even make it to the Arctic, where they settle out on the tundra.[41] Caribou, which are food for Indigenous people, absorb and concentrate POPs when the caribou eat the lichen.

Humans ingest POPs with their food. Most people have detectable levels of POPs.[42] Those living near industrial facilities or waste dumps have higher levels. For example, a global egg-monitoring study found that in Ghana, near an e-waste site, a child eating just one egg would ingest more dioxins than a five-year "tolerable intake" established by the European

Food Safety Authority.[43] Lab studies have linked many POPs with immune suppression and cancer.[44] There is also evidence of cognitive impairment among children.[45] Fortunately, POP concentrations steadily decline when their production stops. Around the world, DDT levels in mothers' breast milk have declined five- to tenfold since 1951.[46]

One class of POP does dissolve in water. These are per- and polyfluoroalkyl substances, PFAS, found in water supplies, as discussed in Chapter 7. These "forever chemicals" do not break down in the environment. PFAS are used in many products, from nonstick cookware to cosmetics to firefighting foam. They do not accumulate in fat tissues, but they bind to blood proteins and accumulate in the liver and other organs. Like other POPs, they suppress the immune system, and they are associated with kidney and testicular cancers.[47] Many PFAS are being phased out of production. The two most commonly used PFAS were discontinued in 2000, and blood levels in the U.S. population have declined since then (Figure 59). But many other PFAS remain in use: an estimated 3,000 PFAS are currently on the global market.[48]

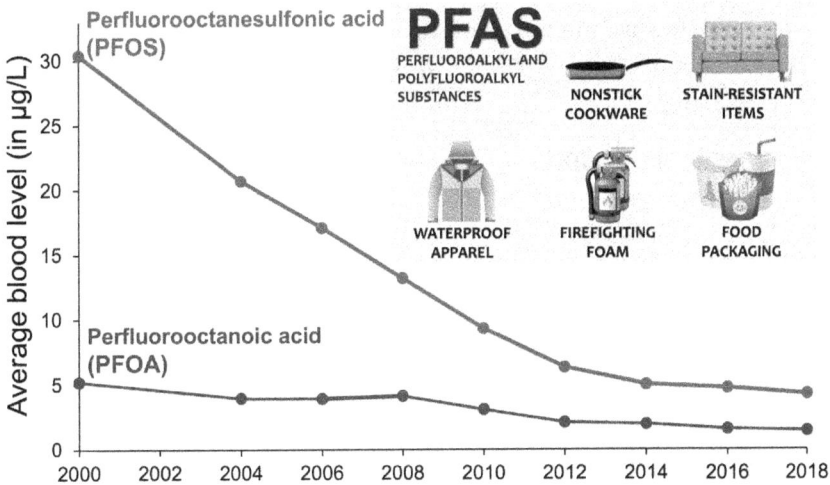

FIGURE 59. Declining blood concentrations in the U.S. population (in microgram per liter, µg/L) of two common but discontinued PFAS: perfluorooctanoic acid (PFOA), used in manufacturing of nonstick cookware, and perfluorooctanesulfonic acid (PFOS), previously used in fabric protectors. People in communities with contaminated drinking water may have as much as 10 times higher levels. Data source: "National Report on Human Exposure to Environmental Chemicals, Biomonitoring Data Tables for Environmental Chemicals," Centers for Disease Control and Prevention, U.S. Department of Health and Human Service, https://www.cdc.gov/exposurereport/data_tables.html.

Pollution by POPs is a worldwide problem. In 2004, an international treaty, the Stockholm Convention on Persistent Organic Pollutants, negotiated under UN auspices, went into effect. It identifies the worst POPs and prohibits or restricts their production and use.[49]

6. What Minerals Are Toxic?

Earth's crust contains minerals that can be harmful. A handful of these pose special health risks to humans. They are released into the environment through natural processes such as rock weathering or volcano eruptions but also through human misuse.

(A) Lead

Lead is hard yet pliable. Since prehistoric times it has been formed into all sorts of utensils. The ancient Greeks realized that drinking acidic beverages from lead vessels could make you ill. But the Romans ignored this lesson and sometimes added lead salts to overly acidic wines to sweeten the flavor. The bones of ancient Romans had high lead levels. Some historians speculate that chronic lead poisoning contributed to the fall of the Roman Empire.[50]

Because lead salts are brightly colored, they were used in paints. During much of the 20th century, the compound tetraethyl lead was added to gasoline to make cars run better.[51] But the lead compound ruins the catalytic converters that were installed in cars to reduce smog-causing air pollution, starting in the 1970s.[52] So leaded gas was phased out, first in Japan, followed by Brazil, Canada, the United States, and the rest of the world. Lead has now been removed from gasoline for vehicles in all countries worldwide, though the aviation industry still uses it in fuels for piston-engine airplanes.[53] Elimination of leaded gasoline had a huge public health benefit because the airborne lead spewing out of exhaust pipes had found its way into people. The positive impact of lead removal was immediate: after 1975, high levels of lead in human blood fell in lockstep with the phaseout of lead in gasoline (Figure 60).[54]

By 2016, blood lead levels in U.S. children aged one to five diminished further to only 0.8 µg/dl (0.8 micrograms lead per deciliter of blood, equivalent to eight parts per billion).[55] Other countries saw similar declines, depending on when they phased out leaded gasoline.[56]

Lead interrupts neurons in the brain. It interferes with children's brain development,[57] reducing their IQ, attention span, and educational attainment, and it increases behavioral problems. These effects can be

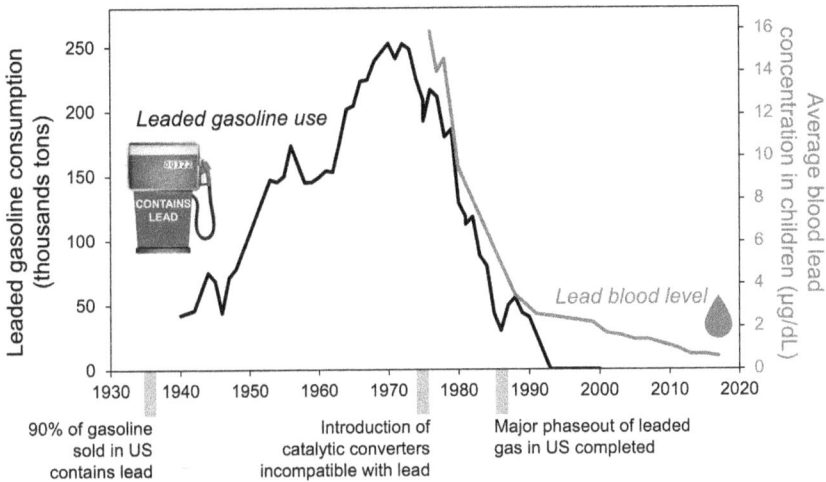

FIGURE 60. Leaded gasoline consumption and average blood lead concentration in children aged one to five years in the United States. Leaded gasoline consumption approximated from Michael J. McFarland, Matt E. Hauer, and Aaron Reuben, "Half of US Population Exposed to Adverse Lead Levels in Early Childhood," *Proceedings of the National Academy of Sciences of the United States of America* 119, no. 11 (March 7, 2022): e2118631119. Blood lead data from "America's Children and the Environment (ACE). Biomonitoring-Lead," Centers for Disease Control and Prevention, National Center for Health Statistics and National Center for Environmental Health, National Health and Nutrition Examination Survey, https://www.epa.gov/americaschildrenenvironment/ace-biomonitoring-lead, and Valerie M. Thomas, Robert H. Socolow, James J. Fanelli, and Thomas G. Spiro, "Effects of Reducing Lead in Gasoline: An Analysis of the International Experience," *Environmental Science & Technology* 33, no. 22 (October 1, 1999): 3942–48.

observed at blood lead levels down to five µg/dl; no safe level of lead has been established.[58] Studies have linked preschool lead exposure to aggressive and delinquent adolescent behavior and later criminal violence.[59] High crime rates during the 1990s in the United States, Canada, and Europe are best explained by high lead levels in the air 20 years earlier, when young men who committed most of the crime would have been infants. Falling violent crime rates paralleled the lead phaseout with a lag of 20 years (Figure 61).[60] Even though reduced lead pollution is not the only factor contributing to the fall in crime, no other factor correlates as well with the crime rates.[61]

But some children continue to be poisoned by lead. Urban soils are often contaminated by present and past uses of lead. Children ingest some of the dust when they play in it.[62] Many children also live in older houses

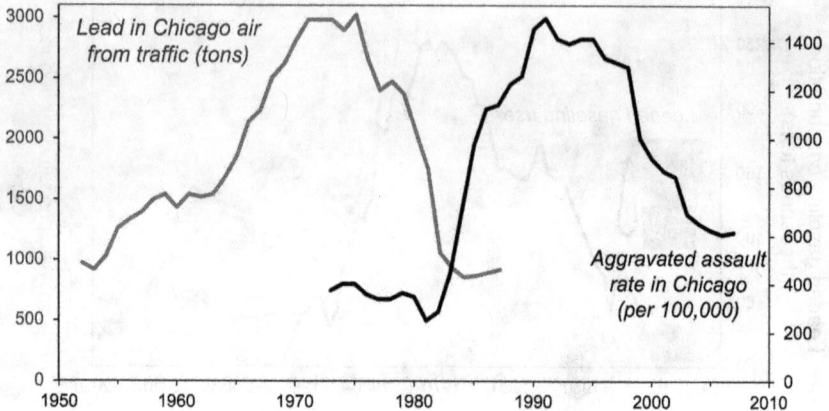

FIGURE 61. The rise and fall of lead in Chicago air was paralleled 20 years later by the rise and fall in reported-to-police violent crime. Similar trends were observed for other cities, with different sizes and socioeconomic characteristics. Adapted from Howard W. Mielke and Sammy Zahran, "The Urban Rise and Fall of Air Lead (Pb) and the Latent Surge and Retreat of Societal Violence," *Environment International* 43 (August 1, 2012): 48–55.

covered with lead paint. The United States only banned lead paint in 1978, though much of Europe started banning it in the 1920s. Over time, lead paint peels and wears off as dust. The simplest remedy is to cover the old paint with fresh paint, sealing the lead in.

Another source of childhood exposure is lead in drinking water due to old lead pipes and lead plumbing solder. Both were outlawed in 1986 in the United States (see Chapter 6). Childhood lead poisoning is worse in low-income countries because of late elimination of leaded gas and the proximity of lead-emitting industries. Many people live near lead-laden waste dumps. Others are exposed to lead through small-scale mining and manufacturing. Lead manufacturing and use worldwide is actually increasing, with the increased use of lead-acid batteries for modern technologies.

Other factors besides lead can harm children's development, so lead poisoning may not be obvious. Most people are unaware of the danger and don't think of testing for lead. Community testing programs are needed. In many cases, local activist groups called attention to lead contamination and brought about corrective action.

(B) Mercury

Mercury, another toxic metal, has a natural cycle in the environment. Coal contains some mercury, which is emitted into the atmosphere when the coal is burned. Volcanoes also emit mercury. Once in the atmosphere, mercury travels far before it is redeposited.[63] Human activities such as mining and coal combustion have increased mercury circulating in the atmosphere and surface waters by a factor of 70 or more.[64]

Mercury damages nerve cells, producing headaches, tremors, and impaired vision.[65] People are exposed through eating mercury-laden fish. Bacteria in sediment convert mercury to methylmercury, which is taken up by fish.[66] All fish contain some mercury, but the level increases when sediments are contaminated by mercury wastes from industry. Waterways are often posted with warnings against eating contaminated fish.

Mercury emissions are regulated globally by the Minamata Convention on Mercury signed by 128 countries.[67] Japan's Minamata Bay was the site of a mass poisoning of people living in fishing villages. They ate fish that accumulated toxic levels of methylmercury from discharges of industrial waste into local waters.[68] Mercury releases have declined in many parts of the world where mercury is no longer used in industrial processes, electrical products, and dental fillings.[69]

But mercury pollution is still a big problem in Asia, Africa, and South America. In Asia, metal mining and coal-fired power plants continue to be large sources of mercury pollution. In Africa and South America, mercury emission is dominated by small-scale gold mines, producing nearly 20 percent of the world's gold supply and nearly 40 percent of global mercury emissions each year.[70] Many miners use mercury to extract the gold and then heat the mixture to drive off the mercury. Usually, they have no protection from the mercury vapor, which is toxic when inhaled. Many of them suffer chronic headaches, tremors, and mental slowing. The mercury also affects villagers where the gold roasting occurs. The miners loft 400 tons of mercury vapor each year.[71] Much of it travels far before being rained out. When it washes into sediment, it adds to the mercury level in fish, exposing people further to mercury. Children born in these communities have high rates of physical and mental disabilities. Efforts are underway to train miners to use non-mercury methods of extracting gold, adopt simple devices for capturing the mercury vapor, and remediate mercury-contaminated soils and waterways.[72]

(C) Arsenic and Fluoride

As described in Chapter 7, arsenic and fluoride are naturally occurring minerals that contaminate water supplies from wells sunk into aquifers that are overpumped for crop irrigation. Filtering the water would protect people.

7. Ecotoxicity

Humans are not the only creatures affected by pollution. When toxic substances build up in the environment, often from sewage or road runoff, wildlife suffers as well. The effect of DDT contamination on Florida alligators, mentioned above in Section 2, is an example.

(A) Tires Versus Coho Salmon

Sometimes animals are more sensitive to toxins than humans. Coho salmon are a good example. Salmon once spawned abundantly in rivers up and down the North American West Coast. They play key ecological roles, bringing nutrients inland from the ocean when they return to their spawning grounds and die. Many animals feed on them, including bears and eagles. Salmon have always been a food source for Native tribes for whom the fish are also a key element in their religious beliefs and practices.

But salmon numbers have plummeted. There are many causes. Overfishing is a major factor. In addition, spawning grounds are sometimes buried in silt from construction projects. Access to spawning grounds has been blocked by dams. Removal of shade trees and bushes from streams has raised water temperatures above salmon tolerance limits. And pollution from storm drains and runoff from farms and roads have harmed aquatic life.[73]

In addition to all of that, scientists recently found that an additive to rubber tires specifically kills coho salmon,[74] one of the major salmon species. When returning from the ocean to spawn, 40–90 percent of coho salmon die if they encounter waters contaminated by urban stormwater runoff. The culprit is the chemical 6PPD (6N-1,3-dimethylbutyl-N-phenyl-p-phenylenediamine) which is added to tires during manufacture to protect them from atmospheric ozone. Ozone attacks the rubber polymer molecules, causing cracks in the tire. When 6PPD is present, the ozone attacks the 6PPD instead, converting it to an altered form, 6PPDQ (6PPD-quinone). It is 6PPDQ that kills coho salmon at quite low concentrations. Other species of salmon are less affected. The reason for the coho sensitivity is not certain, but 6PPDQ could be disrupting the blood-brain barrier of the fish.[75]

Tires of just one car emit a trillion ultrafine particles per kilometer driven.[76] They contain a mix of chemicals, including 6PPDQ; their identities are mostly trade secrets. West Coast fishing groups have sued 13 of the largest tire manufacturers, accusing them of violating the Endangered Species Act by releasing a toxic chemical into the environment.[77] Meanwhile, efforts are underway to reduce the ecotoxicity by treating stormwater before it reaches streams and by reducing the amount of runoff through green infrastructure.[78] Europe is implementing a new rule that would regulate particulate matter emissions from tires and brakes.

(B) Sunscreens Versus Corals

Coral reefs around the world are bleaching and dying from a number of environmental stresses, including rising ocean temperatures (see Chapter 9). Another cause is tourism. Beachgoers and swimmers slather on sunscreens that wash off and damage coral reefs. On the Iranian resort island of Kish, coral bleaching is much greater in winter than summer despite lower water temperatures. The reason is that winter is when most tourists arrive, the summers being too hot for recreation.[79] Some sunscreen ingredients are more toxic to corals than others.[80] Hawai'i has banned two of them, oxybenzone and octinoxate. Sunscreens that don't contain these or other harmful ingredients advertise themselves as "reef safe."[81]

Some commonly used sunscreen ingredients are also endocrine disrupters. The European Commission advised that oxybenzone, homosalate, and octocrylene are not safe for people at the levels commonly found in sunscreens.[82]

8. What's the Solution to Pollution?

In the past, industrial chemicals were often dumped on land and into bodies of water without much thought for the consequences. As awareness grew, governments created environmental agencies that ended this practice and required that dump sites be cleaned up—a tedious and expensive process. Curtailing untreated effluents often required building expensive sewage treatment plants.

In addition to ending the uncontrolled dumping of wastes, governments also restrict the use of harmful substances in the first place. For example, DDT and similar insecticides were banned decades ago in the United States and around the world. A new generation of insecticides called neonicotinoids ("neonics") are, however, much more potent. They were banned in Europe in 2018 and now in many U.S. states because they kill bees and other insects that are food for fish and birds.[83] Another current example is the banning of organohalogen flame retardants in consumer products by the European Union and many U.S. states.[84] These chemicals are of limited effectiveness in fire suppression but leach out of the products into household air and dust. They have been linked to thyroid disruption, cancer, and learning deficits.[85]

Citizen action often spurs cleanup. Environmental activist and consumer advocacy groups prod regulatory agencies to take action against polluters, and they work to persuade major corporations to remove harmful substances from their products. Community groups play a vital role in drawing attention to community-wide contamination, especially in poor and underserved neighborhoods. A local group in Flint, Michigan, exposed the lead contamination of drinking water and pressured the state government to adopt emergency measures (see Chapter 7). India, which has massive pollution problems, has many grassroots environmental organizations focusing on local issues, like the 2018 protest that led to the closure of a controversial copper smelter.[86]

International agreements, like the Stockholm Convention on POPs (Section 5), influence government agencies through the weight of world opinion. But enforcement is up to individual countries, and regulations vary from country to country.

Several European countries have strict regulations based on the "precautionary principle" by which the burden of proof rests with the producers of new products to establish safety in cases where harm is possible. In the United States, on the other hand, it is up to the Environmental Protection Agency to test for safety products already in use. Supporters of the precautionary principle argue that it minimizes the risk of harm to consumers and the public. Its detractors argue that minimizing risk can stifle innovation and the development of new products that might do more good than harm. Establishing a proper balance between risk and benefit is not easy.

Of course, the best course of action is to prevent pollution in the first place. Company leaders are thinking ahead by instituting "green chemistry," redesigning products and processes to avoid releasing harmful substances to the environement.[87] For example, a German tire company manufactures bicycle tires using rubber made from dandelion roots.[88] Reconfiguring the human environment can also help. In the case of runoff contamination of waterways, restored wetlands along roadways can absorb pollutants as well as reduce flooding. Roadways and sidewalks can be repaved with porous concrete or asphalt, which can retard stormwater flows and filter the pollutants they carry.[89]

9. Summary

Many manufactured and naturally occurring substances are harmful to human health, but the extent of harm is highly variable. Once exposure levels are established, they can guide regulatory action for cleanup and for preventing contamination. Endocrine disruption and cancer are the main concerns about continuous environmental exposure. Endocrine disrupters mimic hormones or else block their action, potentially upsetting key biological systems. The chief concern is effects on physical and mental development in children. Chemicals can induce cancer by causing mutations in genes that control cell growth or by causing cell proliferation.

Chemicals that persist in the environment and that build up in the tissues of animals and humans are particularly concerning. Most of these POPs dissolve in oil and build up in fat tissues. One class, PFAS, does not go to fat tissues but sticks to proteins in the body. Many POPs have been connected to endocrine disruption and cancer.

Some minerals are also toxic. Especially harmful are lead, mercury, arsenic, and fluoride. Lead disrupts brain development in children, leading to learning difficulties and violent behavior. Lead exposure came mainly from gasoline, house paint, water pipes, and plumbing solder. Although lead is now widely banned, its legacy lives on through road and house dust that children play in and through antiquated plumbing and poor water management. Monitoring of lead in children, especially in old housing, is still important. Mercury is a potent nerve destroyer. When mercury is used to extract gold in Africa and Latin America, it sickens small-scale gold miners and their communities. Mercury also builds up in fish from mercury-laden sediment, where it is converted by bacteria to methylmercury that enters the food chain. Lake fish need monitoring for mercury levels. Arsenic and fluoride occur naturally in soils and aquifers but can build up in well water when aquifers are overpumped. Poor villagers in agricultural areas are especially at risk. However, they can keep drinking water free of arsenic and fluoride if they use inexpensive filters and test to gauge arsenic and fluoride levels in the water.

Pollutants can also harm aquatic life, as when salmon die from tire chemicals that wash into waterways and corals are bleached by sunscreens washing off beachgoers and divers.

Cleanup and control measures can solve pollution problems. Many waterways are now much cleaner thanks to effluent controls. Government regulations drive these cleanups, but citizen action and environmental organizations play vital roles in getting officials to act. The solution to pollution is a strong community, ready to take action to protect itself. Retention of stormwaters by creating wetlands and using porous pavement can minimize pollution of waterways. Pollution prevention is the best policy. Manufacturers are using green chemistry to avoid releasing harmful substances.

9

What's So Great About Biodiversity?

1. What Is Biodiversity Anyway?

Biodiversity means there are lots of different living things on the earth. They can be plants or animals, and that includes people. And biodiversity can mean different kinds of differences. Often it means different species—organisms that share characteristics and can reproduce with one another. If a species loses all its members, it goes extinct. And today over 1 million plant and animal species face extinction because of environmental pressures.[1]

Biodiversity can also mean different ecosystems. An ecosystem is a geographic area where particular kinds of plants, animals, and other organisms as well as weather and landscape work together. For example, grasslands around the world are similar ecosystems. They have many different grasses and other plants, which harbor all kinds of insects, animals, and birds. Today grasslands are endangered because so much of it is plowed under for farms. The grasses create rich soil, which makes good cropland. But croplands have many fewer kinds of plants than the grasslands they replace. And they harbor fewer kinds of creatures. They are less biodiverse.

Biodiversity is also about relationships among different species. For example, different birds eat different insects which eat different plants. If those plants disappear, so does that insect population and so do their bird predators. On the other hand, if the birds disappear, the insect population can explode and destroy all the plants. There is a complex web of such relationships in an ecosystem. Disrupting that web can have surprising and far-reaching effects. In Section 2 below we consider an example, the effects on the Yellowstone National Park ecosystem of removing and then restoring wolves.

This chapter looks at key ecosystems around the globe, including temperate and tropical forests, grasslands, coral reefs, and kelp forests. All of them are impacted by human activity. Humans are the main drivers of ecosystem change, change that mostly destroys biodiversity. But many people are working to slow biodiversity loss and even reverse it. National and international efforts to protect biodiversity and prevent loss of species include passage of the U.S. Endangered Species Act,[2] adoption of the European Union Birds and Habitats Directives,[3] and creation of the UN Convention on Biological Diversity.[4]

We protect biodiversity because we value the beauty of the natural world and the sense of vigor, harmony, and serenity that it inspires. But biodiversity has other important benefits. It provides food and medicines and purifies our water supply. It can even moderate the climate. Losing these benefits imposes real costs on society and the natural world.

2. Wolves and Biodiversity in Yellowstone Park

Here is an example of biodiversity lost and restored. Wolves that once roamed from the Arctic tundra to Mexico were mostly hunted out of the United States. In 1995, wildlife biologists reintroduced them to

FIGURE 62. Members of the Lamar Canyon wolf pack in Yellowstone National Park. Photo courtesy of Meg Sommers, https://www.megsommers.com.

Yellowstone National Park by releasing 31 wild wolves, some from Canada and some from Montana.[5] Over 90 are now in the park, and more than 500 are in the surrounding area[6] (Figure 62).

Wolves prey on elk. When there were no wolves in Yellowstone, elk numbers exploded. They browsed young trees, especially in river valleys, where they denuded the banks and caused erosion. Coyotes flourished because there was no competition from wolves and decimated small mammal populations. That left little behind for hawks, foxes, and badgers. When wolves were brought back to Yellowstone, the coyote population fell. Elk avoided the valleys where wolves could trap them, thereby allowing trees, shrubs, and flowers to quickly regenerate. Songbirds, bees, and other pollinators came back.[7] Beavers did too, damming streams and creating habitats for amphibians, fish, and reptiles. Wolf kills attracted ravens, magpies, eagles, vultures, coyotes, and bears, who ate the remains of carcasses left by the wolves. The Yellowstone River also changed. With elk gone, new vegetation stabilized the banks, and the river recovered a richer community of aquatic insects and fish. And the people downstream in Billings, Montana, enjoyed cleaner river water.

This is biodiversity in action. It gives us landscapes rich with wildlife, improves the water, and helps store carbon. Also, plants take up carbon dioxide and store the carbon in roots and tree trunks. The richer the variety of plants, the more carbon gets stored away from the atmosphere. That helps to slow global warming. The story of the Yellowstone wolves illustrates how all parts of an ecosystem are interdependent. Removing one species, particularly a top predator like the wolf, had cascading effects on other species. Those effects had not been anticipated when the wolves were killed off. Restoring wolves had many benefits, including the opportunity for Yellowstone visitors to experience a healthier landscape.

But not everyone is happy that the wolves are back. Ranchers fear losing their cows and sheep to the wolves. The success of the reintroduced wolves led to their being delisted as endangered. That prompted the hunting of wolves in the states that border the park. On the other hand, many ranchers also consider themselves stewards of the environment. They work to preserve their lands through rotational grazing, water management, and planting trees. Some partner with environmentalists to find common ground. Still, wolves continue to stir strong feelings, pro and con.[8] National parks are protected areas, valued for the wonders of nature that they preserve. People outside the parks may have a harder time valuing and adopting measures that enhance biodiversity.

3. Wolves and Elephants Are Keystone Species

The wolf is a "keystone" species, one whose removal or restoration has a cascading effect throughout the ecosystem.[9] The term comes from the keystone at the top of an arch, which keeps the arch together.

Another keystone species is the elephant, which keeps the African and Asian grasslands healthy.[10] Elephants dig holes for water during

FIGURE 63. African elephant in Murchison Falls National Park, Uganda, July 30, 2016. Photo credit: Helen Mason/USAID; via Flickr, https://www.flickr.com/photos/usaidafrica/50218546542/in/album-72157668448686988/.

droughts, using their trunks and feet; the holes provide water for other animals as well. As they travel, elephants disperse seeds in their dung. The dung fertilizes the seeds as they sprout. It also feeds dung beetles. The beetles lay their eggs in dung balls, which they bury in the ground so their larvae can feed and grow underground. In the process, the larvae loosen and aerate the packed soil, helping plants grow.

Elephants feed on leaves, breaking branches and pushing down small trees (Figure 63). Fallen branches provide habitat for lizards, spiders, and other small animals. And clearing trees allows more light to reach the ground, helping low-lying shrubs and grasses. Elephants thus maintain the whole grassland ecosystem.

However, the elephants also trample and eat crops if they wander onto farms. The wolf-versus-rancher conflict that exists in the American West plays out as elephant-versus-farmer conflicts in the African and Asian grasslands.[11] To minimize the conflict, beehive fences have been introduced in Kenya, Botswana, Mozambique, Tanzania, Uganda, and Sri Lanka.[12] Beehives are strung along a wire, every 10 meters. When an elephant touches any hive or wire, the whole string of hives is disturbed, releasing bees. Elephants are terrified of bees because they can be painfully stung on the inside of their trunks. The farmers benefit additionally from keeping the bees to pollinate the crops and to make honey, which they can sell.

4. Plants Have Keystone Species Too

The plant world also has keystone species, without which whole eco-systems decline.[13] Plants that support butterflies and bees are particularly important. The caterpillars that turn into butterflies and moths are at the base of food webs. Few animals eat plants directly. Most feed on other animals, which feed on other animals. At the bottom of this chain are animals that feed on caterpillars. Birds are especially reliant on caterpillars: 96 percent of terrestrial birds rear their young on butterfly and moth larvae.[14]

Plants evolve chemicals that repel invaders, which then evolve defenses against those chemicals. The host/invader combinations are specific to each species. So caterpillars feed only on the plants with which they have co-evolved. Those are the keystone plant species for caterpillars. Not all native plants, however, are equally useful to caterpillars. Across the United States, 90 percent of caterpillars feed on just 14 percent of native plants.[15] Oak trees host the largest number of caterpillar species.[16] Willows, pines, poplar, and cherry trees are also important as hosts.

Pollinators are critical for the reproduction of plants. More than 80 percent of the world's flowering plants depend on pollinators, mostly bees.[17] Bees also evolved with the plants they pollinate. Many pollinate a narrow range of plants, which nevertheless nourish important food webs. These are keystone plants as well. Other bees pollinate a wide range of plants. These "generalists" thrive if the keystone plants and their "specialist" bees stay healthy. About 30 percent of the 4,000 species of bees native to North America are specialists.[18] Many are rare and endangered.[19]

Gardeners can help preserve butterflies and bees by cultivating keystone plants. Kits containing locally appropriate keystone native plants are available from the National Wildlife Federation.[20]

5. Will Forests Survive?

The tension between ranching and wolves is an example of the conflict between maintaining natural ecosystems and expanding human use of land and water. Forest use is a prime area of conflict. About one-third of Earth's surface is forest. About one-third of that is boreal forest, the vast stands of cold-resistant conifers stretching across Canada, northern Europe, and Russia. The boreal forests hold twice as much carbon per acre as do tropical forests. They are hugely important for the world's climate, but they are endangered by the world's appetite for timber and paper. Across the north, logging companies are clear-cutting the ancient boreal forest. They generally replant with new trees, forming tree plantations.

The growing trees replace those that were harvested, reabsorbing much of the carbon over time. Logging companies can be certified as sustainable if they follow the sustainability standards of the international Program for the Endorsement of Forest Certification[21] or the Forest Stewardship Council.[22] These programs assure forest stewardship, respect for Aboriginal peoples, compliance with local, provincial, or national environmental laws, and forest worker safety, education, and training. Forest certification is largely about tracking to ensure traceability. It does not assess or decertify lumber obtained from clearcuts or taken without the consent of Aboriginal peoples.

But the second-growth forests are nothing like the old-growth forests, which have trees of different species of varying ages. They also have many dead trees which are home to mosses, fungi, birds, and animals. The second-growth forests are monocultures of one or two species, all of the same age. The carbon they absorb does not include the carbon stored in the rich undergrowth and soils of the old-growth forests they have replaced. And they harbor far less biodiversity.

The huge Canadian boreal forest alone stores twice as much carbon as the world's oil reserves.[23] Eighty percent of the forest carbon is stored in layers of soil, some of it locked there for thousands of years. Logging disturbs the soil and releases much of its carbon, little of which is replaced when new trees grow. Among the animal species that lose habitat to forest clear-cutting are Canada's iconic caribou. They are listed as "threatened" species, and their population has declined by 30 percent in 18 years.[24] Old-growth forests are also more resilient than their replacements, which are more susceptible to insect infestations, intense wildfires, and the effects of global warming. A 2024 study of boreal forests across the Canadian provinces of Quebec and Ontario shows that 35 million acres, roughly the size of New York State, were clear-cut over the previous half century.[25] Industrial logging degraded the whole ecosystem, leaving behind a patchwork of isolated stands of old trees. Of the 21 herds of caribou in the boreal region, 19 were in decline and at risk of extinction.

Sweden, too, while touting its sustainable forestry model, has allowed extensive clear-cutting of its old boreal forest.[26] The forests are certified as sustainable as long as they are replanted, albeit by a monoculture of new trees. And logging the northern forests threatens the Sami Indigenous people, who depend on reindeer herding. Reindeer subsist on lichen that only grows in the old-growth forests.[27]

The old-growth forests that covered much of the United States were richly diverse ecosystems. They provided Native Americans with food and shelter and wood for their fires and for making canoes. Europeans systematically logged the old growth for timber (Figure 64), farmed the cleared

FIGURE 64. Tree clearing in the U.S. Pacific Northwest. Photograph by Alexandra Soldatova.

land, or grew tree plantations. The result was that many native plants and animals disappeared.

In the Northwest of the United States and Canada, logging was a mainstay of the economy. But once the old-growth forests were mostly gone, the logging industry declined, leaving behind high unemployment and shuttered businesses.[28] Out-of-work loggers directed their resentment at environmentalists, who campaigned to save the spotted owl, an endangered species that lives in old-growth forests.[29] But some loggers now join forces with environmentalists to maintain the remaining forests sustainably. They thin the trees selectively to limit fire damage. For example, the Blue Mountain Forest Partners,[30] formed by eastern Oregon loggers and environmentalists, won a federal stewardship contract to clear out small trees from the national forest. The contract saved the sole remaining sawmill in the logging town of John Day from closing.[31]

Forest fires are a natural recurrence and are actually important for forest health. They open up areas for new growth. But in many U.S. forests, aggressive firefighting suppressed this natural rhythm, allowing densely packed saplings and underbrush to accumulate. During droughts, that undergrowth makes the inevitable fires much hotter and more destructive.[32] With global warming, destructive fires intensify. When rains come, the denuded hillsides are more susceptible to landslides and flooding. Selective logging can keep the forests healthier, and it also provides jobs for loggers.[33]

6. Who Profits from the Tropics?

Biodiversity abounds in the tropical rainforests of South America, Africa, and Southeast Asia. Indigenous people always depended on them for food, shelter, and medicines. Many medicinal plants are used today by pharmaceutical companies for drug development.[34]

(A) Amazonia: Jungle Versus Cattle

The Amazon jungle transpires so much water that it produces its own rain. It also produces an atmospheric river of rain clouds that flows southwest to irrigate the Pantanal, the world's largest wetland.[35] The Pantanal sprawls over parts of Bolivia, Brazil, and Paraguay. It provides water for the 22 million people of the Brazilian megacity São Paulo.

Wetlands around the world are richly diverse in plants and animals. Wetlands also filter water effectively and store carbon in their underwater root systems. Yet 35 percent of the world's wetlands have been lost to agriculture and urbanization.[36] The Pantanal has the greatest diversity of aquatic plants on the planet. These plants support 300 species of fish, some 600 species of birds, and over 150 species of mammals.[37] A million tourists a year visit the Pantanal to see this richness. But over 90 percent of the land is in private hands and is mostly devoted to ranching and crops (Figure 65).

Today, drought is more frequent in the Pantanal because of global warming and instabilities of the atmospheric river coming from the Amazon.[38] São Paulo reservoirs are silted up. In 2014, São Paulo ran short of water, forcing schools to close.[39] In 2019 and 2020, fires broke out over vast areas of the Pantanal,[40] stoked by the practice of clearing cropland by burning the stubble left from harvests.[41] Many of the Pantanal's plants and animals were lost. The Paraguay River, a major shipping channel, fell so low that for a time it was unnavigable. Farther downstream, the Paraná River, which carries more than 80 percent of Argentina's agricultural exports to the sea, was 10 feet (3 meters) below normal in 2021, reducing the amount of shipping and doubling costs.[42]

The huge Amazon rainforest itself contains some 2,500 tree species and supports three million species of plants and animals.[43] About two million

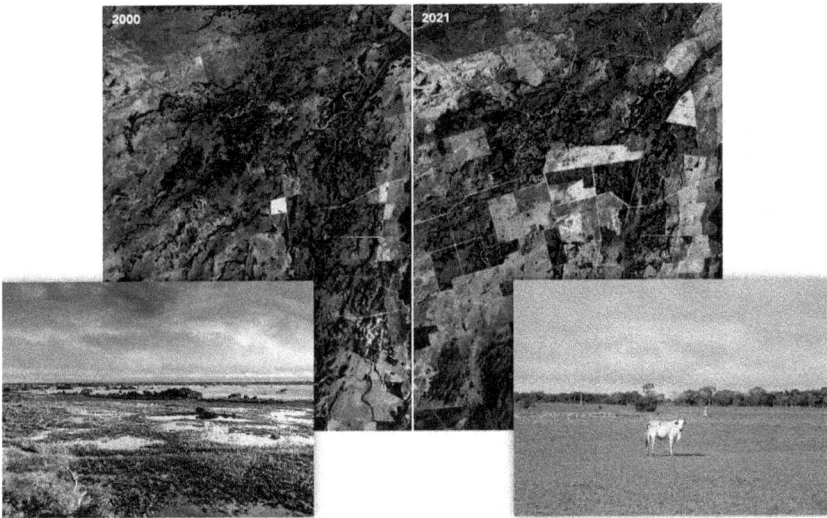

FIGURE 65. The Pantanal was cleared for pastures, as seen from satellite images in 2000 and 2021. NASA Earth Observatory images by Lauren Dauphin, using Landsat data from the U.S. Geological Survey, https://earthobservatory. nasa.gov/images/149398/a-human-fingerprint-on-the-pantanal-inferno. Left photo credit: Filipefrazao, via Wikimedia Commons, https://commons. wikimedia.org/wiki/File:Pantanal,_Mato_Grosso,_Brasil.jpg; https://creative commons.org/licenses/by-sa/3.0/legalcode. Right photo credit: abram, via Flickr, https://www.flickr.com/photos/amlambertson/48294147262/in/album-72157709666142752/; https://creativecommons.org/licenses/by/2.0/.

Indigenous people live there,[44] but the forest is losing ground to logging, farming, and mining, much of it illegal. Roads, both legal and illegal, penetrate more and more of the jungle. Small farmers claim land along the roads and clear it for crops, often using fire to burn the tree remnants. But the soil beneath a rainforest is poor in nutrients, most of which circulate above ground in the jungle. After a few years, heavy rains and erosion deplete the soil, and crop yields fall. Farmers then convert the degraded land to cattle pasture, clearing more forest for crops. Eventually, the small land holders, having cleared much of their land, sell or abandon it to large cattle holders, who in turn consolidate the plots into large areas of pasture.[45] Nearly 17 percent of the rainforest has been lost that way. If that fraction increases to 25 percent, there may not be enough trees cycling moisture through the forest. It might then degrade into tropical grassland and desert.[46]

From 2004 to 2012, Brazil took effective action to slow deforestation (Figure 66). The extent of forest loss fell by three-quarters.[47] After that, the rate of deforestation fluctuated, reflecting political changes, and is now decreasing again, thanks to increased monitoring of illegal logging.[48]

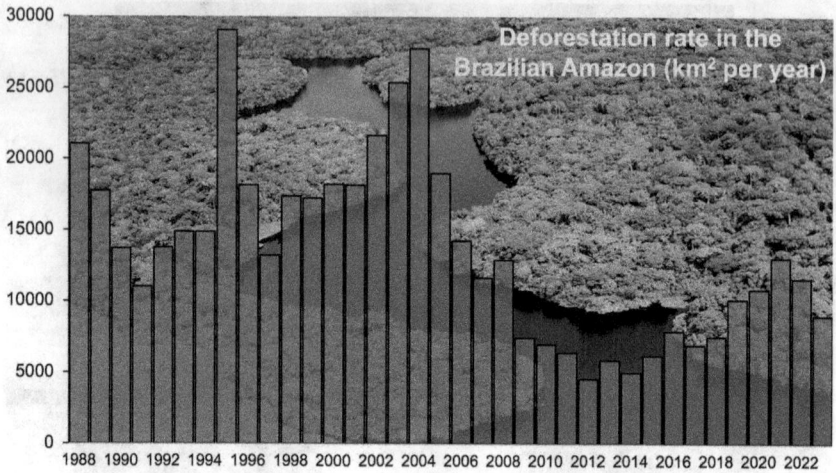

30000
25000
20000
15000
10000
5000
0

Deforestation rate in the Brazilian Amazon (km² per year)

1988 1990 1992 1994 1996 1998 2000 2002 2004 2006 2008 2010 2012 2014 2016 2018 2020 2022

FIGURE 66. Amazon deforestation rates from satellite data: "PRODES-Amazônia. Monitoramento do Desmatamento da Floresta Amazônica Brasileira por Satélite," Brazilian National Institute of Space Research, PRODES satellite monitoring project, accessed June 10, 2024, http://www.obt.inpe.br/OBT/assuntos/programas/amazonia/prodes. Background photograph is an aerial view of the Amazon Rainforest, near Manaus; credit: © 2011CIAT/Neil Palmer via Flickr, https://www.flickr.com/photos/ciat/5641587148/; https://creativecommons.org/licenses/by-sa/2.0/.

There is progress from the cattle ranchers themselves.[49] Prompted by international bans for Brazilian beef over deforestation concerns,[50] farms are adopting sustainable practices. These include rotational grazing on more nutritious grasses, pasture restoration, compliance with environmental legislation, and reforestation.[51] Cattle grow better on smaller but improved pastures, and ranchers' revenues increase.[52]

(B) Sub-Saharan Africa: New Hope from Agroforestry

One-quarter of the world's tropical forest is in Africa, south of the Sahara Desert.[53] There, people use firewood for cooking, adding to the toll of trees felled by mining, logging, and clearing land for agriculture. In Africa, both population growth and forest loss are twice the world average.[54] The continent lost 14 percent of its forest between 1990 and 2020 (slightly more than the 13 percent loss for South America).[55]

Many African countries suffer from ethnic conflict, weak law enforcement, poor administrative authority, and corruption. The Democratic Republic of the Congo, home to much of the forest, suffered from civil war for years. The fighting was spurred on by conflict over mining and logging operations, many of them illegal. In other African countries, corrupt politicians, who view the forest as "free" land, bought votes by selling the land to settlers.

But there is new hope for African forests. Many farmers are using "agroforestry," also known as "evergreen agriculture."[56] Beneficial trees are planted in cropland to maintain a green canopy and restore soils year-round. Most Africans are farmers, but 80 percent of them have less than five acres of land.[57] Most are too poor to buy fertilizer, and their grain yields are very low. To survive, they are forced to grow grain year after year, degrading the soil. They depend on rainwater and suffer badly during droughts and floods, which are more frequent with global warming. But if they plant the right kind of trees, they can shield their crops from excessive heat, better retain the rainwater, and even fertilize and rebuild the soil. Africa has a nitrogen-fixing acacia tree, *Faidherbia albida*,[58] which conveniently goes dormant and drops its leaves just as the tropical rainy season starts. Its leaves regrow at the end of the rains. Farmers plant their crops under the trees just before the rains, and the plants then grow without having to compete for nutrition with the dormant trees (Figure 67).

FIGURE 67. *Faidherbia albida* tree and tomatoes in Salima District, Malawi. Photo credit: Tracy Beedy/International Council for Research in Agroforestry/ Irish Aid via Flickr, https://www.flickr.com/photos/icraf/26627212306/in/ photostream/. Reproduced with permission.

At the end of the rains, the trees, having held back the rainwater with their roots, come to life and shade the maturing crops until they can be harvested. These plants yield grain at triple the usual amounts and need no added fertilizer.[59] And the soils are saved from caking and erosion. As the tree canopies expand, the farmers thin the trees and sell them for timber and wood. That means more farm income. And the downed wood eases the burden of women who have the traditional task of gathering firewood, sometimes carrying it for miles.

Evergreen agriculture has been adopted by more than 300,000 maize (corn) farmers in Zambia and Malawi.[60] It is also spreading in the Sahel, the belt of Africa just below the Saharan desert, where millet and sorghum are the main crops.[61] Land in the Sahel readily converts to desert because of drought and poor farming practices. Farmers across the Sahel had traditionally practiced evergreen agriculture by allowing naturally occurring *Faidherbia albida* seedlings to grow among their crops. But modern laws, intended to protect the forest, actually discouraged this practice by forbidding the cutting or pruning of trees. These laws were relaxed in the 1990s, giving farmers the incentive to revive the practice. Niger and Burkina Faso benefited especially, spreading evergreen agriculture to five million acres of land.[62] These successes are encouraging other countries to adopt evergreen agriculture.

Evergreen agriculture decreases farmers' incentive to clear forest to expand cropland. It also helps with global warming since fields with trees store much more carbon than treeless fields. And forested fields support much greater biodiversity than bare cropland does.

(C) Southeast Asia: The Realm of Palm Oil

In the tropical rainforests of Indonesia and Malaysia, the problem boils down to two words: palm oil. Palm oil is used massively worldwide in prepared foods and cosmetics. It is also blended into diesel fuel, and it counts as a biofuel in some countries to lower their carbon "footprint." The reason palm oil is such an important commodity is because it is very efficient. Oil palm produces more oil per acre than any other plant.[63]

The oil palm is a tropical tree, and tropical rainforest provides the ideal climate to grow it. Southeast Asia rainforests are highly diverse. They include iconic animals, like the orangutan, elephant, rhinoceros, and tiger, which are now endangered by loss of habitat from palm oil cultivation.[64] Palm oil plantations are monocultures. They do not support anything like the rich ecosystems of the rainforests (Figure 68).

To expand palm oil plantations, forests are cleared by setting them on

FIGURE 68. Palm oil plantation replaces tropical rainforest, endangering the orangutan. *Left:* Photo credit: Wikimedia Commons, https://www.jpl.nasa.gov/news/nasa-finds-good-news-on-forests-and-carbon-dioxide. *Middle:* Photo by U.S. Agency for International Development, Indonesia, via Flickr, https://www.flickr.com/photos/usaid-indonesia/4320689115/in/album-72157628034204393/. *Right:* Photo credit: Craig via Wikimedia Commons, https://commons.wikimedia.org/wiki/File:Oilpalm_malaysia.jpg.

fire. That releases massive amounts of CO_2 and smoke. Smoke from fires in Indonesia forms plumes big enough to blot out the sky in Singapore and Malaysia. Indonesia is the biggest palm oil producer. It supplied 59 percent of the world's palm oil in 2024.[65] Occupying 1.3 percent of the earth's land surface, Indonesia's tropical forests hold 10 percent of the world's plant species, 12 percent of mammal species, and 17 percent of all species of birds.[66] But between 2001 and 2023, Indonesia lost 19 percent of its tree cover.[67]

In 2018, Indonesia imposed a moratorium on new licenses for palm oil plantations and conducted a massive review of oil palm licensing data.[68] Deforestation rates decreased, but the audit found that more than 80 percent of the country's palm oil plantations were not complying with regulations on forest destruction.[69] When the moratorium ended, the rate of forest loss in Indonesia began to creep up again. Enforcement is difficult because palm oil is Indonesia's second leading export commodity (coal is the first) and accounts for 10 percent of its exports.[70] When the European Commission decided to ban palm oil–based biofuels by 2030, Indonesia protested and threatened to pull out of the Paris climate agreement. Indonesia requires that its own biodiesel contain at least 35 percent palm oil and plans to increase the blend content.[71]

Oil palm can be grown sustainably, following agroforestry principles,[72] and palm oil companies can be certified as sustainable if they follow rules set by the Roundtable for Sustainable Palm Oil.[73] The rules prohibit further deforestation and set other environmental and worker protections. Companies use the certificates to help market their palm oil products to environmentally conscious consumers.

7. Can Grasslands Stay Green?

Grasslands are found between forests and deserts, in areas too dry to support dense tree cover but moist enough for grasses to grow. Grasses transpire less water than trees. They are brown in dry seasons but turn green when there is rain. They can support grazing animals, like zebra, antelope, and bison. The grazing herds in turn support predators, including wolves, lions, and cheetahs. Grasslands occupy about 12–15 percent of the planet's land surface (Figure 69).[74] They are called prairies in North America, steppes in Asia, savannahs and veldts in Africa, rangelands in Australia, pampas, llanos, and cerrados in South America.

Grasslands are even more endangered than forests. Unlike forests, grasslands develop fertile soils. Their rich tangle of roots harbors beneficial fungi, worms, insects, and microorganisms. Because of the rich soil, humans plow grasslands to plant wheat and other crops, but these crops often require irrigation to supplement scarce rainfall. In North America, European settlers transformed much of the prairie grasslands into agricultural fields. But when drought struck the region in the early 1930s, crops couldn't grow. Bare fields were swept up in powerful dust storms that destroyed farms, making the land uninhabitable for years. (John Steinbeck immortalized the migrant "dust bowl" survivors in his novel *Grapes of Wrath.*[75]) Today the crops are irrigated with water drawn from aquifers below that are pumped unsustainably (see Chapter 6). As a result, some farms are being abandoned again.

Grasslands support grazing herds, and grazing herds benefit grasslands. The animals promote new growth by eating the grass. They break up the soil with their hooves and fertilize it with their excrement. In many areas, humans replaced wildlife with domestic livestock: sheep, goats, llamas, and cattle. If the livestock overgraze the grass, munching down to the roots, the grass dies. The ground is left bare and erodes. Controlling the size of herds and moving them from one area to another to allow the grass to recover is essential to sustaining grasslands. Periodic fires are also important. They clear out dead plant matter and allow new growth. Grasslands are richly biodiverse, but they are losing out to livestock pressure and demand for more cropland.

Before Europeans arrived, millions of bison roamed the North American grasslands, supporting Indigenous tribes for whom bison were essential food. European hunters shot nearly all of them to obtain their hides for the leather trade. Bison hunts were also part of a military campaign to destroy Native tribes and drive the survivors off the land into reservations.[76] The bison were only saved from extinction because the Bronx Zoo purchased a few of them from Texas ranchers at the turn of the 20th

FIGURE 69. Grassland life around the world. Counterclockwise from upper left: buffalo in Yellowstone National Park, USA; rhea in Brazil; zebra in Kenya; kangaroo in Australia; and camels in Altai region of Russia. Photo credit: buffalo: Carol M. Highsmith, https://www.loc.gov/resource/highsm.35332/; rhea: Bernard Dupont, https://flickr.com/photos/65695019@N07/27625818421, https://creativecommons.org/licenses/by-sa/2.0/; zebra herd: sutirta budiman on Unsplash, https://unsplash.com/photos/group-of-zebra-walking-on-wheat-field-Jgiv1rSIpVM; kangaroo: AWS10 via Wikimedia Commons, https://commons.wikimedia.org/wiki/File:Kangaroos_Maranoa.JPG; camels: Kobsev, https://commons.wikimedia.org/wiki/File:Camels_in_Kosh-Agachsky_District.jpg, https://creativecommons.org/licenses/by-sa/3.0/legalcode. Map is from NASA, https://earthobservatory.nasa.gov/biome/biograssland.php.

century to start a captive breeding program.[77] These bison were then released into a new game reserve in Oklahoma, which had previously been home to Apache, Comanche, and Kiowa tribes. Other game reserves were established later, and in 2016, bison were restored to the Flathead reservation in Montana, home of the Blackfeet Nation,[78] and to other tribes in the Great Plains of the United States and Canada. But all the animals remain in fenced rangeland because neighboring ranchers don't want free-roaming bison herds to compete with their cattle for grazing land.

In an effort to preserve a large grassland ecosystem, the American Prairie Reserve[79] ties together a 3-million-acre patchwork of public lands in Montana, with bridging properties bought from private holders. Plowed land on these properties is being restored to native grasses and shrubs; streams are being restored, and fences are being removed. Controlled burns are reintroducing the effects of natural fires. These measures help restore populations of native prairie dogs, ferrets, foxes, pronghorn antelope, and grassland birds. Bison are being reintroduced to build up a sustainable herd. The reserve pays neighboring ranches to introduce "wildlife-friendly" ranching practices, including sustainable cattle grazing, stream restoration, and fencing that allows wildlife to crawl under or jump over without injuring themselves.

Most ranches use barbed wire fencing, which stretches all over the American West. In addition to the injuries they cause, barbed wire fences impede wildlife migration. They are also expensive to maintain and are often destroyed by wildfires. A new and promising approach is "virtual fencing,"[80] which keeps livestock from wandering across invisible lines by issuing warning sounds and mild electric shocks from GPS-enabled collars the animals wear. The lines are set from radio tower base stations, controlled remotely by ranchers. Virtual fences also facilitate rotational grazing to preserve the grasses because virtual fence lines can be reprogrammed to different locations.

8. Destructiveness of Invasive Species

Zebra mussels are small, striped bivalves that are native to the Caspian Sea area of Europe. They were spotted in the U.S. Great Lakes in 1988.[81] Likely, they arrived in the ballast water of a commercial ship. Zebra mussels reproduce at enormous rates, and having no natural predators in North America, they spread rapidly into all the Great Lakes. Then they hitched rides on boats heading for the Mississippi River. Now they are spreading throughout the Mississippi River basin (Figure 70).

Zebra mussels devour plankton floating in the water. They deprive native mussels and plankton-eating fish of food. When these small fish are gone, the whole food chain is disrupted. Sunlight penetrates the water further with plankton gone, allowing algae to grow.[82] Algal blooms become more common, further endangering native species. Zebra mussels are so numerous that they coat the bottoms of boats, which then need frequent cleaning. The mussels clog intake pipes for water purification facilities and for power plant cooling water. The cost to the Great Lakes economy is billions of dollars a year.

Zebra mussels are only one example of invasive species. There are many stories about plants and animals native to one region being released in another. Usually, the natural predators that control their population at home are absent in their new environment. If the introduced species outcompetes the native species, they spread uncontrollably, disrupting the ecosystem and reducing biodiversity.

Australia suffers enormous biodiversity losses from invasive species.

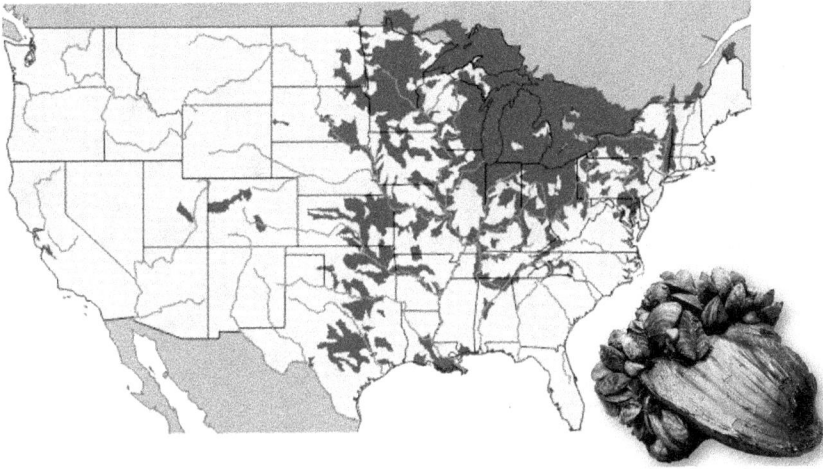

FIGURE 70. Zebra mussels spreading in the United States as of June 2024. Map credit: U.S. Geological Survey, Nonindigenous Aquatic Species Database, https://nas.er.usgs.gov/queries/factsheet.aspx?speciesID=5. Photo shows zebra mussels on fresh water mussel. Photo credit: NOAA, https://www.climate. gov/news-features/featured-images/fending-invaders-warmer-climate.

The continent had evolved a unique ecosystem in the 100 million years since it became a separate land mass. In 1859, a wealthy farmer imported rabbits and released them on his estate for hunting.[83] Lacking predators, their population exploded. Within 50 years, they spread across the continent, destroying crops and native plants, overgrazing the grasses and eroding the soil.[84] Feral cats were released in the late 1800s to control the rabbits as well as rats and mice.[85] Cats proved to be highly adaptable. They in turn spread across the continent, eating most of the small, native animals as they went. Red fox, introduced in 1855 for recreational hunting, also helped wipe out the native small animal population.[86] Very few indigenous small animals are left; some species are now preserved in fenced sanctuaries.

9. Can Coral Reefs Survive?

Life underwater, fresh and salt, is as rich as life on land. In fact, life began in the ocean, home to an amazing array of plants and animals. The aquatic food chain has grazers of algae and plants (small fish, sea urchins) and filter feeders (oysters, clams, sponges), which are eaten by small fish, which are in turn eaten by larger fish and mammals. As with terrestrial ecosystems, disturbance of any part of the food chain can have cascading effects throughout the system.

FIGURE 71. Coral reef in Papahānaumokuākea National Marine Monument, Hawai'i. Photo credit: James Watt/NOAA, https://www.noaa.gov/education/re source-collections/marine-life/coral-reef-ecosystems.

Coral reefs, sometimes called "rainforests of the ocean," teem with life (Figure 71), providing food and shelter for about a quarter of all ocean species.[87] Reefs are built by coral polyps, tiny animals that secrete limestone (calcium carbonate), the same material as in seashells. The corals use the limestone to cement themselves together, eventually forming the reefs. The coral polyps harbor algae that provide the corals with food through photosynthesis. These algae give the corals their bright colors.

Reefs protect coastlines from wave action, erosion, and tropical storms. Healthy reefs spared some Indian Ocean coastlines during a deadly 2004 tsunami that followed a magnitude 9.1 earthquake. Creatures found on reefs produce chemicals used to treat cardiovascular diseases, ulcers, leukemia, lymphoma, and skin cancer.[88] And people in coastal communities depend on reef fish for nourishment. Reefs also enhance local economies through tourism. Close to one billion people live within 100 kilometers of coral reefs and rely on the reef ecosystems for their livelihood: food, income, protection, and cultural practices.[89] Reefs hold sacred meaning for many coastal cultures. They inspire people with a sense of wonder and connectedness to nature.

But coral reefs are in trouble. Runoff from storms and sewage discharge cover reefs in toxic sediment. So does clearing of coastal mangroves for firewood and beach extension since mangroves are effective filters of sediment in runoff. Overnutrition from near-shore agriculture feeds algal blooms that smother the reefs. And overfishing spurs overgrowth of seaweed on which the fish feed. The seaweed blocks the sunlight that the microalgae in the coral need, eventually smothering the reef. Destructive techniques like using dynamite or cyanide to stun and trap fish also destroy the corals. Setting aside protected no-fishing areas provides crucial coral refuges. So marine protection areas are being established around the world (Figure 71).[90]

The biggest threat to corals is global warming because when the temperature gets too high, the polyps lose their algae and "bleach,"[91] turning white. Without nourishment, the polyps die, and the reef starts to break down. In 2016, exceptionally warm water killed one-third of the corals on Australia's Great Barrier Reef.[92] Some corals do survive because their genetic makeup makes them more resistant than the other corals.[93] Given enough time, reefs could adapt to rising temperatures through evolutionary change. But evolution has little chance to save the reefs because the earth's temperature is rising so rapidly. Scientists around the world are trying to speed up this evolution by coral breeding. But it's a race against time.

Reefs can be reconstructed artificially using ordinary rebar (steel) grids. While carrying a small electric current from solar cells on a nearby raft, the rebar attracts calcium and carbonate ions, which form a skin of limestone. The limestone attracts coral larvae, which build new coral reef. The Global Reef Alliance has built over 500 electrified reefs.[94] A success story is the completely eroded beach on an Indonesian island that restored itself in three years after an electrified reef was built in front of it. Fifteen years later, when the Asian tsunami washed over the island, the reef and beach were not damaged. Many small-scale reef restoration projects are underway, often based on coral gardening and spurred by efforts of local communities around the world.[95]

10. And Kelp Forests?

While coral reefs provide tropical coasts with rich biodiversity, giant kelp do this along temperate and polar coastlines.[96] These large brown algae anchor themselves to shallow ocean floors and grow toward the light, protecting coastlines from wave erosion. They are easily torn up by storms, but unlike coral reefs, kelp regrow rapidly, up to two feet a day. So the forest can normally repair itself rapidly. Many fish and invertebrates graze on the kelp, and the fronds provide shelter for fish nurseries of many species. The canopy at the surface provides food and protection for marine mammals and birds. Kelp also stores a lot of carbon dioxide: up to 20 times as much of it per acre as land forests.[97] Kelp is harvested commercially to produce alginate, an emulsifier used in cosmetics and prepared foods.

But kelp forests are also threatened by global warming. Kelp need cool water. They thrive along coasts where cold, nutrient-rich waters rise from deep currents. Ocean heat waves suppress upwelling of cold water, killing the kelp and the creatures relying on it. Recovery is slowed by runoff from near-shore agriculture and cities, which pollutes and clouds the water, dimming the sunlight that kelp need. The heat can also throw ecosystems out of whack. From 2014 to 2016, a massive ocean heat wave triggered a fatal wasting disease in starfish along the coast of Northern California.[98] Starfish eat sea urchins, which are the main grazers of kelp. Without the starfish, the sea urchin population exploded and ate all the kelp. They produced "sea urchin barrens" in which the ocean bottom is carpeted in sea urchin "zombies," a comatose state in which urchin can survive starvation (Figure 72). In areas where the "zombies" are cleared with dredges or by volunteer divers, the kelp are returning.[99] They are helped by sea otters, which love to eat sea urchins.[100] But it will take a long time for the ecosystem to recover from the extensive die-off.

FIGURE 72. Purple sea urchins hibernate on the ocean floor after clearing the majority of nearby kelp along the north coast of California. Photo credit: Steve Lonhart/NOAA, https://www.fisheries.noaa.gov/feature-story/pioneering-project-restore-bull-kelp-forests-greater-farallones-national-marine.

11. Enough Fish for All?

Overfishing is by far the greatest disturbance to aquatic ecosystems. Fish are part of the human diet everywhere. As the human population increases and becomes richer, so does the demand for fish. Per capita fish consumption has doubled since the 1960s.[101] Fish are caught faster than they can reproduce. About one-third of world fish stocks are overfished, and another 57 percent are fished at their maximum sustainable rate.[102]

The waters off Newfoundland once had a rich cod fishery. For hundreds of years, it supported fishermen from as far away as Portugal. But the catch increased hugely in the 1960s, then collapsed, and disappeared by 1992. Stocks have yet to recover (Figure 73).[103] Canada has put the region off-limits to cod fishing.

The most popular and profitable fish are often the largest fish in an area, and often they are the top predators. When they are depleted, smaller fish take over. When the smaller fish are then fished out, even smaller ones take over, with cascading effects throughout the food web.

Overfishing accelerated in the 1960s with the introduction of industrial fishing vessels. Their enormous lines and nets scoop up vast numbers of fish that the ships process at sea.[104] Bottom trawlers drag nets along the

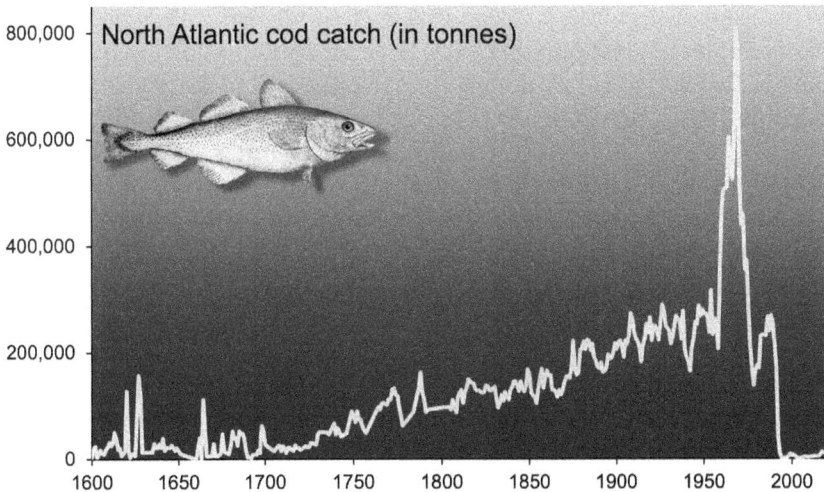

FIGURE 73. Atlantic cod catches in eastern Canada, plotted using data from Rebecca Schijns, Rainer Froese, Jeffrey A. Hutchings, and Daniel Pauly, "Five Centuries of Cod Catches in Eastern Canada," *ICES Journal of Marine Science* 78, no. 8 (August 28, 2021): 2675–83. Atlantic cod image is from NOAA Central Library Historical Fisheries Collection, https://www.noaa.gov/digital-library/collections/3581/item?page=5822.

ocean bottom, scooping up whatever is there. These methods take in a lot of "bycatch"—sea life other than the intended species, including sea turtles, dolphins, seals, and sea birds. An estimated 40 percent of fish catch is bycatch, which is often thrown back in the water injured.[105] Many of the species in the bycatch are also endangered. Trawlers also stir up sediments, which are rich stores of organic carbon, accumulated from the steady rain of dead organisms from above. The stirred-up carbon is converted to CO_2 which eventually escapes into the atmosphere. Trawling produces about as much CO_2 as global air traffic.[106] Governmental support for industrial fishing through loans and subsidies helps drive overfishing and the overproduction of fishing equipment. There are twice as many fishing boats as are needed for the available catch.[107]

To combat overfishing, governments limit fishing in their territorial waters, the area within 200 miles of their shores. But monitoring and enforcing the regulations is often inadequate. Setting aside marine protected areas, where no fishing is allowed, offers better protection. As of 2024, 8 percent of the global ocean is protected; the goal is to increase this number to 30 percent by 2030.[108] These areas can actually increase fish yields because the fish population grows enough to spill over into the unprotected areas. Another approach is to set a sustainable catch and divide up shares among fishing communities. They then have an interest in being stewards of the stock and seeing that no one exceeds their share. An example is the tradable permit system for halibut fishing in the waters off Alaska and British Columbia that provides a well-managed and sustainable halibut supply.[109]

Beyond the 200-mile limit, the oceans are international territory. Protective measures have to be negotiated internationally, and enforcement can be difficult. For example, the International Whaling Commission banned whaling in 1986, exempting only subsistence-level catches by Indigenous communities.[110] But Japan, Norway, and Iceland continue to catch whales, claiming that limited whaling of some species is sustainable.

International fishing is now done on a huge scale, driven by distant-water fishing fleets that harvest productive fisheries far from home. Often the fisheries are just outside, or even inside, the territorial waters of low-income countries that have limited means of enforcement, primarily in the Pacific and Africa.[111] Large fishing vessels are stationed more or less permanently, transferring their catch to a huge "mother ship" from their home country. The mother ship furnishes the vessels with fuel and provisions so they can continue fishing for an entire season, without returning to port. With its hold full, the mother ship returns to port, delivering the fish and restocking for the return to the fishing grounds. This industrial mining of fish stocks impoverishes the local fishing community and deprives the local population of much-needed nutrition. A number of countries operate these distant-water flotillas, but China is by far the biggest player, with at least 3,000 distant-water vessels.[112] China accounts for nearly 40 percent of the world's fishing activities in international waters.[113] Long ago, Chinese fishermen had fished out their territorial waters, which forced them to move on to other territories. Distant-water fishing depends on government subsidies for shipbuilding and maintenance and for the diesel fuel used in the long voyages.[114]

There is widespread violation of territorial limits. Ships often turn off their transponders to avoid being tracked. And transferring fish to a mother ship makes it easy to underreport the catch. But in 2016, the UN organized an international treaty to keep track of illegal fishing vessels and their catch. Countries are required to monitor foreign-flagged ships entering their ports for illegal fishing and to report violations. The treaty has been ratified by 78 countries.[115] Pressure is growing on China to join the treaty.

The demand for seafood exceeds what wild creatures can sustainably supply. The world depends increasingly on fish and shellfish farms, which now supply about 40 percent of the fish market. Aquaculture is discussed in Chapter 10. Meanwhile in 2023, 193 UN member states adopted a "high seas treaty" aimed at protecting biodiversity in the oceans beyond national boundaries.[116]

12. The Human Impact

We humans cover half of the planet's habitable land with cities, roads, and fields for crops and livestock.[117] Human domination of the planet has decimated other living species (Figure 74). Species are becoming extinct at an alarming rate. Since 1970, bird, amphibian, mammal, fish, and reptile populations fell by nearly 70 percent.[118] Flying insects are disappearing,[119] including bees that pollinate food plants.[120] We may be producing a mass extinction on the scale of the one that killed off the dinosaurs 65 million years ago. That one was set off by an asteroid plunging into what was then the Gulf of Mexico, blasting enough dust into the sky to spread around the world and black out the sun for years. Could we fall victim to a mass extinction caused by humans?[121]

In 2022, 190 countries took a hopeful first step toward reversing the global decline in biodiversity.[122] They signed an agreement to protect 30 percent of the planet's land and oceans from further exploitation by 2030. The agreement also promises $30 billion yearly to help low-income countries, many of them in the biologically rich tropics, stem biodiversity loss.

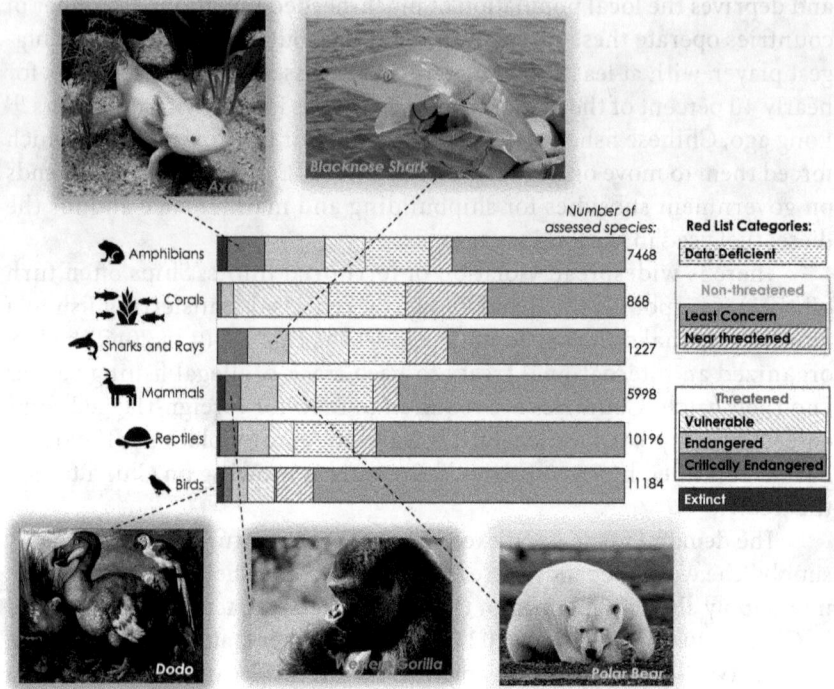

FIGURE 74. Proportion of species in each Red List Category for selected animal groups, from the International Union for Conservation of Nature Red List of Threatened Species, version 2022-1. Photos credit: Axolotl, photo by LaDame-Bucolique, https://commons.wikimedia.org/wiki/File:Axolotl-2193331_1280.webp; Blacknose shark, photo by NOAA, https://commons.wikimedia.org/wiki/File:Carcharhinus_acronotus_noaa.jpg; Polar bear, photo by Susanne Miller, U.S. Fish and Wildlife Service, https://digitalmedia.fws.gov/digital/collection/natdiglib/id/3429; western gorilla, photo by Dozyg, https://commons.wikimedia.org/wiki/File:Gorilla_port_lympne1.jpg; painting of a Dodo bird by Roelant Savery in the late 1620s, from Natural History Museum, London, collection, https://commons.wikimedia.org/wiki/File:Edwards%27_Dodo.jpg.

13. Here's What's Great About Biodiversity

This chapter has looked at biodiversity in key ecosystems around the world, from temperate and tropical forests, to grasslands, coral reefs, and kelp forests. In all of them, biodiversity has been seriously degraded by human activity and is increasingly threatened by further economic development. In many cases, the elimination of key species, like the wolves of Yellowstone, or sea stars in kelp forests, or big fish in the oceans, degrades the whole ecosystem. Invasive species are particularly harmful in disrupting native ecosystems. People around the world are working to limit the damage to all these ecosystems and to restore as much biodiversity as they can, but much greater effort is needed to change the direction in which we are headed.

Biodiversity has many benefits. Areas rich in biodiversity provide food for both wild animals and people. Biodiverse plants clean the water by filtering it through roots and rich soil on its way to aquifers, and they limit flooding by slowing rainwater runoff. Wetlands, rich in biodiversity, filter agricultural runoff and keep lakes and rivers from becoming overfertilized and choked with algae. Mangroves harbor diverse marine life and protect coastal areas from storm surges.

Conserving these "ecosystem services" costs much less than creating substitutes. For example, in the 1800s, New York City built a vast system of reservoirs, aqueducts, and tunnels to create its water supply and expanded the system as the city grew.[123] The city also developed a host of programs to protect its watershed area: buying conservation easements on the land around its reservoirs, incentivizing farmers to avoid using fertilizers and pesticides and to move animals away from streams, and investing in septic tank upgrades in upstream areas. A $1 billion investment, the Watershed Protection Program kept the water clear enough to exempt the city from federal and state filtration requirements.[124] With these measures, New York gave itself clean water and avoided paying more than $10 billion to build a massive filtration plant and another $100 million a year to maintain it.[125]

Resilience, the ability to survive major disturbances, is perhaps the greatest benefit of biodiversity. Potatoes are an example. Some 7,000 years ago, wild potatoes were domesticated on the shores of Lake Titicaca, high in the Andes mountains. Spanish conquistadors took the potato to Europe, where it gradually became popular. Farmers could plant it on land kept fallow to rest the soil after growing grain on it. This practice greatly increased Europe's food supply, especially because potatoes produce more food per planting than do grains. By the end of the 18th century, the potato effectively ended the chronic famines Europe had long suffered.[126] In Ireland, impoverished farmers, about 40 percent of the population, survived on potatoes and milk after their grain crops had been taken by absentee landlords. But hunger came roaring back in the middle of the 19th century when a deadly mold blighted potatoes. All of Europe suffered. In Ireland, a million people, more than 10 percent of the population, died of hunger.[127] Two million more fled Ireland, mostly for the United States.

In the Andes, potato diversity is rich. Weather is harsh in the highlands. Dry spells alternate with slashing rains and floods. In the thin air,

FIGURE 75. Native potato varieties that grow in Peru. Photo credit: International Potato Centre.

temperatures can fluctuate from 75°F (24°C) to below freezing in a few hours. Villages range up and down the steep mountain slopes, and different altitudes harbor different animals and insects. Over time, Native peoples cultivated many different potato varieties; if some didn't survive, others did. Thousands of varieties evolved[128] (Figure 75). Today Peruvian farmers cultivate hundreds of them; Peruvian markets display a remarkable and colorful range of potatoes that are a cornerstone of Peruvian cuisine.

But all of Europe's potatoes were descended from the few samples brought back by the conquistadors, and they were all susceptible to the potato blight. Europe had no resistant varieties to fall back on. This is the great danger of monocultures. Species diversity confers resilience, a principle that applies throughout the living world. It may be the key to our survival in the face of increasing dangers from climate change.

A case in point is the 2021 testimony of a resilient pilot whose small plane developed engine trouble and crashed in the middle of the Amazon jungle. Walking for 36 days to reach help, he used palm branches to shelter at night from the rain and survived on fruit that he saw spider monkeys eating. "If I had fallen somewhere in a deserted plantation site, I wouldn't have water, shelter, or what to eat," he said. "The Amazon is so rich."[129]

14. The Bottom Line

Habitats with diverse species of plants and animals benefit both ecosystems and humanity. They produce food and medicines, store carbon, retain and clean water, and provide resilience against unanticipated threats. And they fill us with a sense of wonder at nature's beauty and bounty.

But biodiverse ecosystems are often degraded by human activity, including logging, land clearing, agricultural monocultures, overfishing, urban development, pollution, and the extirpation of top predators, with cascading effects on the system. And global warming intensifies the threats to biodiversity. Reversing these trends requires concerted action by governments and communities to halt further destruction and rebuild the degraded habitats. Most of all, it requires widespread understanding and appreciation for all that biodiversity gives us.

10

Food

What's for Dinner?

Topics:

1. Where will 10 billion of us get food?
2. Fertilizer: Key to crop abundance but an environmental burden
3. What role do pesticides play?
4. The good and the bad of the Green Revolution
5. Soil is a big deal: Regenerative agriculture
6. Is organic food really good for you and the planet?
7. Livestock: Where's the beef?
8. The trouble with CAFOs
9. What about fish farms?
10. Who's afraid of GMOs?
11. What's next?
   A. Urban farms
   B. Greenhouses and vertical farms
   C. Information technology comes to agriculture: Precision agriculture
   D. Can fake meat save us?
   E. What about insects?
   F. Microbes can make protein too
   G. Real meat and fish from animal cells
   H. Milk too from cell culture
   I. Combating food waste
10. Where are we now?

1. Where Will 10 Billion of Us Get Food?

In 1971, a burning question was whether the planet could feed all its inhabitants, or would famine be the world's fate. That's when Frances Moore Lappé published *Diet for a Small Planet*.[1] Her book started the movement to link food with environmental protection and health. In the following years, it seemed the answer was yes, the planet could feed everyone. Food scarcity diminished as agricultural productivity increased, mainly because of manufactured fertilizer and the "Green Revolution" in the developing world (see below). But even when there is sufficient food globally, hunger persists in various parts of the world plagued by political instability, wars, droughts, and inequitable food distribution. Nearly 800 million people—1 in 10 people globally—experience chronic hunger.[2]

World population was about four billion in 1971, double what it was 40 years earlier and four times what it was in 1800.[3] Till 1800, the population grew very slowly, with high death rates balancing high birth rates. The accelerated growth since 1800 is the result of improved farming practices

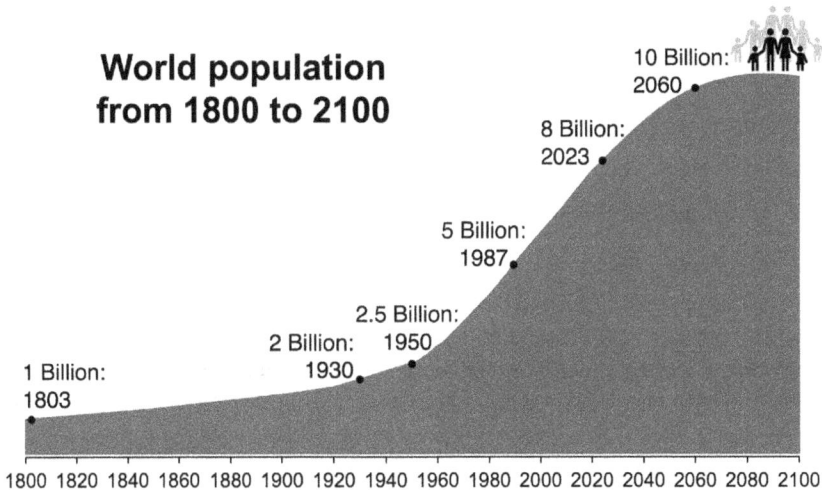

FIGURE 76. World population: historic estimates, present count, and future projection. Data source: United Nations, Department of Economic and Social Affairs, Population Division. Data for the 1800 to 1950 period is from United Nations, "The World at Six Billion. (Table 1)" (October 12, 1999): 5, https://www. un.org/development/desa/pd/sites/www.un.org.development.desa.pd/files/ files/documents/2020/Jan/un_1999_6billion.pdf. Data for the 1950 to 2100 period is from United Nations, "World Population Prospects 2022," United Nations archive (2022), https://population.un.org/wpp/Download/Archive/ Standard/.

and public health measures that lowered death rates dramatically. Birth rates meanwhile remained high. In the 50 years after Lappé's book, the population doubled again. It now stands at eight billion (Figure 76). But today, birth rates are falling everywhere as young people, especially women, seek a better life for themselves with fewer children. Nonetheless, the population is expected to swell by another two billion before leveling off sometime in this century.[4] Will the planet be able to feed not four billion but 10 billion people?

Not only are there more people, but they want richer food. As economies expand and people in the low-income world get wealthier, they spend more on the food they like, especially meat. This trend means that, by 2050, food production would have to increase by at least 50 percent from the 2010 baseline[5] to feed the world's increasing population and appetite, so more crops would be required on more land. But agriculture already takes up 50 percent of all the usable land (see Chapter 9). Expanding the crop production would mean clearing an area nearly twice the size of India[6]—mostly tropical rainforest, which is already in trouble. Alternatively, crop productivity would have to increase. Globally, crop yields have steadily increased since the middle of the last century.[7] But the growth rate is slowing.[8] So we need new ways to provide enough food for the planet while preserving existing native ecosystems.

2. Fertilizer: Key to Crop Abundance but an Environmental Burden

At the turn of the 20th century, Fritz Haber, a German chemist, discovered how to get nitrogen in the air, N_2, to react with hydrogen gas, H_2, to make ammonia, which is the main ingredient in synthetic fertilizer.[9] Applying synthetic fertilizer to their fields allowed farmers to dramatically increase their crop yields. Haber won the 1918 Nobel Prize for his invention.[10] Today, 60 percent of all nitrogen used on crops comes from synthetic fertilizer,[11] and nearly half of the world's population depends on food produced with this additional nitrogen input.[12]

Why is fertilizer needed? Plants need nitrogen to make essential molecules like proteins and DNA, but they can't get it from the nitrogen gas that surrounds the plants. Bacteria learned early on how to break up (or "fix") N_2 and produce ammonia, but plants never picked up this essential trick. Instead, they rely on bacteria in the soil to provide them with "fixed nitrogen" (fixed-N). Fixed-N includes ammonia as well as its oxidation products, like nitrate, that plants can also use (Figure 77). But harvesting a crop depletes the soil's fixed-N supply. Unless fixed-N is added,

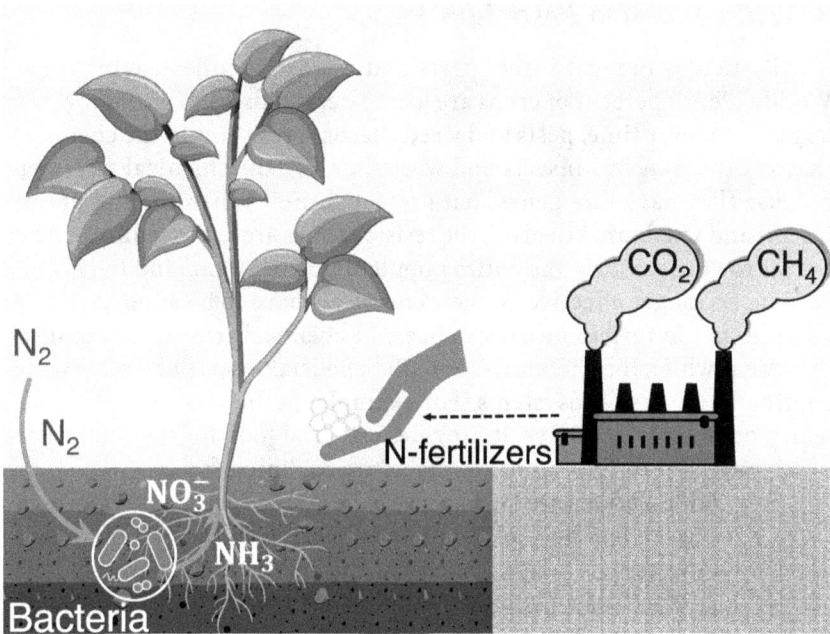

FIGURE 77. Nitrogen for plants is supplied by nitrogen-fixing bacteria or by synthetic fertilizer. Fertilizer production releases CO_2 and methane. (Plant with roots image by Vecteezy, https://www.vecteezy.com/free-vector/plant-roots.)

crops no longer thrive after a few harvests, and the soil must lie "fallow" (unplanted) to allow bacteria time to restore the fixed-N.

Haber's invention freed crops from this nitrogen limitation, but synthetic fertilizer is hitting diminishing returns. Plants take up only as much fixed-N as they can use. Adding more doesn't help. Crop yields level off.[13] And 50 percent of all nitrogen applied to the fields is not used by the plants.[14] Some of the excess turns into nitrous oxide, a powerful greenhouse gas. The rest is converted to nitrate, which washes into rivers and lakes. There, it feeds algal blooms, which suffocate fish, produce toxins, and contaminate beaches and drinking water.[15]

Another problem with synthetic fertilizer is that making it produces a lot of CO_2 and methane (CH_4), accounting for 1–2 percent of global greenhouse gas emissions.[16] That's because the needed hydrogen for ammonia production is obtained from a fossil fuel, natural gas. The reaction produces CO_2 as a by-product, with some CH_4 escaping in the process. These emissions could be avoided by using "green" hydrogen, made by electrolyzing water (discussed in Chapter 4). Some fertilizer manufacturers are moving in this direction.[17]

3. What Role Do Pesticides Play?

Pesticides prevent insect pests and weeds from destroying crops. Worldwide, 20 percent of crops are lost to pests. Losses to weeds are even larger.[18] But over time, pests and weeds become resistant to the chemicals that kill them. A few insects and weeds survive the chemical treatment because they have rare genes that protect them.[19] When the susceptible insects and weeds are killed off, the resistant ones are left to multiply. After a few growing seasons, the entire population is resistant, and the chemicals are no longer effective. So new chemicals have to be applied (Figure 78), and they in turn induce resistance. The chemical arms race is endless.

Meanwhile, the chemicals also kill beneficial insects and plants, disrupting biodiverse ecosystems. For example, herbicides kill milkweed, which often lines roadways. It provides essential food for the caterpillars of migrating butterflies, whose numbers are declining.[20]

Insect populations are falling everywhere.[21] In agricultural areas, car drivers see much less bug splat on windshields than they did years ago. The loss of insects is worrisome because they perform so many essential services. They pollinate plants, decompose dead plants and animals, and build the food chains of fish, birds, and mammals.

FIGURE 78. Pesticide spraying on leaf lettuce in Arizona. Photo by Jeff Vanuga, National Resource Conservation Service, U.S. Department of Agriculture, https://www.usgs.gov/media/images/pesticide-application-leaf-lettuce.

Insects have lost much of their habitat since crops have taken over the grassland, bushes, and trees that used to harbor them. Climate change, urbanization, and pollution all contribute to insect decline. And vast numbers are killed by increasingly powerful insecticides. Currently, the most widely used are neonicotinoid chemicals, called "neonics."[22] They are sprayed on fruit trees and vegetable crops. And seeds of grain crops are coated with neonics to protect the plants as they grow. Coated seed are used for most corn, three-quarters of soybean and cotton, and half of winter wheat crops in the United States.[23] But neonics poison bees and other insects when they feed on the flowers of treated plants.[24] Studies implicate insecticides as the main cause of population declines of the monarch and other butterflies.[25] Insect losses ripple up the food web. In the United States, bird populations have declined 30 percent since 1970.[26]

Neonics are persistent in the environment. They are water soluble and can wash out of soil into nearby fields and waterways, killing insects along the way. The European Union has banned neonics for field applications[27] and for seed treatment.[28] In the United States, some states are beginning to restrict their use.[29]

Instead of massively applying pesticides, many farmers are moving toward integrated pest management (IPM) to control insects and weeds and to protect human health. IPM uses a variety of control measures, like insect traps and releasing pest predators.[30] These measures lower pesticide application to rates sufficient to control a pest population without killing enough of the pests to induce rapid resistance. IPM uses herbicides selectively to target the most harmful weeds. It also suppresses weeds with cover crops. And wild hedgerows are left in place to encourage pollinating insects. Especially when combined with regenerative practices like crop rotation (see below), IPM can increase both crop yield and insect pollinator populations.[31] The farmers also save costs by reducing major pesticide use. Regional IPM centers in the United States were established in 2000[32] to research IPM strategies and to facilitate their adoption by farmers.

4. The Good and the Bad of the Green Revolution

When Frances Moore Lappé published *Diet for a Small Planet* in 1971, mass starvation was a looming threat in low-income countries, where population growth outstripped the food supply. But by then, the "Green Revolution" had begun, with crop yields increasing in Asia and Latin America. Scientists developed new varieties of wheat, rice, and corn that dramatically increased crop production in the tropics, with only a modest increase in agricultural land cultivation. Food prices fell, as did the fraction of undernourished people. The man who led this effort, Norman Borlaug, won the 1970 Nobel Peace Prize for staving off world hunger.[33]

The new plants produced more grain when fertilized and had shorter, stiffer stalks to support the heavier heads. They also grew faster, and more crops could be planted each year. Between 1960 and 2000, yields increased by 200 percent for wheat, 100 percent for rice, 150 percent for corn, and 80 percent for potatoes.[34] But the improved yields required more irrigation, heavy application of fertilizer, and insecticides to protect the crops. Governments generally subsidized the costs. Aquifers were overpumped, soil degraded, and many beneficial insects were poisoned. These problems are highlighted in Chapter 6 for the Punjab, the breadbasket of India. Higher yields encouraged the use of farm equipment, which, along with the fertilizer, increased fossil fuel use, pollution, and greenhouse gas emissions. Agriculture contributed to the ballooning of CO_2 emissions in Asia. In many areas, high-yield crops displaced traditional staple varieties, such as legumes, millet, and vegetables,[35] creating micronutrient deficiencies in the population.[36]

5. Soil Is a Big Deal: Regenerative Agriculture

The soil of grassland is rich and porous from grass roots, fungus, earthworms, and burrowing insects. It stores a lot of carbon and holds a lot of water in its pores. It holds back runoff and reduces flooding. The soil moisture provides cooling on hot days and reduces drought damage. Because of their rich soil, most grasslands have been plowed for crops.

But when left bare after a harvest, the soil turns to dust that blows or washes away, filling waterways with sediment. Loss of soil through erosion is a threat to agriculture everywhere in the world. Bare, caked earth promotes faster runoff and more flooding when the rains come.

During the early decades of the 20th century, American farmers dramatically expanded grain crops in the grasslands of the Great Plains. Starting in 1930, severe drought put bare, degraded soil at the mercy of the region's high winds and produced the "dust bowl." Dust storms brought widespread devastation, bankrupting farms and forcing over 400,000 people to migrate.[37]

Today, erosion is especially severe in sub-Saharan Africa, South America, and Southeast Asia, where clearing of tropical forests to plant crops in the thin soil accelerates land degradation.[38] "Slash and burn" farming, in which vegetation is cut down and burned to prepare the land for planting, is particularly destructive. Entire regions have been degraded. In Madagascar's high central plateau—10 percent of the entire country—the land is denuded and has huge rain gullies running through it.[39]

To combat these destructive trends, farmers are turning to regenerative agriculture[40] to restore and enrich the soil. Regenerative agriculture has four main tools: (1) "no-till" planting, (2) cover crops, (3) crop rotation, and (4) addition of organic matter.

(1) *No-till planting* means not plowing (tilling) the soil. Plowing has been used since time immemorial to prepare soil for planting and to uproot weeds. But plowing exposes bare soil to sun, wind, and rain, which erode the soil and turn it to dust. Plowing also upends the soil ecosystem. It destroys earthworms that digest organic matter. The channels made by earthworms aerate the soil and provide drainage for floodwaters. Plowing tears up plant root systems and the fungal threads ("hyphae") that cling to them.[41] These fungi are fed by the plants and in return bring the plants vital nutrients by decomposing organic matter and soil minerals.[42] Loss of this complex ecosystem exhausts soils after just a few crop plantings.

One-third of U.S. major cropland is now under no-till and another third is under reduced-till management,[43] a step forward in soil conservation. In no-till, planting seeds are directly injected into unplowed fields. But the catch is that the fields are usually sprayed with herbicides to keep the weeds from choking off the new plants. The herbicides also kill earthworms and soil microorganisms, reducing soil richness and fertility. Farmers can opt for integrated weed management strategies to reduce the need for herbicides.[44] These strategies include crop rotation and planting more than one crop at a time ("intercropping") to keep the weeds at bay. Different crops have different defenses of their own against weeds.

(2) *Cover crops* are planted after crops are harvested, instead of leaving the soil bare. Cover crops also help control weeds, reducing the need for herbicides. Planting legumes, like clover or alfalfa, replenishes the soil with nitrogen, reducing the need for fertilizer and increasing the main crop yield by 10–20 percent.[45] The cover crops can also provide forage for livestock. But as of 2023, cover crops were planted on only 5 percent of U.S. cropland.[46]

(3) *Crop rotation* is a traditional way to restore soil by planting different crops in succession in each field. Over time, rotation helps control weeds and insects. Rotating legumes replenishes nitrogen. Switching from two-crop rotation to more diverse rotations that include non-cereal crops, such as potatoes, peanuts, and other legumes, improves yields and soil health over the long term.[47]

(4) *Adding organic matter* to soil enriches it and encourages worms and burrowing insects that leave holes among the roots, improving water retention. Spreading compost, manure, and biochar on the fields improves

plant growth and stores carbon in the root zone.[48] Growing perennial grasses also builds soil organic matter.

So regenerative farming builds soil health and improves crop yields while reducing the need for synthetic fertilizer, pesticides, and herbicides. And it reduces global warming by storing carbon in the soil.

6. Is Organic Food Really Good for You and the Planet?

It depends on the context.[49] Organic farms don't use synthetic products: fertilizer, pesticides, herbicides, antibiotics, growth hormones, or genetically modified organisms (GMOs). Instead, they apply more compost and manure to fertilize the soil and plant legume cover crops. Fields are usually plowed to work in the compost and help control weeds without herbicides. But reduced-till organic farming can also work. Instead of a plow, farmers can use a "roller crimper" that mows down a cover crop and parts the resulting mulch to plant seeds.[50] The sprouts then grow up through the mulch, which keeps down weeds. Organic farmers also use hand weeding.

Organic fruits and vegetables don't contain synthetic herbicide and insecticide residues, while those from conventional farms retain some residue, even after the produce is cleaned. Also, organic produce is healthier for farmworkers and their communities that would otherwise experience toxic exposures to herbicides and insecticides. Organic fruits and vegetables are more nutritious, with higher levels of vitamins and antioxidants. They are also more expensive because they use more labor, especially to control weeds without herbicides. As of 2022, only 2 percent of the world's agricultural land was farmed organically. The fraction was 19 percent in Europe, 9 percent in Asia,[51] and only 1 percent in the United States.[52]

Yields are generally lower for organic than conventional crops because conventional crops are selected for the high yields that synthetic fertilizers and pesticides produce,[53] so organic farms require more land area for the same amount of produce. That's a problem for organic farming because expansion means using more scarce land. However, crop rotation and multi-cropping substantially reduce the yield disadvantage of organic farming.[54]

The organic food label doesn't tell you where the item was produced. It may be from a distant large commercial farm. By some estimates, on average, food travels 1,500 miles in the United States to reach consumers.[55] But there is also a local farm movement whose products are found at farmers' markets in cities. Local farms may or may not be organic, but they offer farm-fresh products. Some sell subscriptions (Community Supported Agriculture), offering regular delivery of produce during the growing season.

7. Livestock: Where's the Beef?

The world pays a high price for meat, especially beef. Twenty percent of irrigation water goes to crops that feed domestic animals (see Chapter 7). Livestock account for 60 percent of agricultural CO_2 emissions.[56] Beef releases 90 times as much CO_2 as peas for the same amount of protein.[57] Livestock need 83 percent of the world's farmland for pasture and fodder, but they provide only 18 percent of the calories and 37 percent of the protein in the human diet.[58]

When they roam pastures, livestock help humans by converting inedible grass into meat. They also help the pastures by stirring up and aerating the soil with their hooves and by fertilizing it with their excrement. As long as livestock do not eat the grass down to the roots, they sustain the land. Well-managed livestock herds are rotated through different patches of grassland to avoid overgrazing.[59] They are good for the environment and are the basis for food production in many traditional societies, like the present-day Maasai of Kenya.

But grazing cannot possibly provide all the meat consumed by humans. Not enough grasslands remain. Beef cattle are raised on pasture only for their first year and a half. For the next three to six months,[60] they are fattened on grains, usually corn and soybeans, to "finish" them before they are slaughtered. They are given antibiotics and hormones to make them grow faster and fatter. Grain-fed beef is marbled with fat, making it tender and flavorful. But the calorie-rich fats contribute to epidemic obesity among meat eaters. The few cattle brought to market as "grass-fed" continue to feed on grass for an additional year. Their meat is leaner and gamier and more nutritious. Because of the longer production time, a herd of grass-fed cows produces less (and more expensive) meat annually than a herd of grain-fed cows.

Grain-fed cows and other livestock compete with humans for valuable cropland. Expansion of livestock to feed the world's increasing appetite for meat means clearing more land for animal feed crops. This land is mostly taken from already threatened rainforests, so eating less meat would (1) help save the remaining rainforests, (2) free up cropland for human food, and (3) combat climate change. We don't have to go completely vegan. A "planet-healthy diet" has mostly vegetables and nuts but allows a beef burger and two servings of fish per week and dairy products daily.[61] Even a modest shift in the direction of less red meat would have major environmental and health benefits.

8. The Trouble with Cafos

Grain-fed beef is "finished" in feedlots. Most cattle, pigs, and chickens—three-quarters of global livestock—are kept in huge "confined animal feeding operations" (CAFOs).[62] CAFOs are highly efficient, producing meat as fast as possible. The speed drives down costs. Because the crowded conditions foster disease, antibiotics are added to the feed. Farm animals consume 70 percent of the antibiotics sold in the United States.[63] This massive use of antibiotics gives rise to antibiotic-resistant bacteria that threaten human and animal health. Outbreaks of human infections with resistant bacteria have been linked to animals being fed antibiotics. Resistant bacteria threaten to render important antibiotics ineffective. European countries restrict farm antibiotics and use two to three times less than does the United States.[64] In response to consumer concerns, U.S. chicken growers have sharply cut back on antibiotics. More than 90 percent of U.S. chickens are now raised without antibiotics that are used in humans.[65] Most of the antibiotics are used on cattle and pigs.

CAFOs produce huge quantities of animal excrement which is collected in manure piles or in lagoons. The manure is applied as fertilizer to farm fields but often exceeds what the fields can use and is washed away by the rains. Sometimes manure lagoons fail and dump the contents into local rivers and lakes. The nitrate and phosphorus from the manure feed algal blooms that choke waterways and kill off fish and aquatic creatures. Every year, waste from CAFOs contributes 10 percent of the nutrients carried down the Mississippi River[66] that produce a large dead zone in the Gulf of Mexico (see Chapter 7).

The manure also pollutes the air with ammonia, which irritates eyes and lungs and produces disease-causing small particles (see Chapter 6). Children living near CAFOs suffer high rates of asthma.[67] And foul odors drift over surrounding communities, whose property values go down.

Animal cruelty is another issue CAFOs raise: cows crowded together, standing in their own feces; chickens in wire "battery cages" 15 inches high with a floor area about the size of printer paper, unable to scratch or even spread their wings[68]; sows in gestation cages, unable to turn around. Both types of cages are banned in Europe and in some states in the United States.[69] Several meat suppliers promise to phase them out. And retail chains like McDonald's are demanding similar action from their suppliers.

9. What About Fish Farms?

The world needs more fish on the table to feed the growing human population, much of which relies on fish. By 1995, fish consumption exceeded that of beef (Figure 79).

But fish catches are declining because of overfishing (see Chapter 9). The gap is filled by farmed fish. Since 2009, half of fish consumed comes from fish farms.[70] Coastlines around the world are dotted with pens in which fish are raised for the commercial market. Ninety percent of the farms are in Asia, where fish have always been an important part of the diet. China alone accounts for 60 percent of farmed fish.[71]

But fish farms have a bad reputation for polluting the water with fish waste, leading to overgrowth of algae. Sometimes the pens break in storms and release farmed fish into the water to compete with or interbreed with wild fish. To combat the spread of disease among fish in the pens, fish farmers add antibiotics that also spread into surrounding waters.[72] Some popular fish, like salmon, are carnivores and are fed fish meal of ground smaller fish, like anchovies. But harvesting so many small fish for feed diminishes the food supply for wild fish. Fortunately, the dominant farmed fish are fast-growing tilapia, catfish, and carp, which are omnivores. They can live on vegetable feed and the waste of other fish, as can shrimp and other shellfish. Today, much of the industry has cleaned up its act.[73] Farms are more efficient and use soybeans and other

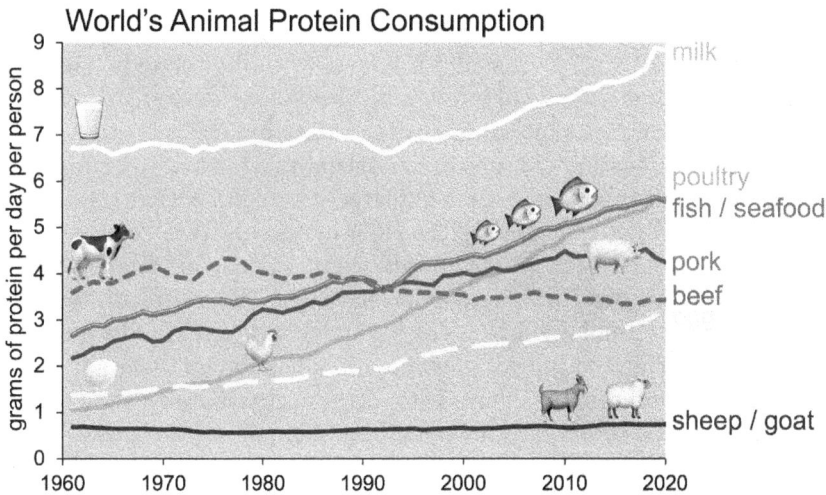

FIGURE 79. Global animal protein consumption. Data from Food and Agriculture Organization of the United Nations, 2023, processed by Our World in Data, https://ourworldindata.org/grapher/animal-protein-consumption.

grains to replace most of the fish meal. Pollution is much lower than it was.

A new approach is inspired by the ancient Chinese practice of growing carp in rice paddies, where the fish eat insects and weeds. The fish fertilize the rice with their excrement before becoming food themselves.[74] Growing fish in rice paddies reduces the need for fertilizer and pesticides and for fish feed. In the new operations, downstream baskets harbor shellfish, which feed on the organic excretions from the fish pens, while lines of kelp use up the nitrate and phosphate from the excretions. Under the pens, sea cucumbers, delicacies in Japan and China, are raised on the heavier wastes falling from above. In other places, shellfish and kelp are grown together to remove fertilizer from runoff.[75]

Farmed fish have a big advantage over farmed land animals. They take less feed because they are buoyant and don't have to fight gravity. And being cold-blooded, they require less energy than warm-blooded land animals. It takes about a pound of feed to produce a pound of fish compared with two pounds of feed per pound of chicken, three for pork, and seven for beef.[76] Fish are far more conserving of Earth's resources than livestock. Even more conserving are shellfish, which are lower on the aquatic food chain and consume fewer nutrients.

10. Who's Afraid of GMOs?

GMOs raise passionate negative feelings. Many people agree with King Charles III of the United Kingdom, who once stated, "Genetic manipulation takes mankind into realms that belong to God, and to God alone."[77] Others are skeptical about the safety of GMOs.[78] Still others object to control of GMO crops by industrial agriculture.[79] Feelings are especially strong in Europe, which has largely banned GMO crops.

GMOs are made by altering the DNA of organisms to express novel traits. Bacteria have been genetically altered for many years to make pharmaceuticals, like insulin.[80] Plant genes have been more difficult to alter, but new gene technology makes the job much easier. Actually, humans have been altering the genetic makeup of plants ever since the advent of agriculture. They crossbred plants with different characteristics and painstakingly selected those with the most desirable properties. This form of genetic modification continues today as plant breeders produce improved hybrid varieties, from naturally occurring variations, like the "Green Revolution" wheat, rice, and corn varieties.

But genetic engineering is much faster and more precise than crossbreeding. It introduces the specific genetic code for a desirable trait.

Crossbreeding instead mixes all the genes of two plants in hopes that the desirable trait will be dominant in some of the daughter plants. It may take several successive crosses to bring this about.[81] On the other hand, genetic engineering requires laboratories and trained scientists. Field tests and safety tests add to the cost of introducing GMO crops. Commercial development of GMO crops is led by large chemical companies. Monsanto (now owned by Bayer) was the first, and anti–GMO sentiment made it notorious.[82] Monsanto focused on improving yields by making crops resistant to pests and weeds. Insect resistance was introduced using genes from a soil bacterium, known as *Bt*. *Bt* itself has been sprayed on plants as a natural pesticide,[83] acceptable to organic farmers. Inserting the *Bt* genes provides plants with their own insecticide. It is more effective than spraying because the spray may not reach insects in hidden parts of the plant, like the kernels in ears of corn. Almost 90 percent of corn and cotton grown in the United States are now *Bt* crops.[84]

To combat weeds, Monsanto introduced its powerful glyphosate herbicide, marketed as "Roundup." Glyphosate kills most plants and is often used to clear unwanted vegetation along roadways and railroad tracks and to control invasive species. It is also used to clear weeds from fields in preparation for "no-till" planting. But it cannot be applied after planting since that would destroy the crop, so Monsanto introduced a crop gene that protects the plant from glyphosate, which can then be used during crop growth. Other companies followed suit, and now in the United States, 90 percent of soybeans, corn, canola, sugar beets, and cotton are from GMO plants that are protected from glyphosate or other herbicides.[85] However, there is increasing concern about links between glyphosate exposure and cancer and liver disease and about ecotoxicity.[86]

As with any other method of pest control, GMO plants encourage the evolution of resistant pests.[87] Overreliance on any one strategy leads to faster resistance. Resistance to several herbicides and insecticides are now common among crop-destroying pests. Farmers are turning instead to the integrated pest and weed management practices described above.[88]

Five countries account for 90 percent of GMO cropland: the United States, Brazil, Argentina, Canada, and India.[89] Genetically modified crops are mostly grown on large commercial farms. Small farms lack the capital for GMO seeds, and the inputs (irrigation, fertilizer, herbicides) needed to produce profitable crops. But small farms are helped by the nonprofit international institutes in Mexico and the Philippines that developed the "Green Revolution" wheat, corn, and rice varieties. Now these institutes are working on traits for drought, flood, and salt resistance to meet the challenges of water scarcity, severe storms, and sea level rise. Both crossbreeding and genetic engineering are used in the search for these traits. As developing nations launch their own labs and train their own scientists, they can focus on improving important local crops. For example, cowpea, an important high-protein staple in much of Africa, has been genetically engineered by Nigerian scientists to resist the maruca pod borer pest, which devastates the crop.[90]

While genetic engineering has mostly focused on protecting crops from insects and weeds, it can also be used to improve nutrient content to combat nutrient deficiency. The best-known example is vitamin A–containing "golden rice," developed as a humanitarian project in the 1990s by German scientists Ingo Potrykus and Peter Beyer.[91] Vitamin A deficiency is the leading cause of childhood blindness in the developing world and a contributor to deaths from infectious diseases. Up to half a million children go blind every year, and half of them die, as a result of vitamin A deficiency.[92] But the use of "golden rice" has been slowed by opposition from anti–GMO activists and by farmers who are concerned about genetic cross contamination and the loss of rice biodiversity.[93] After years of debate, the Philippines cleared golden rice for commercial production in 2022, only to revoke the permit in 2024 after the court concluded that there is no scientific consensus on its safety.[94] So the debate continues.

11. What's Next?

Agriculture needs to meet the challenge of providing enough high-quality food for our ever-shrinking planet without further destroying our natural habitat and its biodiversity. Here are some promising trends.

(A) Urban Farms

Most people live in cities, often far from where their food is grown. Only decades ago, farming was the main way of life everywhere. In 1900, 16 percent of the world's people lived in cities,[95] but 57 percent do so today.[96]

Urban gardens offer city dwellers access to fresh food. By some estimates, nearly a billion people grow food and animals in cities, accounting for 15–20 percent of the global food supply.[97] People all over the world organize and work in community gardens, often with support from municipal governments. These gardens build solidarity and provide fresh produce to marginal communities, often along with other basic services, like health care and social supports. Underutilized land in cities could produce a substantial fraction of our vegetables and fruits, reducing pressures to cultivate more wild lands.[98]

(B) Greenhouses and Vertical Farms

Greenhouses provide plants with well-lit indoor spaces to protect them from the elements. Greenhouses have long been used to grow ornamental plants. Today, they produce crops as well. The Netherlands makes massive use of greenhouses to grow vegetables. Highly productive, greenhouses carefully control temperature and moisture. They supplement natural light with LED lighting, allowing plants to grow at night year-round.[99] Despite its small size, the Netherlands has become the world's second largest exporter of agricultural products (after the United States).[100]

A recent trend is to build "vertical farms" in unused commercial buildings and even surplus shipping containers. Inside these structures, crops are grown in stacked trays containing nutrient solutions instead of soil. This "hydroponic" method uses only a fraction of the water needed for irrigated crops.[101] A plastic film technology from Japan saves even more water than conventional hydroponics.[102] The film holds water strongly so that plants grown through it develop more roots and work harder to absorb nutrient-containing solution placed below. The plants' products are richer in nutrients and flavors than when grown without the film.

Asian countries, with high food demand in their dense cities, are investing heavily in vertical farms. Japan was an early leader but will soon be overtaken by China, which is planning a massive expansion of vertical farming.[103] And instability in world food markets due to pandemics, wars, and climate change is sparking interest around the globe in locally controlled vertical farms.

However, these farms are only useful for growing shallow-rooted vegetables and fruits, like lettuce, tomatoes, and strawberries.

Greenhouses and vertical farms use less water, fertilizer, and pesticides than outdoor farms. But they use a lot of energy for heat and light,[104] most of which is still from fossil fuels. The costs for buildings and operations are also high.

(C) Information Technology Comes to Agriculture: Precision Agriculture

The internet brings important new tools to agriculture. Cell phones are now everywhere. Small farm operators in low-income countries use theirs to sell produce via apps that connect them directly to buyers. The apps allow farmers to bypass middlemen, who would extract substantial profits. The apps post market prices, so farmers know the worth of their produce. Farmers in Mozambique using the app IzyShop increased their revenue up to fivefold.[105]

Besides improving farm income, the apps reduce food wastage, which occurs when middlemen won't buy all the produce farmers have to sell. The excess spoils and must be discarded. Small farms in low-income countries usually lose one-third or more of their crops to spoilage.[106] That depresses farm income and wastes the irrigation water and other resources that produced the spoiled crop. One-quarter of global fresh water is wasted in the production of food that is never consumed.[107] In Colombia, farmers who sell fruit and vegetables through the Frubana app report post-harvest losses of just 3 percent compared with the average of 58 percent for farmers who sell through traditional channels.[108] The apps allow digital payments as well. Farmers build a payment history that allows them to establish creditworthiness to obtain microloans for farm improvements.

Wealthier farmers can buy a range of information technologies to improve profits and reduce environmental impacts. Detailed weather predictions for their locale allow more precise timing of planting, irrigation, and harvesting. Sensors and drones can measure the weight and moisture content of a crop as it is being harvested, providing a map of how the crop yield depends on location in the farm. The map shows exactly where more or less fertilizer and irrigation water are needed for the next planting.[109] Other sensors can map the water content and acidity of the soil itself,[110] showing where lime should be applied to reduce acidity. These data analysis practices, collectively called *precision agriculture*, improve yields, waste fewer resources, and reduce overfertilization.[111]

(D) Can Fake Meat Save Us?

Americans eat about 20 billion beef burgers a year[112]; half of them are sold by fast food chains.[113] Can this staggering number be converted to non-meat alternatives that look and taste like hamburger? Beyond Meat and Impossible Foods are two firms that hope to do just that and earn big profits while protecting the planet by saving water and land.[114] Their burgers are made from high-protein plant sources, primarily peas in one case (Beyond) and soybeans in the other case (Impossible). Other vegetable ingredients are added to enhance flavor and color. Beyond Meat uses beet powder to color its burger red, while Impossible Foods uses leghemoglobin, a plant molecule similar to the hemoglobin in our blood.[115] Vegetable patties have been available for years as hamburger substitutes, but none have gained the acceptance of meat eaters. Beyond and Impossible hoped to do that. Supported by investors and partnerships with restaurants and food chain stores, the sales of vegan meat have been steadily increasing. In 2020, their total U.S. sales came to about a quarter to half a billion burgers.[116] Although impressive, this is still a pittance compared with the 20 billion U.S. beef burgers. And since then, sales have faltered.[117] Questions have been raised about the health effects of the ultra-processed plant protein.[118] Sales are slower still in other countries, where hamburgers are not diet staples as they are in the United States.

(E) What About Insects?

Although most people shy away from eating insects, they have actually been part of the human diet throughout history. Ancient Greeks considered cicadas to be delicacies, and the Bible describes four kinds of locusts that the Hebrews were allowed to eat. Even today, many people regularly consume insects in Asia, Africa, and Latin America.[119] Insects are rich in protein and they grow faster than animals. And they need much less food, water, and space than animals. Insects can feed on food wastes and convert them to fertilizer. Many food companies are now making protein powder from insects for fish and animal feed.[120] Despite initial consumer reluctance, insect protein is likely to make its way into human food as well.

(F) Microbes Can Make Protein Too

Protein made by microbes in industrial fermenters is a promising substitute for meat or plant protein.[121] It can also be used for animal feed, reducing the need for crops. The microbes can be fed nutrients recovered from agricultural and other organic wastes.[122] The fermenters take up less room and use less water than vegetable crops. They make protein much faster than plants since microbes multiply in hours, while plants require a whole growing season. Fermenters don't depend on the weather, and the protein they make is consistent in quality. The microbes can be bacteria, yeast, or fungus. Yeast fermentation has been used for centuries to make wine and beer, so fermenters are a mature technology.[123] A fungus found in soil is used to make UK-based Quorn, the leading imitation meat product produced by fermentation.[124]

(G) Real Meat and Fish from Animal Cells

Fermentation technology can now be used to grow animal cells in tissue culture. The product, cultured meat, is genuine meat, made without the need to raise and kill farm animals.[125] The first cultured beef burger was produced by Dutch scientist Mark Post. He demonstrated his burger on live TV in 2013.[126] It had been made painstakingly in the lab over three months, at a cost of €250,000 ($325,000).

Animal cells are harder to culture than microbes. They require special molecules in the culture medium to direct their growth. So cultured meat is much costlier to produce than microbial protein. While costs have come down with experience and new ideas, it remains unclear whether cell culture can ever compete with meat from livestock. Nevertheless, many companies are vying for the cultured meat market. Scaling up the technology enough to bring costs lower is a major challenge.[127] But in 2021, Believer Meats announced it could make nearly a pound of cultured chicken for $7.70.[128] And the company Eat Just announced plans for a facility capable of making 30 million pounds of cultured meat a year.[129]

As of 2024, cultured meat has been approved for sale in just two countries, Singapore and the United States. Its sale is opposed by farmers, leading to outright bans in Italy[130] and in the states of Alabama, Iowa, and Florida.[131]

Cultured seafood is also on the way.[132] It would help ease the pressure of overfishing on wild sea creature populations. Seafood is somewhat easier to culture than meat.[133] Aquatic animal cells tolerate low temperature, low oxygen conditions, and a wider range of acidity better than land animals do. And seafood tissue is less complex than that of meat. Also, in terms of cost, cultured seafood has an advantage because farmed or wild-caught seafood is more expensive than meat. Wildtype, a cell-based fish developer, has raised major investment capital and has demonstrated its sushi-grade salmon in private tastings.[134] Production costs, currently over $500 per pound, would have to drop 50-fold to achieve parity with farmed salmon.

(H) Milk Too from Cell Culture

Milk from cell culture is coming too. For some time, milk proteins, like whey and casein, have been produced from microbes grown in fermenters.[135] They can be processed into milklike cheese and ice cream. But many companies now aim to produce real milk from cell culture.[136] Real milk has many nutritional components that are absent in products made from microbial milk proteins. An important goal is to make cultured milk with the same properties as human breast milk,[137] as baby formula is often in short supply.

Some companies grow cells from cow mammary glands and trigger them with signal proteins to produce milk.[138] Others are growing special cells from milk itself. In the latter group is Senara, the first cultured milk start-up in Europe.[139] It hopes to collaborate with the dairy industry to integrate the technology with traditional milk production. It remains to be seen which technology succeeds in producing cultured milk at a competitive price and how the dairy industry and consumers will respond to this development.

(I) Combatting Food Waste

One-third of all the food produced worldwide is never consumed.[140] It is wasted. Reducing food waste has huge consequences for the environment. Food conservation, like energy conservation, has immediate environmental benefits. It saves the fertilizer, the pesticides, and the farm machinery fuel that gets spent on the wasted food.

Much food spoils between harvest and market. Small farms, which feed about 70 percent of the world's people,[141] lose produce if they can't distribute it efficiently. As discussed above in the information technology section, small farms can greatly improve efficiency through cell phone technology. Lack of refrigeration is a big contributor to food losses. About one-quarter of the food produced in low-income tropical areas spoils for lack of refrigeration.[142] In Bangladesh, spoilage amounts to half the food produced. To combat this loss, the Golden Harvest food company in Bangladesh bought refrigerated trucks, freezers, and cold storage units to help their suppliers get fresh produce to market.[143] In Rwanda, the UN-supported Africa Center of Excellence for Sustainable Cooling and Cold Chain is developing solar panel–powered freezer chests, battery-operated long-haul refrigerated container trucks, and community cooling hubs.[144]

In high-income countries, a great deal of produce is left unharvested (up to one-third of the total in the United States[145]) when market prices are unfavorable. But at least the unharvested crops are left in the field, returning nutrients to the soil. More serious are losses from unsold food or from overshopping by consumers, most of which ends up in landfills. The food waste in high-income countries is equivalent to the total food production in sub–Saharan Africa.[146]

Many creative efforts to combat the food waste problem are underway. The nonprofit Free-Go has rolled out refrigerators and pantry shelves on the streets of Geneva, Switzerland, where restaurateurs and home cooks can leave food before it goes bad. Passers-by can take it home for free.[147] In the United States, companies like Imperfect Foods and Misfits Market allow customers to buy at a discount perfectly good food that would otherwise be thrown out because it doesn't look quite right.[148] In Canada, the nonprofits Food Stash Foundation,[149] the Leftovers Foundation,[150] and Second Harvest[151] redistribute food free of charge that would otherwise go to the landfill. Many restaurants and grocery stores in the United States cooperate with food banks to get surplus food to those in need.[152]

South Korea claims to have essentially eliminated food waste through a compulsory composting program.[153] Throwing food into landfills is prohibited, and everyone receives bags for their food scraps. These are collected at the curb and the contents are converted into animal feed, biogas, and fertilizer.

If we eliminated food waste across all sectors, we could feed every undernourished person on the planet, twice over.[154] The environment would benefit too.

12. Where Are We Now?

In sum, we are at a critical juncture in food production. Synthetic fertilizer and the Green Revolution saved billions of people from hunger. But growth in crop yields is slowing. The world population continues to grow and will likely reach 10 billion before it levels off. Growing more food currently means clearing more land for agriculture at the expense of already threatened forests. And global warming will add more stress to both agriculture and forests.

At the same time, the environmental damages from current and past practices need to be fixed. Crop rotation, cover crops, and no-till planting can help stop soil loss from erosion. Over time, these methods rebuild soil and reduce the need for herbicides and pesticides. They also reduce the need for fertilizer. Applying less fertilizer, and timing it to the growth of the crops, minimizes excess fertilizer that releases nitrous oxide, a powerful greenhouse gas, and that washes into waterways, promoting destructive algal blooms.

Productivity gains will come from development of drought-, flood-, and salt-tolerant crops, through plant crossbreeding and genetic modification. Genetic engineering can be used to improve the nutritional quality of plants. Greenhouses and vertical farms boost productivity further by protecting plants from the elements and using precise lighting, irrigation, and fertilization. The extra energy required should come from renewable sources. Properly run fish and shellfish farms will make a major contribution to the food supply.

Urban farming offers fresh produce to city dwellers and community gardens. It builds social trust and helps feed marginalized people. Information technologies play a vital role. Smartphone apps help small farms in developing countries market their produce, reduce spoilage, and boost productivity. Precision agriculture, using sensors for crop yield and for soil moisture and acidity, helps limit fertilizer and pesticide additions, thereby reducing energy and environmental impacts.

A major concern is our appetite for meat. A large share of agricultural production goes to feed livestock, especially cattle. Eating less meat would shift agricultural resources to more and better plant-based food for humans. But dietary preferences are hard to change. "Fake meat" from plant or microbial protein may help make this shift. Real meat, fish, and milk made with cell culture are on the horizon, but it may be a long time before they become widely available. Meanwhile, reducing food waste is the most effective way to increase food availability and reduce the environmental costs of food production.

11

Sustainability

What Will We Leave to the Future?

Topics:

1. Sustainability? What is it?
2. Unsustainability: The Great Salt Lake
3. Sustainable business: Action versus "greenwashing"
4. The saga of fossil fuels
5. Environmental justice
6. Carbon footprint and carbon offsets
7. The circular economy
8. Resilience and the long view
9. Summary

---

1. Sustainability? What Is It?

You hear the word "sustainability" everywhere. Sustainable agriculture and sustainable forestry are frequent topics. And so are sustainable manufacturing, sustainable fashion, and sustainable business. Figure 80 shows how often the word is used in printed books. It appeared more and more often after "sustainable development" was introduced into international development negotiations in 1987.[1] Gro Harlem Brundtland, Norway's former prime minister and chair of the World Commission on Environment and Development, defined sustainable development as "development that meets the needs of the present without compromising the ability of future generations to meet their own needs."[2] In short, we want to leave the world at least as well off as we found it. A worthy goal, certainly, but how do we achieve it?

Sustainability Ngram

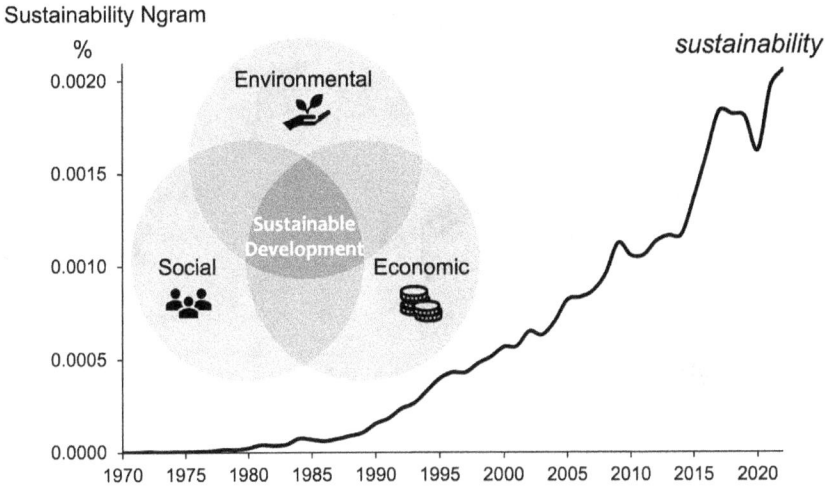

FIGURE 80. How often the term "sustainability" is used in print, from the Google Books Ngram Viewer, http://books.google.com/ngrams. The overlapping spheres represent the three main components of sustainable development: environmental, economic, and social.

2. Unsustainability: The Great Salt Lake

It's hard to be sure whether something is sustainable but easy to see what is not. Pumping aquifers faster than they can recharge is one example (Chapter 7). Cutting down rainforests is another (Chapter 9). So is letting bare fields erode their soil (Chapter 10).

Here is a less obvious but dramatic example. Utah's Great Salt Lake is a wonder of nature. An inland sea with no outlet for its water, it sits under a baking sun much of the year. As the water evaporates, it leaves salts behind. The lake is saltier than the ocean. The shores are white with evaporated salts, which include valuable minerals, such as magnesium and lithium, that are mined there. Tiny brine shrimp and flies thrive in the lake. They provide food for 12 million hungry birds that stop there during migration.[3]

The water level goes up and down from year to year. It is set by the balance between evaporation from the lake and inflow to the lake. The inflow is from rainwater and snowmelt on the nearby mountains. But much of the inflow has been diverted to agriculture and to economic development around rapidly growing Salt Lake City. And global warming has increased the air temperature and lengthened droughts, evaporating water before it reaches the lake.[4] The area of the lake, 3,300 square miles in the 1980s, had shrunk to less than 1,000 square miles in 2022 (Figure 81).[5] And the water is saltier. Soon it will be too salty for the algae, which feed the brine shrimp

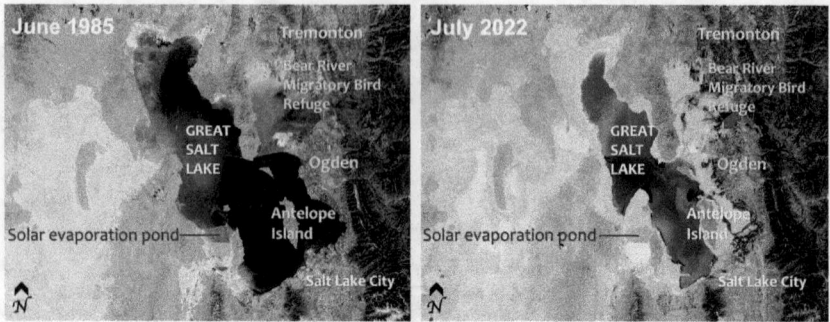

FIGURE 81. Satellite images of the Great Salt Lake in 1985 and 2022. Credit: NASA Earth Observatory images by Joshua Stevens, using Landsat data from the U.S. Geological Survey, https://earthobservatory.nasa.gov/images/150187/the-great-shrinking-lake.

and flies. If these disappear, the flocks of migratory birds will have nothing to eat. Also, the famous Wasatch ski resorts will be in trouble as dust from the lake darkens the snow and hastens its melting.[6] Most ominous of all, the lake's salt contains toxic arsenic, which will contaminate the dust that settles over Salt Lake City.[7]

Can the lake be saved? Just to balance evaporation, the lake would need 30 percent more inflow from the watershed.[8] To bring the lake back to a level needed to cover the already exposed dust spots would take a lot more inflow. Conservation groups have been working for years to alert people to the problem and to press the Utah legislature for action. But water conservation has yet to take hold in Salt Lake City. It uses twice as much water per person as does similarly dry Tucson, Arizona.[9] Lawns are kept watered and green in Salt Lake City, while Tucson has replaced most lawns with desert landscaping. Salt Lake City charges up to five times less for water than Tucson.[10]

Inflow waters are diverted mainly for agriculture. As in the rest of the U.S. Southwest, irrigation and abundant sunshine make commercial crops highly profitable. The principal crop is hay for cattle feed, which is mainly exported. Utah produces less than 3 percent of its own fruits and vegetables, importing the rest.[11] Restoring significant inflow to the Great Salt Lake would require big changes in irrigation practices[12] and in current water rights.[13] Increased publicity about the condition of the Great Salt Lake led the Utah government to adopt significant water conservation legislation in 2022.[14] Whether the Salt Lake region is ultimately sustainable will depend on difficult negotiations among the stakeholders who use the increasingly stressed water supply. Most of the U.S. Southwest faces similar painful negotiations over water.

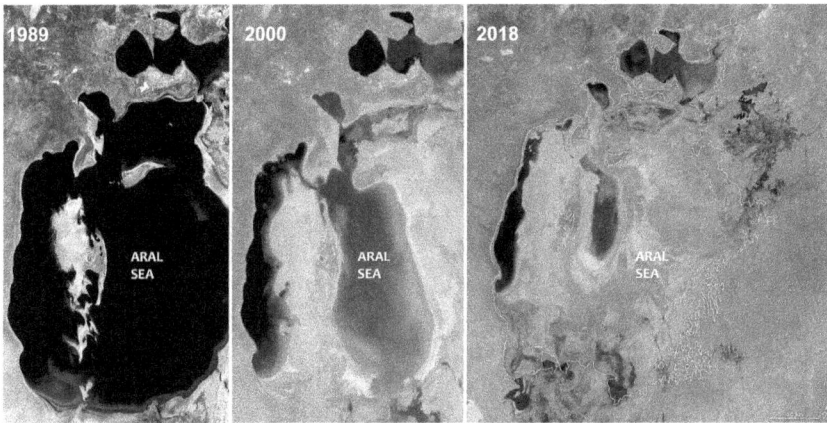

FIGURE 82. Satellite images of the Aral Sea. Credit: NASA/Goddard Space Flight Center, https://earthobservatory.nasa.gov/images/3730/aral-sea and https://earthobservatory.nasa.gov/world-of-change/AralSea.

A much worse case of agriculture-induced drying out is the near disappearance of central Asia's Aral Sea, once the world's fourth largest lake, now reduced to one-tenth of its historic size[15] (Figure 82).

The Aral Sea is shared by Kazakhstan and Uzbekistan. During the Soviet era, the waters of the two rivers feeding the Aral Sea were diverted to expand agricultural production, particularly cotton. Uzbekistan became a leading producer of cotton, which remains the country's main cash crop. Meanwhile, the lake steadily shrank, producing an ecological disaster. As the water diminished, it became steadily saltier. A once thriving fishing industry collapsed as the fish died out. The remaining water was increasingly polluted by runoff from the cotton fields, which required increasing applications of fertilizer and pesticides because of diminishing soil quality. As the lake bed dried out, dust storms filled the air with salt and toxic chemicals, with dire effects on the health of people living in the area.[16]

Only two small portions of the Aral Sea remain. Kazakhstan has begun to refresh the small, remaining northern portion of the lake by improving irrigation channels and building a dam to limit outflow to the southern portion.[17] The small southern portion lies in cotton-dependent Uzbekistan, which has not acted to restore the water.[18]

3. Sustainable Business: Action Versus "Greenwashing"

Sustainability has become a watchword for corporations. They respond to pressures from the public and their own shareholders.

Businesses have started to cut emissions, dispose properly of their waste, and source products from fair-trade organizations. These practices can also benefit their bottom line by saving costs and improving sales. Examples described earlier in Chapter 7 include the Mars Co. project to improve rice farming among its Indian suppliers and L'Oréal's cleaning and reusing all its wastewater. Another example is a new wastewater treatment plant in Ahmedabad, India, to supply recycled wash water for denim manufacture. It was built by retailer Gap Inc. with its textile partner Arvind Ltd.[19] It allows Arvind's denim plant to stop using fresh water from the water-stressed community. The apparel industry is one of the most intensive users of water in the world. Making a pair of jeans takes 7,500 liters of water, seven times what a person needs to drink in a year. And clothing sales have increased 60 percent in the past 15 years.[20]

Many companies have set sustainability goals. Over 400 promised to use only renewable energy by various dates between 2020 and 2050.[21] Another 250-plus companies have pledged that by 2025, they will only use plastic packaging that is reusable, recyclable, or compostable. The packaging initiative is backed by a number of various governmental and financial organizations.[22] But although plastic bottles are easy to recycle, beverage makers are far short of their current recycling targets. In the United States, only 29 percent of plastic bottles were recycled in 2022.[23] The rate is over 70 percent in Europe.[24]

Sustainability pledges make for good public relations and give companies an edge over their competition. But critics charge that the pledges are really "greenwashing." Often the pledges lack detail on how to reach the goals and leave action to sometime in the future. Notably, the median length of time that corporate CEOs stay on the job is five years[25]; they know they will not be around when the pledges come due. Sometimes companies improve their environmental profile by moving polluting operations to other countries or by selling polluting business units to owners who are less environmentally motivated. And sustainability practices that companies advertise may only involve part of their operations while the rest remain polluting.

Increasingly, investors use environmental, social, and governance (ESG) criteria as guides to where to put their money. Corporations prepare sustainability reports on what they are doing with regard to pollution, waste management, energy efficiency, labor standards, customer and community relations, audits, company leadership, and stakeholders' rights.[26] Over 4,300 financial institutions have joined the UN-sponsored Principles for Responsible Investment,[27] promising to follow ESG principles and to report regularly on their progress. But corporations must make profits to survive. To make expensive changes, they need government incentives or regulations. Otherwise, they may be undercut by less motivated competitors. And government measures require political will, which in turn needs an involved public. Tariq Fancy, former chief investment officer of sustainable investing for BlackRock, the largest asset management firm on the planet, argues that sustainable investment is "a dangerous placebo that harms the public interest."[28] It distracts attention from the need to enact needed regulations.

4. The Saga of Fossil Fuels

Fossil fuels are clearly not sustainable. They took millions of years to form. But once dug up and burned, they are gone. And burning them produces the greenhouse gases that warm the globe. Damage from climate change is already apparent, and it will get much worse unless we stop using fossil fuels. If we do, not only would we slow down climate change, but air pollution would mostly stop, improving health and saving millions of lives.

But we can't get rid of fossil fuels, at least not rapidly. We are dependent on them for all aspects of modern life: for heating and cooling, for cooking and cleaning, for transportation and shipping. The economy would grind to a halt without fossil fuels. And the fossil fuel companies work tirelessly against actions that would curb production, as chronicled in Chapter 3. They enjoy large subsidies and are able to keep them in place[29] despite repeated calls for their elimination[30] and an international agreement to phase them out.[31]

Fossil fuel companies are themselves getting into the sustainability act. They invest in renewable energy, hedging their bets against the day when extracting fossil fuels will no longer be profitable. And they advertise their sustainability credentials. Peabody Energy, the largest coal company in the United States, promises "net-zero" greenhouse gas emissions by 2050.[32] It has launched a renewable energy company that will develop enough solar energy and storage batteries to supply 2 million homes.[33] But this impressive amount of energy pales in comparison with Peabody's coal deposits, which it continues to mine and market. Despite its sustainability claims, Peabody was at the top of the list of "most polluting companies" in 2023.[34] All the major oil companies invest in and advertise low-carbon energy projects. Yet almost 90 percent of their investments are for oil production.[35]

Whatever one thinks of their past actions, the coal and oil companies will have to engage in the long path to replacing fossil fuels with clean energy[36] (Figure 83). In addition to their renewable energy investments,

FIGURE 83. The past and the future? Old oil pump with wind turbines in the background in West Texas. Photo by Larry Syverson, via Flickr, https://www.flickr.com/photos/124651729@N04/52289130064/; https://creativecommons.org/licenses/by-sa/2.0/.

they are positioned to advance carbon capture and storage (Chapter 3) and geothermal energy since they excel in the drilling and pipeline technologies.

One company, Danish Oil and Gas Energy, has set an example by transitioning completely to renewable energy and renaming itself Ørsted. (Ørsted was the Danish scientist who discovered the connection between electricity and magnetism.) The largest power provider in Denmark, it reduced its coal use by 80 percent, with plans to phase coal out entirely. It divested its oil and gas operations and is now the world's leading producer of windpower.[37]

5. Environmental Justice

In the summer of 2022, the annual monsoon brought record torrential rains to Pakistan. The spring had been extremely hot, with record temperatures up to 51°C (124°F).[38] The monsoon winds picked up extra moisture from the warmed Arabian Sea to the south. The heat had also increased snowmelt from the Himalayan mountains to the north.[39] Rivers burst their banks, and one-third of the country was soon under water

FIGURE 84. Flood in Pakistan 2022. Photo by Ali Hyder Junejo via Flickr, https://www.flickr.com/photos/193804179@N08/52324916494; https://creativecommons.org/licenses/by/2.0/.

(Figure 84). Over 1,700 people died and over 33 million were displaced.[40] Losses included nearly 1 million livestock and up to 90 percent of the country's main crops.[41] Flood damage is estimated at $30 billion.

Deforestation made matters worse. For decades Pakistan lost about 1 percent of its forest every year, and now less than 5 percent of its land is forested.[42] Vast areas were cleared to produce new farmland to feed a growing population. Torrents of water rushed off bare hillsides, washing away soil and silting up reservoirs and irrigation canals. The country had started an ambitious reforestation plan, with millions of trees planted since 2017.[43] Sadly, many saplings were carried away by the floods.

Yet Pakistan, with 3 percent of the world's population, contributes less than 1 percent of greenhouse gas emissions.[44] Other low-income countries of the Global South also bear the brunt of climate change—drought and flooding, sea level rise, and the threatened disappearance of low-lying islands—even though they contribute little to greenhouse gas emissions. The disparities are stark. Since 1850, the United States, with 4 percent of the world's population, has emitted 20 percent of all greenhouse gases, while China and India, with 17 percent of the population each, have emitted 11 percent and 3.4 percent, respectively, of greenhouse gases.[45]

Recognizing the historical injustice, the high-income countries of the world have established several climate funds, starting in 2009 with a promise to give $100 billion annually in climate aid to low-income countries.[46] But it has taken till 2022 to reach the goal.[47] Moreover, that $100 billion is inflated: just one-quarter of it is designated as grants, and the rest are market-rate loans, which must eventually be repaid by already debt-stressed countries.[48] About two-thirds of the aid has gone for emission-reduction projects and only one-third for climate adaptation.[49]

Environmental injustice also arises within each country. Low-income people bear the brunt of environmental damages. They occupy the most flood-prone areas and make up the bulk of those displaced by rising waters. But even when they occupy higher ground, poor people suffer displacement through "climate gentrification,"[50] when the higher ground becomes more desirable because it is protected from flooding. In coastal areas, high-price seashore properties lose value as the seas rise from global warming.

The Florida coast was once populated by people of color. They were pushed inland, around the turn of the 20th century when people of means moved into new seashore developments.[51] Communities of Black and Hispanic people formed along an elevated stretch of land a few miles east of Miami.[52] Now property values along this ridge are going up as rising sea level threatens coastal property. Wealthier Miami residents, not willing to pay for higher seawalls or the increased cost of flood insurance, are moving up to the ridge, pricing out low-income longtime residents.

Subsistence farmers are particularly affected by both flooding and drought. Many abandon their farms and migrate to overpopulated cities or try and make it to richer countries to work as migrant labor. Poor urban communities are often congested and are hotter than the rest of the city because they lack shade trees and greenery. Poor people also suffer more from pollution than others. Often, they live near mines and smelters, refineries, and chemical plants. They also live on busy roadways, breathing in car and truck exhaust. Their homes are older and expose them to more lead through corroding lead paint or aging lead pipes. They have less access to clean water, especially in low-income countries that lack adequate water treatment or wells. And they have less access to medical care than wealthier people, often delaying medical attention until their conditions become serious, more difficult to treat, and more expensive.

What poor people endure shows where environmental protection is weakest. If their concerns are addressed, society benefits, and the world becomes a more livable place. Environmental justice is drawing increased attention from governments and from environmental organizations that empower vulnerable communities and work for environmental justice in government programs.

Around the world, local groups help poor people to work for better conditions.[53] An example is GreenRoots,[54] an organization that pulls together residents of Chelsea, a poor city sandwiched between Boston's Logan airport and a major road bridge. Its population is heavily Latino, and half are first-generation immigrants. GreenRoots fought off the construction of a diesel power plant next to an elementary school. It helped create walkable green spaces on Chelsea's riverfront, which was otherwise dominated by fuel tanks and piles of road salt. GreenRoots cultivates urban gardens and supplies a local food pantry with its produce. It recruits local youth, who gain growing and harvesting experience and leadership skills.

6. Carbon Footprint and Carbon Offsets

Our carbon footprint is the total amount of greenhouse gases generated by our actions. Dividing the total global emissions, about 40 billion tons,[55] by the world population, eight billion, works out to about five tons per person, the equivalent of two round-trip flights between New York and Singapore.[56] To limit the global temperature rise to 1.5°C, this average needs to be cut nearly in half.[57]

But in the United States, Australia, and Canada, the average footprint is much larger, 15 tons per person, or 45 tons per average household.[58] What activities produce these greenhouse gas emissions? Food for the household contributes around 15 percent to the total, while the home (heating, cooling, maintenance) accounts for 27 percent, and travel accounts for 32 percent.[59] The rest is for goods and services.

So travel produces the biggest share of household emissions. Large emission reductions would come from switching from cars to buses and bicycles or to small electric cars for commuting and shopping. Limiting air travel would help. Home heating and cooling is the next biggest share. So better insulation and more efficient temperature control, using heat pumps, would decrease the carbon footprint a lot. Food is important too. Reducing food waste and eating less meat, which contributes one-third to the total food emission, would have a significant impact.

A number of online calculators or simple questionnaires are available to estimate an individual's own carbon footprint.[60] And there are many actions that can lower an individual's footprint in addition to those listed above. One can remember to turn off the TV and turn out lights in unoccupied rooms, clean and replace home air filters, turn down the thermostat and get outside more. One can also buy more efficient appliances and do the laundry in cold water with cold-water detergents[61] to avoid heating all that water.

Another thing to do is buy "carbon offsets," also called "carbon credits" or "climate contributions."[62] These are shares of projects that reduce greenhouse gas emissions elsewhere or that take up and store CO_2, thereby compensating for the emissions one creates.[63] The projects can involve planting trees, building renewable energy, improving energy efficiency, or capturing methane from landfills. Reforestation in tropical countries with few resources to protect their forests is a popular choice. Some programs are designed to also benefit local and Indigenous communities.

But how do we know that these projects really do lower greenhouse gas concentrations?[64] Here are two issues about whether projects really work as advertised:

- Additionality: Would the carbon targets be met even without the project? For example, California has a law requiring landfills to capture the methane they generate. So a methane-capture project in California would not qualify as an offset since it would have to be done anyway.
- Longevity: Will the project have a lasting effect? Newly planted trees do take up CO_2, but the effect doesn't last if the tree dies before it matures. So a reforestation project must be adequately maintained. And a project to prevent deforestation of a certain area by illegal logging doesn't have much effect if the loggers simply move elsewhere.

Certification programs grapple with these questions and offer assurances through careful monitoring of the offset projects.[65] Their methods are under constant scrutiny.[66] They have sometimes been criticized for overcounting the amount of emission reductions.[67] The stakes are high because major corporations buy offsets to fulfill their "net-zero" emission goals. If the emission savings claimed for the offsets are illusory, then the offsets become just another instance of greenwashing. But certified projects do reduce emissions.[68]

The most important actions are those of corporations, governments, and other organizations.[69] Some of them are moving to cut greenhouse gas emissions, cut pollution, and promote environmental justice. But there is much inertia to overcome. These actors need pressure from society to do the right thing. Many organizations offer a path to get informed and get involved in pressing for action, such as the World Wildlife Fund,[70] the Natural Resource Defense Council,[71] and the Union of Concerned Scientists.[72]

7. The Circular Economy

We need a new way of doing business if we want to stop global warming, eliminate waste and pollution, and prevent further degradation of our environment. These problems stem from our current practice of extracting resources from the earth, consuming what we make, and then throwing the rest away in a linear economy. What if, instead, we designed what we make to be reused or returned to nature in the form we found it? This would be a circular economy, a closed loop of material with no waste. It would be truly sustainable.

Here is a diagram of how a circular economy would work (Figure 85). The left side of the circle indicates what would happen to products when we are finished with them. They would all be collected and recycled, or returned to nature as compost. Recycling would involve remanufacturing or else recovering materials.

The right side of the circle represents the production system. Recovered material would be used as far as possible, while extraction of raw material from the earth would be held to a minimum. New products would be designed for endurance and disassembly and for minimal waste during production. Pollution from manufacturing would be tightly controlled, and product distribution would be as efficient as possible.

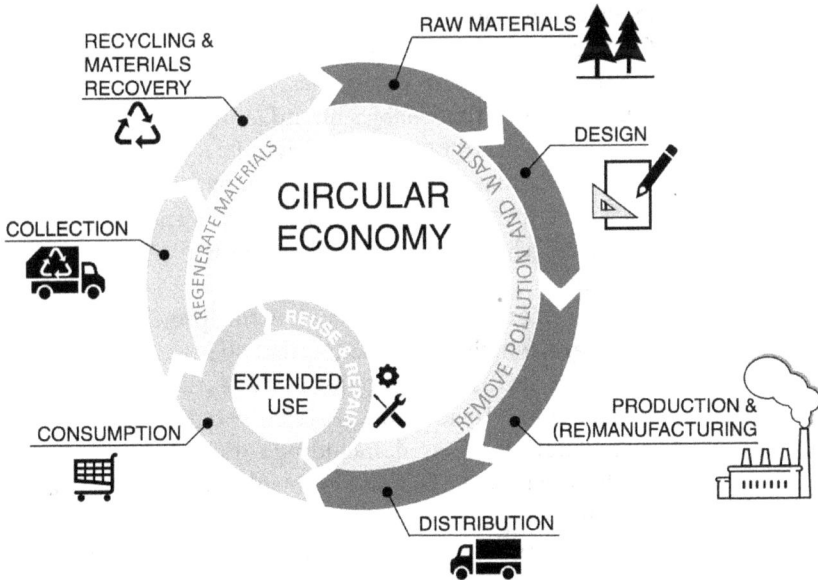

FIGURE 85. The circular economy. Adapted from "The Circular Economy in Philadelphia," Circular Philadelphia, accessed July 10, 2024, https://circular philadelphia.org/the-circular-economy-in-philadelphia/.

The small inner circle represents extended use of products. They would be used, repaired, and reused as long as possible.

There is a broad movement toward a circular economy based on sharing, leasing, reuse, repair, and recycling. The European Commission has a circular economy action plan with targets for waste reduction and reuse.[73] And the Ellen MacArthur Foundation brings together business, government, and nonprofit groups around the world to promote steps toward a circular economy.[74]

But we have a long way to go because material extraction (mines, timber, etc.) keeps increasing worldwide. In 2023, extracted material came to 100 billion tons, having more than tripled since 1970.[75] Only a small fraction of it is cycled back into the economy, and the fraction actually shrank, from 9.1 percent in 2018 to 7.2 percent in 2022.[76] It will take a massive effort over time to reverse these trends. Still, a number of businesses and organizations are pointing the way by introducing products and services whose goal is waste elimination. Examples include:[77]

- Low-cost furniture giant IKEA is establishing secondhand stores to sell used IKEA furniture, which it buys back from customers.
- Burger King fast food chain is introducing reusable packaging for which it adds a small deposit charge, refundable when customers return the boxes and cups. These are cleaned and reprocessed by TerraCycle, a New Jersey–based company that facilitates recycling for consumer goods companies.[78] TerraCycle developed a circular reuse platform that enables manufacturers, retailers, and consumers to shift toward reusable packaging.
- Sportswear giant Adidas is making a shoe out of a single material, thermoplastic polyurethane, which can be melted and recast. It is marketed as the "shoe customers will never own" since Adidas takes them back.[79]
- Another circular economy example is a housing project near Aarhus, Denmark, which is designed so that 90 percent of its building components can be demounted and reused at the building's end of life.[80] In addition, recycled or renewable construction materials are used, including cork and old newspapers for the facades, eelgrass for insulation, and used car tires for underflooring.
- And helping to eliminate waste, there are repair cafés all around Europe and now spreading worldwide. These free meeting places provide tools and tips to people who want to fix appliances, electronics, bicycles, toys, furniture, and clothes rather than throwing them out.[81]

So lots of people are pushing the giant wheel of the circular economy.[82] Their example may inspire enough others to push the wheel up to speed.

8. Resilience and the Long View

Human beings are tremendously resourceful in the face of challenges. Beneath the litany of bad news, people around the globe have improved their living conditions; there are now more middle-class people in India than in the United States.[83] With so many minds newly freed from pre-occupation with survival, the pace of social and technological innovation accelerates.

(A) Empowering Young People and Women

India's Thoughtshop Foundation[84] empowers young people to think and act with "empathy and purpose" through community organizations at 100 locations, from the slums of Kolkata to remote villages in West Bengal. Using cards, games, and illustrated books, Thoughtshop trains young mentors to engage young people in their communities in conversations on taboo topics like gender equality, sexual violence, and early marriage.

Empowering women is the most effective way to improve living conditions in traditional societies. In Dandora, Kenya, one of the poorest and most dangerous neighborhoods of Nairobi, Positive Young Women's Voices runs women's empowerment workshops.[85] They provide training in vocational skills, and dialogues with families and men about gender-based violence. Women taking part receive stipends, often their only income. Positive Young Women's Voices also distributes sanitary pads to combat "menstrual poverty." Women who can't afford the pads often stay home from school or work during their periods and suffer dire economic consequences.

(B) Farms and Gardens

Resilience can be found everywhere. In rural Texas, a one-acre community garden in the middle of a former coal mine helps feed 2,000 people a month at nearby food pantries.[86] In North Carolina, struggling small-scale-farm owners, many of them Black, are benefiting from leasing some of their property for solar panels. The income per acre is greater than what they would get from renting the land for farming. Most solar panel arrays are massive; they are designed to generate grid power. But Ener-Wealth Solutions is building smaller-scale community solar networks[87] with the aim of helping small farm owners stay on their land, and maintain farming communities.

(C) Housing

Housing projects can build in resilience. Hunters Point, a Florida community, is the world's first certified zero-energy residential development. It produces more energy than it consumes. All 86 homes have 14 solar panels and a 12-kilowatt-hour home battery.[88] On a typical afternoon, the panels produce 35 percent more electricity than the house needs.[89] The extra electricity is used to charge the battery and is also sold back to the grid to help it balance supply and demand. When demand is high, the grid can draw on the batteries, which become a virtual power plant. That reduces the need to build additional gas-fired power plants as backup.

The batteries are critical when the grid power goes down. Hurricanes Ian and Idalia left millions of Florida residents without power in 2022 and 2023, respectively But the lights and refrigerators stayed on in Hunters Point. Because the community sits on a low peninsula, its streets are elevated 3.5 feet above ground level, and a low-lying central park drains water off the roads after a flood. The homes are built over first-floor garages, so all the rooms are 17 feet above sea level. The walls are designed to withstand 150-mile-per-hour winds.[90] The solar power and storm-proofing make Hunters Point resilient well into the future.

(D) Restoring Urban Rivers

Bringing nature back to cities is the aim of other resilience projects. Seattle, like most other cities, was built over many streams, sending them into concrete channels and drainage pipes. But in 1999, Chinook salmon, which had spawned in all the streams, were listed under the U.S. Endangered Species Act, which required the city to help them out. Engineers tried reintroducing some curves in the channelized streams and added tree trunks and boulders for habitat, but salmon didn't return.[91]

A city biologist, Katherine Lynch, realized that channelization had scraped away the streams' "hyporheic zone," a biologically rich underlayer of gravel and sediment. Stream water filters down into this layer and mixes with upwelling groundwater. This cool zone regulates stream temperature and aeration as well as the movement of nutrients among the many organisms that live in and above it. With the help of a large group of volunteers, Lynch worked to revive Thornton Creek, which used to drain an 11.6 square mile urban watershed. The channelized creek had become polluted and regularly flooded adjacent roads, yards, and houses after storms. Storm runoff spills rapidly into channelized streams, which lack adjacent wetlands and a hyporheic zone to slow the flow. The city bought some of the streamside lots to create wetlands, scooped out portions of the creek, and layered in sediment and gravel to re-create a hyporheic zone. Stream water was pushed into the zone by adding logs and boulders to slow the flow. The zone was inoculated with microbes and invertebrates collected from a nearby river.[92]

After the restoration, nearby neighborhoods stopped flooding. The city saved money by dredging less often at the stream's outlet, where the fast-flowing water had previously dumped eroded sediment. There is expanded green space. Pollution has dropped significantly thanks to the filtering effect of the hyporheic zone. And three years after the restoration, Chinook salmon began returning to spawn.[93] Thornton Creek is a model for how stream restoration can benefit cities everywhere.

(E) Greening Cities

Here are two examples out of many projects to restore nature to cities. Since 1992, Singapore has had a "green plan" that includes a "city in nature" program.[94] Located close to the equator, Singapore is hot and humid. Because of its rapid economic development, the city has warmed twice as fast as the rest of the world.[95] Its six million people squeeze onto a 710-square-kilometer (274-square-mile) island, making it one of the most densely populated countries in the world. The streets and buildings absorb and trap the heat, which is made worse by the hot air blowing from air conditioners in all the commercial buildings and most of the residential homes.

But since 2006, Singapore has been turning itself into a "garden city," planting millions of trees and covering 47 percent of its area with vegetation.[96] Everywhere there are tree-lined streets, green spaces, and parks. Energy-neutral buildings dot the city (Figure 86). They are covered in greenery and are open to natural breezes, reducing the need for air-conditioning. New buildings are required to have as much greenery as was previously on the lot. Some have rooftop gardens open to the public. The greenery is pleasing to the eye. It also helps cool the building and the surrounding city. That reduces the energy needed for air-conditioning. And the vegetation helps clean the air.

Copenhagen, with greening on its agenda, has built a dramatic waste-to-energy power plant, with a park and grass ski slope on top (Figure 87)! Built on a formerly industrial island, the state-of-the-art power plant burns 450,000 tons of garbage a year, generating electricity for 30,000

FIGURE 86. Singapore's Park Royale Hotel, a dramatic example of its green buildings. Photo credit: Patrick Bingham-Hall/WOHA.

FIGURE 87. CopenHill park and grass ski slope in Copenhagen. Photo by Rasmus Hjortshøj, https://www.rasmushjortshoj.com/architectural-photo-02/copen hill.

homes and heat for 72,000 homes.[97] Covering the plant is CopenHill, a park with hiking trails, a fitness center, and the 1,475-foot (450-meter) artificial ski slope.[98] The park has 7,000 bushes, 300 pine and willow trees, and real grass in addition to the artificial bristles of the ski slope.[99]

(F) Future Generations

Native Americans believe that wise actions now should meet the needs of seven generations into the future. They take inspiration from the Iroquois Confederacy, founded in 1142, and its Great Law of Peace,[100] which also inspired the framers of the U.S. Constitution. The Great Law of Peace emphasizes cooperation and far-seeing leadership.

In 2015, the government of Wales adopted a Well-Being of Future Generations Act.[101] A groundbreaking piece of legislation, it embeds long-term thinking and intergenerational fairness into governance and decision-making. It requires public bodies to conduct regular assessments of their progress toward achieving sustainable development goals and to report publicly on their performance. Wales hopes to set an example of future-oriented collaborative governance for others to follow.[102]

These stories of resilience can inspire us to take the long view, whatever the future brings. When the press of problems weighs us down, we can be sustained by seeing ourselves in the progression of generations that brought us to the present moment and the future generations that succeed us.

9. Summary

The much-used word "sustainability" is hard to pin down, but examples of "unsustainability" are easy to find. The shrinking Great Salt Lake offers a cautionary tale. Businesses tout their sustainable practices, but many of the claims turn out to be greenwashing. Responsible investing is a way to support sustainable businesses.

Changing unsustainable systems is hard. Fossil fuels are a prime example. There is no easy, quick, or painless way to stop burning them, even though they are clearly causing global warming with all its dire consequences. These consequences, as well as pollution, fall most heavily on people with low incomes, so relieving environmental injustice addresses humanity's most basic environmental problems. Complementary individual, corporate, and government actions can reduce our carbon footprint as well as the pollution we produce.

Making our economy circular is the long-term solution to our environmental problems. By reusing and recycling all products, we can minimize both waste and extraction of raw materials. Existing, seemingly intractable, environmental problems are right now being addressed by resilient individuals and organizations that take the long view.

Chapter Notes

Introduction

1. Astronaut Ron Garan, *The Orbital Perspective: Lessons in Seeing the Big Picture from a Journey of 71 Million Miles* (Oakland, CA: Berrett-Koehler Publishers, 2015), eBook Collection (O'Reilly Academic).

2. John Muir, *Wilderness Essays* (Layton, UT: Gibbs Smith, 2011).

3. Rachel Carson, *Silent Spring* (Boston: Houghton Mifflin, 1962).

4. Paul R. Ehrlich, *The Population Bomb*, rev. ed. (Rivercity, MA: Rivercity Press, 1975).

5. Svante Arrhenius, "On the Influence of Carbonic Acid in the Air upon the Temperature of the Ground," *Philosophical Magazine and Journal of Science* 41, no. 251 (April 1, 1896): 237–76, https://doi.org/10.1080/14786449608620846; G.S. Callendar, "The Artificial Production of Carbon Dioxide and Its Influence on Temperature," *Quarterly Journal of the Royal Meteorological Society* 64, no. 275 (April 1, 1938): 223–40, https://doi.org/10.1002/qj.49706427503.

6. Gilbert N. Plass, "The Carbon Dioxide Theory of Climatic Change," *Tellus B: Chemical and Physical Meteorology* 8, no. 2 (May 1, 1956): 140–54, https://doi.org/10.1111/j.2153-3490.1956.tb01206.x.

Chapter 1

1. Iliana Magra, "Mexico Hailstorm Blankets Western Areas Under 3 Feet of Ice," *New York Times*, July 1, 2019, https://www.nytimes.com/2019/07/01/world/americas/mexico-hail-storm-guadalajara.html.

2. Jean Jouzel et al., "Orbital and Millennial Antarctic Climate Variability over the Past 800,000 Years," *Science* 317, no. 5839 (August 10, 2007): 793–96, https://doi.org/10.1126/science.1141038.

3. Andre Berger, "Milankovitch, the Father of Paleoclimate Modeling," *Climate of the Past* 17, no. 4 (August 24, 2021): 1727–33, https://doi.org/10.5194/cp-17-1727-2021.

4. Matthew B. Osman et al., "Globally Resolved Surface Temperatures Since the Last Glacial Maximum," *Nature* 599, no. 7884 (November 10, 2021): 239–44, https://doi.org/10.1038/s41586-021-03984-4.

5. Jessica Stoller-Conrad, "Tree Rings Provide Snapshots of Earth's Past Climate," *Climate Change: Vital Signs of the Planet*, January 25, 2017, https://climate.nasa.gov/news/2540/tree-rings-provide-snapshots-of-earths-past-climate.

6. Holli Riebeek, "Paleoclimatology: The Oxygen Balance," NASA Earth Observatory, May 6, 2005, https://earthobservatory.nasa.gov/features/Paleoclimatology_OxygenBalance.

7. Mauro Rubino et al., "A Revised 1000 Year Atmospheric $\delta[13]C\text{-}CO2$ Record from Law Dome and South Pole, Antarctica," *Journal of Geophysical Research: Atmospheres* 118, no. 15 (August 16, 2013): 8482–99, https://doi.org/10.1002/jgrd.50668.

8. Pierre Friedlingstein et al., "Global Carbon Budget 2022," *Earth System Science Data* 14, no. 11 (November 11, 2022): 4811–900, https://doi.org/10.5194/essd-14-4811-2022. Supplemental data to Global Carbon Budget 2022 (Version 1.0) downloaded from https://doi.org/10.18160/gcp-2022 on October 5, 2023.

9. National Aeronautics and Space Administration, "U.S. Standard Atmosphere, 1976," NASA-TM-X-74335. Washington, D.C.: U.S. Government Printing Office, October 1976.

10. Robert W. Howarth, "Methane Emissions and Climatic Warming Risk from Hydraulic Fracturing and Shale Gas Development: Implications for Policy," *Energy and Emission Control Technologies* 3 (October 8, 2015): 45–54, https://doi.org/10.2147/eect.s61539.

11. Robert B. Jackson et al., "Increasing Anthropogenic Methane Emissions Arise Equally from Agricultural and Fossil Fuel Sources," *Environmental Research Letters* 15, no. 7 (July 1, 2020): 071002, https://doi.org/10.1088/1748-9326/ab9ed2.

12. Hanqin Tian et al., "A Comprehensive Quantification of Global Nitrous Oxide Sources and Sinks," *Nature* 586, no. 7828 (October 7, 2020): 248–56, https://doi.org/10.1038/s41586-020-2780-0.

13. Veerabhadran Ramanathan, "Greenhouse Effect Due to Chlorofluorocarbons: Climatic Implications," *Science* 190, no. 4209 (October 3, 1975): 50–52, https://doi.org/10.1126/science.190.4209.50.

14. Peter G. Simmonds et al., "The Increasing Atmospheric Burden of the Greenhouse Gas Sulfur Hexafluoride (SF6)," *Atmospheric Chemistry and Physics* 20, no. 12 (June 23, 2020): 7271–90, https://doi.org/10.5194/acp-20-7271-2020.

15. Isaac M. Held and Brian J. Soden, "Water Vapor Feedback and Global Warming," *Annual Review of Energy and the Environment* 25 (November 1, 2000): 441–75, https://doi.org/10.1146/annurev.energy.25.1.441.

16. Jean-Baptiste Joseph Fourier, "Remarques générales sur les températures du globe terrestre et des espaces planétaires," *Annales de chimie et de physique* 27 (1824): 136–67.

17. Joseph D. Ortiz and Roland Jackson, "Understanding Eunice Foote's 1856 Experiments: Heat Absorption by Atmospheric Gases," *Notes and Records* 76, no. 1 (August 26, 2020): 67–84, https://doi.org/10.1098/rsnr.2020.0031.

18. John Tyndall, "I. The Bakerian Lecture—On the Absorption and Radiation of Heat by Gases and Vapours, and on the Physical Connexion of Radiation, Absorption, and Conduction," *Philosophical Transactions of the Royal Society of London* 151 (December 31, 1861): 1–36, https://doi.org/10.1098/rstl.1861.0001.

19. Svante Arrhenius, "On the Influence of Carbonic Acid in the Air upon the Temperature of the Ground," *Philosophical Magazine and Journal of Science* 41, no. 251 (April 1, 1896): 237–76, https://doi.org/10.1080/14786449608620846.

20. Geoffrey Supran, Stefan Rahmstorf, and Naomi Oreskes, "Assessing Exxon Mobil's Global Warming Projections," *Science* 379, no. 6628 (January 13, 2023): eabk0063, https://doi.org/10.1126/science.abk0063.

21. Philip Shabecoff, "Global Warming Has Begun, Expert Tells Senate," *New York Times*, June 24, 1988, https://www.nytimes.com/1988/06/24/us/global-warming-has-begun-expert-tells-senate.html.

22. Raymond Clémençon, "30 Years of International Climate Negotiations: Are They Still Our Best Hope?" *Journal of Environment & Development* 32, no. 2 (March 22, 2023): 114–46, https://doi.org/10.1177/10704965231163908.

23. United Nations Environment Programme, *Global Climate Litigation Report: 2023 Status Review*, https://doi.org/10.59117/20.500.11822/43008.

24. Phoebe Keane, "How the Oil Industry Made Us Doubt Climate Change," *BBC News*, September 19, 2020. https://www.bbc.com/news/stories-53640382.

Chapter 2

1. U.S. Department of Health and Human Services, "QuickStats: Deaths Involving Exposure to Excessive Heat, by Sex—National Vital Statistics System, United States, 1999–2020," *Morbidity and Mortality Weekly Report* 71, no. 34 (August 26, 2022): 1097, https://doi.org/10.15585/mmwr.mm7134a5.

2. Joan Ballester et al., "Heat-Related Mortality in Europe During the Summer of 2022," *Nature Medicine* 29 (July 10, 2023): 1857–66, https://doi.org/10.1038/s41591-023-02419-z.

3. Ondřej Lhotka and Jan Kyselý, "The 2021 European Heat Wave in the Context of Past Major Heat Waves," *Earth*

and Space Science 9, no. 11 (November 4, 2022): e2022EA002567, https://doi.org/10.1029/2022ea002567.

4. Daniel J. Vecellio, Qinqin Kong, W. Larry Kenney, and Matthew Huber, "Greatly Enhanced Risk to Humans as a Consequence of Empirically Determined Lower Moist Heat Stress Tolerance," *Proceedings of the National Academy of Sciences of the United States of America* 120, no. 42 (October 9, 2023): e2305427120, https://doi.org/10.1073/pnas.2305427120.

5. Michelle Broder Van Dyke, "14 Stories About the Lahaina Wildfire that Impacted Us," *Spectrum News*, December 22, 2023, https://spectrumlocalnews.com/hi/hawaii/news/2023/12/22/stories-lahaina-wildfire-2023.

6. Jean Lee, Jiachuan Wu, Didi Martinez, and Adiel Kaplan, "'This Is Not a Lahaina Problem': Once Unthinkable, Frequent Fires Are Hawaii's New Normal," *NBC News*, February 3, 2024, https://www.nbcnews.com/specials/hawaii-fire-scientists-warn-escalating-wildfire-threat/index.html.

7. "Wildfire and Acres. Total Wildland Fires and Acres (1983–2022)," National Interagency Fire Center, https://www.nifc.gov/fire-information/statistics/wildfires, accessed October 10, 2023.

8. Mark Binskin, Annabelle Bennett, and Andrew Macintosh, "Royal Commission into National Natural Disaster Arrangements: Report," Royal Commission into National Natural Disaster Arrangements, Commonwealth of Australia, October 30, 2020, https://apo.org.au/node/309191.

9. "Wildfire Graphs. Annual Area Burned in Canada," Canadian Interagency Forest Fire Centre, accessed December 4, 2023, https://ciffc.net/statistics.

10. Barry Saxifrage, "Managed to Death: How Canada Turned Its Forests into a Carbon Bomb," *Bulletin of the Atomic Scientists*, August 28, 2023, https://thebulletin.org/2023/08/managed-to-death-how-canada-turned-its-forests-into-a-carbon-bomb/.

11. Sofia Moutinho, "South American Rainforests Are on the Brink of Becoming Carbon Sources," *Eos, Transactions American Geophysical Union* 104 (October 17, 2023), https://doi.org/10.1029/2023eo230393.

12. Malin L. Pinsky et al., "Greater Vulnerability to Warming of Marine Versus Terrestrial Ectotherms," *Nature* 569, no. 7754 (April 24, 2019): 108–11, https://doi.org/10.1038/s41586-019-1132-4.

13. "Global Sea Level Time Series," NOAA Laboratory for Satellite Altimetry. Data downloaded on October 10, 2023, https://www.star.nesdis.noaa.gov/socd/lsa/SeaLevelRise/LSA_SLR_timeseries.php.

14. Rebecca Lindsey, "Climate Change: Global Sea Level," NOAA Climate, April 19, 2022, https://www.climate.gov/news-features/understanding-climate/climate-change-global-sea-level.

15. Stéphane Hallegatte, Colin Green, Robert J. Nicholls, and Jan Corfee-Morlot, "Future Flood Losses in Major Coastal Cities," *Nature Climate Change* 3 (August 18, 2013): 802–6, https://doi.org/10.1038/nclimate1979.

16. "Sea Ice Index," National Snow and Ice Data Center. Data downloaded from https://nsidc.org/arcticseaicenews/sea-ice-tools/ on October 11, 2023.

17. Joshua D. Stewart et al., "Boom-Bust Cycles in Gray Whales Associated with Dynamic and Changing Arctic Conditions," *Science* 382, no. 6667 (October 12, 2023): 207–11, https://doi.org/10.1126/science.adi1847.

18. "Ice Sheets: Why They Matter," National Snow and Ice Data Center, accessed January 24, 2024, https://nsidc.org/learn/parts-cryosphere/ice-sheets/-why-ice-sheets-matter.

19. Romain Millan et al., "Rapid Disintegration and Weakening of Ice Shelves in North Greenland," *Nature Communications* 14 (November 7, 2023): 6914, https://doi.org/10.1038/s41467-023-42198-2.

20. Benjamin J. Davison et al., "Annual Mass Budget of Antarctic Ice Shelves from 1997 to 2021," *Science Advances* 9, no. 41 (October 12, 2023): eadi0186, https://doi.org/10.1126/sciadv.adi0186.

21. "Slowdown of the Motion of the Ocean," NASA Science Editorial Team, March 18, 2024, https://science.nasa.gov/earth/earth-atmosphere/slowdown-of-the-motion-of-the-ocean/.

22. Peter Ditlevsen and Susanne Ditlevsen, "Warning of a Forthcoming Collapse of the Atlantic Meridional Overturning Circulation," *Nature Com-*

munications 14, no. 4254 (July 25, 2023): 1–12, https://doi.org/10.1038/s41467-023-39810-w.

23. Chuang Zhao et al., "Temperature Increase Reduces Global Yields of Major Crops in Four Independent Estimates," *Proceedings of the National Academy of Sciences of the United States of America* 114, no. 35 (August 15, 2017): 9326–31, https://doi.org/10.1073/pnas.1701762114.

24. Joseph Millard et al., "Key Tropical Crops at Risk from Pollinator Loss Due to Climate Change and Land Use," *Science Advances* 9, no. 41 (October 12, 2023): eadh0756, https://doi.org/10.1126/sciadv.adh0756.

25. "Sky Island Fire Ecology," U.S. National Park Service, https://www.nps.gov/articles/sky-island-fire-ecology.htm.

26. "Climate Change and Fungal Diseases," Centers for Disease Control and Prevention, National Center for Emerging and Zoonotic Infectious Diseases, November 30, 2023, https://www.cdc.gov/fungal/climate.html.

27. Arturo Casadevall, Dimitrios P. Kontoyiannis, and Vincent Robert, "On the Emergence of *Candida auris*: Climate Change, Azoles, Swamps, and Birds," *MBio* 10, no. 4 (July 23, 2019): e01397–19, https://doi.org/10.1128/mbio.01397-19.

28. "Malaria," World Health Organization, December 4, 2023, https://www.who.int/news-room/fact-sheets/detail/malaria.

29. Vera L. Trainer, Raphael M. Kudela, Matthew V. Hunter, Nicolaus G. Adams, and Ryan M. McCabe, "Climate Extreme Seeds a New Domoic Acid Hotspot on the U.S. West Coast," *Frontiers in Climate* 2 (December 14, 2020): 571836, https://doi.org/10.3389/fclim.2020.571836.

30. Ewen C.D. Todd, "Domoic Acid and Amnesic Shellfish Poisoning—A Review," *Journal of Food Protection* 56, no. 1 (January 1, 1993): 69–83, https://doi.org/10.4315/0362-028x-56.1.69.

31. Brooke Jarvis, "Climate Change Is Keeping Therapists Up at Night," *New York Times*, October 25, 2023, https://www.nytimes.com/2023/10/21/magazine/climate-anxiety-therapy.html.

32. Joseph Dodds, "The Psychology of Climate Anxiety," *BJPsych Bulletin* 45, no. 4 (May 19, 2021): 222–26, https://doi.org/10.1192/bjb.2021.18.

33. Alice C. Hill, "Climate Change and U.S. Property Insurance: A Stormy Mix," *Council on Foreign Relations*, August 17, 2023, https://www.cfr.org/article/climate-change-and-us-property-insurance-stormy-mix.

34. Andra J. Garner, "Observed Increases in North Atlantic Tropical Cyclone Peak Intensification Rates," *Scientific Reports* 13, no. 16299 (October 19, 2023): 1–12, https://doi.org/10.1038/s41598-023-42669-y.

35. "Hurricane Otis Causes Catastrophic Damage in Acapulco, Mexico," NOAA, National Environmental Satellite, Data, and Information Service, November 2, 2023, https://www.nesdis.noaa.gov/news/hurricane-otis-causes-catastrophic-damage-acapulco-mexico.

36. Thomas W. Corringham, F. Martin Ralph, Alexander Gershunov, Daniel R. Cayan, and Cary A. Talbot, "Atmospheric Rivers Drive Flood Damages in the Western United States," *Science Advances* 5, no. 12 (December 4, 2019), https://doi.org/10.1126/sciadv.aax4631.

37. Sarah Almukhtar, Blacki Migliozzi, John Schwartz, and Josh Williams, "The Great Flood of 2019: A Complete Picture of a Slow-Motion Disaster," *New York Times*, September 11, 2019, https://www.nytimes.com/interactive/2019/09/11/us/midwest-flooding.html.

38. Emily Fischer and Michael Carlowicz, "Research Shows More People Living in Floodplains," NASA Earth Observatory, September 2021, https://www.earthobservatory.nasa.gov/images/148866/research-shows-more-people-living-in-floodplains.

39. "The Great Texas Freeze: February 11–20, 2021," National Centers for Environmental Information (NCEI), February 24, 2023, https://www.ncei.noaa.gov/news/great-texas-freeze-february-2021.

40. Judah Cohen, Laurie Agel, Mathew Barlow, Chaim I. Garfinkel, and Ian White, "Linking Arctic Variability and Change with Extreme Winter Weather in the United States," *Science* 373, no. 6559 (September 1, 2021): 1116–21, https://doi.org/10.1126/science.abi9167.

41. Kathryn Cawdrey and Michael Carlowicz, "Warming Makes Droughts, Extreme Wet Events More Frequent, Intense," NASA Jet Propulsion Laboratory/California Institute of Technology, March 13, 2023, https://grace.jpl.nasa.

gov/news/151/warming-makes-droughts-extreme-wet-events-more-frequent-intense.

42. Eric Hunt et al., "Agricultural and Food Security Impacts from the 2010 Russia Flash Drought," *Weather and Climate Extremes* 34 (December 1, 2021): 100383, https://doi.org/10.1016/j.wace.2021.100383.

43. Lina Eklund et al., "Societal Drought Vulnerability and the Syrian Climate-Conflict Nexus Are Better Explained by Agriculture than Meteorology," *Communications Earth & Environment* 3 (April 6, 2022): 85, https://doi.org/10.1038/s43247-022-00405-w.

44. "Bangladesh: 2019 Article IV Consultation-Press Release; Staff Report; and Statement by the Executive Director for Bangladesh," International Monetary Fund, September 18, 2019, p. 19, https://www.imf.org/en/Publications/CR/Issues/2019/09/17/Bangladesh-2019-Article-IV-Consultation-Press-Release-Staff-Report-and-Statement-by-the-48682.

45. Pietro De Lellis, Manuel Ruiz Marín, and Maurizio Porfiri, "Modeling Human Migration Under Environmental Change: A Case Study of the Effect of Sea Level Rise in Bangladesh," *Earth's Future* 9, no. 4 (April 1, 2021): e2020EF001931, https://doi.org/10.1029/2020ef001931.

46. Intergovernmental Panel on Climate Change (IPCC), "Summary for Policymakers," in *Climate Change 2021—The Physical Science Basis: Working Group I Contribution to the Sixth Assessment Report of the Intergovernmental Panel on Climate Change*, 3–32 (Cambridge: Cambridge University Press, 2023), https://doi.org/10.1017/9781009157896.001.

47. Pierre Friedlingstein et al., "Global Carbon Budget 2022," *Earth System Science Data* 14, no. 11 (November 11, 2022): 4811–900, https://doi.org/10.5194/essd-14-4811-2022.

48. "Technical Dialogue of the First Global Stocktake. Synthesis Report by the Co-Facilitators on the Technical Dialogue," United Nations Framework Convention on Climate Change, September 8, 2023, https://unfccc.int/documents/631600.

49. Xiao Wu, Erik Sverdrup, Michael D. Mastrandrea, Michael W. Wara, and Stefan Wager, "Low-Intensity Fires Mitigate the Risk of High-Intensity Wildfires in California's Forests," *Science Advances* 9, no. 45 (November 10, 2023): eadi4123, https://doi.org/10.1126/sciadv.adi4123.

50. Yuanyuan Huang et al., "Impacts of Species Richness on Productivity in a Large-Scale Subtropical Forest Experiment," *Science* 362, no. 6410 (October 5, 2018): 80–83, https://doi.org/10.1126/science.aat6405.

51. Simon L. Lewis, Charlotte E. Wheeler, Edward T.A. Mitchard, and Alexander Koch, "Restoring Natural Forests Is the Best Way to Remove Atmospheric Carbon," *Nature* 568 (April 2, 2019): 25–28, https://doi.org/10.1038/d41586-019-01026-8.

52. Lidong Mo et al., "Integrated Global Assessment of the Natural Forest Carbon Potential," *Nature* 624 (November 13, 2023): 92–101, https://doi.org/10.1038/s41586-023-06723-z.

53. Akira Miyawaki, "Creative Ecology: Restoration of Native Forests by Native Trees," *Plant Biotechnology* 16, no. 1 (January 1, 1999): 15–25, https://doi.org/10.5511/plantbiotechnology.16.15.

54. Lela Nargi, "The Miyawaki Method: A Better Way to Build Forests?" *JSTOR Daily*, July 24, 2019, https://daily.jstor.org/the-miyawaki-method-a-better-way-to-build-forests/.

55. Cara Buckley, "Tiny Forests with Big Benefits," *New York Times*, August 26, 2023, https://www.nytimes.com/2023/08/24/climate/tiny-forests-climate-miyawaki.html.

56. "Climate Adaptation & Mitigation," CGIAR Research Initiatives, CGIAR, accessed January 12, 2024, https://www.cgiar.org/research/cgiar-portfolio/-climate-adaptation-mitigation.

57. Jacob Bogage, "Employers Turn to Ice Vests, Sweat Stickers to Cope with Extreme Heat," *Washington Post*, September 8, 2023, https://www.washingtonpost.com/business/2023/09/08/heat-climate-work-tech/.

58. "Orca: The First Large-Scale Plant," *Climeworks*, accessed January 12, 2024, https://climeworks.com/plant-orca.

59. Robert F. Service, "U.S. Unveils Plans for Large Facilities to Capture Carbon Directly from Air," *Science*, August 11, 2023, https://doi.org/10.1126/science.adk2566.

60. "One Atmosphere: An Independent Expert Review on Solar Radiation Modification Research and Deployment," United Nations Environment Programme, 2023, https://wedocs.unep.org/handle/20.500.11822/41903.

61. Ellsworth G. Dutton and John R. Christy, "Solar Radiative Forcing at Selected Locations and Evidence for Global Lower Tropospheric Cooling Following the Eruptions of El Chichón and Pinatubo," *Geophysical Research Letters* 19, no. 23 (December 2, 1992): 2313–16, https://doi.org/10.1029/92gl02495.

Chapter 3

1. "Statistical Review of World Energy 2023," 72nd Edition, *Energy Institute*, accessed October 16, 2023, https://www.energyinst.org/statistical-review.

2. *Ibid.*

3. "Electricity Explained. Electricity in the United States," U.S. Energy Information Administration, https://www.eia.gov/energyexplained/electricity/electricity-in-the-us.php.

4. Scott Nicholson and Garvin Heath, "Life Cycle Emissions Factors for Electricity Generation Technologies," NREL Data Catalog (Golden, CO: National Renewable Energy Laboratory, September 16, 2022), https://doi.org/10.7799/1819907. Data downloaded from https://data.nrel.gov/submissions/171 on October 16, 2023.

5. Jennifer L. Perret et al., "Coal Mine Dust Lung Disease in the Modern Era," *Respirology* 22, no. 4 (March 30, 2017): 662–70, https://doi.org/10.1111/resp.13034.

6. Margaret A. Palmer et al., "Mountaintop Mining Consequences," *Science* 327, no. 5962 (January 8, 2010): 148–49, https://doi.org/10.1126/science.1180543.

7. Christian J. Thomas, Robert K. Shriver, Fabian Nippgen, Matthew Hepler, and Matthew R.V. Ross, "Mines to Forests? Analyzing Long-Term Recovery Trends for Surface Coal Mines in Central Appalachia," *Restoration Ecology* 31, no. 5 (November 9, 2022): e13827, https://doi.org/10.1111/rec.13827.

8. "Exxon Valdez Oil Spill," NOAA Damage Assessment, Remediation, and Restoration Program, August 17, 2020, https://darrp.noaa.gov/oil-spills/exxon-valdez.

9. Richard Steiner, "Lessons from Exxon Valdez, 25 Years Later," *Greenpeace*, March 21, 2014, https://www.greenpeace.org/usa/lessons-from-exxon-valdez-25-years-later/.

10. "Deepwater Horizon—BP Gulf of Mexico Oil Spill," United States Environmental Protection Agency, July 24, 2024, https://www.epa.gov/enforcement/-deepwater-horizon-bp-gulf-mexico-oil-spill.

11. "2011 News & Events. Study on Emissions from Deepwater Horizon Controlled Burns in the Gulf," NOAA Chemical Sciences Laboratory, September 20, 2011, https://csl.noaa.gov/news/2011/105_0920.html.

12. Helen K. White et al., "Impact of the Deepwater Horizon Oil Spill on a Deep-Water Coral Community in the Gulf of Mexico," *Proceedings of the National Academy of Sciences of the United States of America* 109, no. 50 (March 27, 2012): 20303–8, https://doi.org/10.1073/pnas.1118029109.

13. Ron Bousso, "BP Deepwater Horizon Costs Balloon to $65 Billion," *Reuters*, January 16, 2018, https://www.reuters.com/article/idUSKBN1F50O5/.

14. Paul Hammel, "Massive Pipeline Spill Caused by Crack Created During Installation, Third-Party Review Concludes," *Kansas Reflector*, April 21, 2023, https://kansasreflector.com/2023/04/21/-massive-pipeline-spill-caused-by-crack-created-during-installation-third-party-review-concludes/.

15. "A Timeline of Recent Oil Train Crashes in the U.S. and Canada," *Associated Press*, June 3, 2016, https://apnews.com/general-news-84b1e8273d854697b34af57bc60badc2.

16. John P. Rafferty, "9 of the Biggest Oil Spills in History," *Encyclopedia Britannica*, September 1, 2023, https://www.britannica.com/story/9-of-the-biggest-oil-spills-in-history.

17. Melissa Denchak, "Fracking 101," *NRDC: Natural Resources Defense Council*, April 19, 2019, https://www.nrdc.org/stories/fracking-101#what-is.

18. "Hydraulic Fracturing and Health," National Institute of Environmental Health Sciences, https://www.niehs.nih.gov/health/topics/agents/fracking.

19. Nicola Jones, "Canada's Oil Sands

Spew Massive Amounts of Unmonitored Polluting Gases," *Nature*, January 25, 2024, https://doi.org/10.1038/d41586-024-00203-8.

20. Jaclyn Diaz, "The Keystone Pipeline Leaked in Kansas. What Makes This Spill So Bad?" *NPR*, December 17, 2022, https://www.npr.org/2022/12/17/1142675809/-cleanup-for-keystone-pipeline-oil-spill-kansas.

21. Melissa Denchak, "What Is the Keystone XL Pipeline?" *NRDC: Natural Resources Defense Council*, March 15, 2022, https://www.nrdc.org/stories/what-keystone-xl-pipeline#whatis.

22. Aloys Nghiem, Keith Everhart, Eren Çam, and Gergely Molnar, "Natural Gas Is Now Stronger than Ever in the United States Power Sector," *IEA: International Energy Agency*, December 4, 2023, https://www.iea.org/commentaries/natural-gas-is-now-stronger-than-ever-in-the-united-states-power-sector.

23. "Global Methane Tracker 2023," *IEA: International Energy Agency*, February 2023, https://www.iea.org/reports/global-methane-tracker-2023.

24. Global Methane Pledge, accessed February 7, 2023, https://www.globalmethanepledge.org/.

25. Jon Gambrell, Peter Prengaman, and Seth Borenstein, "At COP28 Meeting, Oil Companies Pledge to Combat Methane. Environmentalists Call It a 'Smokescreen,'" *Associated Press*, December 2, 2023, https://apnews.com/article/climate-changemethanecop28-58c756d843fbc696b28a330295505be7.

26. Coco Liu and ClimateWire, "China's Great Green Wall Helps Pull CO2 Out of Atmosphere," *Scientific American*, April 24, 2015, https://www.scientificamerican.com/article/china-s-great-green-wall-helps-pull-co2-out-of-atmosphere/.

27. David J. Tenenbaum, "Biochar: Carbon Mitigation from the Ground Up," *Environmental Health Perspectives* 117, no. 2 (February 1, 2009): A70–73, https://doi.org/10.1289/ehp.117-a70.

28. Warren Cornwall, "An Alkaline Solution. As Alarm About Climate Change Grows, Scientists Explore a Strategy for Drawing Excess Carbon Dioxide into the Ocean," *Science*, November 30, 2023, https://doi.org/10.1126/science.zn8487l.

29. "What Is Marine Permaculture?" Climate Foundation, https://www.climatefoundation.org/what-is-marine-permaculture.html.

30. Jessica F. Green, "Does Carbon Pricing Reduce Emissions? A Review of Ex-Post Analyses," *Environmental Research Letters* 16, no. 4 (March 24, 2021): 043004, https://doi.org/10.1088/1748-9326/abdae9.

31. Patrick Bayer and Michaël Aklin, "The European Union Emissions Trading System Reduced CO2 Emissions Despite Low Prices," *Proceedings of the National Academy of Sciences of the United States of America* 117, no. 16 (April 6, 2020): 8804–12, https://doi.org/10.1073/pnas.1918128117.

32. Jack Ewing and Eric Lipton, "Carmakers Race to Control Next-Generation Battery Technology," *New York Times*, March 7, 2022, https://www.nytimes.com/2022/03/07/business/energy-environment/-next-generation-auto-battery.html.

33. Adele Peters, "These Giant, Glowing Carbon Blocks Bring Clean Energy to Factories," *Fast Company*, November 12, 2023, https://www.fastcompany.com/90951247/-these-giant-glowing-carbon-blocks-bring-clean-energy-to-factories.

34. Casey Crownhart, "These Companies Want to Go Beyond Batteries to Store Energy," *MIT Technology Review*, March 9, 2023, https://www.technologyreview.com/2023/03/09/1069578/these-companies-want-to-go-beyond-batteries-to-store-energy/.

35. Henry Fountain, "Chevron and Others Build an Underground Hydrogen Battery in Utah," *New York Times*, January 12, 2024, https://www.nytimes.com/2024/01/12/climate/green-hydrogen-climate-change.html.

36. "High Voltage Direct Current Electricity—Technical Information," U.K. National Grid, CRFS09/08/13, August 2013, https://www.nationalgrid.com/sites/default/files/documents/13784-High%20Voltage%20Direct%20Current%20Electricity%20-%20technical%20information.pdf.

37. Peter Fairley, "The U.S. Electricity Transmission System Is in Gridlock," *Sierra Club*, September 18, 2023, https://www.sierraclub.org/sierra/2023-3-fall/feature/us-electricity-transmission-system-gridlock.

38. Laura Cozzi, Daniel Wetzel, Gianluca Tonolo, and Jacob Hyppolite II, "For the First Time in Decades, the Number of People Without Access to Electricity Is Set to Increase in 2022," *IEA: International Energy Agency*, November 3, 2022, https://www.iea.org/commentaries/for-the-first-time-in-decades-the-number-of-people-without-access-to-electricity-is-set-to-increase-in-2022.

39. Charles C. Mann, "Solar or Coal? The Energy India Picks May Decide Earth's Fate," *Wired*, January 8, 2020, https://www.wired.com/2015/11/climate-change-in-india/.

40. "ME SOLshare: Peer-to-Peer Smart Village Grids | Bangladesh," United Nations Climate Change, https://unfccc.intclimate-action/momentum-for-change/ict-solutions/solshare.

41. *Ibid.*

42. Ben Zientara, "Solar Panel Payback Period and ROI: How Long Does It Take for Solar Panels to Pay for Themselves?" *SolarReviews*, https://www.solarreviews.com/blog/how-to-calculate-your-solar-payback-period.

43. "Bidirectional Charging and Electric Vehicles for Mobile Storage," U.S. Department of Energy, Office of Federal Energy Management Program, https://www.energy.gov/femp/bidirectional-charging-and-electric-vehicles-mobile-storage.

44. J.D. Dillon, "A Global Look at Residential Solar Adoption Rates," *Power*, July 29, 2022, https://www.powermag.com/a-global-look-at-residential-solar-adoption-rates.

45. "Texas: State Profile and Energy Estimates," U.S. Energy Information Administration, February 9, 2024, https://www.eia.gov/state/?sid=TX#tabs-4.

46. Nancy M. Haegel and Sarah R. Kurtz, "Global Progress Toward Renewable Electricity: Tracking the Role of Solar (Version 3)," *IEEE Journal of Photovoltaics* 13, no. 6 (November 2023): 768–76, https://ieeexplore.ieee.org/document/10244019.

47. *Ibid.*

48. "Latest Talks Between Ethiopia, Sudan and Egypt Over Mega Dam on the Nile End Without Breakthrough," *Associated Press*, September 25, 2023, https://apnews.com/article/ethiopia-egypt-nile-water-dispute-143261644df90d9762a3392c300a4e27.

49. Jacob Kushner, "How Kenya Is Harnessing the Immense Heat from the Earth," *BBC Future*, March 4, 2021, https://www.bbc.com/future/article/20210303-geothermal-the-immense-volcanic-power-beneath-our-feet.

50. Chad Augustine, Sarah Fisher, Jonathan Ho, Ian Warren, and Erik Witter, "Enhanced Geothermal Shot Analysis for the Geothermal Technologies Office," Golden, CO: National Renewable Energy Laboratory, Technical Report NREL/TP-5700–84822, January 2023, https://www.nrel.gov/docs/fy23osti/84822.pdf.

51. Arman Aghahosseini and Christian Breyer, "From Hot Rock to Useful Energy: A Global Estimate of Enhanced Geothermal Systems Potential," *Applied Energy* 279 (December 1, 2020): 115769, https://doi.org/10.1016/j.apenergy.2020.115769.

52. "Hydropower Explained. Tidal Power," U.S. Energy Information Administration, https://www.eia.gov/energyexplained/hydropower/tidal-power.php.

53. "Hydropower Explained. Ocean Thermal Energy Conversion," U.S. Energy Information Administration, https://www.eia.gov/energyexplained/hydropower/-ocean-thermal-energy-conversion.php.

54. Malavika Vyawahare and Climate Wire, "Hawaii First to Harness Deep-Ocean Temperatures for Power," *Scientific American*, August 27, 2015, https://www.scientificamerican.com/article/-hawaii-first-to-harness-deep-ocean-temperatures-for-power/.

55. Brent Wanner and Ryota Taniguchi, "Nuclear Power," *IEA: International Energy Agency*, July 11, 2023, https://www.iea.org/energy-system/electricity/nuclear-power.

56. "Chernobyl Accident 1986," World Nuclear Association, accessed February 12, 2024, https://world-nuclear.org/-information-library/safety-and-security/-safety-of-plants/chernobyl-accident.aspx.

57. "Fukushima Daiichi Accident," World Nuclear Association, accessed February 9, 2024, https://world-nuclear.org/information-library/safety-and-security/safety-of-plants/fukushima-daiichi-accident.aspx.

58. Catherine Clifford, "The Feds Have Collected More than $44 Billion for a Permanent Nuclear Waste Dump—Here's Why We Still Don't Have One," *CNBC*,

December 19, 2021, https://www.cnbc.com/2021/12/18/nuclear-waste-why-theres-no-permanent-nuclear-waste-dump-in-us.html.

59. Sedeer El-Showk, "Final Resting Place," *Science* 375, no. 6583 (February 25, 2022): 806–10, https://www.science.org/doi/epdf/10.1126/science.ada1392.

60. "Nuclear Power in the World Today," World Nuclear Association, accessed February 9, 2024, https://world-nuclear.org/information-library/current-and-future-generation/nuclear-power-in-the-world-today.aspx.

61. "What Is ITER?" ITER Organization, https://www.iter.org/proj/inafewlines.

62. Philip Ball, "The Chase for Fusion Energy," *Nature* 599, no. 599 (November 18, 2021): 362–6, https://www.nature.com/immersive/d41586-021-03401-w/index.html.

63. "Fusion in Brief," Culham Centre for Fusion Energy, UK Atomic Energy Authority, accessed February 9, 2024, https://ccfe.ukaea.uk/fusion-energy/fusion-in-brief/.

64. Christian Schwägerl, "Will Tech Breakthroughs Bring Fusion Energy Closer to Reality?" *Yale Environment 360*, July 6, 2023, https://e360.yale.edu/features/nuclear-fusion-research-startups.

65. Harish K. Jeswani, Andrew Chilvers, and Adisa Azapagic, "Environmental Sustainability of Biofuels: A Review," *Proceedings of the Royal Society A: Mathematical, Physical and Engineering Sciences* 476, no. 2243 (November 25, 2020): 20200351, https://doi.org/10.1098/rspa.2020.0351.

66. Melissa J. Scully, Gregory A. Norris, Tania M. Alarcon Falconi, and David L. MacIntosh, "Carbon Intensity of Corn Ethanol in the United States: State of the Science," *Environmental Research Letters* 16, no. 4 (March 10, 2021): 043001, https://doi.org/10.1088/1748-9326/abde08.

67. Xinyu Liu, Hoyoung Kwon, Michael Wang, and Don O'Connor, "Life Cycle Greenhouse Gas Emissions of Brazilian Sugar Cane Ethanol Evaluated with the GREET Model Using Data Submitted to RenovaBio," *Environmental Science & Technology* 57, no. 32 (August 1, 2023): 11814–22, https://doi.org/10.1021/acs.est.2c08488.

68. Rui Chen et al., "Life Cycle Energy and Greenhouse Gas Emission Effects of Biodiesel in the United States with Induced Land Use Change Impacts," *Bioresource Technology* 251 (March 1, 2018): 249–58, https://doi.org/10.1016/j.biortech.2017.12.031.

69. Hui Xu, Longwen Ou, Yuan Li, Troy R. Hawkins, and Michael Wang, "Life Cycle Greenhouse Gas Emissions of Biodiesel and Renewable Diesel Production in the United States," *Environmental Science & Technology* 56, no. 12 (May 16, 2022): 7512–21, https://doi.org/10.1021/acs.est.2c00289.

70. T. Suganya, M. Varman, H.H. Masjuki, and S. Renganathan, "Macroalgae and Microalgae as a Potential Source for Commercial Applications Along with Biofuels Production: A Biorefinery Approach," *Renewable & Sustainable Energy Reviews* 55 (March 1, 2016): 909–41, https://doi.org/10.1016/j.rser.2015.11.026.

71. Sarah Hurtes and Weiyi Cai, "Europe Is Sacrificing Its Ancient Forests for Energy," *New York Times*, September 16, 2022, https://www.nytimes.com/interactive/2022/09/07/world/europe/eu-logging-wood-pellets.html.

72. Warren Cornwall, "Is Wood a Green Source of Energy? Scientists Are Divided," *Science*, January 5, 2017, https://doi.org/10.1126/science.aal0574.

73. Gabriel Popkin and Erin Schaff, "There's a Booming Business in America's Forests. Some Aren't Happy About It," *New York Times*, November 15, 2022, https://www.nytimes.com/2021/04/19/climate/wood-pellet-industry-climate.html.

74. Michal Lisowyj and Mark Mba Wright, "A Review of Biogas and an Assessment of Its Economic Impact and Future Role as a Renewable Energy Source," *Reviews in Chemical Engineering* 36, no. 3 (September 5, 2018): 401–21, https://doi.org/10.1515/revce-2017-0103.

Chapter 4

1. "What Is the Efficiency of Different Types of Power Plants?" U.S. Energy Information Administration, May 15, 2024, https://www.eia.gov/tools/faqs/faq.php?id=107&t=3.

2. Lindsay Aramayo and Mark Morey,

"Natural Gas Combined-Cycle Power Plants Increased Utilization with Improved Technology," U.S. Energy Information Administration, November 20, 2023, https://www.eia.gov/todayinenergy/detail.php?id=60984.

3. "Combined Heat and Power Technology Fills an Important Energy Niche," U.S. Energy Information Administration, October 4, 2012, https://www.eia.gov/todayinenergy/detail.php?id=8250.

4. Karin Kirk, "Electrifying Transportation Reduces Emissions AND Saves Massive Amounts of Energy," *Yale Climate Connections*, August 7, 2022, https://yaleclimateconnections.org/2022/08/-electrifying-transportation-reduces-emissions-and-saves-massive-amounts-of-energy/.

5. Jan Rosenow, Duncan Gibb, Thomas Nowak, and Richard Lowes, "Heating Up the Global Heat Pump Market," *Nature Energy* 7, no. 10 (September 7, 2022): 901–4, https://doi.org/10.1038/s41560-022-01104-8.

6. "2022 EPA Automotive Trends Report," United States Environmental Protection Agency, data from www.epa.gov/automotive-trends/explore-automotive-trends-data, accessed October 26, 2023.

7. Nils Rokke, "SUV Sales Record Highlights Climate Challenge Ahead," *Forbes*, February 14, 2022, https://www.forbes.com/sites/nilsrokke/2022/02/14/-suv-sales-record-highlights-climate-challenge-ahead.

8. "What Was the Dieselgate Scandal," *Envirotech Online*, December 23, 2022, https://www.envirotech-online.com/news/air-monitoring/6/international-environmental-technology/what-was-the-dieselgate-scandal.

9. "Global EV Outlook 2023," International Energy Agency, Paris, April 2023, https://www.iea.org/reports/global-ev-outlook-2023.

10. "Lithium-Ion Batteries Need to Be Greener and More Ethical," *Nature* 595, no. 7 (June 29, 2021): 7, https://doi.org/10.1038/d41586-021-01735-z.

11. "Alternative Fuels Data Center. Hydrogen Benefits and Considerations," U.S. Department of Energy, Office of Energy Efficiency & Renewable Energy, https://afdc.energy.gov/fuels/hydrogen-benefits.

12. Amela Ajanovic, Marlene Sayer, and Reinhard Haas, "The Economics and the Environmental Benignity of Different Colors of Hydrogen," *International Journal of Hydrogen Energy* 47 no. 57 (July 5, 2022): 24136–54, https://doi.org/10.1016/j.ijhydene.2022.02.094.

13. Robert W. Howarth and Mark Z. Jacobson, "How Green Is Blue Hydrogen?" *Energy Science & Engineering* 9, no. 10 (October 2021): 1676–87, https://doi.org/10.1002/ese3.956.

14. Omar Maiga, Eric Deville, Jérome Laval, Alain Prinzhofer, and Aliou Boubacar Diallo, "Characterization of the Spontaneously Recharging Natural Hydrogen Reservoirs of Bourakebougou in Mali," *Scientific Reports* 13, no. 1 (July 22, 2023): 11876, https://doi.org/10.1038/s41598-023-38977-y.

15. Eric Hand, "Hidden Hydrogen: Earth May Hold Vast Stores of a Renewable, Carbon-Free Fuel," *Science* 379, no. 6633 (February 17, 2023): 630–36, https://www.science.org/doi/epdf/10.1126/science.adh1477.

16. Emily Velasco, "History's Mysteries: Caltech Professor Helps Solve Hindenburg Disaster," California Institute of Technology, May 17, 2021, https://www.caltech.edu/about/news/historys-mysteries-caltech-professor-helps-solve-hindenburg-disaster.

17. Jinsoo Kim, Benjamin K. Sovacool, Morgan Bazilian, Steve Griffiths, Junghwan Lee, Minyoung Yang, and Jordy Lee, "Decarbonizing the Iron and Steel Industry: A Systematic Review of Sociotechnical Systems, Technological Innovations, and Policy Options," *Energy Research & Social Science* 89 (July 2022): 102565, https://doi.org/10.1016/j.erss.2022.102565.

18. *Ibid.*

19. Max Bearak and Giacomo d'Orlando, "Inside the Global Race to Turn Water into Fuel," *New York Times*, March 11, 2023, https://www.nytimes.com/2023/03/11/climate/green-hydrogen-energy.html.

20. "Concrete Needs to Lose Its Colossal Carbon Footprint," *Nature* 597 (September 28, 2021): 593–94, https://doi.org/10.1038/d41586-021-02612-5.

21. Lorraine Boissoneault, "Sticky Rice Mortar, the View from Space, and More Fun Facts About China's Great Wall,"

Smithsonian Magazine, February 16, 2017, https://www.smithsonianmag.com/history/sticky-rice-mortar-view-space-and-more-fun-facts-about-chinas-great-wall-180962197/.

22. Linda M. Seymour, Janille Maragh, Paolo Sabatini, Michel Di Tommaso, James C. Weaver, and Admir Masic, "Hot Mixing: Mechanistic Insights into the Durability of Ancient Roman Concrete," *Science Advances* 9, no. 1 (January 6, 2023): eadd1602, https://doi.org/10.1126/sciadv.add1602.

23. Sabbie A. Miller, Arpad Horvath, and Paulo J.M. Monteiro, "Impacts of Booming Concrete Production on Water Resources Worldwide," *Nature Sustainability* 1 (January 8, 2018): 69–76, https://doi.org/10.1038/s41893-017-0009-5.

24. Sabbie A. Miller and Frances C. Moore, "Climate and Health Damages from Global Concrete Production," *Nature Climate Change* 10, no. 5 (March 23, 2020): 439–43, https://doi.org/10.1038/s41558-020-0733-0.

25. Mike Scott, "Can Artificial Intelligence Pave the Way for Greener Cement and Steel?" *Reuters*, January 8, 2024, https://www.reuters.com/sustainability/climate-energy/can-artificial-intelligence-pave-way-greener-cement-steel-2024-01-08/.

26. Casey Crownhart, "The Climate Solution beneath Your Feet," *MIT Technology Review*, February 9, 2023, https://www.technologyreview.com/2023/02/09/1068083/climate-solution-cement/.

27. Christian Orozco, Somnuk Tangtermsirikul, Takafumi Sugiyama, and Sandhya Babel, "Examining the Endpoint Impacts, Challenges, and Opportunities of Fly Ash Utilization for Sustainable Concrete Construction," *Scientific Reports* 13 (October 25, 2023): 18254, https://doi.org/10.1038/s41598-023-45632-z.

28. Casey Crownhart, "How Electricity Could Help Tackle a Surprising Climate Villain," *MIT Technology Review*, January 3, 2024, https://www.technologyreview.com/2024/01/03/1084734/sublime-systems-cement-climate-change-carbon-footprint/.

29. Dino Grandoni, "Cement Warms the Planet. This Green Version Just Got a Key Nod of Approval," *Washington Post*, July 13, 2023, https://www.washingtonpost.com/climate-solutions/2023/07/13/green-concrete-cement-climate-brimstone/.

30. "Energy System. Industry. Cement," International Energy Agency, July 11, 2023, https://www.iea.org/energy-system/industry/cement.

31. Eli Elinoff, "Concrete and Corruption. Materialising Power and Politics in the Thai Capital," *City* 21 no. 5 (November 13, 2017): 587–96, https://doi.org/10.1080/13604813.2017.1374778.

32. Paulo Sotero, "Petrobras Scandal. Brazilian Political Corruption Scandal," *Britannica*, September 29, 2022, https://www.britannica.com/event/Petrobras-scandal.

33. "Biomass Explained. Waste-to-Energy (Municipal Solid Waste)," U.S. Energy Information Administration, November 6, 2023, https://www.eia.gov/energyexplained/biomass/waste-to-energy.php.

34. "Trends in Solid Waste Management," World Bank, accessed October 28, 2023, https://datatopics.worldbank.org/what-a-waste/trends_in_solid_waste_management.html.

35. Luka Traven, "Busting the Myth: Waste-to-Energy Plants and Public Health," *Archives of Industrial Hygiene and Toxicology* 74, no. 2 (June 26, 2023): 142–43, https://doi.org/10.2478/aiht-2023-74-3733.

36. "Toshima Ward Cleaning Plant—'Waste-to-Energy' from Dealing with Tokyo's Rubbish," Japan Local Government Centre, Council of Local Authorities for International Relations, London, accessed March 6, 2023, https://www.jlgc.org.uk/en/pdfs/casestudies/Toshima.pdf.

37. "Metal Recycling Factsheet," EuRIC AISBL—Recycling: Bridging Circular Economy & Climate Policy, https://circulareconomy.europa.eu/platform/sites/default/files/euric_metal_recycling_factsheet.pdf.

38. "Paper," Institute of Scrap Recycling Industries, accessed March 8, 2024, https://www.isri.org/recycled-commodities/paper.

39. "Energy and the Environment Explained. Recycling and Energy," U.S. Energy Information Administration, August 17, 2022, https://www.eia.gov/energyexplained/energy-and-the-environment/recycling-and-energy.php.

40. Luke Daugherty, "Recycling: A Guide to Saving Energy," *Save on Energy*, January 3, 2024, https://www.saveonenergy.com/resources/recycling-save-energy/.

41. "Tons of Steel Recycled," World Counts, accessed March 8, 2024, https://www.theworldcounts.com/challenges/planet-earth/mining/advantages-of-recycling-steel.

42. "Copper—The World's Most Reusable Resource," Copper Development Association, https://www.copper.org/environment/lifecycle/g_recycl.html.

43. Tong Wang, Peter Berrill, Julie B. Zimmerman, and Edgar G. Hertwich, "Copper Recycling Flow Model for the United States Economy: Impact of Scrap Quality on Potential Energy Benefit," *Environmental Science & Technology* 55, no. 8 (March 30, 2021): 5485–95, https://doi.org/10.1021/acs.est.0c08227.

44. "Aluminium Recycling Factsheet," International Aluminium Institute, October 2020, https://international-aluminium.org/resource/aluminium-recycling-factsheet/.

45. "Facts and Figures About Materials, Waste and Recycling. Other Nonferrous Metals: Material-Specific Data," United States Environmental Protection Agency, November 22, 2023, https://www.epa.gov/facts-and-figures-about-materials-waste-and-recycling/other-nonferrous-metals-material-specific.

46. "Facts and Figures About Materials, Waste and Recycling. Aluminum: Material-Specific Data," United States Environmental Protection Agency, November 22, 2023, https://www.epa.gov/facts-and-figures-about-materials-waste-and-recycling/aluminum-material-specific-data.

47. Brian Taylor, "Europe Records 73 Percent UBC Recycling Rate. Can Recycling Rate Reflects Recyclability of Aluminum, According to Trade Groups," *Recycling Today*, December 15, 2022, https://www.recyclingtoday.com/news/aluminum-can-ubc-recycling-europe-rate-2020/.

48. Zach Winn, "Reducing Methane Emissions at Landfills," *MIT News*, February 2, 2022, https://news.mit.edu/2022/loci-methane-emissions-landfills-0202.

49. Winston Choi-Schagrin and Hiroko Tabuchi, "Trash or Recycling? Why Plastic Keeps Us Guessing," *New York Times*, April 21, 2022, https://www.nytimes.com/interactive/2022/04/21/climate/plastics-recycling-trash-environment.html.

50. Emma Brady, "The Effects of China's Ban on Imported Scrap Plastic on Global Recycling Efforts," *Earth.org*, January 5, 2021, https://earth.org/china-ban-on-imported-scrap-plastic/.

51. Kate O'Neill, "As More Developing Countries Reject Plastic Waste Exports, Wealthy Nations Seek Solutions at Home," *Conversation*, June 5, 2019, https://theconversation.com/as-more-developing-countries-reject-plastic-waste-exports-wealthy-nations-seek-solutions-at-home-117163.

52. "New International Requirements for the Export and Import of Plastic Recyclables and Waste," United States Environmental Protection Agency, February 25, 2024, https://www.epa.gov/hwgenerators/new-international-requirements-export-and-import-plastic-recyclables-and-waste.

53. "Learn About CFLs," United States Environmental Protection Agency, Energy Star, https://www.energystar.gov/products/lighting_fans/light_bulbs/learn_about_cfls.

54. "Lighting Choices to Save You Money," U.S. Department of Energy, Energy Saver, https://www.energy.gov/energysaver/lighting-choices-save-you-money.

55. "Access to Electricity," International Energy Agency, 2022, https://www.iea.org/reports/sdg7-data-and-projections/access-to-electricity.

56. "Accelerating the Global Transition to High-Efficiency Products," United for Efficiency, accessed March 7, 2024, https://united4efficiency.org/about-the-partnership/.

57. Brittney J. Miller, "What Will It Take for Smart Windows to Go Mainstream?" *Smithsonian Magazine*, June 9, 2022, https://www.smithsonianmag.com/innovation/what-will-it-take-for-smart-windows-to-go-mainstream-180980226/.

58. Julia B. Edwards, Alan C. McKinnon, and Sharon L. Cullinane, "Comparative Analysis of the Carbon Footprints of Conventional and Online Retailing: A 'Last Mile' Perspective," *International Journal of Physical Distribution & Logistics*

Management 40, no. 1/2 (February 2, 2010): 103–23, https://doi.org/10.1108/096 00031011018055.

59. Liza Featherstone, "The Scariest Part About Artificial Intelligence," *New Republic*, March 5, 2024, https://newrepublic.com/article/179538/environment-artificial-intelligence-water-energy.

Chapter 5

1. Mike Nichols, 1967, *The Graduate*, United States: Embassy Pictures.

2. Roland Geyer, Jenna R. Jambeck, and Kara Lavender Law, "Production, Use, and Fate of All Plastics Ever Made," *Science Advances* 3, no. 7 (July 19, 2017), https://doi.org/10.1126/sciadv.1700782.

3. "Plastics—The Facts 2022," Plastics Europe AISBL, October 2022, https://plasticseurope.org/knowledge-hub/plastics-the-facts-2022/.

4. Livia Cabernard, Stephan Pfister, Christopher Oberschelp, and Stefanie Hellweg, "Growing Environmental Footprint of Plastics Driven by Coal Combustion," *Nature Sustainability* 5, no. 2 (December 2, 2021): 139–48, https://doi.org/10.1038/s41893-021-00807-2.

5. "The Age of Plastic: From Parkesine to Pollution," Science Museum, London, October 11, 2019, https://www.sciencemuseum.org.uk/objects-and-stories/chemistry/age-plastic-parkesine-pollution.

6. Susan Freinkel, "A Brief History of Plastic's Conquest of the World," *Scientific American*, May 29, 2011, https://www.scientificamerican.com/article/a-brief-history-of-plastic-world-conquest/.

7. Anna Jagger, "Polyethylene: Discovered by Accident 75 Years Ago," *ICIS, Independent Commodity Intelligence Services*, May 8, 2008, https://www.icis.com/explore/resources/news/2008/05/12/9122447/polyethylene-discovered-by-accident-75-years-ago/.

8. "This Month in Physics History. April 6, 1938: Discovery of Teflon," *APS News* 30, no. 4 (April 2021), https://www.aps.org/publications/apsnews/202104/history.cfm.

9. Kiona N. Smith, "Stronger than Steel: How Chemist Stephanie Kwolek Invented Kevlar," *Forbes*, July 31, 2018, https://www.forbes.com/sites/kionasmith/2018/07/31/stronger-than-steel-how-chemist-stephanie-kwolek-invented-kevlar/?sh=239a54f21c3e.

10. Oddvin Sørheim and Kacie Salove, "Meat Packaging for Improved Quality, Reduced Food Waste," National Provisioner, October 15, 2018, https://www.provisioneronline.com/articles/106911-meat-packaging-for-improved-quality-reduced-food-waste.

11. Carmen Ferrara, Giovanni De Feo, and Vincenza Picone, "LCA of Glass Versus PET Mineral Water Bottles: An Italian Case Study," *Recycling* 6, no. 3 (July 15, 2021): 50, https://doi.org/10.3390/recycling6030050.

12. Nikolaos Simantiris, "Single-Use Plastic or Paper Products? A Dilemma that Requires Societal Change," *Cleaner Waste Systems* 7 (April 1, 2024): 100128, https://doi.org/10.1016/j.clwas.2023.100128.

13. Martin B. Hocking, "Paper Versus Polystyrene: A Complex Choice," *Science* 251, no. 4993 (February 1, 1991): 504–5, https://doi.org/10.1126/science.251.4993.504.

14. "Single-Use Plastic Bags and Their Alternatives—Recommendations from Life Cycle Assessments," United Nations Environment Programme, Life Cycle Initiative, 2020, https://www.lifecycleinitiative.org/wp-content/uploads/2021/03/-SUPP-plastic-bags-meta-study-8.3.21.pdf.

15. "Garbage Patches," NOAA Marine Debris Program, https://marinedebris.noaa.gov/discover-marine-debris/garbage-patches.

16. "About. We Are the Ocean Cleanup," Ocean Cleanup, https://theoceancleanup.com/about/.

17. Nick Kilvert, "What Happened to the Ocean Cleanup—The System that Would Rid the Oceans of Plastic?" *ABC News*, March 16, 2023, https://www.abc.net.au/news/science/2023-03-17/ocean-cleanup-plastic-pollution-great-pacific-garbage-patch/102075810#.

18. Marjana Bačić, "Top 10 Ocean Cleaning Startups," *Recycling Startups*, June 22, 2024, https://www.recyclingstartups.org/top/ocean-cleaning/.

19. "Plastic in Our Oceans Is Killing Marine Mammals," WWF Australia, June 26, 2023, https://wwf.org.au/blogs/plastic-in-our-oceans-is-killing-marine-mammals/.

20. Chris Wilcox, Erik Van Sebille, and Britta Denise Hardesty, "Threat of Plastic Pollution to Seabirds Is Global, Pervasive, and Increasing," *Proceedings of the National Academy of Sciences of the United States of America* 112, no. 38 (August 31, 2015): 11899–904, https://doi.org/10.1073/pnas.1502108112.

21. Emily M. Duncan et al., "Microplastic Ingestion Ubiquitous in Marine Turtles," *Global Change Biology* 25, no. 2 (December 4, 2018): 744–52, https://doi.org/10.1111/gcb.14519.

22. Olivia Lai, "The Detrimental Impacts of Plastic Pollution on Animals," *Earth.org*, May 4, 2022, https://earth.org/plastic-pollution-animals/.

23. Zeineb Bouhlel, Jimmy Köpke, Mariam Mina, and Vladimir Smakhtin, "Global Bottled Water Industry: A Review of Impacts and Trends," United Nations, University Institute for Water, Environment and Health, Hamilton, Canada, 2023, https://inweh.unu.edu/-global-bottled-water-industry-a-review-of-impacts-and-trends/.

24. Douglas Main, "Think that Your Plastic Is Being Recycled? Think Again," *MIT Technology Review*, October 12, 2023, https://www.technologyreview.com/2023/10/12/1081129/plastic-recycling-climate-change-microplastics/.

25. Jenny Gesley, "Germany: Lightweight Plastic Bag Ban to Take Effect January 1, 2021," Library of Congress, https://www.loc.gov/item/global-legal-monitor/2021-02-25/germany-lightweight-plastic-bag-ban-to-take-effect-january-1-2022/.

26. "The U.S. Progress with Single-Use Plastic Bans," *Seaside Sustainability*, March 21, 2023, https://www.seasidesustainability.org/post/the-u-s-progress-with-single-use-plastic-bans.

27. Courtney Lindwall, "Single-Use Plastics 101," *Natural Resources Defense Council*, January 9, 2020, https://www.nrdc.org/stories/single-use-plastics-101#corporations.

28. Ali Chamas et al., "Degradation Rates of Plastics in the Environment," *ACS Sustainable Chemistry & Engineering* 8, no. 9 (February 3, 2020): 3494–511, https://dx.doi.org/10.1021/acssuschemeng.9b06635.

29. X. Zhang and X. Peng, "How Long for Plastics to Decompose in the Deep Sea?" *Geochemical Perspectives Letters* 22 (June 27, 2022): 20–25, https://doi.org/10.7185/geochemlet.2222.

30. Imogen E. Napper et al., "Reaching New Heights in Plastic Pollution—Preliminary Findings of Microplastics on Mount Everest," *One Earth* 3, no. 5 (November 1, 2020): 621–30, https://doi.org/10.1016/j.oneear.2020.10.020.

31. Sanae Chiba et al., "Human Footprint in the Abyss: 30 Year Records of Deep-Sea Plastic Debris," *Marine Policy* 96 (October 1, 2018): 204–12. https://doi.org/10.1016/j.marpol.2018.03.022.

32. Chris Skinner, "The Plastocene—Plastic in the Sedimentary Record," *Blogs of the European Geosciences Union*, January 9, 2019, https://blogs.egu.eu/divisions/ssp/2019/01/09/the-plastocene-plastic-in-the-sedimentary-record/.

33. Christina Reed, "Dawn of the Plasticene Age," *New Scientist* 225, no. 3006 (January 31, 2015): 28–32, https://doi.org/10.1016/s0262-4079(15)60215-9.

34. "Plastic Ingestion by People Could Be Equating to a Credit Card a Week," WWF International, June 13, 2019, https://www.wwf.eu/?348458/Plastic-ingestion-by-people-could-be-equating-to-a-credit-card-a-week.

35. Naixin Qian et al., "Rapid Single-Particle Chemical Imaging of Nanoplastics by SRS Microscopy," *Proceedings of the National Academy of Sciences of the United States of America* 121, no. 3 (January 8, 2024): e2300582121, https://doi.org/10.1073/pnas.2300582121.

36. Rewa E. Zurub, Yusmaris Cariaco, Michael G. Wade, and Shannon A. Bainbridge, "Microplastics Exposure: Implications for Human Fertility, Pregnancy and Child Health," *Frontiers in Endocrinology* 14 (January 3, 2024): 1330396, https://doi.org/10.3389/fendo.2023.1330396.

37. Stephanie Wright and Paul J.A. Borm, "Applying Existing Particle Paradigms to Inhaled Microplastic Particles," *Frontiers in Public Health* 10 (May 30, 2022): 868822, https://doi.org/10.3389/fpubh.2022.868822.

38. Claudia Campanale, Carmine Massarelli, Ilaria Savino, Vito Locaputo, and Vito Felice Uricchio, "A Detailed Review Study on Potential Effects of Microplastics and Additives of Concern on Human Health," *International Journal of*

Environmental Research and Public Health 17, no. 4 (February 13, 2020): 1212, https:// doi.org/10.3390/ijerph17041212.

39. A. Dick Vethaak and Juliette Legler, "Microplastics and Human Health. Knowledge Gaps Should Be Addressed to Ascertain the Health Risks of Microplastics," *Science* 371, no. 6530 (February 12, 2021): 672–74, https://doi.org/10.1126/science.abe5041; Elena Molina and Sara Benedé, "Is There Evidence of Health Risks from Exposure to Micro- and Nanoplastics in Foods?" *Frontiers in Nutrition* 9 (June 28, 2022): 910094, https:// doi.org/10.3389/fnut.2022.910094; Elisabeth S. Gruber et al., "To Waste or Not to Waste: Questioning Potential Health Risks of Micro- and Nanoplastics with a Focus on Their Ingestion and Potential Carcinogenicity," *Exposure and Health* 15 (March 22, 2022): 33–51, https://doi.org/10.1007 /s12403-022-00470-8.

40. Jan-Georg Rosenboom, Robert Langer, and Giovanni Traverso, "Bioplastics for a Circular Economy," *Nature Reviews Materials* 7 (January 20, 2022): 117–37, https://doi.org/10.1038 /s41578-021-00407-8.

41. Xiaoying Zhao, Katrina Cornish, and Yael Vodovotz, "Narrowing the Gap for Bioplastic Use in Food Packaging: An Update," *Environmental Science & Technology* 54, no. 8 (March 23, 2020): 4712–32, https://doi.org/10.1021/acs.est.9b03755.

42. "Bioplastics Market Development Update 2023," *European Bioplastics*, accessed March 25, 2024, https://www. european-bioplastics.org/market/.

43. Saahil Desai, "Compostable Plastic Is Garbage," *Atlantic*, July 6, 2023, https://www.theatlantic.com/science/ archive/2023/07/compostable-plastic-trash/674626/.

44. "The New Plastics Economy: Rethinking the Future of Plastics & Catalysing Action," Ellen MacArthur Foundation, 2017, https://www.ellenmacarthurfoundation.org/the-new-plastics-economy-rethinking-the-future-of-plastics-and-catalysing.

45. Winston Choi-Schagrin and Hiroko Tabuchi, "Trash or Recycling? Why Plastic Keeps Us Guessing," *New York Times*, April 21, 2022, https://www.nytimes.com/ interactive/2022/04/21/climate/plastics-recycling-trash-environment.html.

46. "Facts and Figures About Materials, Waste and Recycling. Plastics: Material-Specific Data," United States Environmental Protection Agency, accessed October 20, 2023, https://www.epa.gov/facts-and-figures-about-materials-waste-and-recycling/plastics-material-specific-data.

47. "Plastic Packaging Waste: 38% Recycled in 2020," *Eurostat*, October 20, 2022, https://ec.europa.eu/eurostat/web/ products-eurostat-news/-/ddn-20221020-1.

48. "On the Plastics Crisis," *Nature Sustainability* 6, no. 10 (October 19, 2023): 1137, https://doi.org/10.1038/s418 93-023-01236-z.

49. Robbie A. Clark and Michael P. Shaver, "Depolymerization Within a Circular Plastics System," *Chemical Reviews* 124, no. 5 (February 22, 2024): 2617–50, https://doi.org/10.1021/acs. chemrev.3c00739.

50. "What Are the EPR Directives in the EU?" *Source Intelligence*, March 24, 2023, https://blog.sourceintelligence.com/ what-are-the-epr-directives-in-the-eu.

51. "Extended Producer Responsibility," National Conference of State Legislatures, October 24, 2023, https://www.ncsl. org/environment-and-natural-resources/ extended-producer-responsibility.

52. Samantha Millette, "Deposits by the Numbers," *Resource Recycling News*, June 14, 2023, https://resource-recycling.com/ recycling/2023/04/04/deposits-by-the-numbers/.

53. "Factsheet. Extended Producer Responsibility (EPR) for Used Packaging," EUROPEN: European Organization for Packaging and the Environment, March 16, 2015, https://www.europen-packaging. eu/policy-area/extended-producer-responsibility.

54. Circular Action Alliance, https:// circularactionalliance.org.

55. Brindha Ramasubramanian, Jovan Tan, Vijila Chellappan, and Seeram Ramakrishna, "Recent Advances in Extended Producer Responsibility Initiatives for Plastic Waste Management in Germany and UK," *Materials Circular Economy* 5, no. 1 (May 12, 2023): 6, https:// doi.org/10.1007/s42824-023-00076-8.

56. Yamini Gupt and Samraj Sahay, "Review of Extended Producer Responsibility: A Case Study Approach," *Waste Management & Research* 33, no. 7 (July 1,

2015): 595–611, https://doi.org/10.1177/07
34242x15592275.

57. *Ibid.*

58. "Mycelium, Packaging, and Hope for a Plastic Free Planet," Ecovative, April 21, 2023, https://www.ecovative.com/blogs/blog/mycelium-packaging-plastic-free-planet.

59. John Cumbers, "Ecovative: Growing Better Materials," *Forbes*, May 10, 2023, https://www.forbes.com/sites/johncumbers/2023/05/10/ecovative-growing-better-materials/?sh=1b8f555017b0.

60. Mominul Hoque and Srinivas Janaswamy, "Biodegradable Packaging Films from Banana Peel Fiber," *Sustainable Chemistry and Pharmacy* 37 (February 1, 2024): 101400, https://doi.org/10.1016/j.scp.2023.101400.

61. "Translating Our Science: About Water-Soluble Film," MonoSol, https://www.monosol.com/translating-our-science/.

62. Maher Z. Elsabeé and Entsar S. Abdou, "Chitosan Based Edible Films and Coatings: A Review," *Materials Science and Engineering: C* 33, no. 4 (May 1, 2013): 1819–41, https://doi.org/10.1016/j.msec.2013.01.010.

63. Surya Sasikumar Nair, Joanna Trafiałek, and Wojciech Kolanowski, "Edible Packaging: A Technological Update for the Sustainable Future of the Food Industry," *Applied Sciences* 13, no. 14 (July 15, 2023): 8234, https://doi.org/10.3390/app13148234.

64. Jacqui Palumbo, "Can Seaweed Help Solve the World's Plastic Crisis?" *CNN*, January 4, 2022, https://www.cnn.com/style/article/notpla-seaweed-single-use-plastics/index.html.

65. "Tom Ford Plastic Innovation Accelerator. Powered by Lonely Whale," 2023, https://unwrapthefuture.org/#about-the-program.

66. Jeff Kart, "Winners of the Tom Ford Plastic Innovation Prize Are All Using Seaweed," *Forbes*, March 24, 2023, https://www.forbes.com/sites/jeffkart/2023/03/24/winners-of-the-tom-ford-plastic-innovation-prize-are-all-using-seaweed/?sh=30b3111bb390.

67. "Ooho, the Edible Bubble Made from Seaweed," Notpla, https://www.notpla.com/ooho.

68. Jessica Stewart, "London Marathon Replaces Plastic Bottles with Edible Seaweed Drink Capsules," *My Modern Met*, April 30, 2019, https://mymodernmet.com/ooho-edible-drink-capsule-london-marathon/.

69. Rebecca Smithers, "Carlsberg to Replace Plastic Ring Can Holders with Recyclable Glue," *Guardian*, September 6, 2018, https://www.theguardian.com/food/2018/sep/06/carlsberg-to-replace-plastic-ring-can-holders-with-recyclable-glue.

Chapter 6

1. "Household Air Pollution," World Health Organization, December 15, 2023, https://www.who.int/news-room/fact-sheets/detail/household-air-pollution-and-health.

2. Andrea Pozzer, Susan C. Anenberg, Sagnik Dey, Andy Haines, Jos Lelieveld, and Sourangsu Chowdhury, "Mortality Attributable to Ambient Air Pollution: A Review of Global Estimates," *Geohealth* 7, no. 1 (January 1, 2023): e2022GH000711, https://doi.org/10.1029/2022gh000711.

3. *Ibid.*

4. Katie E. Wyer, David B. Kelleghan, Victoria Blanes-Vidal, Günther Schauberger, and Thomas P. Curran, "Ammonia Emissions from Agriculture and Their Contribution to Fine Particulate Matter: A Review of Implications for Human Health," *Journal of Environmental Management* 323 (December 1, 2022): 116285, https://doi.org/10.1016/j.jenvman.2022.116285.

5. Ana Vicente, Célia Alves, Ana I. Calvo, Ana P. Fernandes, Teresa Nunes, Cristina Monteiro, Susana Marta Almeida, and Casimiro Pio, "Emission Factors and Detailed Chemical Composition of Smoke Particles from the 2010 Wildfire Season," *Atmospheric Environment* 71 (June 1, 2013): 295–303, https://doi.org/10.1016/j.atmosenv.2013.01.062.

6. Jamie Kelly, "Record Breaking PM2.5 Pollution Levels in NYC in Early June 2023 Regular Occurrence in over 350 Cities Worldwide," Centre for Research on Energy and Clean Air (CREA), June 16, 2023, https://energyandcleanair.org/record-breaking-pm2-5-pollution-levels-in-nyc-in-early-june-2023-regular-occurrence-in-over-350-cities-worldwide.

7. Laura Robson-Mainwaring, "The Great Smog of 1952," National Archives, July 19, 2022, https://blog.nationalar chives.gov.uk/the-great-smog-of-1952.

8. "Ozone National Ambient Air Quality Standards (NAAQS)," United States Environmental Protection Agency, https://www.epa.gov/ground-level-ozone-pollution/ozone-national-ambient-air-quality-standards-naaqs.

9. Franziska Rosser and John Balmes, "Ozone and Childhood Respiratory Health: A Primer for U.S. Pediatric Providers and a Call for a More Protective Standard," *Pediatric Pulmonology* 58, no. 5 (May 1, 2023): 1355–66, https://doi.org/10.1002/ppul.26368.

10. "WHO Global Air Quality Guidelines: Particulate Matter (PM2.5 and PM10), Ozone, Nitrogen Dioxide, Sulfur Dioxide and Carbon Monoxide," World Health Organization, Geneva, September 22, 2021, https://www.who.int/publications/i/item/9789240034228.

11. Mark W. Frampton et al., "Nitrogen Dioxide Exposure: Effects on Airway and Blood Cells," *American Journal of Physiology. Lung Cellular and Molecular Physiology* 282, no. 1 (January 1, 2002): L155–65, https://doi.org/10.1152/ajplung.2002.282.1.l155.

12. Joe C. Farman, Brian G. Gardiner, and Jonathan D. Shanklin, "Large Losses of Total Ozone in Antarctica Reveal Seasonal ClOx/NOx Interaction," *Nature* 315, no. 6016 (May 1, 1985): 207–10, https://doi.org/10.1038/315207a0.

13. Mario J. Molina and F.S. Rowland, "Stratospheric Sink for Chlorofluoromethanes: Chlorine Atom-Catalysed Destruction of Ozone," *Nature* 249, no. 5460 (June 28, 1974): 810–12, https://doi.org/10.1038/249810a0; "Scientific Assessment of Ozone Depletion: 1994," World Meteorological Organization, Global Ozone Research and Monitoring Project—Report No. 37, Geneva, 1995, https://csl.noaa.gov/assessments/ozone/1994/copies.html.

14. "About Montreal Protocol," UN Environment Programme (UNEP) Ozon Action, https://www.unep.org/ozonac tion/who-we-are/about-montreal-proto col.

15. Susan Solomon, Diane J. Ivy, Doug. Kinnison, Michael J. Mills, Ryan R. Neely, III, and Anja Schmidt, "Emergence of Healing in the Antarctic Ozone Layer," *Science* 353, no. 6296 (June 30, 2016): 269–74, https://doi.org/10.1126/science.aae0061.

16. Daniel A. Malashock et al., "Global Trends in Ozone Concentration and Attributable Mortality for Urban, Peri-Urban, and Rural Areas Between 2000 and 2019: A Modelling Study," *Lancet, Planetary Health* 6, no. 12 (December 1, 2022): e958–67, https://doi.org/10.1016/s2542-5196(22)00260-1.

17. F. Laden, "A Tale of Six Cities," *Environmental Epidemiology* 3 (October 1, 2019): 221, https://doi.org/10.1097/01.ee9.0000608272.94008.7b.

18. "Particulate Matter (PM) Basics," United States Environmental Protection Agency, https://www.epa.gov/pm-pollution/particulate-matter-pm-basics.

19. Michael T. Young et al., "Blood Pressure Effect of Traffic-Related Air Pollution: A Crossover Trial of In-Vehicle Filtration," *Annals of Internal Medicine* 176, no. 12 (November 28, 2023): 1586–94, https://doi.org/10.7326/m23-1309.

20. Federica Nobile, Anna Forastiere, Paola Michelozzi, Francesco Forastiére, and Massimo Stafoggia, "Long-Term Exposure to Air Pollution and Incidence of Mental Disorders. A Large Longitudinal Cohort Study of Adults Within an Urban Area," *Environment International* 181 (November 1, 2023): 108302, https://doi.org/10.1016/j.envint.2023.108302.

21. Boya Zhang et al., "Comparison of Particulate Air Pollution from Different Emission Sources and Incident Dementia in the U.S.," *JAMA Internal Medicine* 183, no. 10 (October 1, 2023): 1080–89, https://doi.org/10.1001/jamainternmed.2023.3300.

22. Md Mostafijur Rahman et al., "Associations of Autism Spectrum Disorder with PM2.5 Components: A Comparative Study Using Two Different Exposure Models," *Environmental Science & Technology* 57, no. 1 (December 22, 2022): 405–14, https://doi.org/10.1021/acs.est.2c05197.

23. Maryam A. Shehab and Francis D. Pope, "Effects of Short-Term Exposure to Particulate Matter Air Pollution on Cognitive Performance," *Scientific Reports* 9, no. 1 (June 3, 2019): 8237, https://doi.org/10.1038/s41598-019-44561-0.

24. Jia Xu et al., "Reducing Indoor Particulate Air Pollution Improves Student Test Scores: A Randomized Double-Blind Crossover Study," *Environmental Science & Technology* (April 22, 2024), https://doi.org/10.1021/acs.est.3c10372.

25. Lucas Henneman, Christine Choirat, Irene Dedoussi, Francesca Dominici, Jessica Roberts, and Corwin Zigler, "Mortality Risk from United States Coal Electricity Generation," *Science* 382, no. 6673 (November 23, 2023): 941–46, https://doi.org/10.1126/science.adf4915.

26. Annette Peters, "Ambient Air Pollution and Alzheimer's Disease: The Role of the Composition of Fine Particles," *Proceedings of the National Academy of Sciences of the United States of America* 120, no. 3 (January 10, 2023): e2220028120, https://doi.org/10.1073/pnas.2220028120.

27. Xin Liu, Qingtao Jiang, Peihong Wu, Lei Han, and Peng Zhou, "Global Incidence, Prevalence and Disease Burden of Silicosis: 30 Years' Overview and Forecasted Trends," *BMC Public Health* 23 (July 17, 2023): 1366, https://doi.org/10.1186/s12889-023-16295-2.

28. Jay F. Colinet, "The Impact of Black Lung and a Methodology for Controlling Respirable Dust," *Mining, Metallurgy & Exploration* 37, no. 6 (July 30, 2020): 1847–56, https://doi.org/10.1007/s42461-020-00278-7.

29. Richard Schiffman, "A Troubling Look at the Human Toll of Mountaintop Removal Mining," *Yale Environment 360*, November 21, 2017, https://e360.yale.edu/features/a-troubling-look-at-the-human-toll-of-mountaintop-removal-mining.

30. Thomas E. Shriver and Aysha Bodenhamer, "The Enduring Legacy of Black Lung: Environmental Health and Contested Illness in Appalachia," *Sociology of Health & Illness* 40, no. 8 (June 28, 2018): 1361–75, https://doi.org/10.1111/1467-9566.12777.

31. Xinlu Miao et al., "Global, Regional, and National Burden of Non-Communicable Diseases Attributable to Occupational Asbestos Exposure 1990–2019 and Prediction to 2035: Worsening or Improving?" *BMC Public Health* 24 (March 18, 2024): 832, https://doi.org/10.1186/s12889-024-18099-4.

32. Naomi Alpert, Maaike Van Gerwen, and Emanuela Taioli, "Epidemiology of Mesothelioma in the 21st Century in Europe and the United States, 40 Years After Restricted/Banned Asbestos Use," *Translational Lung Cancer Research* 9, no. S1 (February 28, 2020): S28–38, https://doi.org/10.21037/tlcr.2019.11.11.

33. Tony Briscoe, "Los Angeles Gets 'F' Grade for Air Quality Once Again in National Report," *Los Angeles Times*, April 19, 2023, https://www.latimes.com/environment/story/2023-04-19/l-a-gets-failing-grade-for-air-quality-once-again.

34. Katherine Kornei, "Here Are Some of the World's Worst Cities for Air Quality," *Science*, March 21, 2017, https://doi.org/10.1126/science.aal0942.

35. Leigh Hopper, "Improved Air Quality in Los Angeles Linked to Fewer Children Developing Asthma," University of Southern California, Keck School of Medicine, May 22, 2019, https://keck.usc.edu/news/improved-air-quality-in-los-angeles-linked-to-fewer-children-developing-asthma/.

36. Frederica Perera, David Cooley, Alique Berberian, David Mills, and Patrick Kinney, "Co-Benefits to Children's Health of the U.S. Regional Greenhouse Gas Initiative," *Environmental Health Perspectives* 128, no. 7 (July 29, 2020): 077006, https://doi.org/10.1289/ehp6706.

37. Susan C. Anenberg et al., "Long-Term Trends in Urban NO2 Concentrations and Associated Paediatric Asthma Incidence: Estimates from Global Datasets," *Lancet, Planetary Health* 6, no. 1 (January 1, 2022): e49–58, https://doi.org/10.1016/s2542-5196(21)00255-2.

38. Peringe Grennfelt, Anna Engleryd, Martin Forsius, Øystein Hov, Henning Rodhe, and Ellis Cowling, "Acid Rain and Air Pollution: 50 Years of Progress in Environmental Science and Policy," *Ambio* 49 (September 21, 2019): 849–64, https://doi.org/10.1007/s13280-019-01244-4.

39. Rachel Hoesly et al., "Historical (1750–2014) Anthropogenic Emissions of Reactive Gases and Aerosols from the Community Emissions Data System (CEDS)," *Geoscientific Model Development* 11 (January 29, 2018): 369–408, https://doi.org/10.5194/gmd-11-369-2018.

40. Michael Greenstone and Christa Hasenkopf, "Air Quality Life Index | 2023 Annual Update," Energy Policy Institute at the University of Chicago (EPIC), August

2023, https://aqli.epic.uchicago.edu/wp-content/uploads/2023/08/AQLI_2023_Report-Global_v03.5_China_view_spreads.pdf.

41. Paolo Boffetta, Nadia Jourenkova, and Per Gustavsson, "Cancer Risk from Occupational and Environmental Exposure to Polycyclic Aromatic Hydrocarbons," *Cancer Causes Control* 8 (May 1997): 444–72, https://doi.org/10.1023/A:1018465507029.

42. Regina Montero-Montoya, Rocío López-Vargas, and Omar Arellano-Aguilar, "Volatile Organic Compounds in Air: Sources, Distribution, Exposure and Associated Illnesses in Children," *Annals of Global Health* 84, no. 2 (January 27, 2018): 225–38, https://doi.org/10.29024/aogh.910.

43. Roberto Rivera-Luna et al., "Descriptive Epidemiology in Mexican Children with Cancer Under an Open National Public Health Insurance Program," *BMC Cancer* 14 (October 29, 2014): 790, https://doi.org/10.1186/1471-2407-14-790.

44. "'We're Dying Here': The Fight for Life in a Louisiana Fossil Fuel Sacrifice Zone," *Human Rights Watch*, January 25, 2024, https://www.hrw.org/report/2024/01/25/were-dying-here/fight-life-louisiana-fossil-fuel-sacrifice-zone.

45. "Department of Environmental Quality—Monitoring and Enforcement of Air Quality, Report No. 40200007," Performance Audit Services, Louisiana Legislative Auditor, January 20, 2021, https://app2.lla.state.la.us/publicreports.nsf/0/4f3372abddf0f2718625866 30067c25d/$file/00022660a.pdf?openelement&.7773098.

46. "Louisiana Cancer Maps," Louisiana State University, School of Public Health, https://sph.lsuhsc.edu/louisiana-tumor-registry/data-usestatistics/-louisiana-data-interactive-statistics/-louisiana-cancer-maps.

47. "The State of Housing in New Orleans One Year After Katrina," *Opportunity Agenda*, 2006, https://opportunityagenda.org/messaging_reports/one-year-after-katrina/.

48. "Legionellosis," World Health Organization, September 6, 2022, https://www.who.int/news-room/fact-sheets/detail/legionellosis.

49. Mukesh Dherani, Daniel Pope, Maya Mascarenhas, Kirk R. Smith, Martin Weber, and Nigel Bruce, "Indoor Air Pollution from Unprocessed Solid Fuel Use and Pneumonia Risk in Children Aged Under Five Years: A Systematic Review and Meta-Analysis," *Bulletin of the World Health Organization* 86, no. 5 (May 2008): 390–98, https://doi.org/10.2471/BLT.07.044529.

50. "Global Alliance for Clean Cookstoves—Creating a Thriving Global Market for Clean and Efficient Household Cooking Solutions," United Nations Framework Convention on Climate Change, November 25, 2015, https://unfccc.int/news/global-alliance-for-clean-cookstoves.

Chapter 7

1. Peter H. Gleick, "Water Resources," in *Encyclopedia of Climate and Weather*, vol. 2, ed. Stephen H. Schneider (New York: Oxford University Press, 1996), 817–23.

2. Sandra L. Postel, Gretchen C. Daily, and Paul R. Ehrlich, "Human Appropriation of Renewable Fresh Water," *Science* 271, no. 5250 (February 9, 1996): 785–88, http://web.mit.edu/12.000/www/m2012/postel_science.pdf.

3. "Total Water Withdrawal per Capita, AQUASTAT Main Database, 2016," Food and Agriculture Organization of the United Nations (FAO), accessed May 14, 2024, https://data.apps.fao.org/catalog/dataset/829bade5-1bb8-4154-aed3-088e5a3b8d00/resource/d5610feb-00ba-4391-8a11-bdedfda7a89a.

4. Humberto Basilio, "Groundwater Pumping Is Causing Mexico City to Sink," *Eos* 104 (May 5, 2023), https://doi.org/10.1029/2023EO230182.

5. Adam Voiland, "America's Sinking East Coast," NASA Earth Observatory, https://earthobservatory.nasa.gov/images/152452/americas-sinking-east-coast.

6. Mary Ann Capehart, "Drought Diminishes Hydropower Capacity in Western U.S.," University of Arizona, Water Resources Research Center, https://wrrc.arizona.edu/drought-diminishes-hydropower.

7. Henry Fountain, "In a First, U.S. Declares Water Shortage on Colorado River, Forcing Water Cuts," *New York Times*, August 16, 2021, https://www.nytimes.com/2021/08/16/climate/-colorado-river-water-cuts.html.

8. John Mukum Mbaku, "The Controversy over the Grand Ethiopian Renaissance Dam," *Brookings Institution*, August 5, 2020, https://www.brookings.edu/articles/the-controversy-over-the-grand-ethiopian-renaissance-dam.

9. Geological Society of America, "Looming Crisis of the Much Decreased Fresh-Water Supply to Egypt's Nile Delta," *Phys.org*, March 13, 2017, https://phys.org/news/2017-03-looming-crisis-decreased-fresh-water-egypt.html.

10. Elizabeth Manning, "Northwest Tribes Demand Action for Salmon and Orca Restoration," *Earthjustice*, April 25, 2024, https://earthjustice.org/article/northwest-tribes-demand-action-for-salmon-and-orca-restoration.

11. "Water-Use Efficiency," San Diego County Water Authority, January 2024, https://www.sdcwa.org/wp-content/uploads/2020/11/wateruseefficiency-fs.pdf.

12. "Emergency Drought Restrictions Go into Effect for Six Million Southern Californians," *Metropolitan Water District of Southern California*, June 1, 2022, https://www.mwdh2o.com/press-releases/emergency-drought-restrictions-go-into-effect-for-six-million-southern-californians/.

13. Jürgen Förster, "Cooling for Electricity Production Dominates Water Use in Industry," *Eurostat*, Statistics in focus 14/2014, https://ec.europa.eu/eurostat/statistics-explained/index.php?title=Archive:Water_use_in_industry.

14. "What's a Dry Factory?" L'Oréal Group, https://www.loreal.com/en/news/commitments/whats-a-dry-factory/.

15. M.M. Mekonnen and A.Y. Hoekstra, "The Green, Blue and Grey Water Footprint of Crops and Derived Crop Products," *Hydrology and Earth System Sciences* 15, no. 5 (May 25, 2011): 1577–600, https://doi.org/10.5194/hess-15-1577-2011.

16. "Drip Irrigation," University of Rhode Island, Water Quality Program—College of the Environment and Life Sciences, https://web.uri.edu/safewater/protecting-water-quality-at-home/sustainable-landscaping/drip-irrigation.

17. "United States. Description of Cropping Systems, Climate, and Soils," Global Yield Gap Atlas, https://www.yieldgap.org/united-states.

18. Julie Tollefson, "Groundwater Levels Fall Across Western and South-Central Kansas," Kansas Geological Survey, March 10, 2023, https://www.kgs.ku.edu/General/News/2023/water-levels.html.

19. James P. Dobrowolski, "NIFA Impacts: Saving the Ogallala Aquifer, Supporting Farmers," U.S. Department of Agriculture, May 1, 2020, https://www.usda.gov/media/blog/2020/05/01/nifa-impacts-saving-ogallala-aquifer-supporting-farmers.

20. Cristina Novo, "Saudi Arabia's Groundwater to Run Dry," *Smart Water Magazine*, May 30, 2019, https://smartwatermagazine.com/blogs/cristina-novo/-saudi-arabias-groundwater-run-dry.

21. "Pivot Irrigation in Saudi Arabia," NASA Scientific Visualization Studio, May 23, 2013, https://svs.gsfc.nasa.gov/11290.

22. Marie van den Bosch, "Saudi Arabia's 60-Year Battle for Food Security," Arab Gulf States Institute in Washington, May 13, 2024, https://agsiw.org/saudi-arabias-60-year-battle-for-food-security.

23. "Saudi Hay Farm in Arizona Tests State's Supply of Groundwater," *NPR*, November 2, 2015, https://www.npr.org/sections/thesalt/2015/11/02/453885642/saudi-hay-farm-in-arizona-tests-states-supply-of-groundwater.

24. Suman Naishadham, "Arizona to Cancel Leases Allowing Saudi-Owned Farm Access to State's Groundwater," *AP News*, October 3, 2023, https://apnews.com/article/saudi-arabia-drought-arizona-alfalfa-water-agriculture-0d13957edaf882690e15c0bd9ccfa59f#.

25. Sunaina Kumar, "Hope Runs Dry as Groundwater Sources in Punjab Drop to Alarming Levels," *Mongabay-India*, July 5, 2019, https://india.mongabay.com/2019/07/hope-runs-dry-as-groundwater-sources-in-punjab-drop-to-alarming-levels/.

26. Hemant Singh, "Different Types of Agricultural Subsidies Given to Farmers in India," *JagranJosh.com*, May 27, 2016, https://www.jagranjosh.com/general-knowledge/different-types-of-

agricultural-subsidies-given-to-farmers-in-india-1445333409-1.

27. Gene Hettel, "From Crop Production to Market: Improving the Livelihood of Pakistan's Basmati Rice Farmers," *Rice Today*, March 18, 2016, https://ricetoday.irri.org/from-crop-production-to-market-improving-the-livelihood-of-pakistans-basmati-rice-farmers/.

28. "Water Stewardship Position Statement," Mars, https://www.mars.com/about/policies-and-practices/water-stewardship.

29. Mesfin M. Mekonnen and Arjen Y. Hoekstra, "A Global Assessment of the Water Footprint of Farm Animal Products," *Ecosystems* 15 (January 24, 2012): 401–15, https://doi.org/10.1007/s10021-011-9517-8.

30. *Ibid.*

31. Christopher Flavelle and Somini Sengupta, "How America's Diet Is Feeding the Groundwater Crisis," *New York Times*, December 24, 2023, https://www.nytimes.com/interactive/2023/12/24/climate/-groundwater-crisis-chicken-cheese.html.

32. *Ibid.*

33. "Per Capita Meat Consumption by Type, 2021," Food and Agriculture Organization of the United Nations (2023)—with major processing by Our World in Data, https://ourworldindata.org/grapher/per-capita-meat-type.

34. Clara Hernanz Lizarraga and Olivia Solon, "Thirsty Data Centers Are Making Hot Summers Even Scarier," *Bloomberg*, July 26, 2023, https://www.bloomberg.com/news/articles/2023-07-26/extreme-heat-drought-drive-opposition-to-ai-data-centers.

35. David Berreby, "As Use of A.I. Soars, So Does the Energy and Water It Requires," *Yale Environment 360*, February 6, 2024, https://e360.yale.edu/features/artificial-intelligence-climate-energy-emissions.

36. Mike Rogoway, "Google's Water Use Is Soaring in the Dalles, Records Show, with Two More Data Centers to Come," *OregonLive*, December 17, 2022, https://www.oregonlive.com/silicon-forest/2022/12/googles-water-use-is-soaring-in-the-dalles-records-show-with-two-more-data-centers-to-come.html.

37. Cristina Criddle and Kenza Bryan, "AI Boom Sparks Concern over Big Tech's Water Consumption," *Financial Times*, February 24 2024, https://www.ft.com/content/6544119e-a511-4cfa-9243-13b8cf855c13.

38. *Ibid.*

39. Marc-Antoine Eyl-Mazzega and Élise Cassignol, "The Geopolitics of Seawater Desalination," French Institute of International Relations, September 27, 2022, https://www.ifri.org/en/publications/etudes-de-lifri/geopolitics-seawater-desalination.

40. Simon Atkinson, "Solar-Powered Desalination System Provides Villagers with Access to Clean Water for Drinking and Use in Farming," *Membrane Technology* 2020, no. 7 (July 1, 2020): 7–8, https://doi.org/10.1016/s0958-2118(20)30125-7.

41. Arielle Paul, "Dubai's Costly Water World," *New York Times*, November 18, 2023, https://www.nytimes.com/2023/11/18/business/dubai-water-desalination.html.

42. *Ibid.*

43. Maryam R. Al-Shehhi and Yarjan Abdul Samad, "Identifying Algal Bloom 'Hotspots' in Marginal Productive Seas: A Review and Geospatial Analysis," *Remote Sensing* 14, no. 10 (May 20, 2022): 2457, https://doi.org/10.3390/rs14102457.

44. Charles Sheppard, "Coral Reefs in the Gulf Are Mostly Dead Now, but Can We Do Anything About It?" *Marine Pollution Bulletin* 105, no. 2 (April 30, 2016): 593–98, https://doi.org/10.1016/j.marpolbul.2015.09.031.

45. Michael J. McGuire, "Eight Revolutions in the History of U.S. Drinking Water Disinfection," *Journal of the American Water Works Association* 98, no. 3 (March 1, 2006): 123–49, https://doi.org/10.1002/j.1551-8833.2006.tb07612.x.

46. "History of the Clean Water Act," United States Environmental Protection Agency, https://www.epa.gov/laws-regulations/history-clean-water-act.

47. "Water Security Is Critical for Poverty Reduction, but Billions Will Remain Without Water Access Unless Urgent Action Is Taken," World Bank, May 20, 2024, https://www.worldbank.org/en/news/press-release/2024/05/19/water-security-is-critical-for-poverty-reduction.

48. Jennyfer Wolf et al., "Burden of Disease Attributable to Unsafe Drinking Water, Sanitation, and Hygiene in Domestic Settings: A Global Analysis for Selected

Adverse Health Outcomes," *Lancet* 401, no. 10393 (June 5, 2023): 2060–71, https://doi.org/10.1016/s0140-6736(23)00458-0.

49. "Planet Water Foundation's Project 24 Brings Clean Water to Thousands in Need," *GlobeNewswire*, March 17, 2022, https://www.globenewswire.com/en/news-release/2022/03/17/2405440/0/en/Planet-Water-Foundation-s-Project-24-Brings-Clean-Water-to-Thousands-in-Need.html.

50. "AquaTower Community Water Filtration System," *Planet Water Foundation*, https://planet-water.org/community-water-filtration-system/.

51. "Building Access to Clean Water in Support of Sustainable Development Goal 6," UNICEF: United Nations Children's Fund, February 2, 2023, https://www.unicef.org/supply/stories/building-access-clean-water-support-sustainable-development-goal-6.

52. "The 1969 Cuyahoga River Fire," National Park Service, May 3, 2022, https://www.nps.gov/articles/story-of-the-fire.htm.

53. "Bringing 1 River, 21 Subwatersheds, and 10 Miles of Lake Erie Shore Back to Health," Cuyahoga River Area of Concern, https://cuyahogaaoc.org.

54. Diana Ackerman Grunfeld et al., "Underestimated Burden of Per- and Polyfluoroalkyl Substances in Global Surface Waters and Groundwaters," *Nature Geoscience* 17, no. 4 (April 8, 2024): 340–46, https://doi.org/10.1038/s41561-024-01402-8.

55. Delger Erdenesanaa, "PFAS 'Forever Chemicals' Are Pervasive in Water Worldwide, Study Finds," *New York Times*, April 8, 2024, https://www.nytimes.com/2024/04/08/climate/pfas-forever-chemicals-water.html.

56. Peter Jarvis and John Fawell, "Lead in Drinking Water—An Ongoing Public Health Concern?" *Current Opinion in Environmental Science & Health* 20 (April 1, 2021): 100239, https://doi.org/10.1016/j.coesh.2021.100239.

57. Susan J. Masten, Simon H. Davies, and Shawn P. Mcelmurry, "Flint Water Crisis: What Happened and Why?" *Journal of the American Water Works Association* 108, no. 12 (December 1, 2016): 22–34, https://doi.org/10.5942/jawwa.2016.108.0195.

58. "NOAA Forecasts Very Large 'Dead Zone' for Gulf of Mexico," National Oceanic and Atmospheric Administration, National Centers for Coastal Ocean Science, June 10, 2019, https://coastalscience.noaa.gov/news/noaa-forecasts-very-large-dead-zone-for-gulf-of-mexico/.

59. Manvendra Patel et al., "Pharmaceuticals of Emerging Concern in Aquatic Systems: Chemistry, Occurrence, Effects, and Removal Methods," *Chemical Reviews* 119 (March 4, 2019): 3510–673, https://doi.org/10.1021/acs.chemrev.8b00299.

60. E. Shaji et al., "Fluoride Contamination in Groundwater: A Global Review of the Status, Processes, Challenges, and Remedial Measures," *Geoscience Frontiers* 15, no. 2 (March 1, 2024): 101734, https://doi.org/10.1016/j.gsf.2023.101734.

61. Joel Podgorski and Michael Berg, "Global Threat of Arsenic in Groundwater," *Science* 368, no. 6493 (May 22, 2020): 845–50, https://doi.org/10.1126/science.aba1510.

62. Sara V. Flanagan, Richard B. Johnston, and Yan Zheng, "Arsenic in Tube Well Water in Bangladesh: Health and Economic Impacts and Implications for Arsenic Mitigation," *Bulletin of the World Health Organization* 90, no. 11 (November 1, 2012): 839–46, https://doi.org/10.2471/BLT.11.101253.

63. Anand Verma, Bharatesh K. Shetty, Vasudeva Guddattu, Mehul K. Chourasia, and Prachi Pundir, "High Prevalence of Dental Fluorosis Among Adolescents Is a Growing Concern: A School Based Cross-Sectional Study from Southern India," *Environmental Health and Preventive Medicine* 22 (April 4, 2017): 17, https://doi.org/10.1186/s12199-017-0624-9.

64. Andres Jordi, "Tackling Arsenic and Fluoride in Drinking Water," Eawag: Swiss Federal Institute of Aquatic Science and Technology, March 18, 2015, https://www.eawag.ch/en/info/portal/news/news-detail/tackling-arsenic-and-fluoride-in-drinking-water/.

65. Susan S.A. Alkurdi, Raed A. Al-Juboori, Jochen Bundschuh, and Ihsan Hamawand, "Bone Char as a Green Sorbent for Removing Health Threatening Fluoride from Drinking Water," *Environment International* 127 (June 1, 2019): 704–19, https://doi.org/10.1016/j.envint.2019.03.065.

66. "Ocean Acidification," National Oceanic and Atmospheric Administration, April 1, 2020, https://www.noaa.gov/education/resource-collections/ocean-coasts/ocean-acidification.

67. Caitlyn Kennedy, "An Upwelling Crisis: Ocean Acidification," NOAA Climate.gov, October 30, 2009, https://www.climate.gov/news-features/features/upwelling-crisis-ocean-acidification.

68. James C. Orr et al., "Anthropogenic Ocean Acidification 6ver the Twenty-First Century and Its Impact on Calcifying Organisms," *Nature* 437 (September 29, 2005): 681–86, https://doi.org/10.1038/nature04095.

Chapter 8

1. Robert J. Hobbs, Carol A. Thomas, Jennifer Halliwell, and Christopher D. Gwenin, "Rapid Detection of Botulinum Neurotoxins—A Review," *Toxins* 11, no. 7 (July 17, 2019): 418, https://doi.org/10.3390/toxins11070418.

2. Agency for Toxic Substances and Disease Registry (U.S.), "Toxicological Profile for Parathion," NIH, National Center for Biotechnology Information, National Library of Medicine Bookshelf, January 1, 2017, https://www.ncbi.nlm.nih.gov/books/NBK591895/.

3. "Malathion. Technical Fact Sheet," NPIC: National Pesticide Information Center, http://npic.orst.edu/factsheets/archive/malatech.html.

4. "Natural Toxins in Food," World Health Organization, March 10, 2023, https://www.who.int/news-room/-fact-sheets/detail/natural-toxins-in-food.

5. Richard Pérez-Peña, "Decades Later and Far Away, Chernobyl Disaster Still Contaminates Milk," *New York Times*, June 8, 2018, https://www.nytimes.com/2018/06/08/world/europe/chernobyl-nuclear-disaster-radiation-milk.html.

6. Evanthia Diamanti–Kandarakis et al., "Endocrine-Disrupting Chemicals: An Endocrine Society Scientific Statement," *Endocrine Reviews* 30, no. 4 (June 1, 2009): 293–342, https://doi.org/10.1210/er.2009-0002.

7. J.C. Semenza, P.E. Tolbert, C.H. Rubin, L.J. Guillette, and R.J. Jackson, "Reproductive Toxins and Alligator Abnormalities at Lake Apopka, Florida," *Environmental Health Perspectives* 105, no. 10 (October 1, 1997): 1030–32, https://doi.org/10.1289/ehp.971051030.

8. Carrie Arnold, "Consequences of DDT Exposure Could Last Generations," *Scientific American*, July 1, 2021, https://www.scientificamerican.com/article/consequences-of-ddt-exposure-could-last-generations.

9. Cynthia Marie Metz, "Bisphenol A: Understanding the Controversy," *Workplace Health & Safety* 64, no. 1 (January 22, 2016): 28–36, https://doi.org/10.1177/2165079915623790.

10. Muhammad Faisal Manzoor et al., "An Insight into Bisphenol A, Food Exposure and Its Adverse Effects on Health: A Review," *Frontiers in Nutrition* 9 (November 3, 2022): 1047827, https://doi.org/10.3389/fnut.2022.1047827.

11. "Canada Bans Bisphenol A in Baby Products," *Nature* 455 (October 22, 2008): 1020, https://doi.org/10.1038/4551020a.

12. "Bisphenol A: EU Ban on Use in Baby Bottles Enters into Force Next Week. Press Release IP/11/229," European Commission, February 25, 2011, https://ec.europa.eu/commission/presscorner/detail/en/IP_11_229.

13. "Bisphenol A (BPA): Use in Food Contact Application," U.S. Food and Drug Administration, April 20, 2023, https://www.fda.gov/food/food-packaging-other-substances-come-contact-food-information-consumers/bisphenol-bpa-use-food-contact-application.

14. Frederick S. vom Saal et al., "The Conflict Between Regulatory Agencies over the 20,000-Fold Lowering of the Tolerable Daily Intake (TDI) for Bisphenol A (BPA) by the European Food Safety Authority (EFSA)," *Environmental Health Perspectives* 132, no. 4 (April 9, 2024), https://doi.org/10.1289/ehp13812.

15. Tania Estape, "Cancer in the Elderly: Challenges and Barriers," *Asia-Pacific Journal of Oncology Nursing* 5, no. 1 (January 1, 2018): P40–42, https://doi.org/10.4103/apjon.apjon_52_17.

16. Franklyn De Silva and Jane Alcorn, "A Tale of Two Cancers: A Current Concise Overview of Breast and Prostate Cancer," *Cancers* 14, no. 12 (June 15, 2022): 2954, https://doi.org/10.3390/cancers14122954.

17. Josep M. Llovet et al., "Hepatocellular Carcinoma," *Nature Reviews. Disease Primers* 7 (January 21, 2021): 6, https://doi.org/10.1038/s41572-020-00240-3.

18. Freddie Bray, Mathieu Laversanne, Hyuna Sung, Jacques Ferlay, Rebecca L. Siegel, Isabelle Soerjomataram, and Ahmedin Jemal, "Global Cancer Statistics 2022: GLOBOCAN Estimates of Incidence and Mortality Worldwide for 36 Cancers in 185 Countries," *CA: A Cancer Journal for Clinicians* 74, no. 3 (April 4, 2024): 229–63, https://doi.org/10.3322/caac.21834.

19. "How Toxicologists Establish Safe Doses of Chemicals," Toxicology Education Foundation, https://toxedfoundation.org/how-toxicologists-establish-safe-doses/.

20. "Artificial Sweeteners and Cancer," National Cancer Institute, August 29, 2023, https://www.cancer.gov/about-cancer/causes-prevention/risk/diet/artificial-sweeteners-fact-sheet.

21. "Vinyl Chloride," National Cancer Institute, November 3, 2022, https://www.cancer.gov/about-cancer/causes-prevention/risk/substances/vinyl-chloride.

22. "Benzene and Cancer Risk," American Cancer Society, February 1, 2023, https://www.cancer.org/cancer/risk-prevention/chemicals/benzene.html.

23. Xinlu Miao et al., "Global, Regional, and National Burden of Non-Communicable Diseases Attributable to Occupational Asbestos Exposure 1990–2019 and Prediction to 2035: Worsening or Improving?" *BMC Public Health* 24 (March 18, 2024): 832, https://doi.org/10.1186/s12889-024-18099-4.

24. Prabhat Jha, "The Hazards of Smoking and the Benefits of Cessation: A Critical Summation of the Epidemiological Evidence in High-Income Countries," *eLife* 9 (March 24, 2020): e49979, https://doi.org/10.7554/elife.49979.

25. Krishna Chaitanya Thandra, Adam Barsouk, Kalyan Saginala, John Sukumar Aluru, and Alexander Barsouk, "Epidemiology of Lung Cancer," *Contemporary Oncology/Współczesna Onkologia* 25, no. 1 (January 1, 2021): 45–52, https://doi.org/10.5114/wo.2021.103829.

26. Daryoush Shahbazi-Gahrouei, Mehrdad Gholami, and Samaneh Setayandeh, "A Review on Natural Background Radiation," *Advanced Biomedical Research* 2, no. 1 (January 1, 2013): 65, https://doi.org/10.4103/2277-9175.115821.

27. Joe Schwarcz, "Is It True That Bananas Are Radioactive?" McGill University, March 15, 2018, https://www.mcgill.ca/oss/article/you-asked/it-true-banana-radioactive.

28. Anna Grzywa-Celińska, Adam Krusiński, Jadwiga Mazur, Katarzyna Szewczyk, and Krzysztof Kozak, "Radon—The Element of Risk. The Impact of Radon Exposure on Human Health," *Toxics* 8, no. 4 (December 14, 2020): 120, https://doi.org/10.3390/toxics8040120.

29. "Safety of Nuclear Power Reactors," World Nuclear Association, March 2, 2022, https://world-nuclear.org/information-library/safety-and-security/safety-of-plants/safety-of-nuclear-power-reactors.

30. Noboru Takamura, Makiko Orita, Vladimir Saenko, Shunichi Yamashita, Shigenobu Nagataki, and Yuri Demidchik, "Radiation and Risk of Thyroid Cancer: Fukushima and Chernobyl," *Lancet. Diabetes & Endocrinology* 4, no. 8 (August 1, 2016): 647, https://doi.org/10.1016/s2213-8587(16)30112-7.

31. "Strontium-90. A Fission Product with Properties Close to Calcium," Radioactivity.Eu.Com, https://radioactivity.eu.com/articles/phenomenon/strontium_90.

32. Louise Zibold Reiss, "Strontium-90 Absorption by Deciduous Teeth," *Science* 134, no. 3491 (November 24, 1961): 1669–73, https://doi.org/10.1126/science.134.3491.1669.

33. Joseph Mangano, Kelli S. Gaus, Timothy A. Mousseau, and Michael Ketterer, "Strontium-90 in Baby Teeth as a Basis for Estimating U.S. Cancer Deaths from Nuclear Weapons Fallout," *International Journal of Social Determinants of Health and Health Services* 53, no. 3 (January 31, 2023): 374–84, https://doi.org/10.1177/27551938231152771.

34. Robert Alvarez and Joseph Mangano, "The Test Ban Treaty at 60: How Citizen Action Made the World Safer," *Bulletin of the Atomic Scientists*, August 4, 2023, https://thebulletin.org/2023/08/the-test-ban-treaty-at-60-how-citizen-action-made-the-world-safer.

35. "The Nobel Prize in Physiology or

Medicine 1948," Nobel Prize Outreach, June 2, 2024, https://www.nobelprize.org/prizes/medicine/1948/summary.

36. Rachel Carson, *Silent Spring*, Boston: Houghton Mifflin, 1962.

37. "DDT—A Brief History and Status," United States Environmental Protection Agency, March 12, 2024, https://www.epa.gov/ingredients-used-pesticide-products/ddt-brief-history-and-status.

38. "Learn About Polychlorinated Biphenyls," United States Environmental Protection Agency, April 2, 2024, https://www.epa.gov/pcbs/learn-about-polychlorinated-biphenyls.

39. "Learn About Dioxin," United States Environmental Protection Agency, December 7, 2023, https://www.epa.gov/dioxin/learn-about-dioxin.

40. "Dioxins," World Health Organization, November 29, 2023, https://www.who.int/news-room/fact-sheets/detail/dioxins-and-their-effects-on-human-health.

41. Doris Friedrich, "The Problems Won't Go Away: Persistent Organic Pollutants (POPs) in the Arctic," *Arctic Institute*, July 1, 2016, https://www.thearcticinstitute.org/persistent-organic-pollutants-pops-in-the-arctic/.

42. "Human Biomonitoring: Facts and Figures," World Health Organization, Regional Office for Europe, Copenhagen, 2015, https://iris.who.int/handle/10665/164588.

43. Jindrich Petrlik et al., "Monitoring Dioxins and PCBs in Eggs as Sensitive Indicators for Environmental Pollution and Global Contaminated Sites and Recommendations for Reducing and Controlling Releases and Exposure," *Emerging Contaminants* 8 (January 1, 2022): 254–79, https://doi.org/10.1016/j.emcon.2022.05.001.

44. Leila Peivasteh-Roudsari et al., "Origin, Dietary Exposure, and Toxicity of Endocrine-Disrupting Food Chemical Contaminants: A Comprehensive Review," *Heliyon* 9, no. 7 (July 11, 2023): e18140, https://doi.org/10.1016/j.heliyon.2023.e18140.

45. Nathalie Grova, Henri Schroeder, Jean-Luc Olivier, and Jonathan D. Turner, "Epigenetic and Neurological Impairments Associated with Early Life Exposure to Persistent Organic Pollutants," *International Journal of Genomics* 2019

(January 14, 2019): 2085496, https://doi.org/10.1155/2019/2085496.

46. Daniel Smith, "Worldwide Trends in DDT Levels in Human Breast Milk," *International Journal of Epidemiology* 28, no. 2 (April 1, 1999): 179–88, https://doi.org/10.1093/ije/28.2.179; Rainer Malisch et al., "Time Trends in Human Milk Derived from WHO- and UNEP-Coordinated Exposure Studies, Chapter 2: DDT, Beta-HCH and HCB," in *Persistent Organic Pollutants in Human Milk*, ed. R. Malisch, P. Fürst, and K. Šebková (Cham: Springer, October 12, 2023), 485–542, https://doi.org/10.1007/978-3-031-34087-1_13.

47. Alissa Cordner et al., "The True Cost of PFAS and the Benefits of Acting Now," *Environmental Science & Technology* 55, no. 14 (July 7, 2021): 9630–33, https://doi.org/10.1021/acs.est.1c03565.

48. Zhanyun Wang, Jamie C. DeWitt, Christopher P. Higgins, and Ian T. Cousins, "A Never-Ending Story of Per- and Polyfluoroalkyl Substances (PFASs)?" *Environmental Science & Technology* 51, no. 5 (February 22, 2017): 2508–18, https://doi.org/10.1021/acs.est.6b04806.

49. Lisa Melymuk, Jonathan Blumenthal, Ondřej Sáňka, Adriana Shu-Yin, Veena Singla, Kateřina Šebková, Kristi Pullen Fedinick, and Miriam L. Diamond, "Persistent Problem: Global Challenges to Managing PCBs," *Environmental Science & Technology* 56, no. 12 (June 1, 2022): 9029–40, https://doi.org/10.1021/acs.est.2c01204.

50. Michele Augusto Riva, Alessandra Lafranconi, Marco Italo D'orso, and Giancarlo Cesana, "Lead Poisoning: Historical Aspects of a Paradigmatic 'Occupational and Environmental Disease,'" *Safety and Health at Work* 3, no. 1 (March 1, 2012): 11–16, https://doi.org/10.5491/shaw.2012.3.1.11.

51. David Rosner and Gerald Markowitz, "A 'Gift of God'?: The Public Health Controversy over Leaded Gasoline During the 1920s," *American Journal of Public Health* 75, no. 4 (April 1, 1985): 344–52, https://doi.org/10.2105/ajph.75.4.344.

52. Jerome O. Nriagu, "The Rise and Fall of Leaded Gasoline," *Science of the Total Environment* 92 (March 1, 1990): 13–28, https://doi.org/10.1016/0048-9697(90)90318-o.

53. Elizabeth Gamillo, "Leaded Gasoline Use in Vehicles Has Now Officially Ended Worldwide," *Smithsonian Magazine*, August 31, 2021, https://www.smithsonianmag.com/smart-news/worldwide-use-leaded-gasoline-vehicles-now-completely-phased-out-180978549/.

54. Valerie M. Thomas, Robert H. Socolow, James J. Fanelli, and Thomas G. Spiro, "Effects of Reducing Lead in Gasoline: An Analysis of the International Experience," *Environmental Science & Technology* 33, no. 22 (October 1, 1999): 3942–48, https://doi.org/10.1021/es990231; Michael J. McFarland, Matt E. Hauer, and Aaron Reuben, "Half of U.S. Population Exposed to Adverse Lead Levels in Early Childhood," *Proceedings of the National Academy of Sciences of the United States of America* 119, no. 11 (March 7, 2022): e2118631119, https://doi.org/10.1073/pnas.2118631119.

55. Kathryn B. Egan, Cheryl R. Cornwell, Joseph G. Courtney, and Adrienne S. Ettinger, "Blood Lead Levels in U.S. Children Ages 1–11 Years, 1976–2016," *Environmental Health Perspectives* 129, no. 3 (March 17, 2021), https://doi.org/10.1289/ehp7932.

56. Ruth C. Angrand, Geoffrey Collins, Philip J. Landrigan, and Valerie M. Thomas, "Relation of Blood Lead Levels and Lead in Gasoline: An Updated Systematic Review," *Environmental Health* 21 (December 27, 2022): 138, https://doi.org/10.1186/s12940-022-00936-x.

57. Aaron Reuben, Maxwell Elliott, and Avshalom Caspi, "Implications of Legacy Lead for Children's Brain Development," *Nature Medicine* 26 (January 1, 2020): 23–25, https://doi.org/10.1038/s41591-019-0731-9.

58. "Lead Poisoning," World Health Organization, August 11, 2023, https://www.who.int/news-room/fact-sheets/detail/lead-poisoning-and-health.

59. Ted Schwaba, Wiebke Bleidorn, Christopher J. Hopwood, Jochen E. Gebauer, P. Jason Rentfrow, Jeff Potter, and Samuel D. Gosling, "The Impact of Childhood Lead Exposure on Adult Personality: Evidence from the United States, Europe, and a Large-Scale Natural Experiment," *Proceedings of the National Academy of Sciences of the United States of America* 118, no. 29 (July 12, 2021): e2020104118, https://doi.org/10.1073/pnas.2020104118;

John Paul Wright, Bruce P. Lanphear, Kim N. Dietrich, Michelle Bolger, Lisa Tully, Kim M. Cecil, and Catherine Sacarellos, "Developmental Lead Exposure and Adult Criminal Behavior: A 30-Year Prospective Birth Cohort Study," *Neurotoxicology and Teratology* 85 (May 1, 2021): 106960, https://doi.org/10.1016/j.ntt.2021.106960.

60. Howard W. Mielke and Sammy Zahran, "The Urban Rise and Fall of Air Lead (Pb) and the Latent Surge and Retreat of Societal Violence," *Environment International* 43 (August 1, 2012): 48–55, https://doi.org/10.1016/j.envint.2012.03.005.

61. Anthony Higney, Nick Hanley, and Mirko Moro, "The Lead-Crime Hypothesis: A Meta-Analysis," *Regional Science and Urban Economics* 97 (November 1, 2022): 103826, https://doi.org/10.1016/j.regsciurbeco.2022.103826.

62. Howard Mielke, "Lead in the Inner Cities," *American Scientist* 87, no. 1 (January 1, 1999): 62, https://doi.org/10.1511/1999.16.62.

63. Barbara Gworek, Wojciech Dmuchowski, and Aneta H. Baczewska-Dąbrowska, "Mercury in the Terrestrial Environment: A Review," *Environmental Sciences Europe* 32 (October 2, 2020): 128, https://doi.org/10.1186/s12302-020-00401-x.

64. David G. Streets, Hannah M. Horowitz, Daniel J. Jacob, Zifeng Lu, Leonard Levin, Arnout F.H. ter Schure, and Elsie M. Sunderland, "Total Mercury Released to the Environment by Human Activities," *Environmental Science & Technology* 51, no. 11 (April 27, 2017): 5969–77, https://doi.org/10.1021/acs.est.7b00451.

65. Jung-Duck Park and Wei Zheng, "Human Exposure and Health Effects of Inorganic and Elemental Mercury," *Journal of Preventive Medicine and Public Health* 45, no. 6 (November 29, 2012): 344–52, https://doi.org/10.3961/jpmph.2012.45.6.344.

66. Margaret R. Karagas, Anna L. Choi, Emily Oken, Milena Horvat, Rita Schoeny, Elizabeth Kamai, Whitney Cowell, Philippe Grandjean, and Susan Korrick, "Evidence on the Human Health Effects of Low-Level Methylmercury Exposure," *Environmental Health Perspectives* 120, no. 6 (January 24, 2012): 799–806, https://doi.org/10.1289/ehp.1104494.

67. "Minamata Convention on Mercury," United States Environmental Protection Agency, December 12, 2023, https://www.epa.gov/international-cooperation/minamata-convention-mercury.

68. Masazumi Harada, "Minamata Disease: Methylmercury Poisoning in Japan Caused by Environmental Pollution," *Critical Reviews in Toxicology* 25, no. 1 (January 1, 1995): 1–24, https://doi.org/10.3109/10408449509089885.

69. David G. Streets, Hannah M. Horowitz, Zifeng Lu, Leonard Levin, Colin P. Thackray, and Elsie M. Sunderland, "Five Hundred Years of Anthropogenic Mercury: Spatial and Temporal Release Profiles," *Environmental Research Letters* 14 (July 22, 2019): 084004, https://doi.org/10.1088/1748-9326/ab281f.

70. Louisa J. Esdaile and Justin M. Chalker, "The Mercury Problem in Artisanal and Small-Scale Gold Mining," *Chemistry: A European Journal* 24, no. 27 (May 11, 2018): 6905–16, https://doi.org/10.1002/chem.201704840.

71. Justice Afrifa, Yeboah Kwaku Opoku, Eric Ofori Gyamerah, George Ashiagbor, and Rosemary Doe Sorkpor, "The Clinical Importance of the Mercury Problem in Artisanal Small-Scale Gold Mining," *Frontiers in Public Health* 7 (May 28, 2019): 131, https://doi.org/10.3389/fpubh.2019.00131.

72. "Global Mercury Program: Mined Without Mercury Training," Pure Earth, https://www.pureearth.org/global-mercury-program/mined-without-mercury-training/

73. "The Salmon Struggle," State of Salmon in Watersheds Report, 2022, https://stateofsalmon.wa.gov/executive-summary/challenges.

74. Zhenyu Tian et al., "A Ubiquitous Tire Rubber–Derived Chemical Induces Acute Mortality in Coho Salmon," *Science* 371, no. 6525 (January 8, 2021): 185–89, https://doi.org/10.1126/science.abd6951.

75. Stephanie I. Blair, Clyde H. Barlow, and Jenifer K. McIntyre, "Acute Cerebrovascular Effects in Juvenile Coho Salmon Exposed to Roadway Runoff," *Canadian Journal of Fisheries and Aquatic Sciences* 78, no. 2 (February 1, 2021): 103–9, https://doi.org/10.1139/cjfas-2020-0240.

76. Jim Robbins, "Road Hazard: Evidence Mounts on Toxic Pollution from Tires," *Yale Environment 360*, September 19, 2023, https://e360.yale.edu/features/tire-pollution-toxic-chemicals.

77. Perry Wheeler and Glen Spain, "U.S. Fishing Groups Sue Tire Manufacturers over 6PPD Impacts on Salmon, Steelhead," *Earthjustice*, November 8, 2023, https://earthjustice.org/press/2023/u-s-fishing-groups-sue-tire-manufacturers-over-6ppd-impacts-on-salmon-steelhead.

78. Mugdha Flores, "Saving Washington's Salmon from Toxic Tire Dust," Washington State Department of Ecology, January 25, 2023, https://ecology.wa.gov/blog/january-2023/saving-washington-s-salmon-from-toxic-tire-dust.

79. Hamidreza Sharifan, "Alarming the Impacts of the Organic and Inorganic UV Blockers on Endangered Coral's Species in the Persian Gulf: A Scientific Concern for Coral Protection," *Sustainable Futures* 2 (January 1, 2020): 100017, https://doi.org/10.1016/j.sftr.2020.100017.

80. Carys L. Mitchelmore, Emily E. Burns, Annaleise Conway, Andrew Heyes, and Iain A. Davies, "A Critical Review of Organic Ultraviolet Filter Exposure, Hazard, and Risk to Corals," *Environmental Toxicology and Chemistry* 40, no. 4 (February 2, 2021): 967–88, https://doi.org/10.1002/etc.4948.

81. "Your Reef Safe Sunscreen Guide—15 Sunscreens That Are Reef Safe," Hawaii.com, https://www.hawaii.com/reef-safe-sunscreen/.

82. "The Trouble with Ingredients in Sunscreens," EWG's 18th Annual Guide to Sunscreens (2024), Environmental Working Group, https://www.ewg.org/sunscreen/report/the-trouble-with-sunscreen-chemicals/.

83. Erik Stokstad, "European Union Expands Ban of Three Neonicotinoid Pesticides," *Science*, April 27, 2018, https://doi.org/10.1126/science.aau0152.

84. Cheryl Hogue, "New York Bans Televisions with Organohalogen Flame Retardants," *Chemical & Engineering News*, January 5, 2022, https://cen.acs.org/safety/consumer-safety/New-York-bans-televisions-organohalogen/100/web/2022/01; "Overall View on the Current States Laws Against the Flame Retardants Chemical," *Unitec Laboratory Services*, 2020, http://www.unitls.

com/reports-news/the-us-and-canada/51-overall-view-on-the-current-states-laws-against-the-flame-retardants-chemical.html

85. Martin Sharkey, "Flame Retardant Chemicals Can Cause Serious Health Risks—And They Only Slow Fire by a Few Seconds," *Conversation*, November 15, 2023, https://theconversation.com/flame-retardant-chemicals-can-cause-serious-health-risks-and-they-only-slow-fire-by-a-few-seconds-214658.

86. "The Grassroots Movement that Shut Down an Indian Copper Plant," *BBC News*, May 29, 2018, https://www.bbc.com/news/world-asia-india-44286233.

87. "Basics of Green Chemistry," United States Environmental Protection Agency, May 2, 2024, https://www.epa.gov/greenchemistry/basics-green-chemistry.

88. "Urban Taraxagum. Made of Dandelion Rubber," *Continental*, https://www.continental-tires.com/products/b2c/bicycle/tires/urban-taraxagum/.

89. "Soak Up the Rain: Permeable Pavement," United States Environmental Protection Agency, May 23, 2024, https://www.epa.gov/soakuptherain/soak-rain-permeable-pavement.

Chapter 9

1. "UN Report: Nature's Dangerous Decline 'Unprecedented'; Species Extinction Rates 'Accelerating,'" United Nations Sustainable Development Group, May 6, 2019, https://www.un.org/sustainabledevelopment/blog/2019/05/nature-decline-unprecedented-report/.

2. "Laws & Policies: Endangered Species Act," NOAA Fisheries, https://www.fisheries.noaa.gov/topic/laws-policies/endangered-species-act.

3. "The Birds Directive," European Commission, https://environment.ec.europa.eu/topics/nature-and-biodiversity/birds-directive_en; "The Habitats Directive," European Commission, https://environment.ec.europa.eu/topics/nature-and-biodiversity/habitats-directive_en.

4. "The Convention on Biological Diversity: History of the Convention," United Nations Environment Programme, May 22, 2024, https://www.cbd.int/history.

5. "Wolf Restoration," National Park Service, April 27, 2023, https://www.nps.gov/yell/learn/nature/wolf-restoration.htm.

6. "Gray Wolf," National Park Service, March 11, 2024, https://www.nps.gov/yell/learn/nature/wolves.htm.

7. Brodie Farquhar, "Wolf Reintroduction Changes Ecosystem in Yellowstone," *Yellowstone National Park*, June 22, 2023, https://www.yellowstonepark.com/things-to-do/wildlife/wolf-reintroduction-changes-ecosystem/.

8. Grace Hansen, "Yellowstone's Wolves Defied Extinction, but Face New Threats Beyond Park's Borders," *Mongabay*, May 31, 2022, https://news.mongabay.com/2022/05/yellowstones-wolves-defied-extinction-but-face-new-threats-beyond-parks-borders/.

9. Ishana Shukla, Kaitlyn M. Gaynor, Boris Worm, and Chris T. Darimont, "The Diversity of Animals Identified as Keystone Species," *Ecology and Evolution* 13, no. 10 (October 9, 2023): e10561, https://doi.org/10.1002/ece3.10561.

10. Antoinette van de Water, Michelle Henley, Lucy Bates, and Rob Slotow, "The Value of Elephants: A Pluralist Approach," *Ecosystem Services* 58 (December 1, 2022): 101488, https://doi.org/10.1016/j.ecoser.2022.101488.

11. Josh Davis, "Human-Elephant Conflict: How to Live Alongside the Largest Living Land Animal," Natural History Museum, London, https://www.nhm.ac.uk/discover/human-elephant-conflict-how-to-live-alongside-largest-living-land-animal.html.

12. Hannah Thomasy, "Beehive Fences Can Help Mitigate Human-Elephant Conflict," *Mongabay*, September 11, 2019, https://news.mongabay.com/2019/09/beehive-fences-can-help-mitigate-human-elephant-conflict/.

13. "Keystone Plants by Ecoregion," National Wildlife Federation, https://www.nwf.org/Garden-for-Wildlife/About/Native-Plants/keystone-plants-by-ecoregion.

14. Laura Tangley, "Power Plants," *National Wildlife Magazine*, April 1, 2022, https://www.nwf.org/Magazines/National-Wildlife/2022/April-May/Conservation/Keystone-Plants.

15. Jerry Adler, "Meet the Ecologist

Who Wants You to Unleash the Wild on Your Backyard," *Smithsonian Magazine*, April 2020, https://www.smithsonianmag.com/science-nature/meet-ecologist-who-wants-unleash-wild-back yard-180974372/.

16. Desiree L. Narango, Douglas W. Tallamy, and Kimberley J. Shropshire, "Few Keystone Plant Genera Support the Majority of Lepidoptera Species," *Nature Communications* 11 (November 13, 2020): 5751, https://doi.org/10.1038/s41467-020-19565-4.

17. Jeff Ollerton, Rachael Winfree, and Sam Tarrant, "How Many Flowering Plants Are Pollinated by Animals?" *Oikos* 120, no. 3 (February 21, 2011): 321–26, https://doi.org/10.1111/j.1600-0706.2010.18644.x.

18. "What Is the Role of Native Bees in the United States?" U.S. Geological Survey, https://www.usgs.gov/faqs/what-role-native-bees-united-states.

19. Kelsey Kopec and Lori Ann Burd, "Pollinators in Peril. A Systematic Status Review of North American and Hawaiian Native Bees," Center for Biological Diversity, February 2017, https://www.biologicaldiversity.org/campaigns/native_pollinators/pdfs/Pollinators_in_Peril.pdf.

20. "Garden for Wildlife," National Wildlife Federation, https://gardenforwildlife.com.

21. "What Is PEFC?" Programme for the Endorsement of Forest Certification, https://www.pefc.org/discover-pefc/what-is-pefc.

22. "How the FSC System Works," Forest Stewardship Council, https://fsc.org/en/how-the-fsc-system-works.

23. Jennifer Skene, "The Logging Loophole: How the Logging Industry's Unregulated Carbon Emissions Undermine Canada's Climate Goals," Natural Resources Defense Council and Environmental Defence Canada, July 2020, https://naturecanada.ca/wp-content/uploads/2020/07/Boreal-Report-2020.pdf.

24. *Ibid.*

25. Ian Austen and Vjosa Isai, "Canada's Logging Industry Devours Forests Crucial to Fighting Climate Change," *New York Times*, January 4, 2024, https://www.nytimes.com/2024/01/04/world/canada/canada-boreal-forest-logging.html.

26. Erik Hoffner, "Sweden's Green Veneer Hides Unsustainable Logging Practices," *Yale Environment 360*, December 1, 2011, https://e360.yale.edu/features/swedens_green_veneer_hides_unsustainable_logging_practices.

27. Mélissa Godin, "Deforestation Poses 'Existential' Threat to Sweden's Reindeer, Warn Indigenous Herders," *Times*, March 12, 2024, https://time.com/6899748/deforestation-sweden-reindeer-sami-herders/.

28. Connie Y. Chiang and Michael Reese, "Evergreen State: Exploring the History of Washington's Forests," Center for the Study of the Pacific Northwest, University of Washington, Department of History, https://sites.uw.edu/cspn/evergreen-state/.

29. "The Northern Spotted Owl," Forest History Society, https://foresthistory.org/research-explore/us-forest-service-history/policy-and-law/wildlife-management/the-northern-spotted-owl/.

30. "Mission and History," Blue Mountains Forest Partners, https://bluemountainsforestpartners.org/about/.

31. Nicholas Kristof, "They Overcame Mutual Loathing, and Saved a Town," *New York Times*, April 10, 2021, https://www.nytimes.com/2021/04/10/opinion/sunday/loggers-environmentalists-oregon.html.

32. Mark R. Kreider, Philip E. Higuera, Sean A. Parks, William L. Rice, Nadia White, and Andrew J. Larson, "Fire Suppression Makes Wildfires More Severe and Accentuates Impacts of Climate Change and Fuel Accumulation," *Nature Communications* 15 (March 25, 2024): 2412, https://doi.org/10.1038/s41467-024-46702-0.

33. Warren Cornwall, "A Huge Forest Experiment Aims to Reduce Wildfires. Can It Unite Loggers and Environmentalists?" *Science*, September 16, 2021, https://doi.org/10.1126/science.acx9117.

34. Noohi Nasim, Inavolu Sriram Sandeep, and Sujata Mohanty, "Plant-Derived Natural Products for Drug Discovery: Current Approaches and Prospects," *Nucleus* 65 (October 18, 2022): 399–411, https://doi.org/10.1007/s13237-022-00405-3.

35. Michelaina Johnson, "5 Interesting Facts About the Pantanal, the World's Largest Tropical Wetland," World Wildlife Fund, https://www.worldwildlife.org/stories/5-interesting-facts-about-the-

pantanal-the-world-s-largest-tropical-wetland.

36. "Wetlands Disappearing Three Times Faster Than Forests," United Nations Climate Change, October 1, 2018, https://unfccc.int/news/wetlands-disappearing-three-times-faster-than-forests.

37. Walfrido M. Tomas et al., "Sustainability Agenda for the Pantanal Wetland: Perspectives on a Collaborative Interface for Science, Policy, and Decision-Making," *Tropical Conservation Science* 12 (September 18, 2019): 194008291987263, https://doi.org/10.1177/1940082919872634.

38. Paola A. Arias et al., "Interplay Between Climate Change and Climate Variability: The 2022 Drought in Central South America," *Climatic Change* 177 (December 21, 2023): 6, https://doi.org/10.1007/s10584-023-03664-4.

39. Suzanne Ozment and Rafael Feltran-Barbieri, "Help for São Paulo's Complex Water Woes: Protect and Restore Forests," *World Resources Institute*, September 25, 2018, https://www.wri.org/insights/help-sao-paulos-complex-water-woes-protect-and-restore-forests.

40. Ana Ionova, "'Devastating' Fires Engulf Brazilian Pantanal Wetlands—Again," *Mongabay*, December 23, 2020, https://news.mongabay.com/2020/12/devastating-fires-engulf-brazilian-pantanal-wetlands-again/.

41. Newton De Magalhães Neto and Heitor Evangelista, "Human Activity Behind the Unprecedented 2020 Wildfire in Brazilian Wetlands (Pantanal)," *Frontiers in Environmental Science* 10 (June 15, 2022): 888578, https://doi.org/10.3389/fenvs.2022.888578.

42. Daniel Politi, "An Economic Lifeline in South America, the Paraná River, Is Shriveling," *New York Times*, September 4, 2021, https://www.nytimes.com/2021/09/04/world/americas/drought-argentina-parana-river.html.

43. Ashley Thomson, "Biodiversity and the Amazon Rainforest," *Greenpeace*, May 22, 2020, https://www.greenpeace.org/usa/biodiversity-and-the-amazon-rainforest/.

44. Bernardo M. Flores et al., "Critical Transitions in the Amazon Forest System," *Nature* 626 (February 14, 2024): 555–64, https://doi.org/10.1038/s41586-023-06970-0.

45. Adam Voiland, "Making Sense of Amazon Deforestation Patterns," NASA Earth Observatory, November 22, 2019, https://earthobservatory.nasa.gov/images/145888/making-sense-of-amazon-deforestation-patterns.

46. Nikk Ogasa, "The Amazon Might Not Have a 'Tipping Point.' But It's Still in Trouble," *ScienceNews*, June 16, 2023, https://www.sciencenews.org/article/amazon-tipping-trouble-climate-cerrado.

47. "PRODES—Amazônia. Monitoramento do Desmatamento da Floresta Amazônica Brasileira por Satélite," Brazilian National Institute of Space Research, PRODES satellite monitoring project, accessed June 10, 2024, http://www.obt.inpe.br/OBT/assuntos/programas/amazonia/prodes.

48. Sofia Ferreira Santos, "Amazon Rainforest: Deforestation Rate Halved in 2023," *BBC News*, January 12, 2024, https://www.bbc.com/news/world-latin-america-67962297.

49. Maria Fernanda Ribeiro, "In the Amazon, a Farmer Practices the Future of Sustainable Cattle Ranching," *Mongabay*, May 28, 2020, https://news.mongabay.com/2020/05/in-the-amazon-a-farmer-practices-the-future-of-sustainable-cattle-ranching/.

50. Timothy J. Killeen, "National Versus Global Markets—Beef in the Brazilian Amazon," *Mongabay*, October 19, 2023, https://news.mongabay.com/2023/10/national-versus-global-markets-beef-in-the-brazilian-amazon/.

51. Sara Miller Llana, "Saving the Amazon: How Cattle Ranchers Can Halt Deforestation," *Christian Science Monitor*, March 4, 2020, https://www.csmonitor.com/Environment/2020/0304/Saving-the-Amazon-How-cattle-ranchers-can-halt-deforestation.

52. Erasmus K.H.J. Zu Ermgassen et al., "Results from On-the-Ground Efforts to Promote Sustainable Cattle Ranching in the Brazilian Amazon," *Sustainability* 10, no. 4 (April 23, 2018): 1301, https://doi.org/10.3390/su10041301.

53. Rhett A. Butler, "World Rainforest Day: The World's Great Rainforests," *Mongabay*, June 22, 2020, https://news.mongabay.com/2020/06/the-worlds-great-rainforests/.

54. Martina Igini, "Deforestation in

Africa: Causes, Effects, and Solutions," Earth.org, March 24, 2022, https://earth.org/deforestation-in-africa/.

55. Niccolo Conte, "Mapped: 30 Years of Deforestation and Forest Growth, by Country," *Decarbonization Channel*, November 6, 2022, https://decarbonization.visualcapitalist.com/mapped-30-years-of-deforestation-and-forest-growth-by-country/.

56. Héloïse Tschora and Francesco Cherubini, "Co-Benefits and Trade-Offs of Agroforestry for Climate Change Mitigation and Other Sustainability Goals in West Africa," *Global Ecology and Conservation* 22 (June 1, 2020): e00919, https://doi.org/10.1016/j.gecco.2020.e00919.

57. Steve Wiggins and Sharada Keats, "Leaping and Learning: Linking Smallholders to Markets," ODI, May 29, 2013, https://odi.org/en/publications/leaping-and-learning-linking-smallholders-to-markets/.

58. Jonathan D. Haskett, Belay Simane, and Caitlin Smith, "Energy and Climate Change Mitigation Benefits of *Faidherbia albida* Agroforestry in Ethiopia," *Frontiers in Environmental Science* 7 (November 1, 2019): 146, https://doi.org/10.3389/fenvs.2019.00146.

59. Jerry D. Glover, John P. Reganold, and Cindy M. Cox, "Plant Perennials to Save Africa's Soils," *Nature* 489 (September 19, 2012): 359–61, https://doi.org/10.1038/489359a.

60. "Southern Africa," EverGreen Agriculture Partnership, https://evergreenagriculture.net/evergreen-nations/southern-africa.

61. Chris Reij, Gray Tappan, and Melinda Smale, "Re-Greening the Sahel: Farmer-Led Innovation in Burkina Faso and Niger," in *Millions Fed: Proven Successes in Agricultural Development*, ed. David J. Spielman and Rajul Pandya-Lorch (Washington, DC: International Food Policy Research Institute [IFPRI], 2009), 53–58, http://ebrary.ifpri.org/cdm/ref/collection/p15738coll2/id/130817.

62. "Niger's Re-Greening Revolution," World Agroforestry, July 16, 2013, https://www.worldagroforestry.org/news/niger's-re-greening-revolution.

63. "8 Things to Know About Palm Oil," World Wide Fund-UK, https://www.wwf.org.uk/updates/8-things-know-about-palm-oil.

64. Olivia Lai, "Deforestation in Southeast Asia: Causes and Solutions," *Earth.org*, March 7, 2022, https://earth.org/deforestation-in-southeast-asia/.

65. "Palm Oil Explorer," U.S. Department of Agriculture, Foreign Agricultural Service, accessed June 19, 2024, https://ipad.fas.usda.gov/cropexplorer/cropview/commodityView.aspx?cropid=4243000.

66. "Asia and the Pacific National Forestry Programmes: Update 34," Food and Agriculture Organization of the United Nations (FAO), Regional Office for Asia and the Pacific, Bangkok, December 2000, https://www.fao.org/4/x6900e/x6900e0d.htm#10.%20Indonesia.

67. Global Forest Watch Dashboard, "Indonesia," https://www.globalforestwatch.org/dashboards/country/IDN/?map=eyJjYW5Cb3VuZCI6dHJ1ZX0%3D.

68. Bernadette Christina, "Explainer: How Indonesia's Deforestation Persists Despite Moratorium," *Reuters*, June 19, 2024, https://www.reuters.com/business/environment/how-indonesias-deforestation-persists-despite-moratorium-2024-06-20.

69. Hans Nicholas Jong, "81% of Indonesia's Oil Palm Plantations Flouting Regulations, Audit Finds," *Mongabay*, August 25, 2019, https://news.mongabay.com/2019/08/81-of-indonesias-oil-palm-plantations-flouting-regulations-audit-finds/.

70. "Palm Oil in Indonesia," Observatory of Economic Complexity (OEC), accessed June 20, 2024, https://oec.world/en/profile/bilateral-product/palm-oil/reporter/idn.

71. Soni S. Wirawan, Maharani D. Solikhah, Hari Setiapraja, and Agus Sugiyono, "Biodiesel Implementation in Indonesia: Experiences and Future Perspectives," *Renewable & Sustainable Energy Reviews* 189 (January 1, 2024): 113911, https://doi.org/10.1016/j.rser.2023.113911.

72. Grace Dungey, "In Oil Palm-Dominated Malaysia, Agroforestry Orchards Are Oases of Bird Life: Study," *Mongabay*, May 11, 2022, https://news.mongabay.com/2022/05/in-oil-palm-dominated-malaysia-agroforestry-orchards-are-oases-of-bird-life-study/.

73. "A Global Partnership to Make Palm Oil Sustainable," Roundtable on Sustainable Palm Oil (RSPO), https://rspo.org.

74. "Land Cover, 2021," Food and Agriculture Organization of the United Nations, FAOSTAT, https://www.fao.org/faostat/en/#data/LC.

75. John Steinbeck, *Grapes of Wrath*, 1984, https://openlibrary.org/books/OL8459553M/Grapes_of_Wrath.

76. "What Happened to the Bison?" U.S. National Park Service, https://www.nps.gov/articles/000/what-happened-to-the-bison.htm.

77. "Bronx Zoo Bison Join Osage Nation Herd in Oklahoma," Wildlife Conservation Society Newsroom, May 13, 2022, https://newsroom.wcs.org/News-Releases/articleType/ArticleView/articleId/17527/Bronx-Zoo-Bison-Join-Osage-Nation-Herd-in-Oklahoma.aspx.

78. "Bison Range Restoration: Our History," Bison Range, https://bisonrange.org/about/.

79. "America Prairie. History & Values," America Prairie, accessed June 20, 2021, https://americanprairie.org/why-it-matters/.

80. Michelle Nijhuis, "Free the American West from Barbed Wire," *New York Times*, September 26, 2023, https://www.nytimes.com/2023/09/26/opinion/barbed-wire-american-west.html.

81. Mark Hoddle, "Quagga & Zebra Mussels," University of California, Riverside, Center for Invasive Species Research, https://cisr.ucr.edu/invasive-species/quagga-zebra-mussels.

82. Christie A. Bahlai et al., "Cascading Effects: Insights from the U.S. Long Term Ecological Research Network," *Ecosphere* 12, no. 5 (May 17, 2021): e03430, https://doi.org/10.1002/ecs2.3430.

83. Jack Tamisiea, "A 19th Century Farmer May Be to Blame for Australia's Rabbit Scourge," *Science*, August 22, 2022, https://doi.org/10.1126/science.ade5315.

84. Joel M. Alves et al., "A Single Introduction of Wild Rabbits Triggered the Biological Invasion of Australia," *Proceedings of the National Academy of Sciences of the United States of America* 119, no. 35 (August 22, 2022): e2122734119, https://doi.org/10.1073/pnas.2122734119.

85. Peter B.S. Spencer, Andrey A. Yurchenko, Victor A. David, Rachael Scott, Klaus-Peter Koepfli, Carlos Driscoll, Stephen J. O'Brien, and Marilyn Menotti-Raymond, "The Population Origins and Expansion of Feral Cats in Australia," *Journal of Heredity* 107, no. 2 (March 1, 2016): 104–14, https://doi.org/10.1093/jhered/esv095.

86. John C.Z. Woinarski, Andrew A. Burbidge, and Peter L. Harrison, "Ongoing Unraveling of a Continental Fauna: Decline and Extinction of Australian Mammals Since European Settlement," *Proceedings of the National Academy of Sciences of the United States of America* 112, no. 15 (February 9, 2015): 4531–40, https://doi.org/10.1073/pnas.1417301112.

87. "Coral Reef Ecosystems," National Oceanic and Atmospheric Administration (NOAA), February 1, 2019, https://www.noaa.gov/education/resource-collections/marine-life/coral-reef-ecosystems.

88. David J. Newman and Gordon M. Cragg, "Drugs and Drug Candidates from Marine Sources: An Assessment of the Current 'State of Play,'" *Planta Medica* 82, no. 9/10 (February 18, 2016): 775–89, https://doi.org/10.1055/s-0042-101353.

89. Amy Sing Wong, Spyridon Vrontos, and Michelle L. Taylor, "An Assessment of People Living by Coral Reefs over Space and Time," *Global Change Biology* 28, no. 23 (September 28, 2022): 7139–53, https://doi.org/10.1111/gcb.16391.

90. "Marine Protected Areas," Protected Planet, https://www.protected-planet.net/en/thematic-areas/marine-protected-areas.

91. "What Is Coral Bleaching?" Australian Institute of Marine Science, https://www.aims.gov.au/research-topics/environmental-issues/coral-bleaching/what-coral-bleaching.

92. "Coral Bleaching Events," Australian Institute of Marine Science, https://www.aims.gov.au/research-topics/environmental-issues/coral-bleaching/coral-bleaching-events.

93. Danielle C. Claar et al., "Dynamic Symbioses Reveal Pathways to Coral Survival Through Prolonged Heatwaves," *Nature Communications* 11 (December 8, 2020): 6097, https://doi.org/10.1038/s41467-020-19169-y.

94. "Biorock™, Mineral Accretion Technology™, Seament™," Global Coral Reef Alliance, https://www.globalcoral.org/biorock-coral-reef-marine-habitat-restoration/.

95. Lisa Boström-Einarsson et al.,

"Coral Restoration—A Systematic Review of Current Methods, Successes, Failures and Future Directions," *PloS One* 15, no. 1 (January 30, 2020): e0226631, https://doi.org/10.1371/journal.pone.0226631.

96. "Kelp Forest," NOAA National Marine Sanctuaries, https://sanctuaries.noaa.gov/visit/ecosystems/kelpdesc.html.

97. Aaron M. Eger et al., "The Value of Ecosystem Services in Global Marine Kelp Forests," *Nature Communications* 14 (April 18, 2023): 1894, https://doi.org/10.1038/s41467-023-37385-0.

98. Alex Fox, "'This Is Shocking.' An Undersea Plague Is Obliterating a Key Ocean Species," *Science*, January 30, 2019, https://doi.org/10.1126/science.aaw8532.

99. "Pioneering Project to Restore Bull Kelp Forests in Greater Farallones National Marine Sanctuary in California," NOAA Fisheries, March 25, 2024, https://www.fisheries.noaa.gov/feature-story/pioneering-project-restore-bull-kelp-forests-greater-farallones-national-marine.

100. Mallory Pickett and Bob Berwyn, "In the Pacific, Global Warming Disrupted the Ecological Dance of Urchins, Sea Stars and Kelp. Otters Help Restore Balance," *Inside Climate News*, March 16, 2021, https://insideclimatenews.org/news/16032021/pacific-ocean-climate-change-kelp-urchin-sea-otter-sea-stars/.

101. "This Chart Shows Which Countries Consume the Most or Least Fish," World Economic Forum, November 29, 2022, https://www.weforum.org/agenda/2022/11/chart-shows-countries-consume-fish-food-security/.

102. "The State of World Fisheries and Aquaculture 2022. Towards Blue Transformation," Food and Agriculture Organization of the United Nations, FAO (2022), Rome: FAO, https://doi.org/10.4060/cc0461en.

103. Rebecca Schijns, Rainer Froese, Jeffrey A. Hutchings, and Daniel Pauly, "Five Centuries of Cod Catches in Eastern Canada," *ICES Journal of Marine Science* 78, no. 8 (August 28, 2021): 2675–83, https://doi.org/10.1093/icesjms/fsab153.

104. Mansel Blackford, "A Tale of Two Fisheries: Fishing and Over-Fishing in American Waters," Origins: Current Events in Historical Perspective, Ohio State University, September 2008, https://origins.osu.edu/article/tale-two-fisheries-fishing-and-over-fishing-american-waters.

105. "Bycatch—A Sad Topic," World Wide Fund, https://www.fishforward.eu/en/project/by-catch/.

106. Elizabeth Claire Alberts, "How Much Carbon Does Ocean Trawling Put into the Atmosphere?" *Mongabay*, January 19, 2024, https://news.mongabay.com/2024/01/carbon-catch-and-release-study-finds-bottom-trawlers-stir-up-seabed-co2/.

107. Jason Daley, "Twice as Many Fishing Vessels Are Chasing Fewer Fish on the World's Oceans," *Smithsonian Magazine*, May 28, 2019, https://www.smithsonianmag.com/smart-news/twice-many-fishing-vessels-are-chasing-fewer-fish-worlds-oceans-180972294/.

108. "The Marine Protection Atlas," Marine Conservation Institute, June 7, 2024, https://mpatlas.org.

109. Isabel L. Call and Daniel K. Lew, "Tradable Permit Programs: What Are the Lessons for the New Alaska Halibut Catch Sharing Plan?" *Marine Policy* 52 (February 1, 2015): 125–37, https://doi.org/10.1016/j.marpol.2014.10.014.

110. "Commercial Whaling," International Whaling Commission, https://iwc.int/management-and-conservation/whaling/commercial.

111. Liam Campling et al., "A Geopolitical-Economy of Distant Water Fisheries Access Arrangements," *npj Ocean Sustainability* (April 29, 2024): 26, https://doi.org/10.1038/s44183-024-00060-y.

112. Ian Urbina, "How China's Expanding Fishing Fleet Is Depleting the World's Oceans," *Yale Environment 360*, August 17, 2020, https://e360.yale.edu/features/how-chinas-expanding-fishing-fleet-is-depleting-worlds-oceans.

113. Elizabeth Fitt, "Boats Behaving Badly: New Report Analyzes China's Own Fisheries Data," *Mongabay*, April 28, 2022, https://news.mongabay.com/2022/04/boats-behaving-badly-new-report-analyzes-chinas-own-fisheries-data/.

114. Isabel Jarrett, "Most Long-Distance Fishing in Foreign Waters Dominated by Only a Few Governments," *Pew Charitable Trusts*, May 27, 2022, https://www.pewtrusts.org/en/research-and-analysis/issue-briefs/2022/05/most-

long-distance-fishing-in-foreign-waters-dominated-by-only-a-few-governments.

115. "Agreement on Port State Measures (PSMA)," Food and Agriculture Organization of the United Nations, accessed June 17, 2024, https://www.fao.org/port-state-measures/background/parties-psma/en/.

116. "Beyond Borders: Why New 'High Seas' Treaty Is Critical for the World," *UN News*, Global Perspectives, June 19, 2023, https://news.un.org/en/story/2023/06/1137857.

117. Hannah Ritchie and Max Roser, "Half of the World's Habitable Land Is Used for Agriculture," OurWorldInData. org, February 16, 2024, https://ourworldindata.org/global-land-for-agriculture.

118. "Living Planet Report 2022—Building a Nature-Positive Society," ed. R.E.A. Almond, M. Grooten, D. Juffe Bignoli, and T. Petersen (Gland, Switzerland: World Wildlife Fund, 2022), https://livingplanet.panda.org/en-U.S./.

119. William E. Kunin, "Robust Evidence of Declines in Insect Abundance and Biodiversity," *Nature* 574 (October 31, 2019): 641–42, https://doi.org/10.1038/d41586-019-03241-9.

120. Natasha Gilbert, "Global Biodiversity Report Warns Pollinators Are Under Threat," *Nature*, February 26, 2016, https://doi.org/10.1038/nature.2016.19456.

121. Robert H. Cowie, Philippe Bouchet, and Benoît Fontaine, "The Sixth Mass Extinction: Fact, Fiction or Speculation?" *Biological Reviews* 97, no. 2 (January 10, 2022): 640–63, https://doi.org/10.1111/brv.12816.

122. "New International Biodiversity Agreement Strengthens Climate Action," United Nation Climate Change News, December 19, 2022, https://unfccc.int/news/new-international-biodiversity-agreement-strengthens-climate-action.

123. "History of New York City Drinking Water," Official Website of the City of New York, https://www.nyc.gov/site/dep/water/history-of-new-york-citys-drinking-water.page.

124. Winnie Hu, "A Billion-Dollar Investment in New York's Water," *New York Times*, January 18, 2018, https://www.nytimes.com/2018/01/18/nyregion/new-york-city-water-filtration.html.

125. "High Quality NYC Tap Water Receives New Filtration Waiver," Official Website of the City of New York, December 28, 2017, https://www.nyc.gov/office-of-the-mayor/news/779-17/high-quality-nyc-tap-water-receives-new-filtration-waiver.

126. Lukie Pieterse, "The Potato: A Journey Through Time, Cultures, and Challenges," *UN Today*, May 1, 2024, https://untoday.org/the-potato-a-journey-through-time-cultures-and-challenges/.

127. Diego Arguedas Ortiz, "How the Humble Potato Changed the World," *BBC*, March 3, 2020, https://www.bbc.com/travel/article/20200302-the-true-origins-of-the-humble-potato.

128. "Native Potato Varieties," International Potato Center, https://cipotato.org/potato/native-potato-varieties/.

129. Manuela Andreoni, "His Plane Crashed in the Amazon. Then Came the Hard Part," *New York Times*, March 28, 2021, https://www.nytimes.com/2021/03/28/world/americas/brazil-amazon.html.

Chapter 10

1. Frances Moore Lappé, *Diet for a Small Planet* (New York: Ballantine Books, 1971).

2. Sevil Omer, "Global Hunger: 7 Facts You Need to Know," *World Vision*, March 18, 2024, https://www.worldvision.org/-hunger-news-stories/world-hunger-facts.

3. "Historical Estimates of World Population," United States Census Bureau, December 5, 2022, https://www.census.gov/data/tables/time-series/demo/international-programs/historical-est-worldpop.html.

4. "World Population Prospects 2024, Graphs/Profiles," United Nations Department of Economic and Social Affairs, Population Division, 2024, https://population.un.org/wpp/Graphs/DemographicProfiles/Line/900.

5. Michiel van Dijk, Tom Morley, Marie Luise Rau, and Yashar Saghai, "A Meta-Analysis of Projected Global Food Demand and Population at Risk of Hunger for the Period 2010–2050," *Nature Food* 2 (July 21, 2021): 494–501, https://doi.org/10.1038/s43016-021-00322-9.

6. Tim Searchinger, Richard Waite, Craig Hanson, and Janet Ranganathan,

"Creating a Sustainable Food Future: Synthesis Report," World Resources Institute, July 2019, https://research.wri.org/wrr-food.

7. Hannah Ritchie, Pablo Rosado, and Max Roser, "Crop Yields," Our World in Data (2022), https://ourworldindata.org/crop-yields.

8. Toshichika Iizumi and Toru Sakai, "The Global Dataset of Historical Yields for Major Crops 1981–2016," *Scientific Data* 7 (March 20, 2020): 97, https://doi.org/10.1038/s41597-020-0433-7.

9. Jan Willem Erisman, Mark A. Sutton, James Galloway, Zbigniew Klimont, and Wilfried Winiwarter, "How a Century of Ammonia Synthesis Changed the World," *Nature Geoscience* 1 (September 28, 2008): 636–39, https://doi.org/10.1038/ngeo325.

10. "The Nobel Prize in Chemistry 1918," Nobel Prize Outreach, accessed July 14, 2024, https://www.nobelprize.org/prizes/chemistry/1918/summary.

11. Cameron I. Ludemann et al., "A Global FAOSTAT Reference Database of Cropland Nutrient Budgets and Nutrient Use Efficiency (1961–2020): Nitrogen, Phosphorus and Potassium," *Earth System Science Data* 16, no. 1 (January 22, 2024): 525–41, https://doi.org/10.5194/essd-16-525-2024.

12. Xin Zhang et al., "Quantification of Global and National Nitrogen Budgets for Crop Production," *Nature Food* 2, no. 7 (July 15, 2021): 529–40, https://doi.org/10.1038/s43016-021-00318-5.

13. Laila A. Puntel et al., "Modeling Long-Term Corn Yield Response to Nitrogen Rate and Crop Rotation," *Frontiers in Plant Science* 7 (November 11, 2016): 1630, https://doi.org/10.3389/fpls.2016.01630.

14. Prabhu Govindasamy et al., "Nitrogen Use Efficiency—A Key to Enhance Crop Productivity Under a Changing Climate," *Frontiers in Plant Science* 14 (April 18, 2023): 1121073, https://doi.org/10.3389/fpls.2023.1121073.

15. Patricia M. Glibert, Roxane Maranger, Daniel J. Sobota, and Lex Bouwman, "The Haber Bosch–Harmful Algal Bloom (HB–HAB) Link," *Environmental Research Letters* 9, no. 10 (October 1, 2014): 105001, https://doi.org/10.1088/1748-9326/9/10/105001.

16. Stefano Menegat, Alicia Ledo, and Reyes Tirado, "Greenhouse Gas Emissions from Global Production and Use of Nitrogen Synthetic Fertilisers in Agriculture," *Scientific Reports* 12 (August 25, 2022): 14490, https://doi.org/10.1038/s41598-022-18773-w.

17. Nicola Jones, "From Fertilizer to Fuel: Can 'Green' Ammonia Be a Climate Fix?" *Yale Environment 360*, January 20, 2022, https://e360.yale.edu/features/from-fertilizer-to-fuel-can-green-ammonia-be-a-climate-fix.

18. E.-C. Oerke and H.-W. Dehne, "Safeguarding Production—Losses in Major Crops and the Role of Crop Protection," *Crop Protection* 23, no. 4 (April 2004): 275–85, https://doi.org/10.1016/j.cropro.2003.10.001.

19. Nichola J. Hawkins, Chris Bass, Andrea Dixon, and Paul Neve, "The Evolutionary Origins of Pesticide Resistance," *Biological Reviews of the Cambridge Philosophical Society* 94, no. 1 (February 2019): 135–55, https://doi.org/10.1111/brv.12440.

20. John M. Pleasants and Karen S. Oberhauser, "Milkweed Loss in Agricultural Fields Because of Herbicide Use: Effect on the Monarch Butterfly Population," *Insect Conservation and Diversity* 6, no. 2 (March 12, 2012): 135–44, https://doi.org/10.1111/j.1752-4598.2012.00196.x.

21. David L. Wagner, Eliza M. Grames, Matthew L. Forister, May R. Berenbaum, and David Stopak, "Insect Decline in the Anthropocene: Death by a Thousand Cuts," *Proceedings of the National Academy of Sciences of the United States of America* 118, no. 2 (January 11, 2021): e2023989118, https://doi.org/10.1073/pnas.2023989118.

22. Michelle L. Hladik, Anson R. Main, and Dave Goulson, "Environmental Risks and Challenges Associated with Neonicotinoid Insecticides," *Environmental Science & Technology* 52, no. 6 (February 26, 2018): 3329–35, https://doi.org/10.1021/acs.est.7b06388.

23. Claudia Hitaj, David J. Smith, Aimee Code, Seth Wechsler, Paul D. Esker, and Margaret R. Douglas, "Sowing Uncertainty: What We Do and Don't Know About the Planting of Pesticide-Treated Seed," *BioScience* 70, no. 5 (May 2020): 390–403, https://doi.org/10.1093/biosci/biaa019.

24. Ben A. Woodcock, Nicholas J.B.

Isaac, James M. Bullock, David B. Roy, David G. Garthwaite, Andrew Crowe, and Richard F. Pywell, "Impacts of Neonicotinoid Use on Long-Term Population Changes in Wild Bees in England," *Nature Communications* 7 (August 16, 2016): 12459, https://doi.org/10.1038/ncomms12459.

25. Braeden van Deynze, Scott M. Swinton, David A. Hennessy, Nick M. Haddad, and Leslie Ries, "Insecticides, More than Herbicides, Land Use, and Climate, Are Associated with Declines in Butterfly Species Richness and Abundance in the American Midwest," *PloS One* 19, no. 6 (June 20, 2024): e0304319, https://doi.org/10.1371/journal.pone.0304319.

26. Yijia Li, Ruiqing Miao, and Madhu Khanna, "Neonicotinoids and Decline in Bird Biodiversity in the United States," *Nature Sustainability* 3, no. 12 (August 10, 2020): 1027–35, https://doi.org/10.1038/s41893-020-0582-x.

27. Erik Stokstad, "European Union Expands Ban of Three Neonicotinoid Pesticides," *Science*, April 27, 2018, https://doi.org/10.1126/science.aau0152.

28. Britt E. Erickson, "European Union High Court Nixes Neonicotinoid Exemptions," *Chemical & Engineering News*, January 23, 2023, https://cen.acs.org/environment/pesticides/European-Union-high-court-nixes/101/web/2023/01.

29. Paige Bennett, "Vermont Becomes Second State to Ban Bee-Killing Neonic Pesticides," *EcoWatch*, June 18, 2024, https://www.ecowatch.com/vermont-neonics-pesticides-ban-bees-neonicotinoids.html.

30. Marco Barzman, Paolo Bàrberi, A. Nicholas E. Birch, Piet Boonekamp, Silke Dachbrodt-Saaydeh, Benno Graf, Bernd Hommel, et al., "Eight Principles of Integrated Pest Management," *Agronomy for Sustainable Development* 35 (July 24, 2015): 1199–215, https://doi.org/10.1007/s13593-015-0327-9.

31. Jacob R. Pecenka, Laura L. Ingwell, Rick E. Foster, Christian H. Krupke, and Ian Kaplan, "IPM Reduces Insecticide Applications by 95% While Maintaining or Enhancing Crop Yields Through Wild Pollinator Conservation," *Proceedings of the National Academy of Sciences of the United States of America* 118, no. 44 (October 25, 2021): e2108429118, https://doi.org/10.1073/pnas.2108429118.

32. "Regional Integrated Pest Management (IPM) Centers," U.S. Department of Agriculture, National Institute of Food and Agriculture, https://www.nifa.usda.gov/regional-integrated-pest-management-ipm-centers.

33. "The Nobel Peace Prize 1970," Nobel Prize Outreach, accessed July 14, 2024, https://www.nobelprize.org/prizes/peace/1970/summary.

34. Prabhu L. Pingali, "Green Revolution: Impacts, Limits, and the Path Ahead," *Proceedings of the National Academy of Sciences of the United States of America* 109, no. 31 (July 31, 2012): 12302–8, https://doi.org/10.1073/pnas.0912953109.

35. Daisy A. John and Giridhara R. Babu, "Lessons from the Aftermaths of Green Revolution on Food System and Health," *Frontiers in Sustainable Food System* 5 (February 22, 2021): 644559, https://doi.org/10.3389/fsufs.2021.644559.

36. Prabhu Pingali, "Are the Lessons from the Green Revolution Relevant for Agricultural Growth and Food Security in the Twenty-First Century?" in *Agricultural Development in Asia and Africa. Emerging-Economy State and International Policy Studies*, ed. Jonna P. Estudillo, Yoko Kijima, and Tetsushi Sonobe (Singapore: Springer, 2023), 21–32, https://doi.org/10.1007/978-981-19-5542-6_2.

37. "U.S. History Primary Source Timeline. The Dust Bowl," Library of Congress, https://www.loc.gov/classroom-materials/united-states-history-primary-source-timeline/great-depression-and-world-war-ii-1929-1945/dust-bowl/.

38. Pasquale Borrelli et al., "An Assessment of the Global Impact of 21st Century Land Use Change on Soil Erosion," *Nature Communications* 8 (December 8, 2017): 2013, https://doi.org/10.1038/s41467-017-02142-7.

39. Daniel W. Gade, "Deforestation and Its Effects in Highland Madagascar," *Mountain Research and Development* 16, no. 2 (May 1996), 101–16, https://doi.org/10.2307/3674005.

40. George Cusworth and Tara Garnett, "What Is Regenerative Agriculture?" TABLE, University of Oxford, Swedish University of Agricultural Sciences, and Wageningen University and

Research, June 20, 2023, https://www.doi.org/10.56661/2d7b8d1c.

41. Zahangir Kabir, "Tillage or No-Tillage: Impact on Mycorrhizae," *Canadian Journal of Plant Science* 85, no. 1 (2005): 23–29, https://escholarship.org/uc/item/6bv5h1nv.

42. Jincai Shi, Xiaolin Wang, and Ertao Wang, "Mycorrhizal Symbiosis in Plant Growth and Stress Adaptation: From Genes to Ecosystems," *Annual Review of Plant Biology* 74 (May 2023): 569–607, https://doi.org/10.1146/annurev-arplant-061722-090342.

43. "Adoption of Conservation Tillage Has Increased Over the Past Two Decades on Acreage Planted to Major U.S. Cash Crops," U.S. Department of Agriculture, Economic Research Service, October 25, 2022, https://www.ers.usda.gov/data-products/chart-gallery/gallery/chart-detail/?chartId=105042.

44. Haleigh Summers, Heather D. Karsten, William Curran, and Glenna M. Malcolm, "Integrated Weed Management with Reduced Herbicides in a No-Till Dairy Rotation," *Agronomy Journal* 113, no. 4 (July/August 2021): 3418–33, https://doi.org/10.1002/agj2.20757.

45. Yu Peng, Lixin Wang, Pierre-André Jacinthe, and Wei Ren, "Global Synthesis of Cover Crop Impacts on Main Crop Yield," *Field Crops Research* 310 (April 15, 2024): 109343, https://doi.org/10.1016/j.fcr.2024.109343.

46. Jennifer Marston, "Brief: Cover Crop Usage Steady but Still 'Only a Fraction' of Total Acreage in the U.S., Says Purdue's Latest Farmer Survey," *AgFunder News*, August 2, 2023, https://agfundernews.com/cover-crop-usage-steady-but-still-only-a-fraction-of-total-acreage-in-the-us-says-purdues-farmer-survey.

47. Xiaolin Yang et. al., "Diversifying Crop Rotation Increases Food Production, Reduces Net Greenhouse Gas Emissions and Improves Soil Health," *Nature Communications* 15 (January 3, 2024): 198, https://doi.org/10.1038/s41467-023-44464-9.

48. Martin Siedt, Andreas Schäffer, Kilian E.C. Smith, Moritz Nabel, Martina Roß-Nickoll, and Joost T. van Dongen, "Comparing Straw, Compost, and Biochar Regarding Their Suitability as Agricultural Soil Amendments to Affect Soil Structure, Nutrient Leaching, Microbial Communities, and the Fate of Pesticides," *Science of the Total Environment* 751 (January 10, 2021): 141607, https://doi.org/10.1016/j.scitotenv.2020.141607.

49. Verena Seufert and Navin Ramankutty, "Many Shades of Gray—The Context-Dependent Performance of Organic Agriculture," *Science Advances* 3, no. 3 (March 10, 2017): e1602638, https://doi.org/10.1126/sciadv.1602638.

50. "Organic No-Till," Rodale Institute, accessed July 18, 2024, https://rodaleinstitute.org/why-organic/organic-farming-practices/organic-no-till/.

51. "Global Organic Farmland Up 26% in 2022, Reaching 96 Million Hectares," Global Agriculture, February 15, 2024, https://www.globalagriculture.org/whats-new/news/en/34917.html.

52. Sharon Raszap Skorbiansky, Andrea Carlson, and Ashley Spalding, "Rising Consumer Demand Reshapes Landscape for U.S. Organic Farmers," Economic Research Service, U.S. Department of Agriculture, November 14, 2023, https://www.ers.usda.gov/amber-waves/2023/november/rising-consumer-demand-reshapes-landscape-for-u-s-organic-farmers.

53. Samuel Knapp and Marcel G.A. van der Heijden, "A Global Meta-Analysis of Yield Stability in Organic and Conservation Agriculture," *Nature Communications* 9 (September 7, 2018): 3632, https://doi.org/10.1038/s41467-018-05956-1.

54. Lauren C. Ponisio, Leithen K. M'Gonigle, Kevi C. Mace, Jenny Palomino, Perry de Valpine, and Claire Kremen, "Diversification Practices Reduce Organic to Conventional Yield Gap," *Proceedings of the Royal Society B* 282, no. 1799 (January 22, 2015): 20141396, https://doi.org/10.1098/rspb.2014.1396.

55. Linnea Harris, "What Are Food Miles?" *EcoWatch*, March 23, 2022, https://www.ecowatch.com/food-miles-supply-transportation.html.

56. Xiaoming Xu et al., "Global Greenhouse Gas Emissions from Animal-Based Foods Are Twice Those of Plant-Based Foods," *Nature Food* 2 (September 3, 2021): 724–32, https://doi.org/10.1038/s43016-021-00358-x.

57. Hannah Ritchie, "Less Meat Is Nearly Always Better Than Sustainable

Meat, to Reduce Your Carbon Footprint," *Our World in Data*, February 4, 2020, https://ourworldindata.org/less-meat-or-sustainable-meat.

58. J. Poore and T. Nemecek, "Reducing Food's Environmental Impacts Through Producers and Consumers," *Science* 360, no. 6392 (June 1, 2018): 987–92, https://doi.org/10.1126/science.aaq0216.

59. Savannah Bertrand, Anna Sophia Roberts, and Emma Walker, "The Climate and Economic Benefits of Rotational Livestock Grazing. Agriculture and Climate Series," Environmental and Energy Study Institute (EESI), May 3, 2022, https://www.eesi.org/articles/view/the-climate-and-economic-benefits-of-rotational-livestock-grazing.

60. Bruce Hoar and John Angelos, "Beef Cattle Production," UC Davis Western Institute for Food Safety & Security, 2015, http://www.wifss.ucdavis.edu/wp-content/uploads/2015/FDA/fdacoursefinal1/Beef_Food_Animal_Production.pdf.

61. Walter Willett et al., "Food in the Anthropocene: The EAT–Lancet Commission on Healthy Diets from Sustainable Food Systems," *Lancet Commissions* 393, no. 10170 (February 2, 2019): 447–92, https://doi.org/10.1016/S0140-6736(18)31788-4.

62. Hannah Ritchie, "How Many Animals Are Factory-Farmed?" Our World in Data, September 25, 2023, https://ourworldindata.org/how-many-animals-are-factory-farmed.

63. "To Fight Antimicrobial Resistance, Start with Farm Animals," *Scientific American*, March 1, 2023, https://www.scientificamerican.com/article/to-fight-antimicrobial-resistance-start-with-farm-animals/.

64. Chris Dall, "U.S. Lagging Europe in Efforts to Cut Antibiotics in Livestock," CIDRAP News, Center for Infectious Disease Research & Policy Research and Innovation Office, University of Minnesota, December 2, 2022, https://www.cidrap.umn.edu/antimicrobial-stewardship/us-lagging-europe-efforts-cut-antibiotics-livestock.

65. Sameer J. Patel, Matthew Wellington, Rohan M. Shah, and Matthew J. Ferreira, "Antibiotic Stewardship in Food-Producing Animals: Challenges, Progress, and Opportunities," *Clinical Therapeutics* 42, no. 9 (September 2020): 1649–58, https://doi.org/10.1016/j.clinthera.2020.07.004.

66. Patricia M. Glibert, "From Hogs to HABs: Impacts of Industrial Farming in the U.S. on Nitrogen and Phosphorus and Greenhouse Gas Pollution," *Biogeochemistry* 150 (August 10, 2020): 139–80, https://doi.org/10.1007/s10533-020-00691-6.

67. James A. Merchant et al., "Asthma and Farm Exposures in a Cohort of Rural Iowa Children," *Environmental Health Perspectives* 113, no. 3 (December 7, 2004): 350–56, https://doi.org/10.1289/ehp.7240.

68. Ava Mandoli, "More Than 75% of Egg-Laying Hens Live in States with Little-to-No Welfare Protections," *Investigate Midwest*, June 27, 2023, https://investigatemidwest.org/2023/06/27/graphic-more-than-75-of-egg-laying-hens-live-in-states-with-little-to-no-welfare-protections/.

69. Danielle J. Ufer, "Farm Animal Welfare Policies Cover Breeding Sows, Veal Calves, or Laying Hens in 14 U.S. States," U.S. Department of Agriculture, Economic Research Service, April 24, 2023, https://www.ers.usda.gov/amber-waves/2023/april/farm-animal-welfare-policies-cover-breeding-sows-veal-calves-or-laying-hens-in-14-u-s-states/.

70. Rosamond L. Naylor et al., "Feeding Aquaculture in an Era of Finite Resources," *Proceedings of the National Academy of Sciences of the United States of America* 106, no. 36 (September 8, 2009): 15103–10, https://doi.org/10.1073/pnas.0905235106.

71. "The State of World Fisheries and Aquaculture 2022. Towards Blue Transformation," Food and Agriculture Organization of the United Nations, Rome, 2022, https://doi.org/10.4060/cc0461en.

72. Daniel Schar, Eili Y. Klein, Ramanan Laxminarayan, Marius Gilbert, and Thomas P. Van Boeckel, "Global Trends in Antimicrobial Use in Aquaculture," *Scientific Reports* 10 (December 14, 2020): 21878, https://doi.org/10.1038/s41598-020-78849-3.

73. Rosamond L. Naylor et al., "A 20-Year Retrospective Review of Global Aquaculture," *Nature* 591, no. 7851 (March 24, 2021): 551–63, https://doi.org/10.1038/s41586-021-03308-6.

74. Emma Bryce, "Modern Study of the Ancient Practice of Mixing Rice and Fish Farming Uncovers Striking Trends," *Anthropocene Magazine*, March 4, 2022, https://www.anthropocenemag azine.org/2022/03/modern-study-of-the-ancient-practice-of-mixing-rice-and-fish-farming-uncovers-striking-trends/.

75. Luke T. Barrett et al., "Sustainable Growth of Non-Fed Aquaculture Can Generate Valuable Ecosystem Benefits," *Ecosystem Services* 53 (February 1, 2022): 101396, https://doi.org/10.1016/j.ecoser.2021.101396.

76. Joel K. Bourne, Jr., "How to Farm a Better Fish," *National Geographic*, https://www.nationalgeographic.com/foodfeatures/aquaculture.

77. Robert Booth, "Charles Warns GM Farming Will End in Ecological Disaster," *Guardian*, August 12, 2008, https://www.theguardian.com/environment/2008/aug/13/prince.charles.gm.farming.

78. Brian Kennedy and Cary Lynne Thigpen, "Many Publics Around World Doubt Safety of Genetically Modified Foods," *Pew Research Center*, November 11, 2020, https://www.pewresearch.org/short-reads/2020/11/11/many-publics-around-world-doubt-safety-of-genetically-modified-foods.

79. Katherine Dolan, Eva Gelinsky, Nina Holland, Brigitte Reisenberger, Mute Schimpf, Iris Strutzmann, and Dagmar Urban, "Exposed: How Biotech Giants Use Patents and New GMOs to Control the Future of Food," *Corporate Europe Observatory*, October 20, 2022, https://corporateeurope.org/en/2022/10/exposed-how-biotech-giants-use-patents-and-new-gmos-control-future-food.

80. "Science and History of GMOs and Other Food Modification Processes," U.S. Food and Drug Administration, May 3, 2024, https://www.fda.gov/food/agricultural-biotechnology/science-and-history-gmos-and-other-food-modification-processes.

81. "How Does GM Differ from Conventional Plant Breeding?" *Royal Society*, May 2016, https://royalsociety.org/news-resources/projects/gm-plants/how-does-gm-differ-from-conventional-plant-breeding/.

82. Agence-France Presse, "Tens of Thousands March Worldwide Against Monsanto and GM Crops," *Guardian*, May 23, 2015, https://www.theguardian.com/environment/2015/may/24/tens-of-thousands-march-worldwide-against-monsanto-and-gm-crops; Cristina Alesci, "Monsanto CEO Frustrated over 'Polarized' GMO Debate," *CNN Business*, April 18, 2016, https://money.cnn.com/2016/04/18/news/companies/monsanto-ceo-gmo/index.html.

83. Georgina Sanahuja, Raviraj Banakar, Richard M. Twyman, Teresa Capell, and Paul Christou, "*Bacillus thuringiensis*: A Century of Research, Development and Commercial Applications," *Plant Biotechnology Journal* 9, no. 3 (April 2011): 283–300, https://doi.org/10.1111/j.1467-7652.2011.00595.x.

84. "Recent Trends in GE Adoption," U.S. Department of Agriculture, Economic Research Service, October 4, 2023, https://www.ers.usda.gov/data-products/adoption-of-genetically-engineered-crops-in-the-u-s/recent-trends-in-ge-adoption/.

85. "More Than Half of Harvested U.S. Cropland Uses Seed Varieties with at Least One Genetically Modified Trait," U.S. Department of Agriculture, Economic Research Service, August 7, 2023, https://www.ers.usda.gov/data-products/chart-gallery/gallery/chart-detail/?chartId=107037.

86. Jennifer Sass, "ATSDR Report Confirms Glyphosate Cancer Risks," NRDC (Natural Resources Defense Council), April 11, 2019, https://www.nrdc.org/bio/jennifer-sass/atsdr-report-confirms-glyphosate-cancer-risks; Jackson Holtz, "UW Study: Exposure to Chemical in Roundup Increases Risk for Cancer," UW News, University of Washington, February 13, 2019, https://www.washington.edu/news/2019/02/13/uw-study-exposure-to-chemical-in-roundup-increases-risk-for-cancer/; Kate Raphael, "Kids' Glyphosate Exposure Linked to Liver Disease and Metabolic Syndrome," *Environmental Health News*, March 2, 2023, https://www.ehn.org/glyphosate-childrens-health-2659484037.html; P.S. Evalen, E.N. Barnhardt, J. Ryu, and Z.R. Stahlschmidt, "Toxicity of Glyphosate to Animals: A Meta-Analytical Approach," *Environmental Pollution* 347 (April 15, 2024): 123669, https://doi.org/10.1016/j.

envpol.2024.123669; Jarosław Mazuryk, Katarzyna Klepacka, Włodzimierz Kutner, and Piyush Sindhu Sharma, "Glyphosate: Hepatotoxicity, Nephrotoxicity, Hemotoxicity, Carcinogenicity, and Clinical Cases of Endocrine, Reproductive, Cardiovascular, and Pulmonary System Intoxication," *ACS Pharmacology & Translational Science* 7, no. 5 (April 8, 2024): 1205–36, https://doi.org/10.1021/acsptsci.4c00046.

87. Bruce E. Tabashnik, Jeffrey A. Fabrick, and Yves Carrière, "Global Patterns of Insect Resistance to Transgenic *Bt* Crops: The First 25 Years," *Journal of Economic Entomology* 116, no. 2 (April 2023): 297–309, https://doi.org/10.1093/jee/toac183.

88. H. Metcalfe, J. Storkey, R. Hull, J.M. Bullock, A. Whitmore, R.T. Sharp, and A.E. Milne, "Trade-Offs Constrain the Success of Glyphosate-Free Farming," *Scientific Reports* 14 (April 5, 2024): 8001, https://doi.org/10.1038/s41598-024-58183-8.

89. Orla Dwyer, "Q&A: The Evolving Debate About Using Genetically Modified Crops in a Warming World," *Carbon Brief*, May 22, 2024, https://www.carbonbrief.org/qa-the-evolving-debate-about-using-genetically-modified-crops-in-a-warming-world.

90. Joseph Opoku Gakpo, "GMO Cowpea Could Make Protein-Rich Staple Food More Affordable, Say Nigerian Scientists," *Alliance for Science*, December 16, 2021, https://allianceforscience.org/blog/2021/12/gmo-cowpea-could-make-protein-rich-staple-food-more-affordable-say-nigerian-scientists/.

91. Adrian Dubock, "An Overview of Agriculture, Nutrition and Fortification, Supplementation and Biofortification: Golden Rice as an Example for Enhancing Micronutrient Intake," *Agriculture & Food Security* 6 (October 6, 2017): 59, https://doi.org/10.1186/s40066-017-0135-3.

92. "Vitamin A Deficiency," World Health Organization, accessed July 20, 2024, https://www.who.int/data/nutrition/nlis/info/vitamin-a-deficiency.

93. Keith Anthony S. Fabro, "Is the Genetically Modified, Nutrient-Rich Golden Rice as Safe as Promised?" *Mongabay*, September 11, 2023, https://news.mongabay.com/2023/09/is-the-genetically-modified-nutrient-rich-golden-rice-as-safe-as-promised/.

94. Dennis Normile, "What a Philippine Court Ruling Means for Transgenic Golden Rice, Once Hailed as a Dietary Breakthrough," *Science*, May 3, 2024, https://doi.org/10.1126/science.zl7058i.

95. Kees Klein Goldewijk, Arthur Beusen, and Peter Janssen, "Long-Term Dynamic Modeling of Global Population and Built-Up Area in a Spatially Explicit Way: HYDE 3.1," *Holocene* 20, no. 4 (March 22, 2010): 565–73, https://doi.org/10.1177/0959683609356587.

96. "International Data. Percent of Population Living in Urban Areas," Population Reference Bureau, accessed July 21, 2024, https://www.prb.org/international/indicator/urban/table.

97. Florian Thomas Payen et al., "How Much Food Can We Grow in Urban Areas? Food Production and Crop Yields of Urban Agriculture: A Meta-Analysis," *Earth's Future* 10, no. 8 (August 23, 2022): e2022EF002748, https://doi.org/10.1029/2022EF002748.

98. Nicholas Clinton, Michelle Stuhlmacher, Albie Miles, Nazli Uludere Aragon, Melissa Wagner, Matei Georgescu, Chris Herwig, and Peng Gong, "A Global Geospatial Ecosystem Services Estimate of Urban Agriculture," *Earth's Future* 6, no. 1 (January 10, 2018): 40–60, https://doi.org/10.1002/2017EF000536.

99. Niall Patrick Walsh, "How the Dutch Use Architecture to Feed the World," *ArchDaily*, January 24, 2020, https://www.archdaily.com/932301/how-the-dutch-use-architecture-to-feed-the-world.

100. "Netherlands—Country Commercial Guide. Agriculture," International Trade Administration, U.S. Department of Commerce, January 17, 2024, https://www.trade.gov/country-commercial-guides/netherlands-agriculture.

101. Camille Boylan, "The Future of Farming: Hydroponics," Princeton Student Climate Initiative, Princeton University, November 9, 2020, https://psci.princeton.edu/tips/2020/11/9/the-future-of-farming-hydroponics.

102. Mebiol, "Growing Vegetables with Less Water," United Nations Industrial Development Organization Investment and Technology Promotion Office, Tokyo, http://www.unido.or.jp/en/technology_db/4118/.

103. Xin Wen, "Vertical Farming Reaches New Heights in China," *Asia News Network*,

April 14, 2023, https://asianews.network/-vertical-farming-reaches-new-heights-in-china/.

104. Christos Vatistas, Dafni Despoina Avgoustaki, and Thomas Bartzana, "A Systematic Literature Review on Controlled-Environment Agriculture: How Vertical Farms and Greenhouses Can Influence the Sustainability and Footprint of Urban Microclimate with Local Food Production," *Atmosphere* 13, no. 8 (August 8, 2022): 1258, https://doi.org/10.3390/atmos13081258.

105. Kenneth Iversen, Hoi Wai Jackie Cheng, Kristinn Sv. Helgason, and Marcelo LaFleur, "Frontier Technology Issues: Frontier Technologies for Smallholder Farmers: Addressing Information Asymmetries and Deficiencies," United Nations, Department of Economic and Social Affairs, Economic Analysis, November 17, 2021, https://www.un.org/development/desa/dpad/publication/frontier-technology-issues-frontier-technologies-for-smallholder-farmers-addressing-information-asymmetries-and-deficiencies/.

106. "Seeking End to Loss and Waste of Food Along Production Chain," Food and Agriculture Organization of the United Nations, https://www.fao.org/in-action/seeking-end-to-loss-and-waste-of-food-along-production-chain/en/.

107. M. Kummu, H. de Moel, M. Porkka, S. Siebert, O. Varis, and P.J. Ward, "Lost Food, Wasted Resources: Global Food Supply Chain Losses and Their Impacts on Freshwater, Cropland, and Fertiliser Use," *Science of the Total Environment* 438, no. 1 (November 2012): 477–89, https://doi.org/10.1016/j.scitotenv.2012.08.092.

108. James Joiner and Kenechi Okeleke, "E-Commerce in Agriculture: New Business Models for Smallholders' Inclusion into the Formal Economy," *GSMA*, May 29, 2019, https://www.gsma.com/solutions-and-impact/connectivity-for-good/mobile-for-development/gsma_resources/e-commerce-in-agriculture-new-business-models-for-smallholders-inclusion-into-the-formal-economy.

109. James Lowenberg-DeBoer and Bruce Erickson, "Setting the Record Straight on Precision Agriculture Adoption," *Agronomy Journal* 111, no. 4 (July–August 2019): 1552–69, https://doi.org/10.2134/agronj2018.12.0779.

110. Abdellatif Soussi, Enrico Zero, Roberto Sacile, Daniele Trinchero, and Marco Fossa, "Smart Sensors and Smart Data for Precision Agriculture: A Review," *Sensors* 24, no. 8 (April 21, 2024): 2647, https://doi.org/10.3390/s24082647.

111. "Precision Agriculture for Smallholder Farmers," United Nations Development Programme (UNDP), Global Centre for Technology, Innovation and Sustainable Development, October 14, 2021, https://www.undp.org/publications/precision-agriculture-smallholder-farmers.

112. Veronica Fletcher, "America's Burger Loving States," Pantry & Larder, December 27, 2023, https://pantryandlarder.com/americas-burger-loving-states/.

113. Sarah M. Frank, Lindsey Smith Taillie, and Lindsay M. Jaacks, "How Americans Eat Red and Processed Meat: An Analysis of the Contribution of Thirteen Different Food Groups," *Public Health Nutrition* 25, no. 5 (February 21, 2022): 1406–15, https://doi.org/10.1017/S1368980022000416.

114. Sally Ho, "They've Got Beef: Beyond Meat vs. Impossible Foods Burger Showdown: What's the Difference?" *Green Queen*, March 15, 2023, https://www.greenqueen.com.hk/beyond-meat-vs-impossible-foods-burger/.

115. EFSA Panel on Food Additives and Flavourings (FAF) et al., "Safety of Soy Leghemoglobin from Genetically Modified *Komagataella phaffii* as a Food Additive," *EFSA Journal* 22, no. 6 (June 28, 2024): e8822, https://doi.org/10.2903/j.efsa.2024.8822.

116. Karen Formanski, "2021 State of the Industry Report | Plant-Based Meat, Seafood, Eggs, and Dairy," *Good Food Institute*, https://gfi.org/wp-content/uploads/2022/04/2021-Plant-Based-State-of-the-Industry-Report-1.pdf.

117. Matt Reynolds, "Plant-Based Meat Boomed. Here Comes the Bust," *Wired*, April 22, 2024, https://www.wired.com/story/plant-based-meat-sales-2023/.

118. Emily Gelsomin, "Impossible and Beyond: How Healthy Are These Meatless Burgers?" Harvard Health Publishing, Harvard Medical School, January 24, 2022, https://www.health.

harvard.edu/blog/impossible-and-beyond-how-healthy-are-these-meatless-burgers-2019081517448.

119. Tae-Kyung Kim, Hae In Yong, Young-Boong Kim, Hyun-Wook Kim, and Yun-Sang Choi, "Edible Insects as a Protein Source: A Review of Public Perception, Processing Technology, and Research Trends," *Food Science of Animal Resources* 39, no. 4 (August 31, 2019): 521–40, https://doi.org/10.5851/kosfa.2019.e53.

120. Kai Kupferschmidt, "Why Insects Could Be the Ideal Animal Feed," *Science*, October 14, 2015, https://doi.org/10.1126/science.aad4709.

121. Brian Kateman, "Fermentation: The New Game-Changer for Alternative Proteins?" *Forbes*, June 15, 2021, https://www.forbes.com/sites/briankateman/2021/06/07/fermentation-the-new-game-changer-for-alternative-proteins/.

122. Bojana Bajić, Damjan Vučurović, Đurđina Vasić, Rada Jevtić-Mučibabić, and Siniša Dodić, "Biotechnological Production of Sustainable Microbial Proteins from Agro-Industrial Residues and By-Products," *Foods* 12, no. 1 (2023): 107, https://doi.org/10.3390/foods12010107.

123. Jeanne Garbarino, "History and Biochemistry of Fermented Foods," Rockefeller University, https://rockedu.rockefeller.edu/component/biochemistry-fermented-foods/.

124. Tim J.A. Finnigan, Benjamin T. Wall, Peter J. Wilde, Francis B. Stephens, Steve L. Taylor, and Marjorie R. Freedman, "Mycoprotein: The Future of Nutritious Nonmeat Protein, a Symposium Review," *Current Developments in Nutrition* 3, no. 6 (June 2019): nzz021, https://doi.org/10.1093/cdn/nzz021.

125. Elliot Swartz and Claire Bomkamp, "The Science of Cultivated Meat," *Good Food Institute*, https://gfi.org/science/the-science-of-cultivated-meat/.

126. Alok Jha, "First Lab-Grown Hamburger Gets Full Marks for 'Mouth Feel,'" *Guardian*, August 6, 2013, https://www.theguardian.com/science/2013/aug/05/world-first-synthetic-hamburger-mouth-feel.

127. Anmariya Benny, Kathiresan Pandi, and Rituja Upadhyay, "Techniques, Challenges and Future Prospects for Cell-Based Meat," *Food Science and Biotechnology* 31 (July 20, 2022): 1225–42, https://doi.org/10.1007/s10068-022-01136-6.

128. Willow Shah Neville, "6 Cultured Meat Companies Making Waves," *Labiotech*, March 22, 2023, https://www.labiotech.eu/best-biotech/cultured-meat-companies/.

129. Andrew Noyes, "GOOD Meat Partners with Industry Leader to Build the World's First Large-Scale Cultivated Meat Facility," *Business Wire*, May 25, 2022, https://www.businesswire.com/news/home/20220525005345/en/GOOD-Meat-Partners-with-Industry-Leader-to-Build-the-World's-First-Large-Scale-Cultivated-Meat-Facility.

130. Chris McCullough, "European Countries Ban Lab Meat in Move to Support Farmers," *Fence Post*, February 2, 2024, https://www.thefencepost.com/news/european-countries-ban-lab-meat-in-move-to-support-farmers/.

131. Dee-Ann Durbin, "Lab-Grown Meat Isn't on Store Shelves Yet, but Some States Have Already Banned It," *Associated Press*, May 30, 2024, https://apnews.com/article/labgrown-meat-cultivated-ban-8dee6ce8e1282efe953ca4115db4b2c2.

132. Sophie Kevany, "From Petri Dish to Plate: Meet the Company Hoping to Bring Lab-Grown Fish to the Table," *Guardian*, April 28, 2024, https://www.theguardian.com/environment/2024/apr/28/from-petri-dish-to-plate-meet-the-company-hoping-to-bring-lab-grown-fish-to-the-table.

133. Natalie Rubio, Isha Datar, David Stachura, David Kaplan, and Kate Krueger, "Cell-Based Fish: A Novel Approach to Seafood Production and an Opportunity for Cellular Agriculture," *Frontiers in Sustainable Food Systems* 3 (June 11, 2019): 43, https://doi.org/10.3389/fsufs.2019.00043.

134. Brian Kateman, "Cell-Cultured Seafood Isn't Just An Idea; It's a Reality," *Forbes*, June 6, 2022, https://www.forbes.com/sites/briankateman/2022/06/06/cell-cultured-seafood-isnt-just-an-idea-its-a-reality.

135. Kasper Hettinga and Etske Bijl, "Can Recombinant Milk Proteins Replace Those Produced by Animals?" *Current Opinion in Biotechnology* 75 (June 2022): 102690, https://doi.org/10.1016/j.copbio.2022.102690.

136. Randy Diamond, "Will Cell-Based Milk Change the Dairy Industry? This California Lab Could Lead the Way," *Phys. org*, October 13, 2022, https://phys.org/news/2022-10-cell-based-dairy-industry-california-lab.html.

137. Sachin Rawat, "Brewing Milk in Bioreactors. Cellular Agriculture Start-ups Are Culturing Human and Bovine Cells in Bioreactors to Produce More Sustainable Milk Without Animals," *Progress Network*, June 13, 2022, https://theprogressnetwork.org/cell-cultured-milk/.

138. Hyuk Cheol Kwon, Hyun Su Jung, Vahinika Kothuri, and Sung Gu Han, "Current Status and Challenges for Cell-Cultured Milk Technology: A Systematic Review," *Journal of Animal Science and Biotechnology* 15 (June 8, 2024): 81, https://doi.org/10.1186/s40104-024-01039-y.

139. Anay Mridul, "'Blending Tradition and Innovation': Senara Emerges from Stealth as Europe's First Cultured Dairy Startup," *Green Queen*, December 18, 2023, https://www.greenqueen.com.hk/senara-cell-cultured-dairy-lab-grown-milk/.

140. "Nutrition. Food Loss and Waste," Food and Agriculture Organization of the United Nations (FAO), https://www.fao.org/nutrition/capacity-development/food-loss-and-waste/en/.

141. "The 70% Battle: Small Farms Still Feed the World, Open Letter," *Global Agriculture*, September 2, 2022, https://www.globalagriculture.org/whats-new/news/en/34543.html.

142. Massarath Fatima, "Cooling in Developing Countries," *Borgen Project*, December 18, 2018, https://borgenproject.org/cooling-in-developing-countries.

143. USAID Bangladesh, "Cold Chain Bangladesh Alliance. USAID's Assets Amplify Local Partner Investments," U.S. Global Development Lab's Global Partnerships Team, November 2015, https://2017-2020.usaid.gov/sites/default/files/documents/15396/ccba-draft_edited.pdf.

144. Nicola Twilley, "Africa's Cold Rush and the Promise of Refrigeration," *New Yorker*, August 15, 2022, https://www.newyorker.com/magazine/2022/08/22/africas-cold-rush-and-the-promise-of-refrigeration.

145. Gregory A. Baker, Leslie C. Gray, Michael J. Harwood, Travis J. Osland, and Jean Baptiste C. Tooley, "On-Farm Food Loss in Northern and Central California: Results of Field Survey Measurements," *Resources, Conservation and Recycling* 149 (October 2019): 541–49, https://doi.org/10.1016/j.resconrec.2019.03.022.

146. "8 Facts to Know About Food Waste and Hunger," World Food Program USA, March 22, 2022, https://www.wfpusa.org/articles/8-facts-to-know-about-food-waste-and-hunger.

147. Jamey Keaten, "Free Food Fridges Take Off in Parts of Europe in Eco-Friendly Bid to Fight Waste," *Associated Press*, July 28, 2023, https://apnews.com/article/food-waste-switzerland-germany-geneva-austria-refrigerators-environment-fc8484f267f1403a4b76db8b20541f9a.

148. Brian Vines, "Ugly Food Fight: Misfits Market, Imperfect Foods, and the Battle Against Food Waste," *Consumer Reports*, January 12, 2022, https://www.consumerreports.org/health/food-shopping/ugly-food-fight-misfits-market-imperfect-foods-food-waste-a6326488257/.

149. "Mission & Impact," Food Stash Foundation, https://www.foodstash.ca/mission.

150. The Leftovers Foundation, https://rescuefood.ca.

151. "What We Do," Second Harvest, https://secondharvest.ca/about/about.

152. "Fighting Food Waste and Hunger with Food Rescue," Feeding America, https://www.feedingamerica.org/our-work/reduce-food-waste; "Diverting Excess Food to Hungry People," Waste No Food, https://wastenofood.org/about/.

153. Max S. Kim, "South Korea Has Almost Zero Food Waste. Here's What the U.S. Can Learn," *Guardian*, November 20, 2022, https://www.theguardian.com/environment/2022/nov/20/south-korea-zero-food-waste-composting-system.

154. "Food Waste: 13 Facts You Need to Know," UN World Food Programme, July 6, 2023, https://freerice.com/blog/food-waste-13-facts-you-need-know.

Chapter 11

1. Rebecca M. Kulik, "Sustainable Development | Definition, Goals, Origins,

Three Pillars, & Facts," *Encyclopedia Britannica*, May 27, 2024, https://www.britannica.com/topic/sustainable-development.

2. World Commission on Environment and Development, "Report of the World Commission on Environment and Development: Our Common Future," 1987, http://www.un-documents.net/our-common-future.pdf.

3. Anna Johnson, "Great Salt Lake as a 'Pit Stop' for 12 Million Birds," Great Salt Lake Collaborative, April 20, 2023, https://greatsaltlakenews.org/latest-news/utah-public-radio-upr/great-salt-lake-is-a-pit-stop-for-12-million-birds.

4. Dorothy K. Hall, John S. Kimball, Ron Larson, Nicolo E. DiGirolamo, Kimberly A. Casey, and Glynn Hulley, "Intensified Warming and Aridity Accelerate Terminal Lake Desiccation in the Great Basin of the Western United States," *Earth and Space Science* 10, no. 1 (January 6, 2023): e2022EA002630, https://doi.org/10.1029/2022ea002630.

5. "Great Salt Lake Water Levels," Utah Division of Wildlife Resources, Great Salt Lake Ecosystem Program, accessed June 21, 2024, https://wildlife.utah.gov/gslep/about/water-levels.html.

6. Otto I. Lang, Derek Mallia, and S. McKenzie Skiles, "The Shrinking Great Salt Lake Contributes to Record High Dust-on-Snow Deposition in the Wasatch Mountains During the 2022 Snowmelt Season," *Environmental Research Letters* 18, no. 6 (June 15, 2023): 064045, https://doi.org/10.1088/1748-9326/acd409.

7. Carter Williams, "Dust Hot Spots: Where Is Great Salt Lake's Toxic Dust Most Likely to Originate?" University of Utah, College of Science, accessed June 21, 2024, https://science.utah.edu/news/toxic-dust-hot-spots/.

8. Jennifer Alsever, "Who's to Blame for Our Great Salt Lake Problem? And How Can We Fix It?" *Utah Business*, September 2022, https://www.utahbusiness.com/what-to-do-about-the-great-salt-lake-drying-up.

9. *Ibid.*

10. *Ibid.*

11. "Agriculture in Utah," Envision Utah, accessed June 21, 2024, https://yourutahyourfuture.org/topics/agriculture/item/27-background-agriculture-in-utah.

12. Brianna Randall, "Can Farmers Save the Great Salt Lake?" *Reasons to Be Cheerful*, November 17, 2023, https://reasonstobecheerful.world/great-salt-lake-farmers-voluntary-conservation-actions/.

13. Mitchell Lott and Jennifer Morales, "Why Utah Farmers Use So Much Water, and How We Can Get Them to Use Less," Utah State University, Center for Growth and Opportunity, April 13, 2023, https://www.thecgo.org/benchmark/why-utah-farmers-use-so-much-water-and-how-we-can-get-them-to-use-less/.

14. "Protect, Conserve and Invest in Statewide Water Resources," Utah Senate, February 16, 2024, https://senate.utah.gov/utah-legislature-continues-to-protect-conserve-and-invest-in-statewide-water-resources/.

15. "World of Change: Shrinking Aral Sea," *NASA Earth Observatory*, November 7, 2018, https://earthobservatory.nasa.gov/world-of-change/AralSea.

16. Turid Austin Wæhler and Erik Sveberg Dietrichs, "The Vanishing Aral Sea: Health Consequences of an Environmental Disaster," *Journal of the Norwegian Medical Association* 137 (October 3, 2017), https://doi.org/10.4045/tidsskr.17.0597.

17. Xiaolei Wang et al., "Reviving the Aral Sea: A Hydro-Eco-Social Perspective," *Earth's Future* 11, no. 11 (November 22, 2023): e2023EF003657, https://doi.org/10.1029/2023EF003657.

18. Orkhan Huseynli, "The Aral Sea Catastrophe: Understanding One of the Worst Ecological Calamities of the Last Century," *Earth.org*, May 16, 2024, https://earth.org/the-aral-sea-catastrophe-understanding-one-of-the-worst-ecological-calamities-of-the-last-century/.

19. "Arvind and Gap Open World's First Apparel Water Sustainability Hub," *Smart Water Magazine*, January 15, 2024, https://smartwatermagazine.com/news/gap/arvind-and-gap-open-worlds-first-apparel-water-sustainability-hub.

20. "UN Launches Drive to Highlight Environmental Cost of Staying Fashionable," *UN News*, March 25, 2019, https://news.un.org/en/story/2019/03/1035161.

21. "RE100 Members," Climate Group RE100, accessed June 22, 2024, https://www.there100.org/re100-members.

22. "The Global Commitment Five Years In: Learnings to Accelerate Towards a Future Without Plastic Waste or Pollu-

tion," Ellen MacArthur Foundation, Global Commitment, accessed June 22, 2024, https://www.ellenmacarthurfoun dation.org/global-commitment/overview.

23. "NAPCOR's 2022 PET Recycling Report Demonstrates Bottle-to-Bottle Circularity Continues on the Rise," NAP-COR: National Association for PET Container Resources, https://napcor.com/news/2022-pet-recycling-report/.

24. "PET Market in Europe. State of Play. Production, Collection & Recycling Data 2022," Plastics Recyclers Europe (PRE), https://www.plasticsrecyclers.eu/publications/.

25. Joyce Chen, "CEO Tenure Rates," Harvard Law School Forum on Corporate Governance, August 4, 2023, https://corp gov.law.harvard.edu/2023/08/04/ceo-tenure-rates-2/.

26. "What Is ESG Investing and Analysis?" CFA Institute, accessed June 22, 2024, https://www.cfainstitute.org/en/rpc-overview/esg-investing.

27. "About the PRI," Principles for Responsible Investment, accessed June 22, 2024, https://www.unpri.org/about-us/about-the-pri.

28. Caleb Silver, "Why a Former Top Sustainability Investor Says the Industry Is a Dangerous Fraud," *Investopedia*, August 18, 2022, https://www.investo pedia.com/the-green-investor-podcast-episode-19-6500209.

29. "Fossil Fuel Subsidies," European Environmental Agency, November 17, 2023, https://www.eea.europa.eu/en/analysis/indicators/fossil-fuel-subsidies.

30. Sarah Mcfarlane, "Explainer: Global Fossil Fuel Subsidies on the Rise Despite Calls for Phase-Out," *Reuters*, November 23, 2023, https://www.reuters.com/business/environment/global-fossil-fuel-subsidies-rise-despite-calls-phase-out-2023-11-23/.

31. "Experts Call on G7 to Get Serious on Fossil Fuel Subsidy Reform," International Institute for Sustainable Development, April 16, 2024, https://www.iisd.org/articles/press-release/experts-call-g7-fossil-fuel-subsidy-reform.

32. "Statement on Climate Change," Peabody, accessed June 23, 2024, https://www.peabodyenergy.com/Sustainability/climate-change.

33. Louise Boyle, "America's Biggest Coal Producer Is Getting into Solar Power," *Independent*, March 2, 2022, https://www.independent.co.uk/climate-change/news/coal-peabody-solar-power-announcement-b2027204.html#comments-area.

34. Beth Howell, "The Top 14 Most Polluting Companies," *EcoExperts*, October 2, 2023, https://www.theecoexperts.co.uk/blog/most-polluting-companies.

35. "The Oil and Gas Industry in Net Zero Transitions. Executive summary," International Energy Agency, February 2024, https://www.iea.org/reports/the-oil-and-gas-industry-in-net-zero-transitions/executive-summary.

36. Janina Herzog-Hawelka and Joyeeta Gupta, "The Role of (Multi)national Oil and Gas Companies in Leaving Fossil Fuels Underground: A Systematic Literature Review," *Energy Research & Social Science* 103 (September 1, 2023): 103194, https://doi.org/10.1016/j.erss.2023.103194.

37. Nicolas Maennling, "Lessons Learned from an Energy Company's Green Transformation," Columbia Center on Sustainable Investment, Columbia Law School, April 15, 2019, https://ccsi.colum bia.edu/news/lessons-learned-energy-companys-green-transformation.

38. J.S. Nanditha et al., "The Pakistan Flood of August 2022: Causes and Implications," *Earth's Future* 11, no. 3 (March 13, 2023): e2022EF003230, https://doi.org/10.1029/2022EF003230.

39. Yujia You, Mingfang Ting, and Michela Biasutti, "Climate Warming Contributes to the Record-Shattering 2022 Pakistan Rainfall," *npj Climate and Atmospheric Science* 7 (April 13, 2024): 89, https://doi.org/10.1038/s41612-024-006 30-4.

40. "Pakistan: Flood Damages and Economic Losses over USD 30 Billion and Reconstruction Needs Over USD 16 Billion—New Assessment," World Bank, Press Release No: SAR/2022, October 28, 2022, https://www.worldbank.org/en/news/press-release/2022/10/28/pakistan-flood-damages-and-economic-losses-over-usd-30-billion-and-reconstruction-needs-over-usd-16-billion-new-assessme.

41. Faisal Mueen Qamer et al., "A Framework for Multi-Sensor Satellite Data to Evaluate Crop Production Losses: The Case Study of 2022

Pakistan Floods," *Scientific Reports* 13 (March 14, 2023): 4240, https://doi.org/10.1038/s41598-023-30347-y.

42. "Global Forest Resources Assessment 2020. Main report," Food and Agriculture Organization of the United Nations, Rome (2020), https://doi.org/10.4060/ca9825en.

43. Aziz Buneri, "'10 Billion Tree Tsunami' Suffers Setback as Flash Floods Devastate Forests," *Pakistan Today*, May 6, 2023, https://www.pakistantoday.com.pk/2023/05/06/10-billion-tree-tsunami-suffers-setback-as-flash-floods-devastate-forests/.

44. Rob Boyle, "Greenhouse Gas Emissions in Pakistan," *Emission Index*, April 6, 2024, https://www.emission-index.com/countries/pakistan.

45. Simon Evans, "Analysis: Which Countries Are Historically Responsible for Climate Change?" *Carbon Brief*, October 5, 2021, https://www.carbonbrief.org/analysis-which-countries-are-historically-responsible-for-climate-change/.

46. "Climate Action: Finance & Justice," United Nations, https://www.un.org/en/climatechange/raising-ambition/climate-finance.

47. Urmi Goswami and Fermín Koop, "Q&A: COP28 and the 100 Billion U.S. Dollar Climate Finance Commitment," *Clean Energy Wire*, November 29, 2023, https://www.cleanenergywire.org/factsheets/qa-cop28-and-100-billion-us-dollar-climate-finance-commitment.

48. Bertram Zagema, Jan Kowalzig, Lyndsay Walsh, Andrew Hattle, Christopher Roy, and Peter Hans Dejgaard, "Climate Finance Shadow Report 2023. Assessing the Delivery of the $100 Billion Commitment," Oxfam International, June 5, 2023, https://doi.org/10.21201/2023.621500.

49. Irene Casado Sanchez and Jackie Botts, "A Program Meant to Help Developing Nations Fight Climate Change Is Funneling Billions of Dollars Back to Rich Countries," *Reuters*, May 22, 2024, https://www.reuters.com/investigates/special-report/climate-change-loans/.

50. Shelia Hu, "What Is Climate Gentrification?" NRDC (Natural Resources Defense Council), August 27, 2020, https://www.nrdc.org/stories/what-climate-gentrification.

51. Brentin Mock, "How Black Land Became White Sand: The Racial Erosion of the U.S. Coasts," *Grist*, May 30, 2014, https://grist.org/living/how-african-americans-lost-the-coasts-and-how-we-could-make-that-right/.

52. Robynne Boyd, "Has Climate Gentrification Hit Miami? The City Plans to Find Out," NRDC (Natural Resources Defense Council), March 11, 2019, https://www.nrdc.org/stories/has-climate-gentrification-hit-miami-city-plans-find-out.

53. Renee Skelton and Vernice Miller, "The Environmental Justice Movement," NRDC (Natural Resources Defense Council), August 22, 2023, https://www.nrdc.org/stories/environmental-justice-movement.

54. "About Us," GreenRoots, accessed July 26, 2024, https://www.greenrootsej.org/about-us.

55. Pierre Friedlingstein et al., "Global Carbon Budget 2022," *Earth System Science Data* 14, no. 11 (November 11, 2022): 4811–900, https://doi.org/10.5194/essd-14-4811-2022.

56. Laura Cozzi, Olivia Chen, and Hyeji Kim, "The World's Top 1% of Emitters Produce over 1000 Times More CO2 than the Bottom 1%," *International Energy Agency*, February 22, 2023, https://www.iea.org/commentaries/the-world-s-top-1-of-emitters-produce-over-1000-times-more-co2-than-the-bottom-1.

57. "Emissions Gap Report 2023: Broken Record—Temperatures Hit New Highs, Yet World Fails to Cut Emissions (Again)," United Nations Environment Programme, November 20, 2023, https://www.unep.org/resources/emissions-gap-report-2023.

58. Hannah Ritchie and Max Roser, "CO$_2$ Emissions," OurWorldInData.org, January 2024, https://ourworldindata.org/co2-emissions.

59. Angela Druckman and Tim Jackson, "Understanding Households as Drivers of Carbon Emissions," in *Taking Stock of Industrial Ecology*, ed. Roland Clift and Angela Druckman (Cham: Springer, 2016), 181–203, https://doi.org/10.1007/978-3-319-20571-7_9.

60. "How to Calculate Your Carbon Footprint," *Just Energy*, April 9, 2024, https://justenergy.com/blog/how-to-calculate-

your-carbon-footprint/; "Carbon Footprint Calculator," TerraPass, https://terrapass.com/carbon-footprint-calculator/; "UN Carbon Footprint Calculator," United Nations Climate Change, https://offset.climateneutralnow.org/footprintcalc.

61. Craig Bettenhausen, "The Chemistry of Cold-Water Washing," *Chemical & Engineering News*, January 28, 2024, https://cen.acs.org/business/consumer-products/chemistry-cold-water-washing/102/i3?ref.

62. "What Is Offsetting?" United Nations Carbon Offset Platform, https://offset.climateneutralnow.org/aboutoffsetting.

63. Josh Gabbatiss, Daisy Dunne, Aruna Chandrasekhar, Orla Dwyer, Molly Lempriere, Yanine Quiroz, Ayesha Tandon, and Giuliana Viglione, "In-Depth Q&A: Can 'Carbon Offsets' Help to Tackle Climate Change?" *Carbon Brief*, September 24, 2023, https://interactive.carbonbrief.org/carbon-offsets-2023/.

64. Betsy Vereckey, "How to Choose Carbon Offsets that Actually Cut Emissions," *MIT Sloan School of Management*, November 2, 2022, https://mitsloan.mit.edu/ideas-made-to-matter/how-to-choose-carbon-offsets-actually-cut-emissions.

65. Derik Broekhoff, Michael Gillenwater, Tani Colbert-Sangree, and Patrick Cage, "Securing Climate Benefit: A Guide to Using Carbon Offsets," Stockholm Environment Institute & Greenhouse Gas Management Institute, November 13, 2019, https://offsetguide.org/wp-content/uploads/2020/03/Carbon-Offset-Guide_3122020.pdf.

66. Fred Lewsey, "Millions of Carbon Credits Are Generated by Overestimating Forest Preservation," University of Cambridge, August 24, 2023, https://www.cam.ac.uk/stories/carbon-credits-hot-air.

67. Allegra Dawes, "What's Plaguing Voluntary Carbon Markets?" Center for Strategic and International Studies (CSIS), February 2, 2024, https://www.csis.org/analysis/whats-plaguing-voluntary-carbon-markets.

68. Bronson Griscom, "Why We Can't Afford to Dismiss Carbon Offsetting in a Climate Crisis," World Economic Forum, April 22, 2021, https://www.weforum.

org/agenda/2021/04/carbon-offsetting-climate-crisis/.

69. Hidemichi Fujii, Jeremy Webb, Sagadevan Mundree, David Rowlings, Peter Grace, Clevo Wilson, and Shunsuke Managi, "Priority Change and Driving Factors in the Voluntary Carbon Offset Market," *Cleaner Environmental Systems* 13 (June 2024): 100164, https://doi.org/10.1016/j.cesys.2024.100164.

70. "World Wildlife Fund: History," World Wildlife Fund, https://www.worldwildlife.org/about/history.

71. "About NRDC," Natural Resources Defense Council (NRDC), https://www.nrdc.org/about.

72. "Union of Concerned Scientists: About," Union of Concerned Scientists (UCS), https://www.ucsusa.org/about.

73. "Circular Economy Action Plan. The EU's New Circular Action Plan Paves the Way for a Cleaner and More Competitive Europe," European Commission, accessed July 7, 2024, https://environment.ec.europa.eu/strategy/circular-economy-action-plan_en.

74. "About Us," Ellen MacArthur Foundation, https://www.ellenmacarthurfoundation.org/about-us/what-we-do.

75. "The Circularity Gap Report 2023: The Global Economy Is Only 7,2% Circular," Estonian Design Centre, https://ringdisain.ee/en/the-circularity-gap-report-2023-the-global-economy-is-only-72-circular/.

76. "The Circularity Gap Report 2023," Circle Economy Foundation, https://www.circularity-gap.world/2023#download.

77. Sean Fleming, "Circular Economy Examples—How IKEA, Burger King, Adidas and More Are Investing in a Circular Economy," *World Economic Forum*, December 8, 2020, https://www.weforum.org/agenda/2020/12/circular-economy-examples-ikea-burger-king-adidas/.

78. Jessica Perry, "TerraCycle Turns a Profit by Redefining the Value of Waste," *NJBIZ*, April 29, 2024, https://njbiz.com/terracycle-turns-a-profit-by-redefining-the-value-of-waste/.

79. "A Shared Future," Adidas, https://www.adidas.de/en/ultraboost_dna_loop.

80. "Denmark's First Circular Social Housing Project," State of Green, September 4, 2021, https://stateofgreen.com/en/solutions/denmarks-first-circular-social-housing-project/.

81. "Repair Café: About," Repair Café, https://www.repaircafe.org/en/about/.

82. "Case Studies and Examples of Circular Economy in Action," Ellen MacArthur Foundation, https://www.ellenmacarthurfoundation.org/topics/circular-economy-introduction/examples.

83. Sandhya Krishnan, "Understanding India's Evolving Middle Classes," *East Asia Forum*, May 21, 2024, https://doi.org/10.59425/eabc.1716285600.

84. Thoughtshop Foundation, https://thoughtshopfoundation.org.

85. Positive Young Women Voices (PYWV), https://pywv.org.

86. Alejandra Martinez, "At a Shuttered Texas Coal Mine, a 1-Acre Garden Is Helping Feed 2,000 People per Month," *Texas Tribune*, July 14, 2023, https://www.texastribune.org/2023/07/14/texas-coal-mine-garden-nrg-restoration/.

87. Daniel Walton, "Micro Solar Leases: A New Income Stream for Black Farmers in the South?" *Civil Eats*, February 14, 2024, https://civileats.com/2024/02/14/micro-solar-leases-a-new-income-stream-for-black-farmers-in-the-south/.

88. Nicolás Rivero, "Why People Don't Have to Pay Anything for Electricity in This Florida Community," *Washington Post*, January 6, 2024, https://www.washingtonpost.com/climate-solutions/2024/01/06/leed-zero-energy-hunters-point/.

89. "Hunter's Point Residential Community in Florida Pursues Net Positive Power," U.S. Green Building Council, October 24, 2023, https://www.usgbc.org/articles/hunter-s-point-residential-community-florida-pursues-net-positive-power.

90. Alan Naditz, "LEED Zero Certification Brought to the Community Level," *Green Builder Media*, February 28, 2024, https://www.greenbuildermedia.com/blog/leed-zero-certification-brought-to-the-community-level.

91. Erica Gies, "To Revive a River, Restore Its Liver," *Scientific American*, April 1, 2022, https://www.scientificamerican.com/article/to-revive-a-river-restore-its-hidden-gut1/.

92. *Ibid.*

93. "Thornton Creek Salmon Habitat Restoration," Puget Sound Partnership, July 10, 2019, https://innovationstories.psp.wa.gov/2019/07/thornton-creek-salmon-habitat-restoration/.

94. "Singapore, Our City in Nature," National Parks Board of Singapore, March 8, 2023, https://www.nparks.gov.sg/about-us/city-in-nature.

95. Heather Chen, "This Country's Love Affair with Air Conditioning Shows a Catch 22 of Climate Change," *CNN*, June 9, 2023, https://www.cnn.com/2023/06/09/asia/air-conditioning-singapore-climate-change-intl-hnk-dst/index.html.

96. Robin Hicks, "Can Singapore, the City in a Garden, Grow into a City in Nature?" *Eco-Business*, September 19, 2018, https://www.eco-business.com/news/can-singapore-the-city-in-a-garden-grow-into-a-city-in-nature/.

97. Sibylle de Valence, "The Slopes Are Green at Copenhagen's First Ski Hill. Really," *New York Times*, October 24, 2019, https://www.nytimes.com/2019/10/23/travel/copenhagen-ski-hill-powerplant.html.

98. Anne Quito, "CopenHill: The World's Most Consequential Artificial Ski Slope Is Officially Open," *Quartz*, October 4, 2019, https://qz.com/1721236/copenhagens-copenhill-ski-slope-is-officially-open.

99. Hattie Hartman, "BIG's CopenHill Waste-to-Energy Plant-cum-Ski Slope Opens in Copenhagen," *Architects' Journal*, October 11, 2019, https://www.architectsjournal.co.uk/buildings/bigs-copenhill-waste-to-energy-plant-cum-ski-slope-opens-in-copenhagen.

100. Jennifer Davis, "The Haudenosaunee Confederacy and the Constitution," Library of Congress, September 21, 2023, https://blogs.loc.gov/law/2023/09/the-haudenosaunee-confederacy-and-the-constitution/.

101. "The Well-Being of Future Generations," Welsh Government, https://www.gov.wales/well-being-of-future-generations-wales.

102. Jane Davidson, "#FutureGen—Lessons from a Small Country?" *Revue française de civilisation britannique* 28, no. 3 (December 22, 2023), https://doi.org/10.4000/rfcb.11321.

Bibliography

Ackerman, Grunfeld, Diana, Daniel Gilbert, Jennifer Hou, Adele M. Jones, Matthew J. Lee, Tohren C.G. Kibbey, and Denis M. O'Carroll. "Underestimated Burden of Per- and Polyfluoroalkyl Substances in Global Surface Waters and Groundwaters." *Nature Geoscience* 17, no. 4 (April 8, 2024): 340–46. https://doi.org/10.1038/s41561-024-01402-8.

Adidas. "A Shared Future." https://www.adidas.de/en/ultraboost_dna_loop.

Adler, Jerry. "Meet the Ecologist Who Wants You to Unleash the Wild on Your Backyard." *Smithsonian Magazine*. April 2020. https://www.smithsonianmag.com/science-nature/meet-ecologist-who-wants-unleash-wild-backyard-180974372/.

Afrifa, Justice, Yeboah Kwaku Opoku, Eric Ofori Gyamerah, George Ashiagbor, and Rosemary Doe Sorkpor. "The Clinical Importance of the Mercury Problem in Artisanal Small-Scale Gold Mining." *Frontiers in Public Health* 7 (May 28, 2019): 131. https://doi.org/10.3389/fpubh.2019.00131.

Agence France-Presse. "Tens of Thousands March Worldwide Against Monsanto and GM Crops." *Guardian*. May 23, 2015. https://www.theguardian.com/environment/2015/may/24/tens-of-thousands-march-worldwide-against-monsanto-and-gm-crops.

Agency for Toxic Substances and Disease Registry (US). "Toxicological Profile for Parathion." NIH, National Center for Biotechnology Information, National Library of Medicine Bookshelf. January 1, 2017. https://www.ncbi.nlm.nih.gov/books/NBK591895/.

Aghahosseini, Arman, and Christian Breyer. "From Hot Rock to Useful Energy: A Global Estimate of Enhanced Geothermal Systems Potential." *Applied Energy* 279 (December 1, 2020): 115769. https://doi.org/10.1016/j.apenergy.2020.115769.

Ajanovic, Amela, Marlene Sayer, and Reinhard Haas. "The Economics and the Environmental Benignity of Different Colors of Hydrogen." *International Journal of Hydrogen Energy* 47, no. 57 (July 5, 2022): 24136–54. https://doi.org/10.1016/j.ijhydene.2022.02.094.

Alberts, Elizabeth Claire. "How Much Carbon Does Ocean Trawling Put into the Atmosphere?" *Mongabay*. January 19, 2024. https://news.mongabay.com/2024/01/carbon-catch-and-release-study-finds-bottom-trawlers-stir-up-seabed-co2/.

Alesci, Cristina. "Monsanto CEO Frustrated over 'Polarized' GMO Debate." *CNN Business*. April 18, 2016. https://money.cnn.com/2016/04/18/news/companies/monsanto-ceo-gmo/index.html.

Alkurdi, Susan S. A., Raed A. Al-Juboori, Jochen Bundschuh, and Ihsan Hamawand. "Bone Char as a Green Sorbent for Removing Health Threatening Fluoride from Drinking Water." *Environment International* 127 (June 1, 2019): 704–19. https://doi.org/10.1016/j.envint.2019.03.065.

Almond, R.E.A., M. Grooten, D. Juffe Bignoli, and T. Petersen (Eds.). "Living Planet Report 2022—Building a Nature-Positive Society." World Wildlife Fund, Gland, Switzerland. 2022. https://livingplanet.panda.org/en-US/.

Almukhtar, Sara, Blacki Migliozzi, John Schwartz, and Josh Williams. "The Great Flood of 2019: A Complete Picture of a Slow-Motion Disaster." *New York Times*. September 11, 2019. https://www.nytimes.com/interactive/2019/09/11/us/midwest-flooding.html.

Alpert, Naomi, Maaike Van Gerwen, and Emanuela Taioli. "Epidemiology of Mesothelioma in the 21st Century in Europe and the United States, 40 Years After Restricted/Banned Asbestos Use." *Translational Lung Cancer Research* 9, no. S1 (February 28, 2020): S28–38. https://doi.org/10.21037/tlcr.2019.11.11.

Alsever, Jennifer. "Who's to Blame for Our Great Salt Lake Problem? And How Can We Fix It?" *Utah Business.* September 2022. https://www.utahbusiness.com/what-to-do-about-the-great-salt-lake-drying-up.

Al-Shehhi, Maryam R., and Yarjan Abdul Samad. "Identifying Algal Bloom 'Hotspots' in Marginal Productive Seas: A Review and Geospatial Analysis." *Remote Sensing* 14, no. 10 (May 20, 2022): 2457. https://doi.org/10.3390/rs14102457.

Alvarez, Robert, and Joseph Mangano. "The Test Ban Treaty at 60: How Citizen Action Made the World Safer." *Bulletin of the Atomic Scientists.* August 4, 2023. https://thebulletin.org/2023/08/the-test-ban-treaty-at-60-how-citizen-action-made-the-world-safer.

Alves, Joel M., Miguel Carneiro, Jonathan P. Day, John J. Welch, Janine A. Duckworth, Tarnya E. Cox, Mike Letnic, Tanja Strive, Nuno Ferrand, and Francis M. Jiggins. "A Single Introduction of Wild Rabbits Triggered the Biological Invasion of Australia." *Proceedings of the National Academy of Sciences of the United States of America* 119, no. 35 (August 22, 2022): e2122734119. https://doi.org/10.1073/pnas.2122734119.

America Prairie. "America Prairie. History & Values." Accessed June 20, 2021. https://americanprairie.org/why-it-matters/.

American Cancer Society. "Benzene and Cancer Risk." February 1, 2023. https://www.cancer.org/cancer/risk-prevention/chemicals/benzene.html.

Andreoni, Manuela. "His Plane Crashed in the Amazon. Then Came the Hard Part." *New York Times.* March 28, 2021. https://www.nytimes.com/2021/03/28/world/americas/brazil-amazon.html.

Anenberg, Susan C., Arash Mohegh, Daniel L. Goldberg, Gaige H. Kerr, Michael Bräuer, Katrin Burkart, Perry Hystad, Andrew Larkin, Sarah Wozniak, and Lok Lamsal. "Long-Term Trends in Urban NO2 Concentrations and Associated Paediatric Asthma Incidence: Estimates from Global Datasets." *Lancet, Planetary Health* 6, no. 1 (January 1, 2022): e49–58. https://doi.org/10.1016/s2542-5196(21)00255-2.

Angrand, Ruth C., Geoffrey Collins, Philip J. Landrigan, and Valerie M. Thomas. "Relation of Blood Lead Levels and Lead in Gasoline: An Updated Systematic Review." *Environmental Health* 21 (December 27, 2022): 138. https://doi.org/10.1186/s12940-022-00936-x.

APS News. "This Month in Physics History. April 6, 1938: Discovery of Teflon." *APS News* 30, no. 4 (April 2021). https://www.aps.org/publications/apsnews/202104/history.cfm.

Aramayo, Lindsay, and Mark Morey. "Natural Gas Combined-Cycle Power Plants Increased Utilization with Improved Technology." U.S. Energy Information Administration. November 20, 2023. https://www.eia.gov/todayinenergy/detail.php?id=60984.

Arguedas Ortiz, Diego. "How the Humble Potato Changed the World." *BBC.* March 3, 2020. https://www.bbc.com/travel/article/20200302-the-true-origins-of-the-humble-potato.

Arias, Paola A., Juan Antonio Rivera, Anna A. Sörensson, Mariam Zachariah, Clair Barnes, Sjoukje Philip, Sarah Kew, et al. "Interplay Between Climate Change and Climate Variability: The 2022 Drought in Central South America." *Climatic Change* 177 (December 21, 2023): 6. https://doi.org/10.1007/s10584-023-03664-4.

Arnold, Carrie. "Consequences of DDT Exposure Could Last Generations." *Scientific American.* July 1, 2021. https://www.scientificamerican.com/article/consequences-of-ddt-exposure-could-last-generations.

Arrhenius, Svante. "On the Influence of Carbonic Acid in the Air Upon the Temperature of the Ground." *Philosophical Magazine and Journal of Science* 41, no. 251 (April 1, 1896): 237–76. https://doi.org/10.1080/14786449608620846.

Associated Press. "Latest Talks Between Ethiopia, Sudan and Egypt Over Mega Dam on the Nile End Without Breakthrough." September 25, 2023. https://apnews.com/article/ethiopia-egypt-nile-water-dispute-143261644df90d9762a3392c300a4e27.

Associated Press. "A Timeline of Recent Oil Train Crashes in the US and Canada." June 3, 2016. https://apnews.com/general-news-84b1e8273d854697b34af57bc60badc2.

Atkinson, Simon. "Solar-Powered Desalination System Provides Villagers with Access to

Clean Water for Drinking and Use in Farming." *Membrane Technology* 2020, no. 7 (July 1, 2020): 7–8. https://doi.org/10.1016/s0958-2118(20)30125-7.

Augustine, Chad, Sarah Fisher, Jonathan Ho, Ian Warren, and Erik Witter. "Enhanced Geothermal Shot Analysis for the Geothermal Technologies Office." Golden, CO: National Renewable Energy Laboratory, Technical Report NREL/TP-5700–84822. January 2023. https://www.nrel.gov/docs/fy23osti/84822.pdf.

Austen, Ian, and Vjosa Isai. "Canada's Logging Industry Devours Forests Crucial to Fighting Climate Change." *New York Times*. January 4, 2024. https://www.nytimes.com/2024/01/04/world/canada/canada-boreal-forest-logging.html.

Austin Wæhler, Turid, and Erik Sveberg Dietrichs. "The Vanishing Aral Sea: Health Consequences of an Environmental Disaster." *Journal of the Norwegian Medical Association* 137 (October 3, 2017). https://doi.org/10.4045/tidsskr.17.0597.

Australian Institute of Marine Science. "Coral Bleaching Events." https://www.aims.gov.au/research-topics/environmental-issues/coral-bleaching/coral-bleaching-events.

Australian Institute of Marine Science. "What Is Coral Bleaching?" https://www.aims.gov.au/research-topics/environmental-issues/coral-bleaching/what-coral-bleaching.

Bačić, Marjana. "Top 10 Ocean Cleaning Startups." *Recycling Startups*. June 22, 2024. https://www.recyclingstartups.org/top/ocean-cleaning/.

Bahlai, Christie A., Clarisse Hart, Maria T. Kavanaugh, Jeffrey D. White, Roger W. Ruess, Todd J. Brinkman, Hugh W. Ducklow, et al. "Cascading Effects: Insights from the U.S. Long Term Ecological Research Network." *Ecosphere* 12, no. 5 (May 17, 2021): e03430. https://doi.org/10.1002/ecs2.3430.

Bajić, Bojana, Damjan Vučurović, Đurđina Vasić, Rada Jevtić-Mučibabić, and Siniša Dodić. "Biotechnological Production of Sustainable Microbial Proteins from Agro-Industrial Residues and By-Products." *Foods* 12, no. 1 (2023): 107. https://doi.org/10.3390/foods12010107.

Baker, Gregory A., Leslie C. Gray, Michael J. Harwood, Travis J. Osland, and Jean Baptiste C. Tooley. "On-Farm Food Loss in Northern and Central California: Results of Field Survey Measurements." *Resources, Conservation and Recycling* 149 (October 2019): 541–49. https://doi.org/10.1016/j.resconrec.2019.03.022.

Ball, Philip. "The Chase for Fusion Energy." *Nature* 599, no. 599 (November 18, 2021): 362–66. https://www.nature.com/immersive/d41586-021-03401-w/index.html.

Ballester, Joan, Marcos Quijal-Zamorano, Raúl Fernando Méndez Turrubiates, Ferran Pegenaute, François R. Herrmann, Jean Marie Robine, Xavier Basagaña, Cathryn Tonne, Josep M. Antó, and Hicham Achebak. "Heat-Related Mortality in Europe During the Summer of 2022." *Nature Medicine* 29 (July 10, 2023): 1857–66. https://doi.org/10.1038/s41591-023-02419-z.

Barrett, Luke T., Seth J. Theuerkauf, Julie M. Rose, Heidi K. Alleway, Suzanne B. Bricker, Matt Parker, Daniel R. Petrolia, and Robert C. Jones. "Sustainable Growth of Non-Fed Aquaculture Can Generate Valuable Ecosystem Benefits." *Ecosystem Services* 53 (February 1, 2022): 101396. https://doi.org/10.1016/j.ecoser.2021.101396.

Barzman, Marco, Paolo Bàrberi, A. Nicholas E. Birch, Piet Boonekamp, Silke Dachbrodt-Saaydeh, Benno Graf, Bernd Hommel, et al. "Eight Principles of Integrated Pest Management." *Agronomy for Sustainable Development* 35 (July 24, 2015): 1199–215. https://doi.org/10.1007/s13593-015-0327-9.

Basilio, Humberto. "Groundwater Pumping Is Causing Mexico City to Sink." *Eos* 104 (May 5, 2023). https://doi.org/10.1029/2023EO230182.

Bayer, Patrick, and Michaël Aklin. "The European Union Emissions Trading System Reduced CO2 Emissions Despite Low Prices." *Proceedings of the National Academy of Sciences of the United States of America* 117, no. 16 (April 6, 2020): 8804–12. https://doi.org/10.1073/pnas.1918128117.

BBC News. "The Grassroots Movement That Shut Down an Indian Copper Plant." May 29, 2018. https://www.bbc.com/news/world-asia-india-44286233.

Bearak, Max, and Giacomo d'Orlando. "Inside the Global Race to Turn Water into Fuel." *New York Times*. March 11, 2023. https://www.nytimes.com/2023/03/11/climate/green-hydrogen-energy.html.

Bennett, Paige. "Vermont Becomes Second State to Ban Bee-Killing Neonic Pesticides." *EcoWatch.* June 18, 2024. https://www.ecowatch.com/vermont-neonics-pesticides-ban-bees-neonicotinoids.html.

Benny, Anmariya, Kathiresan Pandi, and Rituja Upadhyay. "Techniques, Challenges and Future Prospects for Cell-Based Meat." *Food Science and Biotechnology* 31 (July 20, 2022): 1225–42. https://doi.org/10.1007/s10068-022-01136-6.

Bereiter, Bernhard, Sarah Eggleston, Jochen Schmitt, Christoph Nehrbass-Ahles, Thomas F. Stocker, Hubertus Fischer, Sepp Kipfstuhl, and Jerome Chappellaz. "Antarctic Ice Cores Revised 800KYr CO2 Data." NOAA National Centers for Environmental Information dataset (2015), downloaded on October 5, 2023, from http://ncdc.noaa.gov/paleo/study/17975, which is a supplement to Bereiter, Bernhard, Sarah Eggleston, Jochen Schmitt, Christoph Nehrbass-Ahles, Thomas F. Stocker, Hubertus Fischer, Sepp Kipfstuhl, and Jerome Chappellaz, "Revision of the EPICA Dome C CO2 Record from 800 to 600 Kyr Before Present." *Geophysical Research Letters* 42, no. 2 (January 28, 2015): 542–49. https://doi.org/10.1002/2014gl061957.

Berger, Andre. "Milankovitch, the Father of Paleoclimate Modeling." *Climate of the Past* 17, no. 4 (August 24, 2021): 1727–33. https://doi.org/10.5194/cp-17-1727-2021.

Berreby, David. "As Use of A.I. Soars, So Does the Energy and Water It Requires." *Yale Environment 360.* February 6, 2024. https://e360.yale.edu/features/artificial-intelligence-climate-energy-emissions.

Bertrand, Savannah, Anna Sophia Roberts, and Emma Walker. "The Climate and Economic Benefits of Rotational Livestock Grazing. Agriculture and Climate Series." Environmental and Energy Study Institute (EESI). May 3, 2022. https://www.eesi.org/articles/view/the-climate-and-economic-benefits-of-rotational-livestock-grazing.

Bettenhausen, Craig. "The Chemistry of Cold-Water Washing." *Chemical & Engineering News.* January 28, 2024. https://cen.acs.org/business/consumer-products/chemistry-cold-water-washing/102/i3?ref.

Binskin, Mark, Annabelle Bennett, and Andrew Macintosh. "Royal Commission into National Natural Disaster Arrangements: Report." Royal Commission into National Natural Disaster Arrangements, Commonwealth of Australia. October 30, 2020. https://apo.org.au/node/309191.

Bison Range. "Bison Range Restoration: Our History." https://bisonrange.org/about/.

Blackford, Mansel. "A Tale of Two Fisheries: Fishing and Over-Fishing in American Waters." Origins: Current Events in Historical Perspective, Ohio State University. September 2008. https://origins.osu.edu/article/tale-two-fisheries-fishing-and-over-fishing-american-waters.

Blair, Stephanie I., Clyde H. Barlow, and Jenifer K. McIntyre. "Acute Cerebrovascular Effects in Juvenile Coho Salmon Exposed to Roadway Runoff." *Canadian Journal of Fisheries and Aquatic Sciences* 78, no. 2 (February 1, 2021): 103–9. https://doi.org/10.1139/cjfas-2020-0240.

Blue Mountains Forest Partners. "Mission and History." https://bluemountainsforestpartners.org/about/.

Boffetta, Paolo, Nadia Jourenkova, and Per Gustavsson. "Cancer Risk from Occupational and Environmental Exposure to Polycyclic Aromatic Hydrocarbons." *Cancer Causes Control* 8 (May 1997): 444–72. https://doi.org/10.1023/A:1018465507029.

Bogage, Jacob. "Employers Turn to Ice Vests, Sweat Stickers to Cope with Extreme Heat." *Washington Post.* September 8, 2023. https://www.washingtonpost.com/business/2023/09/08/heat-climate-work-tech/.

Boissoneault, Lorraine. "Sticky Rice Mortar, the View from Space, and More Fun Facts About China's Great Wall." *Smithsonian Magazine.* February 16, 2017. https://www.smithsonianmag.com/history/sticky-rice-mortar-view-space-and-more-fun-facts-about-chinas-great-wall-180962197/.

Booth, Robert. "Charles Warns GM Farming Will End in Ecological Disaster." *Guardian.* August 12, 2008. https://www.theguardian.com/environment/2008/aug/13/prince.charles.gm.farming.

Borrelli, Pasquale, David A. Robinson, Larissa R. Fleischer, Emanuele Lugato, Cristiano Ballabio, Christine Alewell, Katrin Meusburger, et al. "An Assessment of the Global Impact of 21st Century Land Use Change on Soil Erosion." *Nature Communications* 8 (December 8, 2017): 2013. https://doi.org/10.1038/s41467-017-02142-7.

Boström-Einarsson, Lisa, Russell C. Babcock, Elisa Bayraktarov, Daniela Ceccarelli, Nathan Cook, Sebastian C.A. Ferse, Boze Hancock, et al. "Coral Restoration—A Systematic Review of Current Methods, Successes, Failures and Future Directions." *PloS One* 15, no. 1 (January 30, 2020): e0226631. https://doi.org/10.1371/journal.pone.0226631.

Bouhlel, Zeineb, Jimmy Köpke, Mariam Mina, and Vladimir Smakhtin. "Global Bottled Water Industry: A Review of Impacts and Trends." United Nations, University Institute for Water, Environment and Health, Hamilton, Canada, 2023. https://inweh.unu.edu/global-bottled-water-industry-a-review-of-impacts-and-trends/.

Bourne, Joel K., Jr. "How to Farm a Better Fish." *National Geographic.* https://www.nationalgeographic.com/foodfeatures/aquaculture.

Bousso, Ron. "BP Deepwater Horizon Costs Balloon to $65 Billion." *Reuters.* January 16, 2018. https://www.reuters.com/article/idUSKBN1F50O5/.

Boyd, Robynne. "Has Climate Gentrification Hit Miami? The City Plans to Find Out." NRDC (Natural Resources Defense Council). March 11, 2019. https://www.nrdc.org/stories/has-climate-gentrification-hit-miami-city-plans-find-out.

Boylan, Camille. "The Future of Farming: Hydroponics." Princeton Student Climate Initiative, Princeton University. November 9, 2020. https://psci.princeton.edu/tips/2020/11/9/the-future-of-farming-hydroponics.

Boyle, Louise. "America's Biggest Coal Producer Is Getting into Solar Power." *Independent.* March 2, 2022. https://www.independent.co.uk/climate-change/news/coal-peabody-solar-power-announcement-b2027204.html#comments-area.

Boyle, Rob. "Greenhouse Gas Emissions in Pakistan." *Emission Index.* April 6, 2024. https://www.emission-index.com/countries/pakistan.

Brady, Emma. "The Effects of China's Ban on Imported Scrap Plastic on Global Recycling Efforts." *Earth.org.* January 5, 2021. https://earth.org/china-ban-on-imported-scrap-plastic/.

Bray, Freddie, Mathieu Laversanne, Hyuna Sung, Jacques Ferlay, Rebecca L. Siegel, Isabelle Soerjomataram, and Ahmedin Jemal. "Global Cancer Statistics 2022: GLOBOCAN Estimates of Incidence and Mortality Worldwide for 36 Cancers in 185 Countries." *CA: A Cancer Journal for Clinicians* 74, no. 3 (April 4, 2024): 229–63. https://doi.org/10.3322/caac.21834.

Brazilian National Institute of Space Research. "PRODES—Amazônia. Monitoramento do Desmatamento da Floresta Amazônica Brasileira por Satélite." PRODES satellite monitoring project. Accessed June 10, 2024. http://www.obt.inpe.br/OBT/assuntos/programas/amazonia/prodes.

Briscoe, Tony. "Los Angeles Gets 'F' Grade for Air Quality Once Again in National Report." *Los Angeles Times.* April 19, 2023. https://www.latimes.com/environment/story/2023-04-19/l-a-gets-failing-grade-for-air-quality-once-again.

Broder van Dyke, Michelle. "14 Stories About the Lahaina Wildfire That Impacted Us." *Spectrum News,* December 22, 2023. https://spectrumlocalnews.com/hi/hawaii/news/2023/12/22/stories-lahaina-wildfire-2023.

Broekhoff, Derik, Michael Gillenwater, Tani Colbert-Sangree, and Patrick Cage. "Securing Climate Benefit: A Guide to Using Carbon Offsets." Stockholm Environment Institute & Greenhouse Gas Management Institute. November 13, 2019. https://offsetguide.org/wp-content/uploads/2020/03/Carbon-Offset-Guide_3122020.pdf.

Bryce, Emma. "Modern Study of the Ancient Practice of Mixing Rice and Fish Farming Uncovers Striking Trends." *Anthropocene Magazine.* March 4, 2022. https://www.anthropocenemagazine.org/2022/03/modern-study-of-the-ancient-practice-of-mixing-rice-and-fish-farming-uncovers-striking-trends/.

Buckley, Cara. "Tiny Forests with Big Benefits." *New York Times.* August 26, 2023. https://www.nytimes.com/2023/08/24/climate/tiny-forests-climate-miyawaki.html.

Buneri, Aziz. "'10 Billion Tree Tsunami' Suffers Setback as Flash Floods Devastate

Forests." *Pakistan Today.* May 6, 2023. https://www.pakistantoday.com.pk/2023/05/06/10-billion-tree-tsunami-suffers-setback-as-flash-floods-devastate-forests/

Bureau of Reclamation, Lower Colorado Region/Lower Colorado River Operations. "Lake Mead at Hoover Dam, End of Month Elevation (Feet)." Accessed November 14, 2023. https://www.usbr.gov/lc/region/g4000/hourly/mead-elv.html.

Butler, Rhett A. "World Rainforest Day: The World's Great Rainforests." *Mongabay.* June 22, 2020. https://news.mongabay.com/2020/06/the-worlds-great-rainforests/.

Cabernard, Livia, Stephan Pfister, Christopher Oberschelp, and Stefanie Hellweg. "Growing Environmental Footprint of Plastics Driven by Coal Combustion." *Nature Sustainability* 5, no. 2 (December 2, 2021): 139–48. https://doi.org/10.1038/s41893-021-00807-2.

Cady-Pereira, Karen E., Vivienne H. Payne, Jessica L. Neu, Kevin W. Bowman, Kazuyuki Miyazaki, Eloïse A. Marais, Susan Kulawik, Zitely A. Tzompa-Sosa, and Jennifer D. Hegarty. "Seasonal and Spatial Changes in Trace Gases Over Megacities from Aura TES Observations: Two Case Studies." *Atmospheric Chemistry and Physics* 17, no. 15 (August 7, 2017): 9379–98. https://doi.org/10.5194/acp-17-9379-2017.

Call, Isabel L., and Daniel K. Lew. "Tradable Permit Programs: What Are the Lessons for the New Alaska Halibut Catch Sharing Plan?" *Marine Policy* 52 (February 1, 2015): 125–37. https://doi.org/10.1016/j.marpol.2014.10.014.

Callendar, G.S. "The Artificial Production of Carbon Dioxide and Its Influence on Temperature." *Quarterly Journal of the Royal Meteorological Society* 64, no. 275 (April 1, 1938): 223–40. https://doi.org/10.1002/qj.49706427503.

Campanale, Claudia, Carmine Massarelli, Ilaria Savino, Vito Locaputo, and Vito Felice Uricchio. "A Detailed Review Study on Potential Effects of Microplastics and Additives of Concern on Human Health." *International Journal of Environmental Research and Public Health* 17, no. 4 (February 13, 2020): 1212. https://doi.org/10.3390/ijerph17041212.

Campling, Liam, Elizabeth Havice, John Virdin, Gabrielle Carmine, Mialy Andriamahefazafy, Mads Barbesgaard, Siddharth Chakravarty, et al. "A Geopolitical-Economy of Distant Water Fisheries Access Arrangements." *npj Ocean Sustainability* (April 29, 2024): 26. https://doi.org/10.1038/s44183-024-00060-y.

Canadian Interagency Forest Fire Centre. "Wildfire Graphs. Annual Area Burned in Canada." Accessed December 4, 2023. https://ciffc.net/statistics.

Capehart, Mary Ann. "Drought Diminishes Hydropower Capacity in Western U.S." Water Resources Research Center, University of Arizona. https://wrrc.arizona.edu/drought-diminishes-hydropower.

Carson, Rachel. *Silent Spring.* Boston: Houghton Mifflin, 1962.

Casadevall, Arturo, Dimitrios P. Kontoyiannis, and Vincent Robert. "On the Emergence of *Candida auris*: Climate Change, Azoles, Swamps, and Birds." *MBio* 10, no. 4 (July 23, 2019): e01397–19. https://doi.org/10.1128/mbio.01397-19.

Casado Sanchez, Irene, and Jackie Botts. "A Program Meant to Help Developing Nations Fight Climate Change Is Funneling Billions of Dollars Back to Rich Countries." *Reuters.* May 22, 2024. https://www.reuters.com/investigates/special-report/climate-change-loans/.

Cawdrey, Kathryn, and Michael Carlowicz. "Warming Makes Droughts, Extreme Wet Events More Frequent, Intense." NASA's Jet Propulsion Laboratory/California Institute of Technology. March 13, 2023. https://grace.jpl.nasa.gov/news/151/warming-makes-droughts-extreme-wet-events-more-frequent-intense.

Centers for Disease Control and Prevention, National Center for Emerging and Zoonotic Infectious Diseases. "Climate Change and Fungal Diseases." November 30, 2023. https://www.cdc.gov/fungal/climate.html

CFA Institute. "What Is ESG Investing and Analysis?" Accessed June 22, 2024. https://www.cfainstitute.org/en/rpc-overview/esg-investing.

CGIAR Research Initiatives, CGIAR. "Climate Adaptation & Mitigation." Accessed January 12, 2024. https://www.cgiar.org/research/cgiar-portfolio/climate-adaptation-mitigation.

Chamas, Ali, Hyunjin Moon, Jiajia Zheng, Yang Qiu, Tarnuma Tabassum, Jun Hee Jang, Mahdi Abu-Omar, Susannah L. Scott, and Sangwon Suh. "Degradation Rates of Plastics in the Environment." *ACS Sustainable Chemistry & Engineering* 8, no. 9 (February 3, 2020): 3494–511. https://dx.doi.org/10.1021/acssuschemeng.9b06635.

Chen, Heather. "This Country's Love Affair with Air Conditioning Shows a Catch 22 of Climate Change." *CNN.* June 9, 2023. https://www.cnn.com/2023/06/09/asia/air-conditioning-singapore-climate-change-intl-hnk-dst/index.html.

Chen, Joyce. "CEO Tenure Rates." Harvard Law School Forum on Corporate Governance. August 4, 2023. https://corpgov.law.harvard.edu/2023/08/04/ceo-tenure-rates-2/.

Chen, Rui, Zhangcai Qin, Jeongwoo Han, Michael Wang, Farzad Taheripour, Wallace Tyner, Don O'Connor, and James Duffield. "Life Cycle Energy and Greenhouse Gas Emission Effects of Biodiesel in the United States with Induced Land Use Change Impacts." *Bioresource Technology* 251 (March 1, 2018): 249–58. https://doi.org/10.1016/j.biortech.2017.12.031.

Chiang, Connie Y., and Michael Reese. "Evergreen State: Exploring the History of Washington's Forests." Center for the Study of the Pacific Northwest, Department of History, University of Washington. https://sites.uw.edu/cspn/evergreen-state/.

Chiba, Sanae, Hideaki Saito, Ruth Fletcher, Takayuki Yogi, Makino Kayo, Shin Miyagi, Moritaka Ogido, and Katsunori Fujikura. "Human Footprint in the Abyss: 30 Year Records of Deep-Sea Plastic Debris." *Marine Policy* 96 (October 1, 2018): 204–12. https://doi.org/10.1016/j.marpol.2018.03.022.

Choi-Schagrin, Winston, and Hiroko Tabuchi. "Trash or Recycling? Why Plastic Keeps Us Guessing." *New York Times.* April 21, 2022. https://www.nytimes.com/interactive/2022/04/21/climate/plastics-recycling-trash-environment.html.

Christina, Bernadette. "Explainer: How Indonesia's Deforestation Persists Despite Moratorium." *Reuters.* June 19, 2024. https://www.reuters.com/business/environment/how-indonesias-deforestation-persists-despite-moratorium-2024-06-20.

Circle Economy Foundation. "The Circularity Gap Report 2023." https://www.circularity-gap.world/2023#download.

Circular Action Alliance. https://circularactionalliance.org.

Claar, Danielle C., Samuel Starko, Kristina L. Tietjen, Hannah E. Epstein, Ross Cunning, Kim M. Cobb, Andrew C. Baker, Ruth D. Gates, and Julia K. Baum. "Dynamic Symbioses Reveal Pathways to Coral Survival Through Prolonged Heatwaves." *Nature Communications* 11 (December 8, 2020): 6097. https://doi.org/10.1038/s41467-020-19169-y.

Clark, Robbie A., and Michael P. Shaver. "Depolymerization Within a Circular Plastics System." *Chemical Reviews* 124, no. 5 (February 22, 2024): 2617–50. https://doi.org/10.1021/acs.chemrev.3c00739.

Clémençon, Raymond. "30 Years of International Climate Negotiations: Are They Still Our Best Hope?" *Journal of Environment & Development* 32, no. 2 (March 22, 2023): 114–46. https://doi.org/10.1177/10704965231163908.

Clifford, Catherine. "The Feds Have Collected More than $44 Billion for a Permanent Nuclear Waste Dump—Here's Why We Still Don't Have One." *CNBC.* December 19, 2021. https://www.cnbc.com/2021/12/18/nuclear-waste-why-theres-no-permanent-nuclear-waste-dump-in-us.html.

Climate Foundation. "What Is Marine Permaculture?" https://www.climatefoundation.org/what-is-marine-permaculture.html.

Climate Group RE100. "RE100 Members." Accessed June 22, 2024. https://www.there100.org/re100-members.

Climeworks. "Orca: The First Large-Scale Plant." Accessed January 12, 2024. https://climeworks.com/plant-orca.

Clinton, Nicholas, Michelle Stuhlmacher, Albie Miles, Nazli Uludere Aragon, Melissa Wagner, Matei Georgescu, Chris Herwig, and Peng Gong. "A Global Geospatial Ecosystem Services Estimate of Urban Agriculture." *Earth's Future* 6, no. 1 (January 10, 2018): 40–60. https://doi.org/10.1002/2017EF000536.

Cohen, Judah, Laurie Agel, Mathew Barlow, Chaim I. Garfinkel, and Ian White. "Linking Arctic Variability and Change with Extreme Winter Weather in the United States." *Science* 373, no. 6559 (September 1, 2021): 1116–21. https://doi.org/10.1126/science.abi9167.

Colinet, Jay F. "The Impact of Black Lung and a Methodology for Controlling Respirable

Dust." *Mining, Metallurgy & Exploration* 37, no. 6 (July 30, 2020): 1847–56. https://doi. org/10.1007/s42461-020-00278-7.

Conte, Niccolo. "Mapped: 30 Years of Deforestation and Forest Growth, by Country." *Decarbonization Channel.* November 6, 2022. https://decarbonization.visualcapitalist. com/mapped-30-years-of-deforestation-and-forest-growth-by-country/.

Continental. "Urban Taraxagum. Made of Dandelion Rubber." https://www.continental-tires.com/products/b2c/bicycle/tires/urban-taraxagum/.

Copper Development Association Inc. "Copper—The World's Most Reusable Resource." https://www.copper.org/environment/lifecycle/g_recycl.html.

Cordner, Alissa, Gretta Goldenman, Linda S. Birnbaum, Phil Brown, Mark F. Miller, Rosie Mueller, Sharyle Patton, Derrick H. Salvatore, and Leonardo Trasande. "The True Cost of PFAS and the Benefits of Acting Now." *Environmental Science & Technology* 55, no. 14 (July 7, 2021): 9630–33. https://doi.org/10.1021/acs.est.1c03565.

Cornwall, Warren. "An Alkaline Solution. As Alarm About Climate Change Grows, Scientists Explore a Strategy for Drawing Excess Carbon Dioxide into the Ocean." *Science.* November 30, 2023. https://doi.org/10.1126/science.zn8487l.

Cornwall, Warren. "A Huge Forest Experiment Aims to Reduce Wildfires. Can It Unite Loggers and Environmentalists?" *Science.* September 16, 2021. https://doi.org/10.1126/ science.acx9117.

Cornwall, Warren. "Is Wood a Green Source of Energy? Scientists Are Divided." *Science.* January 5, 2017. https://doi.org/10.1126/science.aal0574.

Corringham, Thomas W., F. Martin Ralph, Alexander Gershunov, Daniel R. Cayan, and Cary A. Talbot. "Atmospheric Rivers Drive Flood Damages in the Western United States." *Science Advances* 5, no. 12 (December 4, 2019). https://doi.org/10.1126/sciadv. aax4631.

Cowie, Robert H., Philippe Bouchet, and Benoît Fontaine. "The Sixth Mass Extinction: Fact, Fiction or Speculation?" *Biological Reviews* 97, no. 2 (January 10, 2022): 640–63. https://doi.org/10.1111/brv.12816.

Cozzi, Laura, Daniel Wetzel, Gianluca Tonolo, and Jacob Hyppolite II. "For the First Time in Decades, the Number of People Without Access to Electricity Is Set to Increase in 2022." *IEA: International Energy Agency.* November 3, 2022. https://www.iea.org/ commentaries/for-the-first-time-in-decades-the-number-of-people-without-access-to-electricity-is-set-to-increase-in-2022.

Cozzi, Laura, Olivia Chen, and Hyeji Kim. "The World's Top 1% of Emitters Produce Over 1000 Times More CO2 than the Bottom 1%." *International Energy Agency.* February 22, 2023. https://www.iea.org/commentaries/the-world-s-top-1-of-emitters-produce-over-1000-times-more-co2-than-the-bottom-1.

Criddle, Cristina, and Kenza Bryan. "AI Boom Sparks Concern Over Big Tech's Water Consumption." *Financial Times.* February 24 2024. https://www.ft.com/content/6544119e-a511-4cfa-9243-13b8cf855c13.

Crownhart, Casey. "The Climate Solution Beneath Your Feet." *MIT Technology Review.* February 9, 2023. https://www.technologyreview.com/2023/02/09/1068083/climate-solution-cement/.

Crownhart, Casey. "How Electricity Could Help Tackle a Surprising Climate Villain." *MIT Technology Review.* January 3, 2024. https://www.technologyreview. com/2024/01/03/1084734/sublime-systems-cement-climate-change-carbon-footprint/.

Crownhart, Casey. "These Companies Want to Go Beyond Batteries to Store Energy." *MIT Technology Review.* March 9, 2023. https://www.technologyreview. com/2023/03/09/1069578/these-companies-want-to-go-beyond-batteries-to-store-energy/.

Cumbers, John. "Ecovative: Growing Better Materials." *Forbes.* May 10, 2023. https:// www.forbes.com/sites/johncumbers/2023/05/10/ecovative-growing-better-materials/?sh=1b8f555017b0.

Cusworth, George, and Tara Garnett. "What Is Regenerative Agriculture?" TABLE, University of Oxford, Swedish University of Agricultural Sciences, and Wageningen University and Research. June 20, 2023. https://www.doi.org/10.56661/2d7b8d1c.

Cuyahoga River Area of Concern. "Bringing 1 River, 21 Subwatersheds, and 10 Miles of Lake Erie Shore Back to Health." https://cuyahogaaoc.org.

Daley, Jason. "Twice as Many Fishing Vessels Are Chasing Fewer Fish on the World's Oceans." *Smithsonian Magazine.* May 28, 2019. https://www.smithsonianmag.com/smart-news/twice-many-fishing-vessels-are-chasing-fewer-fish-worlds-oceans-180972294/.

Dall, Chris. "US Lagging Europe in Efforts to Cut Antibiotics in Livestock." CIDRAP News, Center for Infectious Disease Research & Policy Research and Innovation Office, University of Minnesota. December 2, 2022. https://www.cidrap.umn.edu/antimicrobial-stewardship/us-lagging-europe-efforts-cut-antibiotics-livestock.

Daugherty, Luke. "Recycling: A Guide to Saving Energy." *Save on Energy.* January 3, 2024. https://www.saveonenergy.com/resources/recycling-save-energy/

Davidson, Jane. "#FutureGen—Lessons from a Small Country?" *Revue française de civilisation britannique* 28, no. 3 (December 22, 2023). https://doi.org/10.4000/rfcb.11321.

Davis, Jennifer. "The Haudenosaunee Confederacy and the Constitution." *Library of Congress.* September 21, 2023. https://blogs.loc.gov/law/2023/09/the-haudenosaunee-confederacy-and-the-constitution/.

Davis, Josh. "Human-Elephant Conflict: How to Live Alongside the Largest Living Land Animal." *Natural History Museum,* London. https://www.nhm.ac.uk/discover/human-elephant-conflict-how-to-live-alongside-largest-living-land-animal.html.

Davison, Benjamin J., Anna E. Hogg, Noel Gourmelen, Livia Jakob, Jan Wuite, Thomas Nagler, Chad A. Greene, Julia Andreasen, and Marcus E. Engdahl. "Annual Mass Budget of Antarctic Ice Shelves from 1997 to 2021." *Science Advances* 9, no. 41 (October 12, 2023): eadi0186. https://doi.org/10.1126/sciadv.adi0186.

Dawes, Allegra. "What's Plaguing Voluntary Carbon Markets?" Center for Strategic and International Studies (CSIS). February 2, 2024. https://www.csis.org/analysis/whats-plaguing-voluntary-carbon-markets.

De Lellis, Pietro, Manuel Ruiz Marín, and Maurizio Porfiri. "Modeling Human Migration Under Environmental Change: A Case Study of the Effect of Sea Level Rise in Bangladesh." *Earth's Future* 9, no. 4 (April 1, 2021): e2020EF001931. https://doi.org/10.1029/2020ef001931.

De Magalhães Neto, Newton, and Heitor Evangelista. "Human Activity Behind the Unprecedented 2020 Wildfire in Brazilian Wetlands (Pantanal)." *Frontiers in Environmental Science* 10 (June 15, 2022): 888578. https://doi.org/10.3389/fenvs.2022.888578.

Denchak, Melissa. "Fracking 101." *NRDC: Natural Resources Defense Council.* April 19, 2019. https://www.nrdc.org/stories/fracking-101#what-is.

Denchak, Melissa. "What Is the Keystone XL Pipeline?" *NRDC: Natural Resources Defense Council.* March 15, 2022. https://www.nrdc.org/stories/what-keystone-xl-pipeline#whatis.

De Silva, Franklyn, and Jane Alcorn. "A Tale of Two Cancers: A Current Concise Overview of Breast and Prostate Cancer." *Cancers* 14, no. 12 (June 15, 2022): 2954. https://doi.org/10.3390/cancers14122954.

de Valence, Sibylle. "The Slopes Are Green at Copenhagen's First Ski Hill. Really." *New York Times.* October 24, 2019. https://www.nytimes.com/2019/10/23/travel/copenhagen-ski-hill-powerplant.html.

Dherani, Mukesh, Daniel Pope, Maya Mascarenhas, Kirk R. Smith, Martin Weber, and Nigel Bruce. "Indoor Air Pollution from Unprocessed Solid Fuel Use and Pneumonia Risk in Children Aged Under Five Years: A Systematic Review and Meta-Analysis." *Bulletin of the World Health Organization* 86, no. 5 (May 2008): 390–98. https://doi.org/10.2471/BLT.07.044529.

Diamanti–Kandarakis, Evanthia, Jean-Pierre Bourguignon, Linda C. Giudice, Russ Hauser, Gail S. Prins, Ana M. Soto, R. Thomas Zoeller, and Andrea C. Gore. "Endocrine-Disrupting Chemicals: An Endocrine Society Scientific Statement." *Endocrine Reviews* 30, no. 4 (June 1, 2009): 293–342. https://doi.org/10.1210/er.2009-0002.

Diamond, Randy. "Will Cell-Based Milk Change the Dairy Industry? This California Lab Could Lead the Way." *Phys.org.* October 13, 2022. https://phys.org/news/2022-10-cell-based-dairy-industry-california-lab.html.

Diaz, Jaclyn. "The Keystone Pipeline Leaked in Kansas. What Makes This Spill So Bad?" *NPR*. December 17, 2022. https://www.npr.org/2022/12/17/1142675809/cleanup-for-keystone-pipeline-oil-spill-kansas.

Dillon, J.D. "A Global Look at Residential Solar Adoption Rates." *POWER*. July 29, 2022. https://www.powermag.com/a-global-look-at-residential-solar-adoption-rates.

Ditlevsen, Peter, and Susanne Ditlevsen. "Warning of a Forthcoming Collapse of the Atlantic Meridional Overturning Circulation." *Nature Communications* 14, no. 4254 (July 25, 2023): 1–12. https://doi.org/10.1038/s41467-023-39810-w.

Dobrowolski, James P. "NIFA Impacts: Saving the Ogallala Aquifer, Supporting Farmers." U.S. Department of Agriculture. May 1, 2020. https://www.usda.gov/media/blog/2020/05/01/nifa-impacts-saving-ogallala-aquifer-supporting-farmers.

Dodds, Joseph. "The Psychology of Climate Anxiety." *BJPsych Bulletin* 45, no. 4 (May 19, 2021): 222–26. https://doi.org/10.1192/bjb.2021.18.

Dolan, Katherine, Eva Gelinsky, Nina Holland, Brigitte Reisenberger, Mute Schimpf, Iris Strutzmann, and Dagmar Urban. "Exposed: How Biotech Giants Use Patents and New GMOs to Control the Future of Food." *Corporate Europe Observatory*. October 20, 2022. https://corporateeurope.org/en/2022/10/exposed-how-biotech-giants-use-patents-and-new-gmos-control-future-food.

Druckman, Angela, and Tim Jackson. "Understanding Households as Drivers of Carbon Emissions." In *Taking Stock of Industrial Ecology*, edited by Roland Clift and Angela Druckman, 181–203. Cham: Springer, 2016. https://doi.org/10.1007/978-3-319-20571-7_9.

Dubock, Adrian. "An Overview of Agriculture, Nutrition and Fortification, Supplementation and Biofortification: Golden Rice as an Example for Enhancing Micronutrient Intake." *Agriculture & Food Security* 6 (October 6, 2017): 59. https://doi.org/10.1186/s40066-017-0135-3.

Duncan, Emily M., Annette C. Broderick, Wayne J. Fuller, Tamara S. Galloway, Matthew H. Godfrey, Mark Hamann, Colin J. Limpus, Penelope K. Lindeque, Andrew G. Mayes, Lucy C.M. Omeyer, David Santillo, Robin T.E. Snape, and Brendan J. Godley. "Microplastic Ingestion Ubiquitous in Marine Turtles." *Global Change Biology* 25, no. 2 (December 4, 2018): 744–52. https://doi.org/10.1111/gcb.14519.

Dungey, Grace. "In Oil Palm-Dominated Malaysia, Agroforestry Orchards Are Oases of Bird Life: Study." *Mongabay*. May 11, 2022. https://news.mongabay.com/2022/05/in-oil-palm-dominated-malaysia-agroforestry-orchards-are-oases-of-bird-life-study/.

Durbin, Dee-Ann. "Lab-Grown Meat Isn't on Store Shelves Yet, but Some States Have Already Banned It." *Associated Press*. May 30, 2024. https://apnews.com/article/labgrown-meat-cultivated-ban-8dee6ce8e1282efe953ca4115db4b2c2.

Dutton, Ellsworth G., and John R. Christy. "Solar Radiative Forcing at Selected Locations and Evidence for Global Lower Tropospheric Cooling Following the Eruptions of El Chichón and Pinatubo." *Geophysical Research Letters* 19, no. 23 (December 2, 1992): 2313–16. https://doi.org/10.1029/92gl02495.

Dwyer, Orla. "Q&A: The Evolving Debate About Using Genetically Modified Crops in a Warming World." *Carbon Brief*. May 22, 2024. https://www.carbonbrief.org/qa-the-evolving-debate-about-using-genetically-modified-crops-in-a-warming-world.

Ecovative. "Mycelium, Packaging, and Hope for a Plastic Free Planet." April 21 2023. https://www.ecovative.com/blogs/blog/mycelium-packaging-plastic-free-planet.

Edwards, Julia B., Alan C. McKinnon, and Sharon L. Cullinane. "Comparative Analysis of the Carbon Footprints of Conventional and Online Retailing: A 'Last' Mile Perspective." *International Journal of Physical Distribution & Logistics Management* 40, no. 1/2 (February 2, 2010): 103–23. https://doi.org/10.1108/09600031011018055.

EFSA Panel on Food Additives and Flavourings (FAF), Maged Younes, Gabriele Aquilina, Gisela Degen, Karl-Heinz Engel, Paul Fowler, Maria Jose Frutos Fernandez, et al. "Safety of Soy Leghemoglobin from Genetically Modified *Komagataella phaffii* as a Food Additive." *EFSA Journal* 22, no. 6 (June 28, 2024): e8822. https://doi.org/10.2903/j.efsa.2024.8822.

Egan, Kathryn B., Cheryl R. Cornwell, Joseph G. Courtney, and Adrienne S. Ettinger.

"Blood Lead Levels in U.S. Children Ages 1–11 Years, 1976–2016." *Environmental Health Perspectives* 129, no. 3 (March 17, 2021). https://doi.org/10.1289/ehp7932.

Eger, Aaron M., Ezequiel M. Marzinelli, Rodrigo Beas-Luna, Caitlin O. Blain, Laura K. Blamey, Jarrett E.K. Byrnes, Paul E. Carnell, et al. "The Value of Ecosystem Services in Global Marine Kelp Forests." *Nature Communications* 14 (April 18, 2023): 1894. https://doi.org/10.1038/s41467-023-37385-0.

Ehrlich, Paul R. *The Population Bomb.* Rev. ed. Rivercity, MA: Rivercity Press, 1975.

Eklund, Lina, Ole Magnus Theisen, Matthias Baumann, Andreas Forø Tollefsen, Tobias Kuemmerle, and Jonas Østergaard Nielsen. "Societal Drought Vulnerability and the Syrian Climate-Conflict Nexus Are Better Explained by Agriculture than Meteorology." *Communications Earth & Environment* 3 (April 6, 2022): 85. https://doi.org/10.1038/s43247-022-00405-w.

Elinoff, Eli. "Concrete and Corruption. Materialising Power and Politics in the Thai Capital." *City* 21 no. 5 (November 13, 2017): 587–96. https://doi.org/10.1080/13604813.2017.1374778.

Ellen MacArthur Foundation. "About Us." https://www.ellenmacarthurfoundation.org/about-us/what-we-do.

Ellen MacArthur Foundation. "Case Studies and Examples of Circular Economy in Action." https://www.ellenmacarthurfoundation.org/topics/circular-economy-introduction/examples.

Ellen MacArthur Foundation. "The Global Commitment Five Years In: Learnings to Accelerate Towards a Future Without Plastic Waste or Pollution." Accessed June 22, 2024. https://www.ellenmacarthurfoundation.org/global-commitment/overview.

Ellen MacArthur Foundation. "The New Plastics Economy: Rethinking the Future of Plastics & Catalysing Action." 2017. https://www.ellenmacarthurfoundation.org/the-new-plastics-economy-rethinking-the-future-of-plastics-and-catalysing.

Elsabeé, Maher Z., and Entsar S. Abdou. "Chitosan Based Edible Films and Coatings: A Review." *Materials Science and Engineering: C* 33, no. 4 (May 1, 2013): 1819–41. https://doi.org/10.1016/j.msec.2013.01.010.

El-Showk, Sedeer. "Final Resting Place." *Science* 375, no. 6583 (February 25, 2022): 806–10. https://www.science.org/doi/epdf/10.1126/science.ada1392.

Emmerich, Roland. 2004. *The Day After Tomorrow.* United States: Twentieth Century Fox.

Energy Institute. "Statistical Review of World Energy 2023, 72nd Edition." https://www.energyinst.org/statistical-review.

Environmental Working Group. "The Trouble with Ingredients in Sunscreens." EWG's 18th Annual Guide to Sunscreens (2024). https://www.ewg.org/sunscreen/report/the-trouble-with-sunscreen-chemicals/.

Envirotech Online. "What Was the Dieselgate Scandal." December 23, 2022. https://www.envirotech-online.com/news/air-monitoring/6/international-environmental-technology/what-was-the-dieselgate-scandal.

Envision Utah. "Agriculture in Utah." Accessed June 21, 2024. https://yourutahyourfuture.org/topics/agriculture/item/27-background-agriculture-in-utah.

Erdenesanaa, Delger. "PFAS 'Forever Chemicals' Are Pervasive in Water Worldwide, Study Finds." *New York Times.* April 8, 2024. https://www.nytimes.com/2024/04/08/climate/-pfas-forever-chemicals-water.html.

Erickson, Britt E. "European Union High Court Nixes Neonicotinoid Exemptions." *Chemical & Engineering News.* January 23, 2023. https://cen.acs.org/environment/pesticides/European-Union-high-court-nixes/101/web/2023/01.

Erisman, Jan Willem, Mark A. Sutton, James Galloway, Zbigniew Klimont, and Wilfried Winiwarter. "How a Century of Ammonia Synthesis Changed the World." *Nature Geoscience* 1 (September 28, 2008): 636–39. https://doi.org/10.1038/ngeo325.

Esdaile, Louisa J., and Justin M. Chalker. "The Mercury Problem in Artisanal and Small-Scale Gold Mining." *Chemistry: A European Journal* 24, no. 27 (May 11, 2018): 6905–16. https://doi.org/10.1002/chem.201704840.

Estape, Tania. "Cancer in the Elderly: Challenges and Barriers." *Asia-Pacific Journal of*

Oncology Nursing 5, no. 1 (January 1, 2018): P40–42. https://doi.org/10.4103/apjon. apjon_52_17.

Estonian Design Centre. "The Circularity Gap Report 2023: The Global Economy Is Only 7,2% Circular." https://ringdisain.ee/en/the-circularity-gap-report-2023-the-global-economy-is-only-72-circular/.

EuRIC AISBL–Recycling: Bridging Circular Economy & Climate Policy. "Metal Recycling Factsheet." https://circulareconomy.europa.eu/platform/sites/default/files/euric_metal_recycling_factsheet.pdf

European Bioplastics. "Bioplastics Market Development Update 2023." Accessed March 25, 2024. https://www.european-bioplastics.org/market/

European Commission. "The Birds Directive." https://environment.ec.europa.eu/topics/nature-and-biodiversity/birds-directive_en.

European Commission. "Bisphenol A: EU Ban on Use in Baby Bottles Enters into Force Next Week. Press Release IP/11/229." February 25, 2011. https://ec.europa.eu/commission/presscorner/detail/en/IP_11_229.

European Commission. "Circular Economy Action Plan. The EU's New Circular Action Plan Paves the Way for a Cleaner and More Competitive Europe." Accessed July 7, 2024. https://environment.ec.europa.eu/strategy/circular-economy-action-plan_en.

European Commission. "The Habitats Directive." https://environment.ec.europa.eu/topics/nature-and-biodiversity/habitats-directive_en.

European Environmental Agency. "Fossil Fuel Subsidies." November 17, 2023. https://www.eea.europa.eu/en/analysis/indicators/fossil-fuel-subsidies.

EUROPEN: European Organization for Packaging and the Environment. "Factsheet. Extended Producer Responsibility (EPR) for Used Packaging." March 16, 2015. https://www.europen-packaging.eu/policy-area/extended-producer-responsibility.

Eurostat. "Plastic Packaging Waste: 38% Recycled in 2020." October 20, 2022. https://ec.europa.eu/eurostat/web/products-eurostat-news/-/ddn-20221020-1.

Evalen, P.S., E.N. Barnhardt, J. Ryu, and Z.R. Stahlschmidt. "Toxicity of Glyphosate to Animals: A Meta-Analytical Approach." *Environmental Pollution* 347 (April 15, 2024): 123669. https://doi.org/10.1016/j.envpol.2024.123669.

Evans, Simon. "Analysis: Which Countries Are Historically Responsible for Climate Change?" *Carbon Brief.* October 5, 2021. https://www.carbonbrief.org/analysis-which-countries-are-historically-responsible-for-climate-change/.

EverGreen Agriculture Partnership. "Southern Africa." https://evergreenagriculture.net/evergreen-nations/southern-africa.

Ewing, Jack, and Eric Lipton. "Carmakers Race to Control Next-Generation Battery Technology." *New York Times.* March 7, 2022. https://www.nytimes.com/2022/03/07/business/energy-environment/next-generation-auto-battery.html.

Eyl-Mazzega, Marc-Antoine, and Élise Cassignol. "The Geopolitics of Seawater Desalination." French Institute of International Relationships. September 27, 2022. https://www.ifri.org/en/publications/etudes-de-lifri/geopolitics-seawater-desalination.

Fabro, Keith Anthony S. "Is the Genetically Modified, Nutrient-Rich Golden Rice as Safe as Promised?" *Mongabay.* September 11, 2023. https://news.mongabay.com/2023/09/is-the-genetically-modified-nutrient-rich-golden-rice-as-safe-as-promised/.

Fairley, Peter. "The US Electricity Transmission System Is in Gridlock." *Sierra Club.* September 18, 2023. https://www.sierraclub.org/sierra/2023-3-fall/feature/us-electricity-transmission-system-gridlock.

Farman, Joe C., Brian G. Gardiner, and Jonathan D. Shanklin. "Large Losses of Total Ozone in Antarctica Reveal Seasonal ClOx/NOx Interaction." *Nature* 315, no. 6016 (May 1, 1985): 207–10. https://doi.org/10.1038/315207a0.

Farquhar, Brodie. "Wolf Reintroduction Changes Ecosystem in Yellowstone." *Yellowstone National Park.* June 22, 2023. https://www.yellowstonepark.com/things-to-do/wildlife/wolf-reintroduction-changes-ecosystem/.

Fatima, Massarath. "Cooling in Developing Countries." *Borgen Project.* December 18, 2018. https://borgenproject.org/cooling-in-developing-countries.

Featherstone, Liza. "The Scariest Part About Artificial Intelligence." *New Republic.* March

5, 2024. https://newrepublic.com/article/179538/environment-artificial-intelligence-water-energy.

Feeding America. "Fighting Food Waste and Hunger with Food Rescue." https://www.feedingamerica.org/our-work/reduce-food-waste.

Fernanda Ribeiro, Maria. "In the Amazon, a Farmer Practices the Future of Sustainable Cattle Ranching." *Mongabay.* May 28, 2020. https://news.mongabay.com/2020/05/in-the-amazon-a-farmer-practices-the-future-of-sustainable-cattle-ranching/.

Ferrara, Carmen, Giovanni De Feo, and Vincenza Picone. "LCA of Glass Versus PET Mineral Water Bottles: An Italian Case Study." *Recycling* 6, no. 3 (July 15, 2021): 50. https://doi.org/10.3390/recycling6030050.

Ferreira Santos, Sofia. "Amazon Rainforest: Deforestation Rate Halved in 2023." *BBC News.* January 12, 2024. https://www.bbc.com/news/world-latin-america-67962297.

Finnigan, Tim J.A., Benjamin T. Wall, Peter J. Wilde, Francis B. Stephens, Steve L. Taylor, and Marjorie R. Freedman. "Mycoprotein: The Future of Nutritious Nonmeat Protein, a Symposium Review." *Current Developments in Nutrition* 3, no. 6 (June 2019): nzz021. https://doi.org/10.1093/cdn/nzz021.

Fischer, Emily, and Michael Carlowicz. "Research Shows More People Living in Floodplains." NASA Earth Observatory. September 2021. https://www.earthobservatory.nasa.gov/images/148866/research-shows-more-people-living-in-floodplains.

Fitt, Elizabeth. "Boats Behaving Badly: New Report Analyzes China's Own Fisheries Data." *Mongabay.* April 28, 2022. https://news.mongabay.com/2022/04/boats-behaving-badly-new-report-analyzes-chinas-own-fisheries-data/.

Flanagan, Sara V., Richard B. Johnston, and Yan Zheng. "Arsenic in Tube Well Water in Bangladesh: Health and Economic Impacts and Implications for Arsenic Mitigation." *Bulletin of the World Health Organization* 90, no. 11 (November 1, 2012): 839–46. https://doi.org/10.2471/BLT.11.101253.

Flavelle, Christopher, and Somini Sengupta. "How America's Diet Is Feeding the Groundwater Crisis." *New York Times.* December 24, 2023. https://www.nytimes.com/interactive/2023/12/24/climate/groundwater-crisis-chicken-cheese.html.

Fleming, Sean. "Circular Economy Examples—How IKEA, Burger King, Adidas and More Are Investing in a Circular Economy." *World Economic Forum.* December 8, 2020. https://www.weforum.org/agenda/2020/12/circular-economy-examples-ikea-burger-king-adidas/.

Fletcher, Veronica. "America's Burger Loving States." Pantry & Larder. December 27, 2023. https://pantryandlarder.com/americas-burger-loving-states/.

Flores, Bernardo M., Encarni Montoya, Boris Sakschewski, Nathália Nascimento, Arie Staal, Richard A. Betts, Carolina Levis, et al. "Critical Transitions in the Amazon Forest System." *Nature* 626 (February 14, 2024): 555–64. https://doi.org/10.1038/s41586-023-06970-0.

Flores, Mugdha. "Saving Washington's Salmon from Toxic Tire Dust." Washington State Department of Ecology. January 25, 2023. https://ecology.wa.gov/blog/january-2023/saving-washington-s-salmon-from-toxic-tire-dust.

Food and Agriculture Organization of the United Nations (FAO). "Agreement on Port State Measures (PSMA)." Accessed June 17, 2024. https://www.fao.org/port-state-measures/background/parties-psma/en/.

Food and Agriculture Organization of the United Nations (FAO). "Asia and the Pacific National Forestry Programmes: Update 34." Regional Office for Asia and the Pacific, Bangkok. December 2000. https://www.fao.org/4/x6900e/x6900e0d.htm#10.%20Indonesia.

Food and Agriculture Organization of the United Nations (FAO). "Land Cover, 2021." FAOSTAT. https://www.fao.org/faostat/en/#data/LC.

Food and Agriculture Organization of the United Nations (FAO). "Nutrition. Food Loss and Waste." https://www.fao.org/nutrition/capacity-development/food-loss-and-waste/en/.

Food and Agriculture Organization of the United Nations (FAO). "Per Capita Meat Consumption by Type, 2021." With major processing by Our World in Data. https://ourworldindata.org/grapher/per-capita-meat-type.

Food and Agriculture Organization of the United Nations (FAO). "Seeking End to Loss and Waste of Food Along Production Chain." https://www.fao.org/in-action/seeking-end-to-loss-and-waste-of-food-along-production-chain/en/.

Food and Agriculture Organization of the United Nations (FAO). "The State of World Fisheries and Aquaculture 2022. Towards Blue Transformation." FAO (2022), Rome. https://doi.org/10.4060/cc0461en.

Food and Agriculture Organization of the United Nations (FAO). "Total Water Withdrawal per Capita, AQUASTAT Main Database, 2016." Accessed May 14, 2024. https://data.apps.fao.org/catalog/dataset/829bade5-1bb8-4154-aed3-088e5a3b8d00/resource/d5610feb-00ba-4391-8a11-bdedfda7a89a.

Food Stash Foundation. "Mission & Impact." https://www.foodstash.ca/mission.

Forest History Society. "The Northern Spotted Owl." https://foresthistory.org/research-explore/us-forest-service-history/policy-and-law/wildlife-management/the-northern-spotted-owl/.

Forest Stewardship Council. "How the FSC System Works." https://fsc.org/en/how-the-fsc-system-works.

Formanski, Karen. "2021 State of the Industry Report | Plant-Based Meat, Seafood, Eggs, and Dairy." *Good Food Institute*. https://gfi.org/wp-content/uploads/2022/04/2021-Plant-Based-State-of-the-Industry-Report-1.pdf.

Förster, Jürgen. "Cooling for Electricity Production Dominates Water Use in Industry." *Eurostat*, Statistics in focus 14/2014. https://ec.europa.eu/eurostat/statistics-explained/index.php?title=Archive:Water_use_in_industry.

Fountain, Henry. "Chevron and Others Build an Underground Hydrogen Battery in Utah." *New York Times*. January 12, 2024. https://www.nytimes.com/2024/01/12/climate/green-hydrogen-climate-change.html.

Fountain, Henry. "In a First, U.S. Declares Water Shortage on Colorado River, Forcing Water Cuts." *New York Times*. August 16, 2021. https://www.nytimes.com/2021/08/16/climate/colorado-river-water-cuts.html.

Fourier, Jean-Baptiste Joseph. "Remarques générales sur les températures du globe terrestre et des espaces planetaires." *Annales de chimie et de physique* 27 (1824): 136–67.

Fox, Alex. "'This Is Shocking.' An Undersea Plague Is Obliterating a Key Ocean Species." *Science*. January 30, 2019. https://doi.org/10.1126/science.aaw8532.

Frampton, Mark W., Joseph Boscia, Norbert J. Roberts, Jr., Mitra Azadniv, Alfonso Torres, Christopher Cox, Paul E. Morrow, et al. "Nitrogen Dioxide Exposure: Effects on Airway and Blood Cells." *American Journal of Physiology. Lung Cellular and Molecular Physiology* 282, no. 1 (January 1, 2002): L155–65. https://doi.org/10.1152/ajplung.2002.282.1.l155.

Frank, Sarah M., Lindsey Smith Taillie, and Lindsay M. Jaacks, "How Americans Eat Red and Processed Meat: An Analysis of the Contribution of Thirteen Different Food Groups." *Public Health Nutrition* 25, no. 5 (February 21, 2022): 1406–15. https://doi.org/10.1017/S1368980022000416.

Freinkel, Susan. "A Brief History of Plastic's Conquest of the World." *Scientific American*. May 29, 2011. https://www.scientificamerican.com/article/a-brief-history-of-plastic-world-conquest/.

Friedlingstein, Pierre, Michael O'Sullivan, Matthew W. Jones, Robbie M. Andrew, Luke Gregor, Judith Hauck, Corinne Le Quéré, et al. "Global Carbon Budget 2022." *Earth System Science Data* 14, no. 11 (November 11, 2022): 4811–900. https://doi.org/10.5194/essd-14-4811-2022.

Friedrich, Doris. "The Problems Won't Go Away: Persistent Organic Pollutants (POPs) in the Arctic." *Arctic Institute*. July 1, 2016. https://www.thearcticinstitute.org/persistent-organic-pollutants-pops-in-the-arctic/.

Fujii, Hidemichi, Jeremy Webb, Sagadevan Mundree, David Rowlings, Peter Grace, Clevo Wilson, and Shunsuke Managi. "Priority Change and Driving Factors in the Voluntary Carbon Offset Market." *Cleaner Environmental Systems* 13 (June 2024): 100164. https://doi.org/10.1016/j.cesys.2024.100164.

Gabbatiss, Josh, Daisy Dunne, Aruna Chandrasekhar, Orla Dwyer, Molly Lempriere, Yanine Quiroz, Ayesha Tandon, and Giuliana Viglione. "In-Depth Q&A: Can 'Carbon

Offsets' Help to Tackle Climate Change?" *Carbon Brief.* September 24, 2023. https://interactive.carbonbrief.org/carbon-offsets-2023/.

Gade, Daniel W. "Deforestation and Its Effects in Highland Madagascar." *Mountain Research and Development* 16, no. 2 (May 1996): 101–16. https://doi.org/10.2307/3674005.

Gambrell, Jon, Peter Prengaman, and Seth Borenstein. "At COP28 Meeting, Oil Companies Pledge to Combat Methane. Environmentalists Call It a 'Smokescreen.'" *Associated Press.* December 2, 2023. https://apnews.com/article/climate-changemethanecop28-58c756d8 43fbc696b28a330295505be7.

Gamillo, Elizabeth. "Leaded Gasoline Use in Vehicles Has Now Officially Ended Worldwide." *Smithsonian Magazine.* August 31, 2021. https://www.smithsonianmag.com/smart-news/worldwide-use-leaded-gasoline-vehicles-now-completely-phased-out-180978549/.

Garan, Ron. *The Orbital Perspective: Lessons in Seeing the Big Picture from a Journey of 71 Million Miles.* Oakland, CA: Berrett-Koehler Publishers, 2015, eBook Collection (O'Reilly Academic).

Garbarino, Jeanne. "History and Biochemistry of Fermented Foods." Rockefeller University. https://rockedu.rockefeller.edu/component/biochemistry-fermented-foods/.

Garner, Andra J. "Observed Increases in North Atlantic Tropical Cyclone Peak Intensification Rates." *Scientific Reports* 13, no. 16299 (October 19, 2023): 1–12. https://doi.org/10.1038/s41598-023-42669-y.

Gelsomin, Emily. "Impossible and Beyond: How Healthy Are These Meatless Burgers?" Harvard Health Publishing, Harvard Medical School. January 24, 2022. https://www.health.harvard.edu/blog/impossible-and-beyond-how-healthy-are-these-meatless-burgers-2019081517448.

Geological Society of America. "Looming Crisis of the Much Decreased Fresh-Water Supply to Egypt's Nile Delta." *Phys.org.* March 13, 2017. https://phys.org/news/2017-03-looming-crisis-decreased-fresh-water-egypt.html.

Gesley, Jenny. "Germany: Lightweight Plastic Bag Ban to Take Effect January 1, 2021." Retrieved from Library of Congress. https://www.loc.gov/item/global-legal-monitor/2021-02-25/germany-lightweight-plastic-bag-ban-to-take-effect-january-1-2022/.

Geyer, Roland, Jenna R. Jambeck, and Kara Lavender Law. "Production, Use, and Fate of All Plastics Ever Made" *Science Advances* 3, no. 7 (July 19, 2017). https://doi.org/10.1126/sciadv.1700782.

Gies, Erica. "To Revive a River, Restore Its Liver." *Scientific American.* April 1, 2022. https://www.scientificamerican.com/article/to-revive-a-river-restore-its-hidden-gut1/.

Gilbert, Natasha. "Global Biodiversity Report Warns Pollinators Are Under Threat." *Nature,* February 26, 2016. https://doi.org/10.1038/nature.2016.19456.

Gleick, Peter H. "Water Resources." In *Encyclopedia of Climate and Weather,* vol. 2, edited by Stephen H. Schneider, 817–23. New York: Oxford University Press, 1996.

Glibert, Patricia M. "From Hogs to HABs: Impacts of Industrial Farming in the US on Nitrogen and Phosphorus and Greenhouse Gas Pollution." *Biogeochemistry* 150 (August 10, 2020): 139–80. https://doi.org/10.1007/s10533-020-00691-6.

Glibert, Patricia M., Roxane Maranger, Daniel J. Sobota, and Lex Bouwman. "The Haber Bosch–Harmful Algal Bloom (HB–HAB) Link." *Environmental Research Letters* 9, no. 10 (October 1, 2014): 105001. https://doi.org/10.1088/1748-9326/9/10/105001.

Global Agriculture. "Global Organic Farmland Up 26% in 2022, Reaching 96 Million Hectares." February 15, 2024. https://www.globalagriculture.org/whats-new/news/en/34917.html.

Global Agriculture. "The 70% Battle: Small Farms Still Feed the World, Open Letter." September 2, 2022. https://www.globalagriculture.org/whats-new/news/en/34543.html.

Global Coral Reef Alliance. "Biorock™, Mineral Accretion Technology™, Seament™." https://www.globalcoral.org/biorock-coral-reef-marine-habitat-restoration/.

Global Forest Watch Dashboard. "Indonesia." https://www.globalforestwatch.org/dashboards/country/IDN/?map=eyJjYW5Cb3VuZCI6dHJ1ZX0%3D.

Global Methane Pledge. Accessed February 7, 2023. https://www.globalmethanepledge.org/.

Global Yield Gap Atlas. "United States. Description of Cropping Systems, Climate, and Soils." https://www.yieldgap.org/united-states.

GlobeNewswire. "Planet Water Foundation's Project 24 Brings Clean Water to Thousands in Need." March 17, 2022. https://www.globenewswire.com/en/news-release/2022/03/17/2405440/0/en/Planet-Water-Foundation-s-Project-24-Brings-Clean-Water-to-Thousands-in-Need.html.

Glover, Jerry D., John P. Reganold, and Cindy M. Cox. "Plant Perennials to Save Africa's Soils." *Nature* 489 (September 19, 2012): 359–61. https://doi.org/10.1038/489359a.

Godin, Mélissa. "Deforestation Poses 'Existential' Threat to Sweden's Reindeer, Warn Indigenous Herders." *Times.* March 12, 2024. https://time.com/6899748/deforestation-sweden-reindeer-sami-herders/.

Goswami, Urmi, and Fermín Koop. "Q&A: COP28 and the 100 Billion U.S. Dollar Climate Finance Commitment." *Clean Energy Wire.* November 29, 2023. https://www.cleanenergywire.org/factsheets/qa-cop28-and-100-billion-us-dollar-climate-finance-commitment.

Govindasamy, Prabhu, Senthilkumar K. Muthusamy, Muthukumar Bagavathiannan, Jake Mowrer, Prasanth Tej Kumar Jagannadham, Aniruddha Maity, Hanamant M. Halli, et al. "Nitrogen Use Efficiency—A Key to Enhance Crop Productivity Under a Changing Climate." *Frontiers in Plant Science* 14 (April 18, 2023): 1121073. https://doi.org/10.3389/fpls.2023.1121073.

Grandoni, Dino. "Cement Warms the Planet. This Green Version Just Got a Key Nod of Approval." *Washington Post.* July 13, 2023. https://www.washingtonpost.com/climate-solutions/2023/07/13/green-concrete-cement-climate-brimstone/.

Green, Jessica F. "Does Carbon Pricing Reduce Emissions? A Review of Ex-Post Analyses." *Environmental Research Letters* 16, no. 4 (March 24, 2021): 043004. https://doi.org/10.1088/1748-9326/abdae9.

GreenRoots. "About Us." Accessed July 26, 2024. https://www.greenrootsej.org/about-us.

Greenstone, Michael, and Christa Hasenkopf. "Air Quality Life Index | 2023 Annual Update." The Energy Policy Institute at the University of Chicago (EPIC), August 2023. https://aqli.epic.uchicago.edu/wp-content/uploads/2023/08/AQLI_2023_Report-Global_v03.5_China_view_spreads.pdf.

Grennfelt, Peringe, Anna Engleryd, Martin Forsius, Øystein Hov, Henning Rodhe, and Ellis Cowling. "Acid Rain and Air Pollution: 50 Years of Progress in Environmental Science and Policy." *Ambio* 49 (September 21, 2019): 849–64. https://doi.org/10.1007/s13280-019-01244-4.

Griscom, Bronson. "Why We Can't Afford to Dismiss Carbon Offsetting in a Climate Crisis." *World Economic Forum.* April 22, 2021. https://www.weforum.org/agenda/2021/04/carbon-offsetting-climate-crisis/.

Grova, Nathalie, Henri Schroeder, Jean-Luc Olivier, and Jonathan D. Turner. "Epigenetic and Neurological Impairments Associated with Early Life Exposure to Persistent Organic Pollutants." *International Journal of Genomics* 2019 (January 14, 2019): 2085496. https://doi.org/10.1155/2019/2085496.

Gruber, Elisabeth S., Vanessa Stadlbauer, Verena Pichler, Katharina Resch-Fauster, Andrea Todorovic, Thomas C. Meisel, Sibylle Trawoeger, Oldamur Hollóczki, Suzanne D. Turner, Wolfgang Wadsak, A. Dick Vethaak, and Lukas Kenner. "To Waste or Not to Waste: Questioning Potential Health Risks of Micro- and Nanoplastics with a Focus on Their Ingestion and Potential Carcinogenicity." *Exposure and Health* 15 (March 22, 2022): 33–51. https://doi.org/10.1007/s12403-022-00470-8.

Grzywa-Celińska, Anna, Adam Krusiński, Jadwiga Mazur, Katarzyna Szewczyk, and Krzysztof Kozak. "Radon—The Element of Risk. The Impact of Radon Exposure on Human Health." *Toxics* 8, no. 4 (December 14, 2020): 120. https://doi.org/10.3390/toxics8040120.

Gupt, Yamini, and Samraj Sahay. "Review of Extended Producer Responsibility: A Case Study Approach." *Waste Management & Research* 33, no. 7 (July 1, 2015): 595–611. https://doi.org/10.1177/0734242x15592275.

Gworek, Barbara, Wojciech Dmuchowski, and Aneta H. Baczewska-Dąbrowska. "Mercury in the Terrestrial Environment: A Review." *Environmental Sciences Europe* 32 (October 2, 2020): 128. https://doi.org/10.1186/s12302-020-00401-x.

Haegel, Nancy M., and Sarah R. Kurtz. "Global Progress Toward Renewable Electricity: Tracking the Role of Solar (Version 3)." *IEEE Journal of Photovoltaics* 13, no. 6 (November 2023): 768–76. https://ieeexplore.ieee.org/document/10244019.

Hall, Dorothy K., John S. Kimball, Ron Larson, Nicolo E. DiGirolamo, Kimberly A. Casey, and Glynn Hulley. "Intensified Warming and Aridity Accelerate Terminal Lake Desiccation in the Great Basin of the Western United States." *Earth and Space Science* 10, no. 1 (January 6, 2023): e2022EA002630. https://doi.org/10.1029/2022ea002630.

Hallegatte, Stéphane, Colin Green, Robert J. Nicholls, and Jan Corfee-Morlot. "Future Flood Losses in Major Coastal Cities." *Nature Climate Change* 3 (August 18, 2013): 802–6. https://doi.org/10.1038/nclimate1979.

Hammel, Paul. "Massive Pipeline Spill Caused by Crack Created During Installation, Third-Party Review Concludes." *Kansas Reflector*. April 21, 2023. https://kansasreflector.com/2023/04/21/massive-pipeline-spill-caused-by-crack-created-during-installation-third-party-review-concludes/.

Hand, Eric. "Hidden Hydrogen: Earth May Hold Vast Stores of a Renewable, Carbon-Free Fuel." *Science* 379, no. 6633 (February 17, 2023): 630–36. https://www.science.org/doi/epdf/10.1126/science.adh1477.

Hansen, Grace. "Yellowstone's Wolves Defied Extinction, but Face New Threats Beyond Park's Borders." *Mongabay*. May 31, 2022. https://news.mongabay.com/2022/05/yellowstones-wolves-defied-extinction-but-face-new-threats-beyond-parks-borders/.

Harada, Masazumi. "Minamata Disease: Methylmercury Poisoning in Japan Caused by Environmental Pollution." *Critical Reviews in Toxicology* 25, no. 1 (January 1, 1995): 1–24. https://doi.org/10.3109/10408449509089885.

Harris, Linnea. "What Are Food Miles?" *EcoWatch*. March 23, 2022. https://www.ecowatch.com/food-miles-supply-transportation.html.

Hartman, Hattie. "BIG's CopenHill Waste-to-Energy Plant-cum-Ski Slope Opens in Copenhagen." *Architects' Journal*. October 11, 2019. https://www.architectsjournal.co.uk/buildings/bigs-copenhill-waste-to-energy-plant-cum-ski-slope-opens-in-copenhagen.

Haskett, Jonathan D., Belay Simane, and Caitlin Smith. "Energy and Climate Change Mitigation Benefits of *Faidherbia albida* Agroforestry in Ethiopia." *Frontiers in Environmental Science* 7 (November 1, 2019): 146. https://doi.org/10.3389/fenvs.2019.00146.

Hawaii.com. "Your Reef Safe Sunscreen Guide—15 Sunscreens That Are Reef Safe." https://www.hawaii.com/reef-safe-sunscreen/.

Hawkins, Nichola J., Chris Bass, Andrea Dixon, and Paul Neve. "The Evolutionary Origins of Pesticide Resistance." *Biological Reviews of the Cambridge Philosophical Society* 94, no. 1 (February 2019): 135–55. https://doi.org/10.1111/brv.12440.

Held, Isaac M., and Brian J. Soden. "Water Vapor Feedback and Global Warming." *Annual Review of Energy and the Environment* 25 (November 1, 2000): 441–75. https://doi.org/10.1146/annurev.energy.25.1.441.

Henneman, Lucas, Christine Choirat, Irene Dedoussi, Francesca Dominici, Jessica Roberts, and Corwin Zigler. "Mortality Risk from United States Coal Electricity Generation." *Science* 382, no. 6673 (November 23, 2023): 941–46. https://doi.org/10.1126/science.adf4915.

Herzog-Hawelka, Janina, and Joyeeta Gupta. "The Role of (Multi)national Oil and Gas Companies in Leaving Fossil Fuels Underground: A Systematic Literature Review." *Energy Research & Social Science* 103 (September 1, 2023): 103194. https://doi.org/10.1016/j.erss.2023.103194.

Hettel, Gene. "From Crop Production to Market: Improving the Livelihood of Pakistan's Basmati Rice Farmers." *Rice Today*. March 18, 2016. https://ricetoday.irri.org/from-crop-production-to-market-improving-the-livelihood-of-pakistans-basmati-rice-farmers/.

Hettinga, Kasper, and Etske Bijl. "Can Recombinant Milk Proteins Replace Those Produced by Animals?" *Current Opinion in Biotechnology* 75 (June 2022): 102690. https://doi.org/10.1016/j.copbio.2022.102690.

Hicks, Robin. "Can Singapore, the City in a Garden, Grow into a City in Nature?" *Eco-

Business. September 19, 2018. https://www.eco-business.com/news/can-singapore-the-city-in-a-garden-grow-into-a-city-in-nature/.

Higney, Anthony, Nick Hanley, and Mirko Moro. "The Lead-Crime Hypothesis: A Meta-Analysis." *Regional Science and Urban Economics* 97 (November 1, 2022): 103826. https://doi.org/10.1016/j.regsciurbeco.2022.103826.

Hill, Alice C. "Climate Change and U.S. Property Insurance: A Stormy Mix." *Council on Foreign Relations.* August 17, 2023. https://www.cfr.org/article/climate-change-and-us-property-insurance-stormy-mix.

Hitaj, Claudia, David J. Smith, Aimee Code, Seth Wechsler, Paul D. Esker, and Margaret R. Douglas. "Sowing Uncertainty: What We Do and Don't Know About the Planting of Pesticide-Treated Seed." *BioScience* 70, no. 5 (May 2020): 390–403. https://doi.org/10.1093/biosci/biaa019.

Hladik, Michelle L., Anson R. Main, and Dave Goulson. "Environmental Risks and Challenges Associated with Neonicotinoid Insecticides." *Environmental Science & Technology* 52, no. 6 (February 26, 2018): 3329–35. https://doi.org/10.1021/acs.est.7b06388.

Ho, Sally. "They've Got Beef: Beyond Meat vs. Impossible Foods Burger Showdown: What's the Difference?" *Green Queen.* March 15, 2023. https://www.greenqueen.com.hk/beyond-meat-vs-impossible-foods-burger/.

Hoar, Bruce, and John Angelos. "Beef Cattle Production." UC Davis Western Institute for Food Safety & Security. 2015. http://www.wifss.ucdavis.edu/wp-content/uploads/2015/FDA/fdacoursefinal1/Beef_Food_Animal_Production.pdf.

Hobbs, Robert J., Carol A. Thomas, Jennifer Halliwell, and Christopher D. Gwenin. "Rapid Detection of Botulinum Neurotoxins—A Review." *Toxins* 11, no. 7 (July 17, 2019): 418. https://doi.org/10.3390/toxins11070418.

Hocking, Martin B. "Paper Versus Polystyrene: A Complex Choice." *Science* 251, no. 4993 (February 1, 1991): 504–5. https://doi.org/10.1126/science.251.4993.504.

Hoddle, Mark. "Quagga & Zebra Mussels." University of California, Riverside, Center for Invasive Species Research. https://cisr.ucr.edu/invasive-species/quagga-zebra-mussels.

Hoesly, Rachel, Steven J. Smith, Leyang Feng, Zbigniew Klimont, Greet Janssens-Maenhout, Tyler Pitkanen, Jonathan J. Seibert, et al. "Historical (1750–2014) Anthropogenic Emissions of Reactive Gases and Aerosols from the Community Emissions Data System (CEDS)." *Geoscientific Model Development* 11 (January 29, 2018): 369–408. https://doi.org/10.5194/gmd-11-369-2018.

Hoffner, Erik. "Sweden's Green Veneer Hides Unsustainable Logging Practices." *Yale Environment 360.* December 1, 2011. https://e360.yale.edu/features/swedens_green_veneer_hides_unsustainable_logging_practices.

Hogue, Cheryl. "New York Bans Televisions with Organohalogen Flame Retardants." *Chemical & Engineering News.* January 5, 2022. https://cen.acs.org/safety/consumer-safety/New-York-bans-televisions-organohalogen/100/web/2022/01.

Holtz, Jackson. "UW Study: Exposure to Chemical in Roundup Increases Risk for Cancer." UW News, University of Washington. February 13, 2019. https://www.washington.edu/news/2019/02/13/uw-study-exposure-to-chemical-in-roundup-increases-risk-for-cancer/.

Hopper, Leigh. "Improved Air Quality in Los Angeles Linked to Fewer Children Developing Asthma." University of Southern California, Keck School of Medicine. May 22, 2019. https://keck.usc.edu/news/improved-air-quality-in-los-angeles-linked-to-fewer-children-developing-asthma/.

Hoque, Mominul, and Srinivas Janaswamy. "Biodegradable Packaging Films from Banana Peel Fiber." *Sustainable Chemistry and Pharmacy* 37 (February 1, 2024): 101400. https://doi.org/10.1016/j.scp.2023.101400.

Howarth, Robert W. "Methane Emissions and Climatic Warming Risk from Hydraulic Fracturing and Shale Gas Development: Implications for Policy." *Energy and Emission Control Technologies* 3 (October 8, 2015): 45–54. https://doi.org/10.2147/eect.s61539.

Howarth, Robert W., and Mark Z. Jacobson. "How Green Is Blue Hydrogen?" *Energy Science & Engineering* 9, no. 10 (October 2021): 1676–87. https://doi.org/10.1002/ese3.956.

Howell, Beth. "The Top 14 Most Polluting Companies." *EcoExperts.* October 2, 2023. https://www.theecoexperts.co.uk/blog/most-polluting-companies.

Hu, Shelia. "What Is Climate Gentrification?" NRDC (Natural Resources Defense Council). August 27, 2020. https://www.nrdc.org/stories/what-climate-gentrification.

Hu, Winnie. "A Billion-Dollar Investment in New York's Water." *New York Times*. January 18, 2018. https://www.nytimes.com/2018/01/18/nyregion/new-york-city-water-filtration.html.

Huang, Yuanyuan, Yuxin Chen, Nadia Castro-Izaguirre, Martin Baruffol, Matteo Brezzi, Anne Lang, Ying Li, Werner Härdtle, Goddert Von Oheimb, Xuefei Yang, et al. "Impacts of Species Richness on Productivity in a Large-Scale Subtropical Forest Experiment." *Science* 362, no. 6410 (October 5, 2018): 80–83. https://doi.org/10.1126/science.aat6405.

Human Rights Watch. "'We're Dying Here': The Fight for Life in a Louisiana Fossil Fuel Sacrifice Zone." January 25, 2024. https://www.hrw.org/report/2024/01/25/were-dying-here/fight-life-louisiana-fossil-fuel-sacrifice-zone.

Hunt, Eric, Francesco Femia, Caitlin Werrell, Jordan I. Christian, Jason A. Otkin, Jeff Basara, Martha Anderson, Tyler White, Christopher Hain, Robb Randall, and Katie McGaughey. "Agricultural and Food Security Impacts from the 2010 Russia Flash Drought." *Weather and Climate Extremes* 34 (December 1, 2021): 100383. https://doi.org/10.1016/j.wace.2021.100383.

Hunter, Mitchell C., Richard G. Smith, Meagan E. Schipanski, Lesley W. Atwood, and David A. Mortensen. "Agriculture in 2050: Recalibrating Targets for Sustainable Intensification." *BioScience* 67, no. 4 (April 2017): 386–91. https://doi.org/10.1093/biosci/bix010.

Hurtes, Sarah, and Weiyi Cai. "Europe Is Sacrificing Its Ancient Forests for Energy." *New York Times*. September 16, 2022. https://www.nytimes.com/interactive/2022/09/07/world/europe/eu-logging-wood-pellets.html.

Huseynli, Orkhan. "The Aral Sea Catastrophe: Understanding One of the Worst Ecological Calamities of the Last Century." *Earth.Org*. May 16, 2024. https://earth.org/the-aral-sea-catastrophe-understanding-one-of-the-worst-ecological-calamities-of-the-last-century/.

Igini, Martina. "Deforestation in Africa: Causes, Effects, and Solutions." *Earth.org*. March 24, 2022. https://earth.org/deforestation-in-africa/.

Iizumi, Toshichika, and Toru Sakai. "The Global Dataset of Historical Yields for Major Crops 1981–2016." *Scientific Data* 7 (March 20, 2020): 97. https://doi.org/10.1038/s41597-020-0433-7.

Institute of Scrap Recycling Industries. "Paper." Accessed March 8, 2024. https://www.isri.org/recycled-commodities/paper.

Intergovernmental Panel on Climate Change (IPCC). "Summary for Policymakers." In *Climate Change 2021—The Physical Science Basis: Working Group I Contribution to the Sixth Assessment Report of the Intergovernmental Panel on Climate Change*, 3–32. Cambridge: Cambridge University Press, 2023. https://doi.org/10.1017/9781009157896.001.

International Aluminium Institute. "Aluminium Recycling Factsheet." October 2020. https://international-aluminium.org/resource/aluminium-recycling-fact-sheet/.

International Energy Agency. "Access to Electricity." 2022. https://www.iea.org/reports/sdg7-data-and-projections/access-to-electricity.

International Energy Agency. "Cement." July 11, 2023. https://www.iea.org/energy-system/industry/cement.

International Energy Agency. "Global EV Outlook 2023." April 2023. https://www.iea.org/reports/global-ev-outlook-2023.

International Energy Agency. "Global Methane Tracker 2023." February 2023. https://www.iea.org/reports/global-methane-tracker-2023.

International Energy Agency. "The Oil and Gas Industry in Net Zero Transitions. Executive summary." February 2024. https://www.iea.org/reports/the-oil-and-gas-industry-in-net-zero-transitions/executive-summary.

International Institute for Sustainable Development. "Experts Call on G7 to Get Serious on Fossil Fuel Subsidy Reform." April 16, 2024. https://www.iisd.org/articles/press-release/experts-call-g7-fossil-fuel-subsidy-reform.

International Monetary Fund. "Bangladesh: 2019 Article IV Consultation-Press Release;

Staff Report; and Statement by the Executive Director for Bangladesh." September 18, 2019, p. 19. https://www.imf.org/en/Publications/CR/Issues/2019/09/17/Bangladesh-2019-Article-IV-Consultation-Press-Release-Staff-Report-and-Statement-by-the-48682.

International Potato Center. "Native Potato Varieties." https://cipotato.org/potato/native-potato-varieties/.

International Whaling Commission. "Commercial Whaling." https://iwc.int/management-and-conservation/whaling/commercial.

Ionova, Ana. "'Devastating' Fires Engulf Brazilian Pantanal Wetlands—Again." *Mongabay*. December 23, 2020. https://news.mongabay.com/2020/12/devastating-fires-engulf-brazilian-pantanal-wetlands-again/.

ITER Organization. "What Is ITER?" https://www.iter.org/proj/inafewlines.

Iversen, Kenneth, Hoi Wai Jackie Cheng, Kristinn Sv. Helgason, and Marcelo LaFleur. "Frontier Technology Issues: Frontier Technologies for Smallholder Farmers: Addressing Information Asymmetries and Deficiencies." United Nations, Department of Economic and Social Affairs, Economic Analysis. November 17, 2021. https://www.un.org/development/desa/dpad/publication/frontier-technology-issues-frontier-technologies-for-smallholder-farmers-addressing-information-asymmetries-and-deficiencies/.

Jackson, Robert B., Marielle Saunois, Philippe Bousquet, Josep G. Canadell, Benjamin Poulter, Ann R. Stavert, Peter Bergamaschi, Yosuke Niwa, Arjo Segers, and Aki Tsuruta. "Increasing Anthropogenic Methane Emissions Arise Equally from Agricultural and Fossil Fuel Sources." *Environmental Research Letters* 15, no. 7 (July 1, 2020): 071002. https://doi.org/10.1088/1748-9326/ab9ed2.

Jagger, Anna. "Polyethylene: Discovered by Accident 75 Years Ago." *ICIS, Independent Commodity Intelligence Services*. May 8, 2008. https://www.icis.com/explore/resources/news/2008/05/12/9122447/polyethylene-discovered-by-accident-75-years-ago/.

Japan Local Government Centre. "Toshima Ward Cleaning Plant—'Waste-to-Energy' from Dealing with Tokyo's Rubbish." Council of Local Authorities for International Relations, London. Accessed March 6, 2023. https://www.jlgc.org.uk/en/pdfs/casestudies/Toshima.pdf.

Jarrett, Isabel. "Most Long-Distance Fishing in Foreign Waters Dominated by Only a Few Governments." *Pew Charitable Trusts*. May 27, 2022. https://www.pewtrusts.org/en/research-and-analysis/issue-briefs/2022/05/most-long-distance-fishing-in-foreign-waters-dominated-by-only-a-few-governments.

Jarvis, Brooke. "Climate Change Is Keeping Therapists Up at Night." *New York Times*. October 25, 2023. https://www.nytimes.com/2023/10/21/magazine/climate-anxiety-therapy.html.

Jarvis, Peter, and John Fawell. "Lead in Drinking Water—An Ongoing Public Health Concern?" *Current Opinion in Environmental Science & Health* 20 (April 1, 2021): 100239. https://doi.org/10.1016/j.coesh.2021.100239.

Jeswani, Harish K., Andrew Chilvers, and Adisa Azapagic. "Environmental Sustainability of Biofuels: A Review." *Proceedings of the Royal Society A: Mathematical, Physical and Engineering Sciences* 476, no. 2243 (November 25, 2020): 20200351. https://doi.org/10.1098/rspa.2020.0351.

Jha, Alok. "First Lab-Grown Hamburger Gets Full Marks for 'Mouth Feel.'" *Guardian*. August 6, 2013. https://www.theguardian.com/science/2013/aug/05/world-first-synthetic-hamburger-mouth-feel.

Jha, Prabhat. "The Hazards of Smoking and the Benefits of Cessation: A Critical Summation of the Epidemiological Evidence in High-Income Countries." *eLife* 9 (March 24, 2020): e49979. https://doi.org/10.7554/elife.49979.

John, Daisy A., and Giridhara R. Babu. "Lessons from the Aftermaths of Green Revolution on Food System and Health." *Frontiers in Sustainable Food System* 5 (February 22, 2021): 644559. https://doi.org/10.3389/fsufs.2021.644559.

Johnson, Anna. "Great Salt Lake as a 'Pit Stop' for 12 Million Birds." Great Salt Lake Collaborative. April 20, 2023. https://greatsaltlakenews.org/latest-news/utah-public-radio-upr/great-salt-lake-is-a-pit-stop-for-12-million-birds.

Johnson, Michelaina. "5 Interesting Facts About the Pantanal, the World's Largest Tropical Wetland." World Wildlife Fund. https://www.worldwildlife.org/stories/5-interesting-facts-about-the-pantanal-the-world-s-largest-tropical-wetland.

Joiner, James, and Kenechi Okeleke. "E-Commerce in Agriculture: New Business Models for Smallholders' Inclusion into the Formal Economy." *GSMA*. May 29, 2019. https://www.gsma.com/solutions-and-impact/connectivity-for-good/mobile-for-development/gsma_resources/e-commerce-in-agriculture-new-business-models-for-smallholders-inclusion-into-the-formal-economy.

Jones, Nicola. "Canada's Oil Sands Spew Massive Amounts of Unmonitored Polluting Gases." *Nature*. January 25, 2024. https://doi.org/10.1038/d41586-024-00203-8.

Jones, Nicola. "From Fertilizer to Fuel: Can 'Green' Ammonia Be a Climate Fix?" *Yale Environment 360*. January 20, 2022. https://e360.yale.edu/features/from-fertilizer-to-fuel-can-green-ammonia-be-a-climate-fix.

Jordi, Andres. "Tackling Arsenic and Fluoride in Drinking Water." Eawag: Swiss Federal Institute of Aquatic Science and Technology. March 18, 2015. https://www.eawag.ch/en/info/portal/news/news-detail/tackling-arsenic-and-fluoride-in-drinking-water/.

Jouzel, Jean, and Valerie Masson-Delmotte. "EPICA Dome C Ice Core 800KYr Deuterium Data and Temperature Estimates." *PANGAEA* (2007). https://doi.org/10.1594/PANGAEA.683655.

Jouzel, Jean, Valérie Masson-Delmotte, O. Cattani, G. Dreyfus, S. Falourd, G.F. Hoffmann, B. Minster, et al. "Orbital and Millennial Antarctic Climate Variability over the Past 800,000 Years." *Science* 317, no. 5839 (August 10, 2007): 793–96. https://doi.org/10.1126/science.1141038.

Just Energy. "How to Calculate Your Carbon Footprint." April 9, 2024. https://justenergy.com/blog/how-to-calculate-your-carbon-footprint/.

Kabir, Zahangir. "Tillage or No-Tillage: Impact on Mycorrhizae." *Canadian Journal of Plant Science* 85, no. 1 (2005): 23–29. https://escholarship.org/uc/item/6bv5h1nv.

Karagas, Margaret R., Anna L. Choi, Emily Oken, Milena Horvat, Rita Schoeny, Elizabeth Kamai, Whitney Cowell, Philippe Grandjean, and Susan Korrick. "Evidence on the Human Health Effects of Low-Level Methylmercury Exposure." *Environmental Health Perspectives* 120, no. 6 (January 24, 2012): 799–806. https://doi.org/10.1289/ehp.1104494.

Kart, Jeff. "Winners of the Tom Ford Plastic Innovation Prize Are All Using Seaweed." *Forbes*. March 24, 2023. https://www.forbes.com/sites/jeffkart/2023/03/24/winners-of-the-tom-ford-plastic-innovation-prize-are-all-using-seaweed/?sh=30b3111bb390.

Kateman, Brian. "Cell-Cultured Seafood Isn't Just an Idea; It's a Reality." *Forbes*. June 6, 2022. https://www.forbes.com/sites/briankateman/2022/06/06/cell-cultured-seafood-isnt-just-an-idea-its-a-reality.

Kateman, Brian. "Fermentation: The New Game-Changer for Alternative Proteins?" *Forbes*. June 15, 2021. https://www.forbes.com/sites/briankateman/2021/06/07/fermentation-the-new-game-changer-for-alternative-proteins/.

Keane, Phoebe. "How the Oil Industry Made Us Doubt Climate Change." *BBC News*. September 19, 2020. https://www.bbc.com/news/stories-53640382.

Keaten, Jamey. "Free Food Fridges Take Off in Parts of Europe in Eco-Friendly Bid to Fight Waste." *Associated Press*. July 28, 2023. https://apnews.com/article/food-waste-switzerland-germany-geneva-austria-refrigerators-environment-fc8484f267f1403a4b76db8b20541f9a.

Kelly, Jamie. "Record Breaking PM2.5 Pollution Levels in NYC in Early June 2023 Regular Occurrence in over 350 Cities Worldwide." Centre for Research on Energy and Clean Air (CREA), June 16, 2023. https://energyandcleanair.org/record-breaking-pm2-5-pollution-levels-in-nyc-in-early-june-2023-regular-occurrence-in-over-350-cities-worldwide.

Kennedy, Brian, and Cary Lynne Thigpen. "Many Publics Around World Doubt Safety of Genetically Modified Foods." *Pew Research Center*. November 11, 2020. https://www.pewresearch.org/short-reads/2020/11/11/many-publics-around-world-doubt-safety-of-genetically-modified-foods.

Kennedy, Caitlyn. "An Upwelling Crisis: Ocean Acidification." NOAA Climate.gov. October

30, 2009. https://www.climate.gov/news-features/features/upwelling-crisis-ocean-acidification.

Kevany, Sophie. "From Petri Dish to Plate: Meet the Company Hoping to Bring Lab-Grown Fish to the Table." *Guardian*. April 28, 2024. https://www.theguardian.com/environment/2024/apr/28/from-petri-dish-to-plate-meet-the-company-hoping-to-bring-lab-grown-fish-to-the-table.

Killeen, Timothy J. "National Versus Global Markets—Beef in the Brazilian Amazon." *Mongabay*. October 19, 2023. https://news.mongabay.com/2023/10/national-versus-global-markets-beef-in-the-brazilian-amazon/.

Kilvert, Nick. "What Happened to the Ocean Cleanup—The System that Would Rid the Oceans of Plastic?" *ABC News*. March 16, 2023. https://www.abc.net.au/news/science/2023-03-17/ocean-cleanup-plastic-pollution-great-pacific-garbage-patch/102075810#.

Kim, Jinsoo, Benjamin K. Sovacool, Morgan Bazilian, Steve Griffiths, Junghwan Lee, Minyoung Yang, and Jordy Lee. "Decarbonizing the Iron and Steel Industry: A Systematic Review of Sociotechnical Systems, Technological Innovations, and Policy Options." *Energy Research & Social Science* 89 (July 2022): 102565. https://doi.org/10.1016/j.erss.2022.102565.

Kim, Max S. "South Korea Has Almost Zero Food Waste. Here's What the US Can Learn." *Guardian*. November 20, 2022. https://www.theguardian.com/environment/2022/nov/20/south-korea-zero-food-waste-composting-system.

Kim, Tae-Kyung, Hae In Yong, Young-Boong Kim, Hyun-Wook Kim, and Yun-Sang Choi. "Edible Insects as a Protein Source: A Review of Public Perception, Processing Technology, and Research Trends." *Food Science of Animal Resources* 39, no. 4 (August 31, 2019): 521–40. https://doi.org/10.5851/kosfa.2019.e53.

Kirk, Karin. "Electrifying Transportation Reduces Emissions AND Saves Massive Amounts of Energy." *Yale Climate Connections*. August 7, 2022. https://yaleclimateconnections.org/2022/08/electrifying-transportation-reduces-emissions-and-saves-massive-amounts-of-energy/.

Klein Goldewijk, Kees, Arthur Beusen, and Peter Janssen. "Long-Term Dynamic Modeling of Global Population and Built-Up Area in a Spatially Explicit Way: HYDE 3.1." *Holocene* 20, no. 4 (March 22, 2010): 565–73. https://doi.org/10.1177/0959683609356587.

Knapp, Samuel, and Marcel G.A. van der Heijden. "A Global Meta-Analysis of Yield Stability in Organic and Conservation Agriculture." *Nature Communications* 9 (September 7, 2018): 3632. https://doi.org/10.1038/s41467-018-05956-1.

Kopec, Kelsey, and Lori Ann Burd. "Pollinators in Peril. A Systematic Status Review of North American and Hawaiian Native Bees." Center for Biological Diversity. February 2017. https://www.biologicaldiversity.org/campaigns/native_pollinators/pdfs/Pollinators_in_Peril.pdf.

Kornei, Katherine. "Here Are Some of the World's Worst Cities for Air Quality." *Science*. March 21, 2017. https://doi.org/10.1126/science.aal0942.

Kreider, Mark R., Philip E. Higuera, Sean A. Parks, William L. Rice, Nadia White, and Andrew J. Larson. "Fire Suppression Makes Wildfires More Severe and Accentuates Impacts of Climate Change and Fuel Accumulation." *Nature Communications* 15 (March 25, 2024): 2412. https://doi.org/10.1038/s41467-024-46702-0.

Krishnan, Sandhya. "Understanding India's Evolving Middle Classes." *East Asia Forum*. May 21, 2024. https://doi.org/10.59425/eabc.1716285600.

Kristof, Nicholas. "They Overcame Mutual Loathing, and Saved a Town." *New York Times*. April 10, 2021. https://www.nytimes.com/2021/04/10/opinion/sunday/loggers-environmentalists-oregon.html.

Kulik, Rebecca M. "Sustainable Development | Definition, Goals, Origins, Three Pillars, & Facts." *Encyclopedia Britannica*. May 27, 2024. https://www.britannica.com/topic/sustainable-development.

Kumar, Sunaina. "Hope Runs Dry as Groundwater Sources in Punjab Drop to Alarming Levels." *Mongabay-India*. July 5, 2019. https://india.mongabay.com/2019/07/hope-runs-dry-as-groundwater-sources-in-punjab-drop-to-alarming-levels/.

Kummu, M., H. de Moel, M. Porkka, S. Siebert, O. Varis, and P.J. Ward. "Lost Food, Wasted

Resources: Global Food Supply Chain Losses and Their Impacts on Freshwater, Cropland, and Fertiliser Use." *Science of the Total Environment* 438, no. 1 (November 2012): 477–89. https://doi.org/10.1016/j.scitotenv.2012.08.092.

Kunin, William E. "Robust Evidence of Declines in Insect Abundance and Biodiversity." *Nature* 574 (October 31, 2019): 641–42. https://doi.org/10.1038/d41586-019-03241-9.

Kupferschmidt, Kai. "Why Insects Could Be the Ideal Animal Feed." *Science*. October 14, 2015. https://doi.org/10.1126/science.aad4709.

Kushner, Jacob. "How Kenya Is Harnessing the Immense Heat from the Earth." *BBC Future*. March 4, 2021. https://www.bbc.com/future/article/20210303-geothermal-the-immense-volcanic-power-beneath-our-feet.

Kwon, Hyuk Cheol, Hyun Su Jung, Vahinika Kothuri, and Sung Gu Han. "Current Status and Challenges for Cell-Cultured Milk Technology: A Systematic Review." *Journal of Animal Science and Biotechnology* 15 (June 8, 2024): 81. https://doi.org/10.1186/s40104-024-01039-y.

Laden, F. "A Tale of Six Cities." *Environmental Epidemiology* 3 (October 1, 2019): 221. https://doi.org/10.1097/01.ee9.0000608272.94008.7b.

Lai, Olivia. "Deforestation in Southeast Asia: Causes and Solutions." *Earth.org*. March 7, 2022. https://earth.org/deforestation-in-southeast-asia/.

Lai, Olivia. "The Detrimental Impacts of Plastic Pollution on Animals." *Earth.org*. May 4, 2022. https://earth.org/plastic-pollution-animals/.

Lan, Xin, Kirk W. Thoning, and Edward J. Dlugokencky. "Trends in Globally-Averaged CH4, N2O, and SF6 Determined from NOAA Global Monitoring Laboratory measurements." Version 2023–09. https://doi.org/10.15138/P8XG-AA10.

Lang, Otto I., Derek Mallia, and S. McKenzie Skiles. "The Shrinking Great Salt Lake Contributes to Record High Dust-on-Snow Deposition in the Wasatch Mountains During the 2022 Snowmelt Season." *Environmental Research Letters* 18, no. 6 (June 15, 2023): 064045. https://doi.org/10.1088/1748-9326/acd409.

Lappé, Frances Moore. *Diet for a Small Planet*. New York: Ballantine Books. 1971.

Lee, Jean, Jiachuan Wu, Didi Martinez, and Adiel Kaplan. "'This Is Not a Lahaina Problem': Once Unthinkable, Frequent Fires Are Hawaii's New Normal." *NBC News*. February 3, 2024. https://www.nbcnews.com/specials/hawaii-fire-scientists-warn-escalating-wildfire-threat/index.html.

Leftovers Foundation. https://rescuefood.ca.

Lewis, Simon L., Charlotte E. Wheeler, Edward T.A. Mitchard, and Alexander Koch, "Restoring Natural Forests Is the Best Way to Remove Atmospheric Carbon." *Nature* 568 (April 2, 2019): 25–28. https://doi.org/10.1038/d41586-019-01026-8.

Lewsey, Fred. "Millions of Carbon Credits Are Generated by Overestimating Forest Preservation." University of Cambridge. August 24, 2023. https://www.cam.ac.uk/stories/carbon-credits-hot-air.

Lhotka, Ondřej, and Jan Kyselý. "The 2021 European Heat Wave in the Context of Past Major Heat Waves." *Earth and Space Science* 9, no. 11 (November 4, 2022): e2022EA002567. https://doi.org/10.1029/2022ea002567.

Li, Yijia, Ruiqing Miao, and Madhu Khanna. "Neonicotinoids and Decline in Bird Biodiversity in the United States." *Nature Sustainability* 3, no. 12 (August 10, 2020): 1027–35. https://doi.org/10.1038/s41893-020-0582-x.

Library of Congress. "U.S. History Primary Source Timeline. The Dust Bowl." https://www.loc.gov/classroom-materials/united-states-history-primary-source-timeline/great-depression-and-world-war-ii-1929-1945/dust-bowl/.

Lindsey, Rebecca. "Climate Change: Global Sea Level." NOAA Climate.gov. April 19, 2022. https://www.climate.gov/news-features/understanding-climate/climate-change-global-sea-level.

Lindwall, Courtney. "Single-Use Plastics 101." *Natural Resources Defense Council*. January 9, 2020. https://www.nrdc.org/stories/single-use-plastics-101#corporations.

Lisowyj, Michal, and Mark Mba Wright. "A Review of Biogas and an Assessment of Its Economic Impact and Future Role as a Renewable Energy Source." *Reviews in Chemical Engineering* 36, no. 3 (September 5, 2018): 401–21. https://doi.org/10.1515/revce-2017-0103.

Liu, Coco, and ClimateWire. "China's Great Green Wall Helps Pull CO2 Out of Atmosphere." *Scientific American*. April 24, 2015. https://www.scientificamerican.com/article/china-s-great-green-wall-helps-pull-co2-out-of-atmosphere/.

Liu, Xin, Qingtao Jiang, Peihong Wu, Lei Han, and Peng Zhou. "Global Incidence, Prevalence and Disease Burden of Silicosis: 30 Years' Overview and Forecasted Trends." *BMC Public Health* 23 (July 17, 2023): 1366. https://doi.org/10.1186/s12889-023-16295-2.

Liu, Xinyu, Hoyoung Kwon, Michael Wang, and Don O'Connor. "Life Cycle Greenhouse Gas Emissions of Brazilian Sugar Cane Ethanol Evaluated with the GREET Model Using Data Submitted to RenovaBio." *Environmental Science & Technology* 57, no. 32 (August 1, 2023): 11814–22. https://doi.org/10.1021/acs.est.2c08488.

Lizarraga, Clara Hernanz, and Olivia Solon. "Thirsty Data Centers Are Making Hot Summers Even Scarier." *Bloomberg*. July 26, 2023. https://www.bloomberg.com/news/articles/2023-07-26/extreme-heat-drought-drive-opposition-to-ai-data-centers.

Llovet, Josep M., Robin Kate Kelley, Augusto Villanueva, Amit G. Singal, Eli Pikarsky, Sasan Roayaie, Riccardo Lencioni, Kazuhiko Koike, Jessica Zucman-Rossi, and Richard S. Finn. "Hepatocellular Carcinoma." *Nature Reviews. Disease Primers* 7 (January 21, 2021): 6. https://doi.org/10.1038/s41572-020-00240-3.

L'Oréal Group. "What's a Dry Factory?" https://www.loreal.com/en/news/commitments/whats-a-dry-factory/.

Lott, Mitchell, and Jennifer Morales. "Why Utah Farmers Use So Much Water, and How We Can Get Them to Use Less." Utah State University, Center for Growth and Opportunity. April 13, 2023. https://www.thecgo.org/benchmark/why-utah-farmers-use-so-much-water-and-how-we-can-get-them-to-use-less/.

Louisiana Legislative Auditor. "Department of Environmental Quality—Monitoring and Enforcement of Air Quality, Report No. 40200007." Performance Audit Services. January 20, 2021. https://app2.lla.state.la.us/publicreports.nsf/0/4f3372abddf0f271862586630067c25d/$file/00022660a.pdf?openelement&.7773098.

Louisiana State University, School of Public Health. "Louisiana Cancer Maps." https://sph.lsuhsc.edu/louisiana-tumor-registry/data-usestatistics/louisiana-data-interactive-statistics/louisiana-cancer-maps.

Lowenberg-DeBoer, James, and Bruce Erickson. "Setting the Record Straight on Precision Agriculture Adoption." *Agronomy Journal* 111, no. 4 (July–August 2019): 1552–69. https://doi.org/10.2134/agronj2018.12.0779.

Ludemann, Cameron I., Nathan Wanner, Pauline Chivenge, Achim Dobermann, Rasmus Einarsson, Patricio Grassini, Armelle Gruere, et al. "A Global FAOSTAT Reference Database of Cropland Nutrient Budgets and Nutrient Use Efficiency (1961–2020): Nitrogen, Phosphorus and Potassium." *Earth System Science Data* 16, no. 1 (January 22, 2024): 525–41. https://doi.org/10.5194/essd-16-525-2024.

Maennling, Nicolas. "Lessons Learned from an Energy Company's Green Transformation." Columbia Center on Sustainable Investment, Columbia Law School. April 15, 2019. https://ccsi.columbia.edu/news/lessons-learned-energy-companys-green-transformation.

Magra, Iliana. "Mexico Hailstorm Blankets Western Areas Under 3 Feet of Ice." *New York Times*. July 1, 2019. https://www.nytimes.com/2019/07/01/world/americas/mexico-hailstorm-guadalajara.html.

Maiga, Omar, Eric Deville, Jérome Laval, Alain Prinzhofer, and Aliou Boubacar Diallo. "Characterization of the Spontaneously Recharging Natural Hydrogen Reservoirs of Bourakebougou in Mali." *Scientific Reports* 13, no. 1 (July 22, 2023): 11876. https://doi.org/10.1038/s41598-023-38977-y.

Main, Douglas. "Think that Your Plastic Is Being Recycled? Think Again." *MIT Technology Review*. October 12, 2023. https://www.technologyreview.com/2023/10/12/1081129/plastic-recycling-climate-change-microplastics/.

Malashock, Daniel A., Marissa N. Delang, Jacob S. Becker, Marc L. Serre, J. Jason West, Kai-Lan Chang, Owen R. Cooper, and Susan C. Anenberg. "Global Trends in Ozone Concentration and Attributable Mortality for Urban, Peri-Urban, and Rural Areas Between 2000 and 2019: A Modelling Study." *Lancet, Planetary Health* 6, no. 12 (December 1, 2022): e958–67. https://doi.org/10.1016/s2542-5196(22)00260-1.

Malisch, Rainer, Björn Hardebusch, Ralf Lippold, F.X. Rolaf van Leeuwen, Gerald Moy, Angelika Tritscher, Kateřina Šebková, Jana Klánová, and Jiří Kalina, "Time Trends in Human Milk Derived from WHO- and UNEP-Coordinated Exposure Studies, Chapter 2: DDT, Beta-HCH and HCB." In *Persistent Organic Pollutants in Human Milk*, edited by R. Malisch, P. Fürst, and K. Šebková, 485–542. Cham: Springer, October 12, 2023. https://doi.org/10.1007/978-3-031-34087-1_13.

Mandoli, Ava. "More Than 75% of Egg-Laying Hens Live in States with Little-to-No Welfare Protections." *Investigate Midwest.* June 27, 2023. https://investigatemidwest. org/2023/06/27/graphic-more-than-75-of-egg-laying-hens-live-in-states-with-little-to-no-welfare-protections/.

Mangano, Joseph, Kelli S. Gaus, Timothy A. Mousseau, and Michael Ketterer. "Strontium-90 in Baby Teeth as a Basis for Estimating U.S. Cancer Deaths from Nuclear Weapons Fallout." *International Journal of Social Determinants of Health and Health Services* 53, no. 3 (January 31, 2023): 374–84. https://doi.org/10.1177/27551938231152771.

Mann, Charles C. "Solar or Coal? The Energy India Picks May Decide Earth's Fate." *Wired.* January 8, 2020. https://www.wired.com/2015/11/climate-change-in-india/.

Manning, Elizabeth. "Northwest Tribes Demand Action for Salmon and Orca Restoration." *Earthjustice.* April 25, 2024. https://earthjustice.org/article/northwest-tribes-demand-action-for-salmon-and-orca-restoration.

Manzoor, Muhammad Faisal, Tayyaba Tariq, Birjees Fatima, Amna Sahar, Farwa Tariq, Seemal Munir, Sipper Khan, et al. "An Insight into Bisphenol A, Food Exposure and Its Adverse Effects on Health: A Review." *Frontiers in Nutrition* 9 (November 3, 2022): 1047827. https://doi.org/10.3389/fnut.2022.1047827.

Marine Conservation Institute. "The Marine Protection Atlas." June 7, 2024. https:// mpatlas.org.

Mars. "Water Stewardship Position Statement." https://www.mars.com/about/policies-and-practices/water-stewardship.

Marston, Jennifer. "Brief: Cover Crop Usage Steady but Still 'Only a Fraction' of Total Acreage in the US, Says Purdue's Latest Farmer Survey." *AgFunderNews.* August 2, 2023. https://agfundernews.com/cover-crop-usage-steady-but-still-only-a-fraction-of-total-acreage-in-the-us-says-purdues-farmer-survey.

Martinez, Alejandra. "At a Shuttered Texas Coal Mine, a 1-Acre Garden Is Helping Feed 2,000 People per Month." *Texas Tribune.* July 14, 2023. https://www.texastribune. org/2023/07/14/texas-coal-mine-garden-nrg-restoration/.

Masten, Susan J., Simon H. Davies, and Shawn P. Mcelmurry. "Flint Water Crisis: What Happened and Why?" *Journal of the American Water Works Association* 108, no. 12 (December 1, 2016): 22–34. https://doi.org/10.5942/jawwa.2016.108.0195.

Mazuryk, Jarosław, Katarzyna Klepacka, Włodzimierz Kutner, and Piyush Sindhu Sharma. "Glyphosate: Hepatotoxicity, Nephrotoxicity, Hemotoxicity, Carcinogenicity, and Clinical Cases of Endocrine, Reproductive, Cardiovascular, and Pulmonary System Intoxication." *ACS Pharmacology & Translational Science* 7, no. 5 (April 8, 2024): 1205–36. https://doi.org/10.1021/acsptsci.4c00046.

Mbaku, John Mukum. "The Controversy Over the Grand Ethiopian Renaissance Dam." *Brookings Institution.* August 5, 2020. https://www.brookings.edu/articles/the-controversy-over-the-grand-ethiopian-renaissance-dam.

McCullough, Chris. "European Countries Ban Lab Meat in Move to Support Farmers." *Fence Post.* February 2, 2024. https://www.thefencepost.com/news/european-countries-ban-lab-meat-in-move-to-support-farmers/.

McFarland, Michael J., Matt E. Hauer, and Aaron Reuben. "Half of US Population Exposed to Adverse Lead Levels in Early Childhood." *Proceedings of the National Academy of Sciences of the United States of America* 119, no. 11 (March 7, 2022): e2118631119. https://doi. org/10.1073/pnas.2118631119.

Mcfarlane, Sarah. "Explainer: Global Fossil Fuel Subsidies on The Rise Despite Calls for Phase-Out." *Reuters.* November 23, 2023. https://www.reuters.com/business/ environment/global-fossil-fuel-subsidies-rise-despite-calls-phase-out-2023-11-23/.

McGuire, Michael J. "Eight Revolutions in the History of US Drinking Water Disinfection."

Journal of the American Water Works Association 98, no. 3 (March 1, 2006): 123–49. https://doi.org/10.1002/j.1551-8833.2006.tb07612.x.

McLinden, Mark O., Christopher J. Seeton, and Andy Pearson. "New Refrigerants and System Configurations for Vapor-Compression Refrigeration." *Science* 370, no. 6518 (November 13, 2020): 791–96. https://doi.org/10.1126/science.abe3692.

Mebiol. "Growing Vegetables with Less Water." United Nations Industrial Development Organization Investment and Technology Promotion Office, Tokyo. http://www.unido.or.jp/en/technology_db/4118/.

Mekonnen, Mesfin M., and Arjen Y. Hoekstra. "A Global Assessment of the Water Footprint of Farm Animal Products." *Ecosystems* 15 (January 24, 2012): 401–15. https://doi.org/10.1007/s10021-011-9517-8.

Mekonnen, M.M., and A.Y. Hoekstra. "The Green, Blue and Grey Water Footprint of Crops and Derived Crop Products." *Hydrology and Earth System Sciences* 15, no. 5 (May 25, 2011): 1577–600. https://doi.org/10.5194/hess-15-1577-2011.

Melymuk, Lisa, Jonathan Blumenthal, Ondřej Sáňka, Adriana Shu-Yin, Veena Singla, Kateřina Šebková, Kristi Pullen Fedinick, and Miriam L. Diamond. "Persistent Problem: Global Challenges to Managing PCBs." *Environmental Science & Technology* 56, no. 12 (June 1, 2022): 9029–40. https://doi.org/10.1021/acs.est.2c01204.

Menegat, Stefano, Alicia Ledo, and Reyes Tirado. "Greenhouse Gas Emissions from Global Production and Use of Nitrogen Synthetic Fertilisers in Agriculture." *Scientific Reports* 12 (August 25, 2022): 14490. https://doi.org/10.1038/s41598-022-18773-w.

Merchant, James A., Allison L. Naleway, Erik R. Svendsen, Kevin M. Kelly, Leon F. Burmeister, Ann M. Stromquist, Craig D. Taylor, Peter S. Thorne, Stephen J. Reynolds, Wayne T. Sanderson, and Elizabeth A. Chrischilles. "Asthma and Farm Exposures in a Cohort of Rural Iowa Children." *Environmental Health Perspectives* 113, no. 3 (December 7, 2004): 350–56. https://doi.org/10.1289/ehp.7240.

Metcalfe, H., J. Storkey, R. Hull, J.M. Bullock, A. Whitmore, R.T. Sharp, and A.E. Milne. "Trade-Offs Constrain the Success of Glyphosate-Free Farming." *Scientific Reports* 14 (April 5, 2024): 8001. https://doi.org/10.1038/s41598-024-58183-8.

Metropolitan Water District of Southern California. "Emergency Drought Restrictions Go into Effect for Six Million Southern Californians." June 1, 2022. https://www.mwdh2o.com/press-releases/emergency-drought-restrictions-go-into-effect-for-six-million-southern-californians/.

Metz, Cynthia Marie. "Bisphenol A: Understanding the Controversy." *Workplace Health & Safety* 64, no. 1 (January 22, 2016): 28–36. https://doi.org/10.1177/2165079915623790.

Miao, Xinlu, Teng Yao, Chenxian Dong, Zuhai Chen, Wanting Wei, Zhengyang Shi, Tongtong Xu, et al. "Global, Regional, and National Burden of Non-Communicable Diseases Attributable to Occupational Asbestos Exposure 1990–2019 and Prediction to 2035: Worsening or Improving?" *BMC Public Health* 24 (March 18, 2024): 832. https://doi.org/10.1186/s12889-024-18099-4.

Mielke, Howard. "Lead in the Inner Cities." *American Scientist* 87, no. 1 (January 1, 1999): 62. https://doi.org/10.1511/1999.16.62.

Mielke, Howard W., and Sammy Zahran. "The Urban Rise and Fall of Air Lead (Pb) and the Latent Surge and Retreat of Societal Violence." *Environment International* 43 (August 1, 2012): 48–55. https://doi.org/10.1016/j.envint.2012.03.005.

Millan, R., E. Jager, J. Mouginot, M.H. Wood, S.H. Larsen, P. Mathiot, N.C. Jourdain, and A. Bjørk. "Rapid Disintegration and Weakening of Ice Shelves in North Greenland." *Nature Communications* 14 (November 7, 2023): 6914. https://doi.org/10.1038/s41467-023-42198-2.

Millard, Joseph, Charlotte L. Outhwaite, Silvia Ceaușu, Luísa G. Carvalheiro, Felipe Deodato Da Silva E Silva, Lynn V. Dicks, Jeff Ollerton, and Tim Newbold. "Key Tropical Crops at Risk from Pollinator Loss Due to Climate Change and Land Use." *Science Advances* 9, no. 41 (October 12, 2023): eadh0756. https://doi.org/10.1126/sciadv.adh0756.

Miller, Brittney J. "What Will It Take for Smart Windows to Go Mainstream?" *Smithsonian Magazine.* June 9, 2022. https://www.smithsonianmag.com/innovation/what-will-it-take-for-smart-windows-to-go-mainstream-180980226/.

Miller, Sabbie A., Arpad Horvath, and Paulo J.M. Monteiro. "Impacts of Booming Concrete Production on Water Resources Worldwide." *Nature Sustainability* 1 (January 8, 2018): 69–76. https://doi.org/10.1038/s41893-017-0009-5.

Miller, Sabbie A., and Frances C. Moore. "Climate and Health Damages from Global Concrete Production." *Nature Climate Change* 10, no. 5 (March 23, 2020): 439–43. https://doi.org/10.1038/s41558-020-0733-0.

Miller Llana, Sara. "Saving the Amazon: How Cattle Ranchers Can Halt Deforestation." *Christian Science Monitor*. March 4, 2020. https://www.csmonitor.com/Environment/2020/0304/Saving-the-Amazon-How-cattle-ranchers-can-halt-deforestation.

Millette, Samantha. "Deposits by the Numbers." *Resource Recycling News*. June 14, 2023. https://resource-recycling.com/recycling/2023/04/04/deposits-by-the-numbers/.

Mitchelmore, Carys L., Emily E. Burns, Annaleise Conway, Andrew Heyes, and Iain A. Davies. "A Critical Review of Organic Ultraviolet Filter Exposure, Hazard, and Risk to Corals." *Environmental Toxicology and Chemistry* 40, no. 4 (February 2, 2021): 967–88. https://doi.org/10.1002/etc.4948.

Miyawaki, Akira. "Creative Ecology: Restoration of Native Forests by Native Trees." *Plant Biotechnology* 16, no. 1 (January 1, 1999): 15–25. https://doi.org/10.5511/plantbiotechnology.16.15.

Mo, Lidong, Constantin M. Zohner, Peter B. Reich, Jingjing Liang, Sergio de Miguel, Gert-Jan Nabuurs, Susanne S. Renner, Johan van den Hoogen, Arnan Araza, Martin Herold, et al. "Integrated Global Assessment of the Natural Forest Carbon Potential." *Nature* 624 (November 13, 2023): 92–101. https://doi.org/10.1038/s41586-023-067 23-z.

Mock, Brentin. "How Black Land Became White Sand: The Racial Erosion of the U.S. Coasts." *Grist*. May 30, 2014. https://grist.org/living/how-african-americans-lost-the-coasts-and-how-we-could-make-that-right/.

Molina, Elena, and Sara Benedé. "Is There Evidence of Health Risks from Exposure to Micro- and Nanoplastics in Foods?" *Frontiers in Nutrition* 9 (June 28, 2022): 910094. https://doi.org/10.3389/fnut.2022.910094.

Molina, Mario J., and F.S. Rowland. "Stratospheric Sink for Chlorofluoromethanes: Chlorine Atom-Catalysed Destruction of Ozone." *Nature* 249, no. 5460 (June 28, 1974): 810–12. https://doi.org/10.1038/249810a0.

MonoSol. "Translating Our Science: About Water-Soluble Film." https://www.monosol.com/translating-our-science/.

Montero-Montoya, Regina, Rocío López-Vargas, and Omar Arellano-Aguilar. "Volatile Organic Compounds in Air: Sources, Distribution, Exposure and Associated Illnesses in Children." *Annals of Global Health* 84, no. 2 (January 27, 2018): 225–38. https://doi.org/10.29024/aogh.910.

Morice, Colin P., John J. Kennedy, Nick A. Rayner, Jonathan P. Winn, Emma Hogan, Rachel E. Killick, Robert J.H. Dunn, Timothy J. Osborn, Phil D. Jones, and Ian R. Simpson. "An Updated Assessment of Near-Surface Temperature Change from 1850: The HADCRUT5 Data Set." *Journal of Geophysical Research: Atmospheres* 126, no. 3 (February 16, 2021): e2019JD032361. https://doi.org/10.1029/2019jd032361.

Moutinho, Sofia. "South American Rainforests Are on the Brink of Becoming Carbon Sources." *Eos, Transactions American Geophysical Union* 104 (October 17, 2023). https://doi.org/10.1029/2023eo230393.

Mridul, Anay. "'Blending Tradition and Innovation': Senara Emerges from Stealth as Europe's First Cultured Dairy Startup." *Green Queen*. December 18, 2023. https://www.greenqueen.com.hk/senara-cell-cultured-dairy-lab-grown-milk/.

Mueen Qamer, Faisal, Sawaid Abbas, Bashir Ahmad, Abid Hussain, Aneel Salman, Sher Muhammad, Muhammad Nawaz, Sravan Shrestha, Bilal Iqbal, and Sunil Thapa. "A Framework for Multi-Sensor Satellite Data to Evaluate Crop Production Losses: The Case Study of 2022 Pakistan Floods." *Scientific Reports* 13 (March 14, 2023): 4240. https://doi.org/10.1038/s41598-023-30347-y.

Muir, John. *Wilderness Essays*. Layton, UT: Gibbs Smith, 2011.

Naditz, Alan. "LEED Zero Certification Brought to the Community Level." *Green Builder*

Media. February 28, 2024. https://www.greenbuildermedia.com/blog/leed-zero-certifica
tion-brought-to-the-community-level.

Naishadham, Suman. "Arizona to Cancel Leases Allowing Saudi-Owned Farm Access
to State's Groundwater." *AP News*. October 3, 2023. https://apnews.com/article/saudi-
arabia-drought-arizona-alfalfa-water-agriculture-0d13957edaf882690e15c0bd9ccfa
59f#.

Nanditha, J. S., Anuj Prakash Kushwaha, Rajesh Singh, Iqura Malik, Hiren Solanki, Dipesh
Singh Chuphal, Swarup Dangar, Shanti Shwarup Mahto, Urmin Vegad, and Vimal
Mishra. "The Pakistan Flood of August 2022: Causes and Implications." *Earth's Future*
11, no. 3 (March 13, 2023): e2022EF003230. https://doi.org/10.1029/2022EF003230.

NAPCOR: National Association for PET Container Resources. "NAPCOR's 2022 PET
Recycling Report Demonstrates Bottle-to-Bottle Circularity Continues on the Rise."
https://napcor.com/news/2022-pet-recycling-report/.

Napper, Imogen E., Bede F.R. Davies, Heather Clifford, Sandra Elvin, Heather J. Koldewey,
Paul A. Mayewski, Kimberley R. Miner, Mariusz Potocki, Aurora C. Elmore, Ananta P.
Gajurel, and Richard C. Thompson. "Reaching New Heights in Plastic Pollution—Preliminary Findings of Microplastics on Mount Everest." *One Earth* 3, no. 5 (November 1,
2020): 621–30. https://doi.org/10.1016/j.oneear.2020.10.020.

Narango, Desiree L., Douglas W. Tallamy, and Kimberley J. Shropshire. "Few Keystone
Plant Genera Support the Majority of Lepidoptera Species." *Nature Communications* 11
(November 13, 2020): 5751. https://doi.org/10.1038/s41467-020-19565-4.

Nargi, Lela. "The Miyawaki Method: A Better Way to Build Forests?" *JSTOR Daily*. July 24,
2019. https://daily.jstor.org/the-miyawaki-method-a-better-way-to-build-forests/.

NASA Earth Observatory. "Artificial Archipelagos, Dubai, United Arab Emirates." https://
earthobservatory.nasa.gov/images/42477/artificial-archipelagos-dubai-united-arab-
emirates.

NASA Earth Observatory. "World of Change: Shrinking Aral Sea." November 7, 2018.
https://earthobservatory.nasa.gov/world-of-change/AralSea.

NASA Science Editorial Team. "Slowdown of the Motion of the Ocean." March 18, 2024. https://
science.nasa.gov/earth/earth-atmosphere/slowdown-of-the-motion-of-the-ocean/.

NASA Scientific Visualization Studio. "Pivot Irrigation in Saudi Arabia." May 23, 2013.
https://svs.gsfc.nasa.gov/11290.

Nasim, Noohi, Inavolu Sriram Sandeep, and Sujata Mohanty. "Plant-Derived Natural
Products for Drug Discovery: Current Approaches and Prospects." *Nucleus* 65 (October
18, 2022): 399–411. https://doi.org/10.1007/s13237-022-00405-3.

National Aeronautics and Space Administration. "U.S. Standard Atmosphere, 1976."
NASA-TM-X-74335. Washington, D.C.: U.S. Government Printing Office, October 1976.

National Cancer Institute. "Artificial Sweeteners and Cancer." August 29, 2023. https://
www.cancer.gov/about-cancer/causes-prevention/risk/diet/artificial-sweeteners-
fact-sheet.

National Cancer Institute. "Vinyl Chloride." November 3, 2022. https://www.cancer.
gov/about-cancer/causes-prevention/risk/substances/vinyl-chloride.

National Centers for Environmental Information (NCEI). "The Great Texas Freeze: February 11–20, 2021." February 24, 2023. https://www.ncei.noaa.gov/news/great-texas-freeze-
february-2021.

National Conference of State Legislatures. "Extended Producer Responsibility." October 24, 2023. https://www.ncsl.org/environment-and-natural-resources/extended-
producer-responsibility.

National Institute of Environmental Health Sciences. "Hydraulic Fracturing and Health."
https://www.niehs.nih.gov/health/topics/agents/fracking.

National Interagency Fire Center. "Wildfire and Acres. Total Wildland Fires and Acres (1983–
2022)." Accessed October 10, 2023. https://www.nifc.gov/fire-information/statistics/
wildfires.

National Oceanic and Atmospheric Administration. "Coral Reef Ecosystems." February 1, 2019. https://www.noaa.gov/education/resource-collections/marine-life/
coral-reef-ecosystems.

National Oceanic and Atmospheric Administration. "NOAA Forecasts Very Large 'Dead Zone' for Gulf of Mexico." June 10, 2019. https://coastalscience.noaa.gov/news/noaa-forecasts-very-large-dead-zone-for-gulf-of-mexico/.

National Oceanic and Atmospheric Administration. "Ocean Acidification." April 1, 2020. https://www.noaa.gov/education/resource-collections/ocean-coasts/ocean-acidification.

National Park Service. "Gray Wolf." March 11, 2024. https://www.nps.gov/yell/learn/nature/wolves.htm.

National Park Service. "The 1969 Cuyahoga River Fire." May 3, 2022. https://www.nps.gov/articles/story-of-the-fire.htm.

National Park Service. "Wolf Restoration." April 27, 2023. https://www.nps.gov/yell/learn/nature/wolf-restoration.htm.

National Parks Board of Singapore. "Singapore, Our City in Nature." March 8, 2023. https://www.nparks.gov.sg/about-us/city-in-nature.

National Pesticide Information Center. "Malathion. Technical Fact Sheet." http://npic.orst.edu/factsheets/archive/malatech.html.

National Snow and Ice Data Center. "Ice Sheets: Why They Matter." https://nsidc.org/learn/parts-cryosphere/ice-sheets/why-ice-sheets-matter.

National Snow and Ice Data Center. "Sea Ice Index." https://nsidc.org/arcticseaicenews/sea-ice-tools/.

National Wildlife Federation. "Garden for Wildlife." https://gardenforwildlife.com.

National Wildlife Federation. "Keystone Plants by Ecoregion." https://www.nwf.org/Garden-for-Wildlife/About/Native-Plants/keystone-plants-by-ecoregion.

Natural Resources Defense Council (NRDC). "About NRDC." https://www.nrdc.org/about.

Nature. "Canada Bans Bisphenol A in Baby Products." *Nature* 455 (October 22, 2008): 1020. https://doi.org/10.1038/4551020a.

Nature. "Concrete Needs to Lose Its Colossal Carbon Footprint." *Nature* 597 (September 28, 2021): 593–94. https://doi.org/10.1038/d41586-021-02612-5.

Nature. "Lithium-Ion Batteries Need to Be Greener and More Ethical." *Nature* 595, no. 7 (June 29, 2021): 7. https://doi.org/10.1038/d41586-021-01735-z.

Nature Sustainability. "On the Plastics Crisis." *Nature Sustainability* 6, no. 10 (October 19, 2023): 1137. https://doi.org/10.1038/s41893-023-01236-z.

Naylor, Rosamond L., Ronald W. Hardy, Alejandro H. Buschmann, Simon R. Bush, Ling Cao, Dane H. Klinger, David C. Little, Jane Lubchenco, Sandra E. Shumway, and Max Troell. "A 20-Year Retrospective Review of Global Aquaculture." *Nature* 591, no. 7851 (March 24, 2021): 551–63. https://doi.org/10.1038/s41586-021-03308-6.

Naylor, Rosamond L., Ronald W. Hardy, Dominique P. Bureau, Alice Chiu, Matthew Elliott, Anthony P. Farrell, Ian Forster, et al. "Feeding Aquaculture in an Era of Finite Resources." *Proceedings of the National Academy of Sciences of the United States of America* 106, no. 36 (September 8, 2009): 15103–10. https://doi.org/10.1073/pnas.0905235106.

Neukom, Raphael, Luis A. Barboza, Michael P. Erb, Feng Shi, Julien Emile-Geay, Michael N. Evans, Jörg Franke, et al. "Consistent Multidecadal Variability in Global Temperature Reconstructions and Simulations over the Common Era." *Nature Geoscience* 12, no. 8 (July 24, 2019): 643–49. https://doi.org/10.1038/s41561-019-0400-0.

Neukom, Raphael, Luis A. Barboza, Michael P. Erb, Feng Shi, Julien Emile-Geay, Michael N. Evans, Jörg Franke, et al. "NOAA/WDS Paleoclimatology—PAGES2k Common Era Surface Temperature Reconstructions." *NOAA National Centers for Environmental Information* (July 24, 2019). https://doi.org/10.25921/tkxp-vn12.

Newman, David J., and Gordon M. Cragg. "Drugs and Drug Candidates from Marine Sources: An Assessment of the Current 'State of Play.'" *Planta Medica* 82, no. 9/10 (February 18, 2016): 775–89. https://doi.org/10.1055/s-0042-101353.

Nghiem, Aloys, Keith Everhart, Eren Çam, and Gergely Molnar. "Natural Gas Is Now Stronger than Ever in the United States Power Sector." *IEA: International Energy Agency*. December 4, 2023. https://www.iea.org/commentaries/natural-gas-is-now-stronger-than-ever-in-the-united-states-power-sector.

Nichols, Mike. 1967. *The Graduate*. United States: Embassy Pictures.

Nicholson, Scott, and Garvin Heath. "Life Cycle Emissions Factors for Electricity Generation Technologies." NREL Data Catalog. Golden, CO: National Renewable Energy Laboratory. September 16, 2022. https://doi.org/10.7799/1819907. Data downloaded from https://data.nrel.gov/submissions/171.

Nijhuis, Michelle. "Free the American West from Barbed Wire." *New York Times*. September 26, 2023. https://www.nytimes.com/2023/09/26/opinion/barbed-wire-american-west.html.

NOAA, National Environmental Satellite, Data, and Information Service. "Hurricane Otis Causes Catastrophic Damage in Acapulco, Mexico." November 2, 2023. https://www.nesdis.noaa.gov/news/hurricane-otis-causes-catastrophic-damage-acapulco-mexico.

NOAA Chemical Sciences Laboratory. "2011 News & Events. Study on Emissions from Deepwater Horizon Controlled Burns in the Gulf." September 20, 2011. https://csl.noaa.gov/news/2011/105_0920.html.

NOAA Damage Assessment, Remediation, and Restoration Program. "Exxon Valdez Oil Spill." August 17, 2020. https://darrp.noaa.gov/oil-spills/exxon-valdez.

NOAA Fisheries. "Laws & Policies: Endangered Species Act." https://www.fisheries.noaa.gov/topic/laws-policies/endangered-species-act.

NOAA Fisheries. "Pioneering Project to Restore Bull Kelp Forests in Greater Farallones National Marine Sanctuary in California." March 25, 2024. https://www.fisheries.noaa.gov/feature-story/pioneering-project-restore-bull-kelp-forests-greater-farallones-national-marine.

NOAA Global Monitoring Laboratory. "Global Climate Change. Vital Signs of the Planet." https://climate.nasa.gov/vital-signs/carbon-dioxide.

NOAA Laboratory for Satellite Altimetry. "Global Sea Level Time Series." https://www.star.nesdis.noaa.gov/socd/lsa/SeaLevelRise/LSA_SLR_timeseries.php.

NOAA Marine Debris Program. "Garbage Patches." https://marinedebris.noaa.gov/discover-marine-debris/garbage-patches.

NOAA National Marine Sanctuaries. "Kelp Forest." https://sanctuaries.noaa.gov/visit/ecosystems/kelpdesc.html.

Nobel Prize Outreach. "The Nobel Peace Prize 1970." Accessed July 14, 2024. https://www.nobelprize.org/prizes/peace/1970/summary.

Nobel Prize Outreach. "The Nobel Prize in Chemistry 1918." Accessed July 14, 2024. https://www.nobelprize.org/prizes/chemistry/1918/summary.

Nobel Prize Outreach. "The Nobel Prize in Physiology or Medicine 1948." https://www.nobelprize.org/prizes/medicine/1948/summary.

Nobile, Federica, Anna Forastiere, Paola Michelozzi, Francesco Forastiére, and Massimo Stafoggia. "Long-Term Exposure to Air Pollution and Incidence of Mental Disorders. A Large Longitudinal Cohort Study of Adults Within an Urban Area." *Environment International* 181 (November 1, 2023): 108302. https://doi.org/10.1016/j.envint.2023.108302.

Normile, Dennis. "What a Philippine Court Ruling Means for Transgenic Golden Rice, Once Hailed as a Dietary Breakthrough." *Science*. May 3, 2024. https://doi.org/10.1126/science.zl7058i.

Notpla. "Ooho, the Edible Bubble Made from Seaweed." https://www.notpla.com/ooho.

Novo, Cristina. "Saudi Arabia's Groundwater to Run Dry." *Smart Water Magazine*, May 30, 2019. https://smartwatermagazine.com/blogs/cristina-novo/saudi-arabias-groundwater-run-dry.

Noyes, Andrew. "GOOD Meat Partners with Industry Leader to Build the World's First Large-Scale Cultivated Meat Facility." *Business Wire*. May 25, 2022. https://www.businesswire.com/news/home/20220525005345/en/GOOD-Meat-Partners-with-Industry-Leader-to-Build-the-World's-First-Large-Scale-Cultivated-Meat-Facility.

NPR. "Saudi Hay Farm in Arizona Tests State's Supply Of Groundwater." November 2, 2015. https://www.npr.org/sections/thesalt/2015/11/02/453885642/saudi-hay-farm-in-arizona-tests-states-supply-of-groundwater.

Nriagu, Jerome O. "The Rise and Fall of Leaded Gasoline." *Science of the Total Environment* 92 (March 1, 1990): 13–28. https://doi.org/10.1016/0048-9697(90)90318-o.

Observatory of Economic Complexity (OEC). "Palm Oil in Indonesia." Accessed June 20, 2024. https://oec.world/en/profile/bilateral-product/palm-oil/reporter/idn.

Ocean Cleanup. "About. We Are the Ocean Cleanup." https://theoceancleanup.com/about/.

Oerke, E.-C., and H.-W. Dehne. "Safeguarding Production—Losses in Major Crops and the Role of Crop Protection." *Crop Protection* 23, no. 4 (April 2004): 275–85. https://doi.org/10.1016/j.cropro.2003.10.001.

Official Website of the City of New York. "High Quality NYC Tap Water Receives New Filtration Waiver." December 28, 2017. https://www.nyc.gov/office-of-the-mayor/news/779-17/high-quality-nyc-tap-water-receives-new-filtration-waiver.

Official Website of the City of New York. "History of New York City Drinking Water." https://www.nyc.gov/site/dep/water/history-of-new-york-citys-drinking-water.page.

Ogasa, Nikk. "The Amazon Might Not Have a 'Tipping Point.' But It's Still in Trouble." *ScienceNews*. June 16, 2023. https://www.sciencenews.org/article/amazon-tipping-trouble-climate-cerrado.

Ollerton, Jeff, Rachael Winfree, and Sam Tarrant. "How Many Flowering Plants Are Pollinated by Animals?" *Oikos* 120, no. 3 (February 21, 2011): 321–26. https://doi.org/10.1111/j.1600-0706.2010.18644.x.

Omer, Sevil. "Global Hunger: 7 Facts You Need to Know." *World Vision*. March 18, 2024. https://www.worldvision.org/hunger-news-stories/world-hunger-facts.

O'Neill, Kate. "As More Developing Countries Reject Plastic Waste Exports, Wealthy Nations Seek Solutions at Home." *Conversation*. June 5, 2019. https://theconversation.com/as-more-developing-countries-reject-plastic-waste-exports-wealthy-nations-seek-solutions-at-home-117163.

Opoku Gakpo, Joseph. "GMO Cowpea Could Make Protein-Rich Staple Food More Affordable, Say Nigerian Scientists." *Alliance for Science*. December 16, 2021. https://allianceforscience.org/blog/2021/12/gmo-cowpea-could-make-protein-rich-staple-food-more-affordable-say-nigerian-scientists/.

Opportunity Agenda. "The State of Housing in New Orleans One Year After Katrina." 2006. https://opportunityagenda.org/messaging_reports/one-year-after-katrina/.

Orozco, Christian, Somnuk Tangtermsirikul, Takafumi Sugiyama, and Sandhya Babel. "Examining the Endpoint Impacts, Challenges, and Opportunities of Fly Ash Utilization for Sustainable Concrete Construction." *Scientific Reports* 13 (October 25, 2023): 18254. https://doi.org/10.1038/s41598-023-45632-z.

Orr, James C., Victoria J. Fabry, Olivier Aumont, Laurent Bopp, Scott C. Doney, Richard A. Feely, Anand Gnanadesikan, et al. "Anthropogenic Ocean Acidification over the Twenty-First Century and Its Impact on Calcifying Organisms." *Nature* 437 (September 29, 2005): 681–86. https://doi.org/10.1038/nature04095.

Ortiz, Joseph D., and Roland Jackson. "Understanding Eunice Foote's 1856 Experiments: Heat Absorption by Atmospheric Gases." *Notes and Records* 76, no. 1 (August 26, 2020): 67–84. https://doi.org/10.1098/rsnr.2020.0031.

Osman, Matthew B., Jessica E. Tierney, Jiang Zhu, Robert Tardif, Gregory J. Hakim, Jonathan King, and Christopher J. Poulsen. "Globally Resolved Surface Temperatures Since the Last Glacial Maximum." *Nature* 599, no. 7884 (November 10, 2021): 239–44. https://doi.org/10.1038/s41586-021-03984-4.

Ozment, Suzanne, and Rafael Feltran-Barbieri. "Help for São Paulo's Complex Water Woes: Protect and Restore Forests." *World Resources Institute*. September 25, 2018. https://www.wri.org/insights/help-sao-paulos-complex-water-woes-protect-and-restore-forests.

PAGES2k Consortium: Raphael Neukom, Luis A. Barboza, Michael P. Erb, Feng Shi, Julien Emile-Geay, Michael N. Evans, Jörg Franke, et al. "Consistent Multidecadal Variability in Global Temperature Reconstructions and Simulations over the Common Era." *Nature Geoscience* 12, no. 8 (July 24, 2019): 643–49. https://doi.org/10.1038/s41561-019-0400-0.

Palmer, M.A., E.S. Bernhardt, W.H. Schlesinger, K.N. Eshleman, E. Foufoula-Georgiou, M.S. Hendryx, A.D. Lemly, G.E. Likens, O.L. Loucks, M.E. Power, P.S. White, and P.R. Wilcock. "Mountaintop Mining Consequences." *Science* 327, no. 5962 (January 8, 2010): 148–49. https://doi.org/10.1126/science.1180543.

Palumbo, Jacqui. "Can Seaweed Help Solve the World's Plastic Crisis?" *CNN*. January 4,

2022. https://www.cnn.com/style/article/notpla-seaweed-single-use-plastics/index. html.

Park, Jung-Duck, and Wei Zheng. "Human Exposure and Health Effects of Inorganic and Elemental Mercury." *Journal of Preventive Medicine and Public Health* 45, no. 6 (November 29, 2012): 344–52. https://doi.org/10.3961/jpmph.2012.45.6.344.

Patel, Manvendra, Rahul Kumar, Kamal Kishor, Todd Mlsna, Charles U. Pittman, Jr., and Dinesh Mohan. "Pharmaceuticals of Emerging Concern in Aquatic Systems: Chemistry, Occurrence, Effects, and Removal Methods." *Chemical Reviews* 119 (March 4, 2019): 3510–673. https://doi.org/10.1021/acs.chemrev.8b00299.

Patel, Sameer J., Matthew Wellington, Rohan M. Shah, and Matthew J. Ferreira. "Antibiotic Stewardship in Food-Producing Animals: Challenges, Progress, and Opportunities." *Clinical Therapeutics* 42, no. 9 (September 2020): 1649–58. https://doi.org/10.1016/j. clinthera.2020.07.004.

Paul, Arielle. "Dubai's Costly Water World." *New York Times.* November 18, 2023. https:// www.nytimes.com/2023/11/18/business/dubai-water-desalination.html.

Payen, Florian Thomas, Daniel L. Evans, Natalia Falagán, Charlotte A. Hardman, Sofia Kourmpetli, Lingxuan Liu, Rachel Marshall, Bethan R. Mead, and Jessica A.C. Davies. "How Much Food Can We Grow in Urban Areas? Food Production and Crop Yields of Urban Agriculture: A Meta-Analysis." *Earth's Future* 10, no. 8 (August 23, 2022): e2022EF002748. https://doi.org/10.1029/2022EF002748.

Peabody. "Statement on Climate Change." Accessed June 23, 2024. https://www.peabody energy.com/Sustainability/climate-change.

Pecenka, Jacob R., Laura L. Ingwell, Rick E. Foster, Christian H. Krupke, and Ian Kaplan. "IPM Reduces Insecticide Applications by 95% While Maintaining or Enhancing Crop Yields Through Wild Pollinator Conservation." *Proceedings of the National Academy of Sciences of the United States of America* 118, no. 44 (October 25, 2021): e2108429118. https://doi.org/10.1073/pnas.2108429118.

Peivasteh-Roudsari, Leila, Raziyeh Barzegar-Bafrouei, Kurush Aghbolagh Sharifi, Shamimeh Azimisalim, Marziyeh Karami, Solmaz Abedinzadeh, Shabnam Asadinezhad, et al. "Origin, Dietary Exposure, and Toxicity of Endocrine-Disrupting Food Chemical Contaminants: A Comprehensive Review." *Heliyon* 9, no. 7 (July 11, 2023): e18140, https:// doi.org/10.1016/j.heliyon.2023.e18140.

Peng, Yu, Lixin Wang, Pierre-André Jacinthe, and Wei Ren. "Global Synthesis of Cover Crop Impacts on Main Crop Yield." *Field Crops Research* 310 (April 15, 2024): 109343. https://doi.org/10.1016/j.fcr.2024.109343.

Perera, Frederica, David Cooley, Alique Berberian, David Mills, and Patrick Kinney. "Co-Benefits to Children's Health of the U.S. Regional Greenhouse Gas Initiative." *Environmental Health Perspectives* 128, no. 7 (July 29, 2020): 077006. https://doi.org/10.1289/ ehp6706.

Pérez-Peña, Richard. "Decades Later and Far Away, Chernobyl Disaster Still Contaminates Milk." *New York Times.* June 8, 2018. https://www.nytimes.com/2018/06/08/world/ europe/chernobyl-nuclear-disaster-radiation-milk.html.

Perret, Jennifer L., Brian Plush, Philippe Lachapelle, Timothy S.C. Hinks, Clare Walter, Philip Clarke, Louis Irving, Pat Brady, Shyamali C. Dharmage, and Alastair Stewart. "Coal Mine Dust Lung Disease in the Modern Era." *Respirology* 22, no. 4 (March 30, 2017): 662–70. https://doi.org/10.1111/resp.13034.

Perry, Jessica. "TerraCycle Turns a Profit by Redefining the Value of Waste." *NJBIZ.* April 29, 2024. https://njbiz.com/terracycle-turns-a-profit-by-redefining-the-value-of-waste/.

Peters, Adele. "These Giant, Glowing Carbon Blocks Bring Clean Energy to Factories." *Fast Company.* November 12, 2023. https://www.fastcompany.com/90951247/these-giant-glowing-carbon-blocks-bring-clean-energy-to-factories.

Peters, Annette. "Ambient Air Pollution and Alzheimer's Disease: The Role of the Composition of Fine Particles." *Proceedings of the National Academy of Sciences of the United States of America* 120, no. 3 (January 10, 2023): e2220028120. https://doi.org/10.1073/ pnas.2220028120.

Petrlik, Jindrich, Lee Bell, Joe DiGangi, Serge Molly Allo'o Allo'o, Gilbert Kuepouo,

Griffins Ochieng Ochola, Valeriya Grechko, et al. "Monitoring Dioxins and PCBs in Eggs as Sensitive Indicators for Environmental Pollution and Global Contaminated Sites and Recommendations for Reducing and Controlling Releases and Exposure." *Emerging Contaminants* 8 (January 1, 2022): 254–79. https://doi.org/10.1016/j.emcon.2022.05.001.

Pickett, Mallory, and Bob Berwyn. "In the Pacific, Global Warming Disrupted the Ecological Dance of Urchins, Sea Stars and Kelp. Otters Help Restore Balance." *Inside Climate News.* March 16, 2021. https://insideclimatenews.org/news/16032021/pacific-ocean-climate-change-kelp-urchin-sea-otter-sea-stars/.

Pieterse, Lukie. "The Potato: A Journey Through Time, Cultures, and Challenges." *UN Today.* May 1, 2024. https://untoday.org/the-potato-a-journey-through-time-cultures-and-challenges/.

Pingali, Prabhu. "Are the Lessons from the Green Revolution Relevant for Agricultural Growth and Food Security in the Twenty-First Century?" In *Agricultural Development in Asia and Africa. Emerging-Economy State and International Policy Studies*, edited by Jonna P. Estudillo, Yoko Kijima, and Tetsushi Sonobe, 21–32. Singapore: Springer, 2023. https://doi.org/10.1007/978-981-19-5542-6_2.

Pingali, Prabhu L. "Green Revolution: Impacts, Limits, and the Path Ahead." *Proceedings of the National Academy of Sciences of the United States of America* 109, no. 31 (July 31, 2012): 12302–8. https://doi.org/10.1073/pnas.0912953109.

Pinsky, Malin L., Anne Maria Eikeset, Douglas J. McCauley, Jonathan L. Payne, and Jennifer M. Sunday. "Greater Vulnerability to Warming of Marine Versus Terrestrial Ectotherms." *Nature* 569, no. 7754 (April 24, 2019): 108–11. https://doi.org/10.1038/s41586-019-1132-4.

Planet Water Foundation. "AquaTower Community Water Filtration System." https://planet-water.org/community-water-filtration-system/.

Plass, Gilbert N. "The Carbon Dioxide Theory of Climatic Change." *Tellus B: Chemical and Physical Meteorology* 8, no. 2 (May 1, 1956): 140–54. https://doi.org/10.1111/j.2153-3490.1956.tb01206.x.

Plastics Europe AISBL. "Plastics—The Facts 2022." October 2022. https://plasticseurope.org/knowledge-hub/plastics-the-facts-2022/.

Plastics Recyclers Europe (PRE). "PET Market in Europe. State of Play. Production, Collection & Recycling Data 2022." https://www.plasticsrecyclers.eu/publications/.

Pleasants, John M., and Karen S. Oberhauser. "Milkweed Loss in Agricultural Fields Because of Herbicide Use: Effect on the Monarch Butterfly Population." *Insect Conservation and Diversity* 6, no. 2 (March 12, 2012): 135–44. https://doi.org/10.1111/j.1752-4598.2012.00196.x.

Podgorski, Joel, and Michael Berg. "Global Threat of Arsenic in Groundwater." *Science* 368, no. 6493 (May 22, 2020): 845–50. https://doi.org/10.1126/science.aba1510.

Politi, Daniel. "An Economic Lifeline in South America, the Paraná River, Is Shriveling." *New York Times.* September 4, 2021. https://www.nytimes.com/2021/09/04/world/americas/drought-argentina-parana-river.html.

Ponisio, Lauren C., Leithen K. M'Gonigle, Kevi C. Mace, Jenny Palomino, Perry de Valpine, and Claire Kremen. "Diversification Practices Reduce Organic to Conventional Yield Gap." *Proceedings of the Royal Society B* 282, no. 1799 (January 22, 2015): 20141396. https://doi.org/10.1098/rspb.2014.1396.

Poore, J., and T. Nemecek. "Reducing Food's Environmental Impacts Through Producers and Consumers." *Science* 360, no. 6392 (June 1, 2018): 987–92. https://doi.org/10.1126/science.aaq0216.

Popkin, Gabriel, and Erin Schaff. "There's a Booming Business in America's Forests. Some Aren't Happy About It." *New York Times.* November 15, 2022. https://www.nytimes.com/2021/04/19/climate/wood-pellet-industry-climate.html.

Population Reference Bureau. "International Data. Percent of Population Living in Urban Areas." Accessed July 21, 2024. https://www.prb.org/international/indicator/urban/table.

Positive Young Women Voices (PYWV). https://pywv.org.

Postel, Sandra L. Gretchen C. Daily, and Paul R. Ehrlich. "Human Appropriation of

Renewable Fresh Water." *Science* 271, no. 5250 (February 9, 1996): 785–88. http://web. mit.edu/12.000/www/m2012/postel_science.pdf.

Pozzer, Andrea, Susan C. Anenberg, Sagnik Dey, Andy Haines, Jos Lelieveld, and Sourangsu Chowdhury. "Mortality Attributable to Ambient Air Pollution: A Review of Global Estimates." *Geohealth* 7, no. 1 (January 1, 2023): e2022GH000711. https://doi. org/10.1029/2022gh000711.

Principles for Responsible Investment. "About the PRI." Accessed June 22, 2024. https:// www.unpri.org/about-us/about-the-pri.

Programme for the Endorsement of Forest Certification. "What Is PEFC?" https://www. pefc.org/discover-pefc/what-is-pefc.

Protected Planet. "Marine Protected Areas." https://www.protectedplanet.net/en/thematic-areas/marine-protected-areas.

Puget Sound Partnership. "Thornton Creek Salmon Habitat Restoration." July 10, 2019. https:// innovationstories.psp.wa.gov/2019/07/thornton-creek-salmon-habitat-restoration/.

Puntel, Laila A., John E. Sawyer, Daniel W. Barker, Ranae Dietzel, Hanna Poffenbarger, Michael J. Castellano, Kenneth J. Moore, Peter Thorburn, and Sotirios V. Archontoulis. "Modeling Long-Term Corn Yield Response to Nitrogen Rate and Crop Rotation." *Frontiers in Plant Science* 7 (November 11, 2016): 1630. https://doi.org/10.3389/fpls.2016.01630.

Pure Earth. "Global Mercury Program: Mined Without Mercury Training." https://www. pureearth.org/global-mercury-program/mined-without-mercury-training/.

Qian, Naixin, Xin Gao, Xiaoqi Lang, Huiping Deng, Teodora Maria Bratu, Qixuan Chen, Phoebe Stapleton, Beizhan Yan, and Wei Min. "Rapid Single-Particle Chemical Imaging of Nanoplastics by SRS Microscopy." *Proceedings of the National Academy of Sciences of the United States of America* 121, no. 3 (January 8, 2024): e2300582121. https:// doi.org/10.1073/pnas.2300582121.

Quito, Anne. "CopenHill: The World's Most Consequential Artificial Ski Slope Is Officially Open." *Quartz.* October 4, 2019. https://qz.com/1721236/copenhagens-copenhill-ski-slope-is-officially-open.

Radioactivity.Eu.Com. "Strontium-90. A Fission Product with Properties Close to Calcium." https://radioactivity.eu.com/articles/phenomenon/strontium_90.

Rafferty, John P. "9 of the Biggest Oil Spills in History." *Encyclopedia Britannica.* September 1, 2023. https://www.britannica.com/story/9-of-the-biggest-oil-spills-in-history.

Rahman, Md Mostafijur, Sarah A. Carter, Jane C. Lin, Ting Chow, Xin Yu, Mayra P. Martinez, Zhanghua Chen, et al. "Associations of Autism Spectrum Disorder with PM2.5 Components: A Comparative Study Using Two Different Exposure Models." *Environmental Science & Technology* 57, no. 1 (December 22, 2022): 405–14. https://doi. org/10.1021/acs.est.2c05197.

Ramanathan, Veerabhadran. "Greenhouse Effect Due to Chlorofluorocarbons: Climatic Implications." *Science* 190, no. 4209 (October 3, 1975): 50–52. https://doi.org/10.1126/science.190.4209.50.

Ramasubramanian, Brindha, Jovan Tan, Vijila Chellappan, and Seeram Ramakrishna. "Recent Advances in Extended Producer Responsibility Initiatives for Plastic Waste Management in Germany and UK." *Materials Circular Economy* 5, no. 1 (May 12, 2023): 6. https://doi.org/10.1007/s42824-023-00076-8.

Randall, Brianna. "Can Farmers Save the Great Salt Lake?" *Reasons to Be Cheerful.* November 17, 2023. https://reasonstobecheerful.world/great-salt-lake-farmers-voluntary-conservation-actions/.

Raphael, Kate. "Kids' Glyphosate Exposure Linked to Liver Disease and Metabolic Syndrome." *Environmental Health News.* March 02, 2023. https://www.ehn.org/glyphosate-childrens-health-2659484037.html.

Raszap Skorbiansky, Sharon, Andrea Carlson, and Ashley Spalding. "Rising Consumer Demand Reshapes Landscape for U.S. Organic Farmers." Economic Research Service, U.S. Department of Agriculture. November 14, 2023. https://www.ers.usda. gov/amber-waves/2023/november/rising-consumer-demand-reshapes-landscape-for-u-s-organic-farmers.

Rawat, Sachin. "Brewing Milk in Bioreactors. Cellular Agriculture Startups Are Culturing Human and Bovine Cells in Bioreactors to Produce More Sustainable Milk Without Animals." *Progress Network*. June 13, 2022. https://theprogressnetwork. org/cell-cultured-milk/.

Reed, Christina. "Dawn of the Plasticene Age." *New Scientist* 225, no. 3006 (January 31, 2015): 28–32. https://doi.org/10.1016/s0262-4079(15)60215-9.

Reij, Chris, Gray Tappan, and Melinda Smale. "Re-Greening the Sahel: Farmer-Led Innovation in Burkina Faso and Niger." In *Millions Fed: Proven Successes in Agricultural Development*, edited by David J. Spielman and Rajul Pandya-Lorch, 53–58. Washington, DC: International Food Policy Research Institute (IFPRI), 2009. http://ebrary.ifpri.org/cdm/ref/collection/p15738coll2/id/130817.

Repair Café. "Repair Café: About." https://www.repaircafe.org/en/about/.

Reuben, Aaron, Maxwell Elliott, and Avshalom Caspi. "Implications of Legacy Lead for Children's Brain Development." *Nature Medicine* 26 (January 1, 2020): 23–25. https://doi.org/10.1038/s41591-019-0731-9.

Reynolds, Matt. "Plant-Based Meat Boomed. Here Comes the Bust." *Wired*. April 22, 2024. https://www.wired.com/story/plant-based-meat-sales-2023/.

Riebeek, Holli. "Paleoclimatology: The Oxygen Balance." NASA Earth Observatory. May 6, 2005. https://earthobservatory.nasa.gov/features/Paleoclimatology_OxygenBalance.

Ritchie, Hannah. "How Many Animals Are Factory-Farmed?" *OurWorldInData.org*. September 25, 2023. https://ourworldindata.org/how-many-animals-are-factory-farmed.

Ritchie, Hannah. "Less Meat Is Nearly Always Better than Sustainable Meat, to Reduce Your Carbon Footprint." *OurWorldInData.org*. February 4, 2020. https://ourworldindata.org/less-meat-or-sustainable-meat.

Ritchie, Hannah, and Max Roser. "CO_2 Emissions." *OurWorldInData.org*. January 2024. https://ourworldindata.org/co2-emissions.

Ritchie, Hannahm, and Max Roser. "Half of the World's Habitable Land Is Used for Agriculture." *OurWorldInData.org*. February 16, 2024. https://ourworldindata.org/global-land-for-agriculture.

Ritchie, Hannah, Pablo Rosado, and Max Roser. "Crop Yields." *OurWorldInData.org*. 2022. https://ourworldindata.org/crop-yields.

Riva, Michele Augusto, Alessandra Lafranconi, Marco Italo D'orso, and Giancarlo Cesana. "Lead Poisoning: Historical Aspects of a Paradigmatic 'Occupational and Environmental Disease.'" *Safety and Health at Work* 3, no. 1 (March 1, 2012): 11–16. https://doi.org/10.5491/shaw.2012.3.1.11.

Rivera-Luna, Roberto, Jaime Shalkow-Klincovstein, Liliana Velasco-Hidalgo, Rocío Cárdenas-Cardós, Marta Zapata-Tarrés, Alberto Olaya-Vargas, Marco R. Aguilar-Ortiz, et al. "Descriptive Epidemiology in Mexican Children with Cancer Under an Open National Public Health Insurance Program." *BMC Cancer* 14 (October 29, 2014): 790. https://doi.org/10.1186/1471-2407-14-790.

Rivero, Nicolás. "Why People Don't Have to Pay Anything for Electricity in This Florida Community." *Washington Post*. January 6, 2024. https://www.washingtonpost.com/climate-solutions/2024/01/06/leed-zero-energy-hunters-point/.

Robbins, Jim. "Road Hazard: Evidence Mounts on Toxic Pollution from Tires." *Yale Environment 360*. September 19, 2023. https://e360.yale.edu/features/tire-pollution-toxic-chemicals.

Robson-Mainwaring, Laura. "The Great Smog of 1952." *National Archives*. July 19, 2022. https://blog.nationalarchives.gov.uk/the-great-smog-of-1952.

Rodale Institute. "Organic No-Till." Accessed July 18, 2024. https://rodaleinstitute.org/why-organic/organic-farming-practices/organic-no-till/.

Rogoway, Mike. "Google's Water Use Is Soaring in the Dalles, Records Show, with Two More Data Centers to Come." *OregonLive*. December 17, 2022. https://www.oregonlive.com/silicon-forest/2022/12/googles-water-use-is-soaring-in-the-dalles-records-show-with-two-more-data-centers-to-come.html.

Rokke, Nils. "SUV Sales Record Highlights Climate Challenge Ahead." *Forbes*. February 14,

2022. https://www.forbes.com/sites/nilsrokke/2022/02/14/suv-sales-record-highlights-climate-challenge-ahead.

Rosenboom, Jan-Georg, Robert Langer, and Giovanni Traverso. "Bioplastics for a Circular Economy." *Nature Reviews Materials* 7 (January 20, 2022): 117–37. https://doi.org/10.1038/s41578-021-00407-8.

Rosenow, Jan, Duncan Gibb, Thomas Nowak, and Richard Lowes. "Heating Up the Global Heat Pump Market." *Nature Energy* 7, no. 10 (September 7, 2022): 901–4. https://doi.org/10.1038/s41560-022-01104-8.

Rosner, David, and Gerald Markowitz. "A 'Gift of God'?: The Public Health Controversy over Leaded Gasoline During the 1920s." *American Journal of Public Health* 75, no. 4 (April 1, 1985): 344–52. https://doi.org/10.2105/ajph.75.4.344.

Rosser, Franziska, and John Balmes. "Ozone and Childhood Respiratory Health: A Primer for US Pediatric Providers and a Call for a More Protective Standard." *Pediatric Pulmonology* 58, no. 5 (May 1, 2023): 1355–66. https://doi.org/10.1002/ppul.26368.

Roundtable on Sustainable Palm Oil (RSPO). "A Global Partnership to Make Palm Oil Sustainable." https://rspo.org.

Royal Society. "How Does GM Differ from Conventional Plant Breeding?" May 2016. https://royalsociety.org/news-resources/projects/gm-plants/how-does-gm-differ-from-conventional-plant-breeding/.

Rubino, Mauro, David M. Etheridge, Cathy M. Trudinger, Colin E. Allison, Mark O. Battle, Ray L. Langenfelds, L. Paul Steele, et al. "A Revised 1000 Year Atmospheric δ13C-CO2 Record from Law Dome and South Pole, Antarctica." *Journal of Geophysical Research: Atmospheres* 118, no. 15 (August 16, 2013): 8482–99. https://doi.org/10.1002/jgrd.50668.

Rubio, Natalie, Isha Datar, David Stachura, David Kaplan, and Kate Krueger. "Cell-Based Fish: A Novel Approach to Seafood Production and an Opportunity for Cellular Agriculture." *Frontiers in Sustainable Food Systems* 3 (June 11, 2019): 43. https://doi.org/10.3389/fsufs.2019.00043.

San Diego County Water Authority. "Water-Use Efficiency." January 2024. https://www.sdcwa.org/wp-content/uploads/2020/11/wateruseefficiency-fs.pdf.

Sanahuja, Georgina, Raviraj Banakar, Richard M. Twyman, Teresa Capell, and Paul Christou. "*Bacillus thuringiensis*: A Century of Research, Development and Commercial Applications." *Plant Biotechnology Journal* 9, no. 3 (April 2011): 283–300. https://doi.org/10.1111/j.1467-7652.2011.00595.x.

Sasikumar Nair, Surya, Joanna Trafiałek, and Wojciech Kolanowski. "Edible Packaging: A Technological Update for the Sustainable Future of the Food Industry." *Applied Sciences* 13, no. 14 (July 15, 2023): 8234. https://doi.org/10.3390/app13148234.

Sass, Jennifer. "ATSDR Report Confirms Glyphosate Cancer Risks." NRDC (Natural Resources Defense Council). April 11, 2019. https://www.nrdc.org/bio/jennifer-sass/atsdr-report-confirms-glyphosate-cancer-risks.

Saxifrage, Barry. "Managed to Death: How Canada Turned Its Forests into a Carbon Bomb." *Bulletin of the Atomic Scientists.* August 28, 2023. https://thebulletin.org/2023/08/managed-to-death-how-canada-turned-its-forests-into-a-carbon-bomb/.

Schar, Daniel, Eili Y. Klein, Ramanan Laxminarayan, Marius Gilbert, and Thomas P. Van Boeckel. "Global Trends in Antimicrobial Use in Aquaculture." *Scientific Reports* 10 (December 14, 2020): 21878. https://doi.org/10.1038/s41598-020-78849-3.

Schiffman, Richard. "A Troubling Look at the Human Toll of Mountaintop Removal Mining." *Yale Environment 360.* November 21, 2017. https://e360.yale.edu/features/a-troubling-look-at-the-human-toll-of-mountaintop-removal-mining.

Schijns, Rebecca, Rainer Froese, Jeffrey A. Hutchings, and Daniel Pauly. "Five Centuries of Cod Catches in Eastern Canada." *ICES Journal of Marine Science* 78, no. 8 (August 28, 2021): 2675–83. https://doi.org/10.1093/icesjms/fsab153.

Schwaba, Ted, Wiebke Bleidorn, Christopher J. Hopwood, Jochen E. Gebauer, P. Jason Rentfrow, Jeff Potter, and Samuel D. Gosling. "The Impact of Childhood Lead Exposure on Adult Personality: Evidence from the United States, Europe, and a Large-Scale Natural Experiment." *Proceedings of the National Academy of Sciences of the United*

States of America 118, no. 29 (July 12, 2021): e2020104118. https://doi.org/10.1073/pnas.2020104118.

Schwägerl, Christian. "Will Tech Breakthroughs Bring Fusion Energy Closer to Reality?" *Yale Environment 360*. July 6, 2023. https://e360.yale.edu/features/nuclear-fusion-research-startups.

Schwarcz, Joe. "Is It True that Bananas Are Radioactive?" McGill University. March 15, 2018. https://www.mcgill.ca/oss/article/you-asked/it-true-banana-radioactive.

Science Museum, London. "The Age of Plastic: From Parkesine to Pollution." October 11, 2019. https://www.sciencemuseum.org.uk/objects-and-stories/chemistry/age-plastic-parkesine-pollution.

Scientific American. "To Fight Antimicrobial Resistance, Start with Farm Animals." March 1, 2023. https://www.scientificamerican.com/article/to-fight-antimicrobial-resistance-start-with-farm-animals/.

Scott, Mike. "Can Artificial Intelligence Pave the Way for Greener Cement and Steel?" *Reuters*. January 8, 2024. https://www.reuters.com/sustainability/climate-energy/can-artificial-intelligence-pave-way-greener-cement-steel-2024-01-08/.

Scully, Melissa J., Gregory A. Norris, Tania M. Alarcon Falconi, and David L. MacIntosh. "Carbon Intensity of Corn Ethanol in the United States: State of the Science." *Environmental Research Letters* 16, no. 4 (March 10, 2021): 043001. https://doi.org/10.1088/1748-9326/abde08.

Searchinger, Tim, Richard Waite, Craig Hanson, and Janet Ranganathan. "Creating a Sustainable Food Future: Synthesis Report." World Resources Institute. July 2019. https://research.wri.org/wrr-food.

Seaside Sustainability. "The U.S. Progress with Single-Use Plastic Bans." March 21, 2023. https://www.seasidesustainability.org/post/the-u-s-progress-with-single-use-plastic-bans.

Second Harvest. "What We Do." https://secondharvest.ca/about/about.

Semenza, J.C., P.E. Tolbert, C.H. Rubin, L.J. Guillette, and R.J. Jackson. "Reproductive Toxins and Alligator Abnormalities at Lake Apopka, Florida." *Environmental Health Perspectives* 105, no. 10 (October 1, 1997): 1030–32. https://doi.org/10.1289/ehp.971051030.

Service, Robert F. "U.S. Unveils Plans for Large Facilities to Capture Carbon Directly from Air." *Science*. August 11, 2023. https://doi.org/10.1126/science.adk2566.

Seufert, Verena, and Navin Ramankutty. "Many Shades of Gray—The Context-Dependent Performance of Organic Agriculture." *Science Advances* 3, no. 3 (March 10, 2017): e1602638. https://doi.org/10.1126/sciadv.1602638.

Seymour, Linda M., Janille Maragh, Paolo Sabatini, Michel Di Tommaso, James C. Weaver, and Admir Masic. "Hot Mixing: Mechanistic Insights into the Durability of Ancient Roman Concrete." *Science Advances* 9, no. 1 (January 6, 2023): eadd1602. https://doi.org/10.1126/sciadv.add1602.

Shabecoff, Philip. "Global Warming Has Begun, Expert Tells Senate." *New York Times*. June 24, 1988. https://www.nytimes.com/1988/06/24/us/global-warming-has-begun-expert-tells-senate.html.

Shah Neville, Willow. "6 Cultured Meat Companies Making Waves." *Labiotech*. March 22, 2023. https://www.labiotech.eu/best-biotech/cultured-meat-companies/.

Shahbazi-Gahrouei, Daryoush, Mehrdad Gholami, and Samaneh Setayandeh. "A Review on Natural Background Radiation." *Advanced Biomedical Research* 2, no. 1 (January 1, 2013): 65. https://doi.org/10.4103/2277-9175.115821.

Shaji, E., K.V. Sarath, M. Santosh, P.K. Krishnaprasad, B.K. Arya, and Manisha S. Babu. "Fluoride Contamination in Groundwater: A Global Review of the Status, Processes, Challenges, and Remedial Measures." *Geoscience Frontiers* 15, no. 2 (March 1, 2024): 101734. https://doi.org/10.1016/j.gsf.2023.101734.

Sharifan, Hamidreza. "Alarming the Impacts of the Organic and Inorganic UV Blockers on Endangered Coral's Species in the Persian Gulf: A Scientific Concern for Coral Protection." *Sustainable Futures* 2 (January 1, 2020): 100017. https://doi.org/10.1016/j.sftr.2020.100017.

Sharkey, Martin. "Flame Retardant Chemicals Can Cause Serious Health Risks—And

They Only Slow Fire by a Few Seconds." *Conversation*. November 15, 2023. https://theconversation.com/flame-retardant-chemicals-can-cause-serious-health-risks-and-they-only-slow-fire-by-a-few-seconds-214658.

Shehab, Maryam A., and Francis D. Pope. "Effects of Short-Term Exposure to Particulate Matter Air Pollution on Cognitive Performance." *Scientific Reports* 9, no. 1 (June 3, 2019): 8237. https://doi.org/10.1038/s41598-019-44561-0.

Sheppard, Charles. "Coral Reefs in the Gulf Are Mostly Dead Now, but Can We Do Anything About It?" *Marine Pollution Bulletin* 105, no. 2 (April 30, 2016): 593–98. https://doi.org/10.1016/j.marpolbul.2015.09.031.

Shi, Jincai, Xiaolin Wang, and Ertao Wang. "Mycorrhizal Symbiosis in Plant Growth and Stress Adaptation: From Genes to Ecosystems." *Annual Review of Plant Biology* 74 (May 2023): 569–607. https://doi.org/10.1146/annurev-arplant-061722-090342.

Shriver, Thomas E., and Aysha Bodenhamer. "The Enduring Legacy of Black Lung: Environmental Health and Contested Illness in Appalachia." *Sociology of Health & Illness* 40, no. 8 (June 28, 2018): 1361–75. https://doi.org/10.1111/1467-9566.12777.

Shukla, Ishana, Kaitlyn M. Gaynor, Boris Worm, and Chris T. Darimont. "The Diversity of Animals Identified as Keystone Species." *Ecology and Evolution* 13, no. 10 (October 9, 2023): e10561. https://doi.org/10.1002/ece3.10561.

Siedt, Martin, Andreas Schäffer, Kilian E.C. Smith, Moritz Nabel, Martina Roß-Nickoll, and Joost T. van Dongen. "Comparing Straw, Compost, and Biochar Regarding Their Suitability as Agricultural Soil Amendments to Affect Soil Structure, Nutrient Leaching, Microbial Communities, and the Fate of Pesticides." *Science of the Total Environment* 751 (January 10, 2021): 141607. https://doi.org/10.1016/j.scitotenv.2020.141607.

Silver, Caleb. "Why a Former Top Sustainability Investor Says the Industry Is a Dangerous Fraud." *Investopedia*. August 18, 2022. https://www.investopedia.com/the-green-investor-podcast-episode-19-6500209.

Simantiris, Nikolaos. "Single-Use Plastic or Paper Products? A Dilemma That Requires Societal Change." *Cleaner Waste Systems* 7 (April 1, 2024): 100128. https://doi.org/10.1016/j.clwas.2023.100128.

Simmonds, Peter G., Matthew Rigby, Alistair J. Manning, Sunyoung Park, Kieran M. Stanley, Archie McCulloch, Stephan Henne, et al. "The Increasing Atmospheric Burden of the Greenhouse Gas Sulfur Hexafluoride (SF6)." *Atmospheric Chemistry and Physics* 20, no. 12 (June 23, 2020): 7271–90. https://doi.org/10.5194/acp-20-7271-2020.

Sing Wong, Amy, Spyridon Vrontos, and Michelle L. Taylor. "An Assessment of People Living by Coral Reefs over Space and Time." *Global Change Biology* 28, no. 23 (September 28, 2022): 7139–53. https://doi.org/10.1111/gcb.16391.

Singh, Hemant. "Different Types of Agricultural Subsidies Given to Farmers in India." *JagranJosh.com*. May 27, 2016. https://www.jagranjosh.com/general-knowledge/-different-types-of-agricultural-subsidies-given-to-farmers-in-india-1445333409-1.

Skelton, Renee, and Vernice Miller. "The Environmental Justice Movement." NRDC (Natural Resources Defense Council). August 22, 2023. https://www.nrdc.org/stories/environmental-justice-movement.

Skene, Jennifer. "The Logging Loophole: How the Logging Industry's Unregulated Carbon Emissions Undermine Canada's Climate Goals." Natural Resources Defense Council and Environmental Defence Canada. July 2020. https://naturecanada.ca/wp-content/uploads/2020/07/Boreal-Report-2020.pdf.

Skinner, Chris. "The Plastocene—Plastic in the Sedimentary Record." *Blogs of the European Geosciences Union*. January 9, 2019. https://blogs.egu.eu/divisions/ssp/2019/01/09/the-plastocene-plastic-in-the-sedimentary-record/.

Smart Water Magazine. "Arvind and Gap Open World's First Apparel Water Sustainability Hub." January 15, 2024. https://smartwatermagazine.com/news/gap/arvind-and-gap-open-worlds-first-apparel-water-sustainability-hub.

Smith, Daniel. "Worldwide Trends in DDT Levels in Human Breast Milk." *International Journal of Epidemiology* 28, no. 2 (April 1, 1999): 179–88. https://doi.org/10.1093/ije/28.2.179.

Smith, Kiona N. "Stronger than Steel: How Chemist Stephanie Kwolek Invented Kevlar."

Forbes. July 31, 2018. https://www.forbes.com/sites/kionasmith/2018/07/31/stronger-than-steel-how-chemist-stephanie-kwolek-invented-kevlar/?sh=239a54f21c3e.

Smithers, Rebecca. "Carlsberg to Replace Plastic Ring Can Holders with Recyclable Glue." *Guardian.* September 6, 2018. https://www.theguardian.com/food/2018/sep/06/carlsberg-to-replace-plastic-ring-can-holders-with-recyclable-glue.

Solomon, Susan, Diane J. Ivy, Doug. Kinnison, Michael J. Mills, Ryan R. Neely, III, and Anja Schmidt. "Emergence of Healing in the Antarctic Ozone Layer." *Science* 353, no. 6296 (June 30, 2016): 269–74. https://doi.org/10.1126/science.aae0061.

Sørheim, Oddvin, and Kacie Salove. "Meat Packaging for Improved Quality, Reduced Food Waste." National Provisioner. October 15, 2018. https://www.provisioneronline.com/articles/106911-meat-packaging-for-improved-quality-reduced-food-waste.

Sotero, Paulo. "Petrobras Scandal. Brazilian Political Corruption Scandal." *Britannica.* September 29, 2022. https://www.britannica.com/event/Petrobras-scandal.

Source Intelligence. "What Are the EPR Directives in the EU?" March 24, 2023. https://blog.sourceintelligence.com/what-are-the-epr-directives-in-the-eu.

Soussi, Abdellatif, Enrico Zero, Roberto Sacile, Daniele Trinchero, and Marco Fossa. "Smart Sensors and Smart Data for Precision Agriculture: A Review." *Sensors* 24, no. 8 (April 21, 2024): 2647. https://doi.org/10.3390/s24082647.

Spencer, Peter B.S., Andrey A. Yurchenko, Victor A. David, Rachael Scott, Klaus-Peter Koepfli, Carlos Driscoll, Stephen J. O'Brien, and Marilyn Menotti-Raymond. "The Population Origins and Expansion of Feral Cats in Australia." *Journal of Heredity* 107, no. 2 (March 1, 2016): 104–14. https://doi.org/10.1093/jhered/esv095.

State of Green. "Denmark's First Circular Social Housing Project." September 4, 2021. https://stateofgreen.com/en/solutions/denmarks-first-circular-social-housing-project/.

State of Salmon in Watersheds. "The Salmon Struggle." State of Salmon in Watersheds Report 2022. https://stateofsalmon.wa.gov/executive-summary/challenges.

Steinbeck, John. *Grapes of Wrath.* 1984. https://openlibrary.org/books/OL8459553M/Grapes_of_Wrath.

Steiner, Richard. "Lessons from Exxon Valdez, 25 Years Later." *Greenpeace.* March 21, 2014. https://www.greenpeace.org/usa/lessons-from-exxon-valdez-25-years-later/.

Stewart, Jessica. "London Marathon Replaces Plastic Bottles with Edible Seaweed Drink Capsules." *My Modern Met.* April 30, 2019. https://mymodernmet.com/ooho-edible-drink-capsule-london-marathon/.

Stewart, Joshua D., Trevor W. Joyce, John W. Durban, John Calambokidis, Deborah Fauquier, Holly Fearnbach, Jacqueline M. Grebmeier, Morgan Lynn, Manfredi, Wayne L. Perryman, M. Tim Tinker, and David W. Weller. "Boom-Bust Cycles in Gray Whales Associated with Dynamic and Changing Arctic Conditions." *Science* 382, no. 6667 (October 12, 2023): 207–11. https://doi.org/10.1126/science.adi1847.

Stokstad, Erik. "European Union Expands Ban of Three Neonicotinoid Pesticides." *Science.* April 27, 2018. https://doi.org/10.1126/science.aau0152.

Stoller-Conrad, Jessica. "Tree Rings Provide Snapshots of Earth's Past Climate." *Climate Change: Vital Signs of the Planet.* January 25, 2017. https://climate.nasa.gov/news/2540/tree-rings-provide-snapshots-of-earths-past-climate.

Streets, David G., Hannah M. Horowitz, Daniel J. Jacob, Zifeng Lu, Leonard Levin, Arnout F.H. ter Schure, and Elsie M. Sunderland. "Total Mercury Released to the Environment by Human Activities." *Environmental Science & Technology* 51, no. 11 (April 27, 2017): 5969–77. https://doi.org/10.1021/acs.est.7b00451.

Streets, David G., Hannah M. Horowitz, Zifeng Lu, Leonard Levin, Colin P. Thackray, and Elsie M. Sunderland. "Five Hundred Years of Anthropogenic Mercury: Spatial and Temporal Release Profiles." *Environmental Research Letters* 14 (July 22, 2019): 084004. https://doi.org/10.1088/1748-9326/ab281f.

Suganya, T., M. Varman, H.H. Masjuki, and S. Renganathan. "Macroalgae and Microalgae as a Potential Source for Commercial Applications Along with Biofuels Production: A Biorefinery Approach." *Renewable & Sustainable Energy Reviews* 55 (March 1, 2016): 909–41. https://doi.org/10.1016/j.rser.2015.11.026.

Summers, Haleigh, Heather D. Karsten, William Curran, and Glenna M. Malcolm.

"Integrated Weed Management with Reduced Herbicides in a No-Till Dairy Rotation." *Agronomy Journal* 113, no. 4 (July/August 2021): 3418–33. https://doi.org/10.1002/agj2.20757.

Supran, Geoffrey, Stefan Rahmstorf, and Naomi Oreskes. "Assessing ExxonMobil's Global Warming Projections." *Science* 379, no. 6628 (January 13, 2023): eabk0063. https://doi.org/10.1126/science.abk0063.

Swartz, Elliot, and Claire Bomkamp. "The Science of Cultivated Meat." *Good Food Institute.* https://gfi.org/science/the-science-of-cultivated-meat/.

Tabashnik, Bruce E., Jeffrey A. Fabrick, and Yves Carrière. "Global Patterns of Insect Resistance to Transgenic *Bt* Crops: The First 25 Years." *Journal of Economic Entomology* 116, no. 2 (April 2023): 297–309. https://doi.org/10.1093/jee/toac183.

Takamura, Noboru, Makiko Orita, Vladimir Saenko, Shunichi Yamashita, Shigenobu Nagataki, and Yuri Demidchik. "Radiation and Risk of Thyroid Cancer: Fukushima and Chernobyl." *Lancet. Diabetes & Endocrinology* 4, no. 8 (August 1, 2016): 647. https://doi.org/10.1016/s2213-8587(16)30112-7.

Tamisiea, Jack. "A 19th Century Farmer May Be to Blame for Australia's Rabbit Scourge." *Science.* August 22, 2022. https://doi.org/10.1126/science.ade5315.

Tangley, Laura. "Power Plants." *National Wildlife Magazine.* April 1, 2022. https://www.nwf.org/Magazines/National-Wildlife/2022/April-May/Conservation/Keystone-Plants.

Taylor, Brian. "Europe Records 73 Percent UBC Recycling Rate. Can Recycling Rate Reflects Recyclability of Aluminum, According to Trade Groups." *Recycling Today.* December 15, 2022. https://www.recyclingtoday.com/news/aluminum-can-ubc-recycling-europe-rate-2020/.

Tenenbaum, David J. "Biochar: Carbon Mitigation from the Ground Up." *Environmental Health Perspectives* 117, no. 2 (February 1, 2009): A70–73. https://doi.org/10.1289/ehp.117-a70.

TerraPass. "Carbon Footprint Calculator." https://terrapass.com/carbon-footprint-calculator/.

Thandra, Krishna Chaitanya, Adam Barsouk, Kalyan Saginala, John Sukumar Aluru, and Alexander Barsouk. "Epidemiology of Lung Cancer." *Contemporary Oncology/Współczesna Onkologia* 25, no. 1 (January 1, 2021): 45–52. https://doi.org/10.5114/wo.2021.103829.

Thomas, Christian J., Robert K. Shriver, Fabian Nippgen, Matthew Hepler, and Matthew R.V. Ross. "Mines to Forests? Analyzing Long-Term Recovery Trends for Surface Coal Mines in Central Appalachia." *Restoration Ecology* 31, no. 5 (November 9, 2022): e13827. https://doi.org/10.1111/rec.13827.

Thomas, Valerie M., Robert H. Socolow, James J. Fanelli, and Thomas G. Spiro. "Effects of Reducing Lead in Gasoline: An Analysis of the International Experience." *Environmental Science & Technology* 33, no. 22 (October 1, 1999): 3942–48. https://doi.org/10.1021/es990231.

Thomasy, Hannah. "Beehive Fences Can Help Mitigate Human-Elephant Conflict." *Mongabay.* September 11, 2019. https://news.mongabay.com/2019/09/beehive-fences-can-help-mitigate-human-elephant-conflict/.

Thomson, Ashley. "Biodiversity and the Amazon Rainforest." *Greenpeace.* May 22, 2020. https://www.greenpeace.org/usa/biodiversity-and-the-amazon-rainforest/.

Thoreau, Henry David. *Walden.* Boston: Beacon Press, 2017.

Thoughtshop Foundation. https://thoughtshopfoundation.org.

Tian, Hanqin, Rongting Xu, Josep G. Canadell, Rona L. Thompson, Wilfried Winiwarter, Parvadha Suntharalingam, Eric A. Davidson, et al. "A Comprehensive Quantification of Global Nitrous Oxide Sources and Sinks." *Nature* 586, no. 7828 (October 7, 2020): 248–56. https://doi.org/10.1038/s41586-020-2780-0.

Tian, Zhenyu, Haoqi Zhao, Katherine T. Peter, Melissa Gonzalez, Jill Wetzel, Christopher Wu, Ximin Hu, et al. "A Ubiquitous Tire Rubber–Derived Chemical Induces Acute Mortality in Coho Salmon." *Science* 371, no. 6525 (January 8, 2021): 185–89. https://doi.org/10.1126/science.abd6951.

Todd, Ewen C.D. "Domoic Acid and Amnesic Shellfish Poisoning—A Review." *Journal of Food Protection* 56, no. 1 (January 1, 1993): 69–83. https://doi.org/10.4315/0362-028x-56.1.69.

Tollefson, Julie. "Groundwater Levels Fall Across Western and South-Central Kansas." Kansas Geological Survey, March 10, 2023. https://www.kgs.ku.edu/General/News/2023/water-levels.html.

Tom Ford Plastic Innovation Accelerator. Powered by Lonely Whale. 2023. https://unwrapthefuture.org/#about-the-program.

Tomas, Walfrido M., Fabio De Oliveira Roque, Ronaldo G. Morato, Patricia Emilia Medici, Rafael M. Chiaravalloti, Fernando R. Tortato, Jerry M.F. Penha, et al. "Sustainability Agenda for the Pantanal Wetland: Perspectives on a Collaborative Interface for Science, Policy, and Decision-Making." *Tropical Conservation Science* 12 (September 18, 2019): 194008291987263. https://doi.org/10.1177/1940082919872634.

Toxicology Education Foundation. "How Toxicologists Establish Safe Doses of Chemicals." https://toxedfoundation.org/how-toxicologists-establish-safe-doses/.

Trainer, Vera L., Raphael M. Kudela, Matthew V. Hunter, Nicolaus G. Adams, and Ryan M. McCabe. "Climate Extreme Seeds a New Domoic Acid Hotspot on the US West Coast." *Frontiers in Climate* 2 (December 14, 2020): 571836. https://doi.org/10.3389/fclim.2020.571836.

Traven, Luka. "Busting the Myth: Waste-to-Energy Plants and Public Health." *Archives of Industrial Hygiene and Toxicology* 74, no. 2 (June 26, 2023): 142–43. https://doi.org/10.2478/aiht-2023-74-3733.

Tschora, Héloïse, and Francesco Cherubini. "Co-Benefits and Trade-Offs of Agroforestry for Climate Change Mitigation and Other Sustainability Goals in West Africa." *Global Ecology and Conservation* 22 (June 1, 2020): e00919. https://doi.org/10.1016/j.gecco.2020.e00919.

Twilley, Nicola. "Africa's Cold Rush and the Promise of Refrigeration." *New Yorker.* August 15, 2022. https://www.newyorker.com/magazine/2022/08/22/africas-cold-rush-and-the-promise-of-refrigeration.

Tyndall, John. "I. The Bakerian Lecture.—On the Absorption and Radiation of Heat by Gases and Vapours, and on the Physical Connexion of Radiation, Absorption, and Conduction." *Philosophical Transactions of the Royal Society of London* 151 (December 31, 1861): 1–36. https://doi.org/10.1098/rstl.1861.0001.

Ufer, Danielle J. "Farm Animal Welfare Policies Cover Breeding Sows, Veal Calves, or Laying Hens in 14 U.S. States." U.S. Department of Agriculture, Economic Research Service. April 24, 2023. https://www.ers.usda.gov/amber-waves/2023/april/farm-animal-welfare-policies-cover-breeding-sows-veal-calves-or-laying-hens-in-14-u-s-states/.

UK Atomic Energy Authority. Culham Centre for Fusion Energy. "Fusion in Brief." Accessed February 9, 2024. https://ccfe.ukaea.uk/fusion-energy/fusion-in-brief/.

U.K. National Grid. "High Voltage Direct Current Electricity—Technical Information." CRFS09/08/13. August 2013. https://www.nationalgrid.com/sites/default/files/documents/13784-High%20Voltage%20Direct%20Current%20Electricity%20-%20technical%20information.pdf.

UN News. "UN Launches Drive to Highlight Environmental Cost of Staying Fashionable." March 25, 2019. https://news.un.org/en/story/2019/03/1035161.

UN News, Global Perspectives. "Beyond Borders: Why New 'High Seas' Treaty Is Critical for the World." June 19, 2023. https://news.un.org/en/story/2023/06/1137857.

UN World Food Programme. "Food Waste: 13 Facts You Need to Know." July 6, 2023. https://freerice.com/blog/food-waste-13-facts-you-need-know.

U.S. Department of Energy, Office of Federal Energy Management Program. "Bidirectional Charging and Electric Vehicles for Mobile Storage." https://www.energy.gov/femp/bidirectional-charging-and-electric-vehicles-mobile-storage.

Union of Concerned Scientists (UCS). "Union of Concerned Scientists: About." https://www.ucsusa.org/about.

Unitec Laboratory Services. "Overall View on the Current States Laws Against the Flame Retardants Chemical." 2020. http://www.unitls.com/reports-news/the-us-and-canada/51-overall-view-on-the-current-states-laws-against-the-flame-retardants-chemical.html.

United for Efficiency. "Accelerating the Global Transition to High-Efficiency Products." Accessed March 7, 2024. https://united4efficiency.org/about-the-partnership/.

United Nations. "Climate Action: Finance & Justice." https://www.un.org/en/climate change/raising-ambition/climate-finance.

United Nations Carbon Offset Platform. "What Is Offsetting?" https://offset.climate neutralnow.org/aboutoffsetting.

United Nations Children's Fund. "Building Access to Clean Water in Support of Sustainable Development Goal 6." February 2, 2023. https://www.unicef.org/supply/stories/building-access-clean-water-support-sustainable-development-goal-6.

United Nations Climate Change. "ME SOLshare: Peer-to-Peer Smart Village Grids | Bangladesh." https://unfccc.int/climate-action/momentum-for-change/ict-solutions/solshare.

United Nations Climate Change. "UN Carbon Footprint Calculator." https://offset.climate neutralnow.org/footprintcalc.

United Nations Climate Change. "Wetlands Disappearing Three Times Faster than Forests." October 1, 2018. https://unfccc.int/news/wetlands-disappearing-three-times-faster-than-forests.

United Nations Climate Change News. "New International Biodiversity Agreement Strengthens Climate Action." December 19, 2022. https://unfccc.int/news/new-international-biodiversity-agreement-strengthens-climate-action.

United Nations Department of Economic and Social Affairs. "World Population Prospects 2024, Graphs/Profiles." United Nations Department of Economic and Social Affairs, Population Division (2024). https://population.un.org/wpp/Graphs/DemographicProfiles/Line/900.

United Nations Development Programme. "Precision Agriculture for Smallholder Farmers." UNDP, Global Centre for Technology, Innovation and Sustainable Development. October 14, 2021. https://www.undp.org/publications/precision-agriculture-smallholder-farmers.

United Nations Environment Programme. "The Convention on Biological Diversity: History of the Convention." May 22, 2024. https://www.cbd.int/history.

United Nations Environment Programme. "Emissions Gap Report 2023: Broken Record—Temperatures Hit New Highs, Yet World Fails to Cut Emissions (Again)." November 20, 2023. https://www.unep.org/resources/emissions-gap-report-2023.

United Nations Environment Programme. Global Climate Litigation Report: 2023 Status Review. https://doi.org/10.59117/20.500.11822/43008.

United Nations Environment Programme. "One Atmosphere: An Independent Expert Review on Solar Radiation Modification Research and Deployment." 2023. https://wedocs.unep.org/handle/20.500.11822/41903.

United Nations Environment Programme. "Single-Use Plastic Bags and Their Alternatives—Recommendations from Life Cycle Assessments." Life Cycle Initiative, 2020. https://www.lifecycleinitiative.org/wp-content/uploads/2021/03/SUPP-plastic-bags-meta-study-8.3.21.pdf.

United Nations Environment Programme OzonAction. "About Montreal Protocol." https://www.unep.org/ozonaction/who-we-are/about-montreal-protocol.

United Nations Framework Convention on Climate Change. "Global Alliance for Clean Cookstoves—Creating a Thriving Global Market for Clean and Efficient Household Cooking Solutions." November 25, 2015. https://unfccc.int/news/global-alliance-for-clean-cookstoves.

United Nations Framework Convention on Climate Change. "Technical Dialogue of the First Global Stocktake. Synthesis Report by the Co-Facilitators on the Technical Dialogue." September 8, 2023. https://unfccc.int/documents/631600.

United Nations Sustainable Development Group. "UN Report: Nature's Dangerous Decline 'Unprecedented'; Species Extinction Rates 'Accelerating.'" May 6, 2019. https://www.un.org/sustainabledevelopment/blog/2019/05/nature-decline-unprecedented-report/.

United States Census Bureau. "Historical Estimates of World Population." December 5, 2022. https://www.census.gov/data/tables/time-series/demo/international-programs/-historical-est-worldpop.html.

United States Environmental Protection Agency. "Basics of Green Chemistry." May 2, 2024. https://www.epa.gov/greenchemistry/basics-green-chemistry.

United States Environmental Protection Agency. "DDT—A Brief History and Status." March 12, 2024. https://www.epa.gov/ingredients-used-pesticide-products/ddt-brief-history-and-status.

United States Environmental Protection Agency. "Deepwater Horizon—BP Gulf of Mexico Oil Spill." July 24, 2024. https://www.epa.gov/enforcement/deepwater-horizon-bp-gulf-mexico-oil-spill.

United States Environmental Protection Agency. "Facts and Figures About Materials, Waste and Recycling. Aluminum: Material-Specific Data." November 22, 2023. https://www.epa.gov/facts-and-figures-about-materials-waste-and-recycling/aluminum-material-specific-data.

United States Environmental Protection Agency. "Facts and Figures About Materials, Waste and Recycling. Other Nonferrous Metals: Material-Specific Data." November 22, 2023. https://www.epa.gov/facts-and-figures-about-materials-waste-and-recycling/-other-nonferrous-metals-material-specific.

United States Environmental Protection Agency. "Facts and Figures About Materials, Waste and Recycling. Plastics: Material-Specific Data." October 20, 2023. https://www.epa.gov/facts-and-figures-about-materials-waste-and-recycling/plastics-material-specific-data.

United States Environmental Protection Agency. "History of the Clean Water Act." https://www.epa.gov/laws-regulations/history-clean-water-act.

United States Environmental Protection Agency. "Learn About Dioxin." December 7, 2023. https://www.epa.gov/dioxin/learn-about-dioxin.

United States Environmental Protection Agency. "Learn About Polychlorinated Biphenyls." April 2, 2024. https://www.epa.gov/pcbs/learn-about-polychlorinated-biphenyls.

United States Environmental Protection Agency. "Minamata Convention on Mercury." December 12, 2023. https://www.epa.gov/international-cooperation/minamata-convention-mercury.

United States Environmental Protection Agency. "New International Requirements for the Export and Import of Plastic Recyclables and Waste." February 25, 2024. https://www.epa.gov/hwgenerators/new-international-requirements-export-and-import-plastic-recyclables-and-waste.

United States Environmental Protection Agency. "Ozone National Ambient Air Quality Standards (NAAQS)." https://www.epa.gov/ground-level-ozone-pollution/ozone-national-ambient-air-quality-standards-naaqs.

United States Environmental Protection Agency. "Particulate Matter (PM) Basics." https://www.epa.gov/pm-pollution/particulate-matter-pm-basics.

United States Environmental Protection Agency. "Soak Up the Rain: Permeable Pavement." May 23, 2024. https://www.epa.gov/soakuptherain/soak-rain-permeable-pavement.

United States Environmental Protection Agency. "2022 EPA Automotive Trends Report." Accessed October 26, 2023. www.epa.gov/automotive-trends/explore-automotive-trends-data.

United States Environmental Protection Agency, Energy Star. "Learn About CFLs." https://www.energystar.gov/products/lighting_fans/light_bulbs/learn_about_cfls.

University of Rhode Island. "Drip Irrigation." Water Quality Program—College of the Environment and Life Sciences. https://web.uri.edu/safewater/protecting-water-quality-at-home/sustainable-landscaping/drip-irrigation.

Urbina, Ian. "How China's Expanding Fishing Fleet Is Depleting the World's Oceans." *Yale Environment 360.* August 17, 2020. https://e360.yale.edu/features/how-chinas-expanding-fishing-fleet-is-depleting-worlds-oceans.

U.S. Department of Agriculture. "Adoption of Conservation Tillage Has Increased Over the Past Two Decades on Acreage Planted to Major U.S. Cash Crops." USDA Economic

Research Service. October 25, 2022. https://www.ers.usda.gov/data-products/chart-gallery/gallery/chart-detail/?chartId=105042.

U.S. Department of Agriculture. "More than Half of Harvested U.S. Cropland Uses Seed Varieties with at Least One Genetically Modified Trait." USDA Economic Research Service. August 7, 2023. https://www.ers.usda.gov/data-products/chart-gallery/gallery/chart-detail/?chartId=107037.

U.S. Department of Agriculture. "Palm Oil Explorer." Foreign Agricultural Service. Accessed June 19, 2024. https://ipad.fas.usda.gov/cropexplorer/cropview/commodityView.aspx?cropid=4243000.

U.S. Department of Agriculture, "Recent Trends in GE Adoption." USDA Economic Research Service. October 4, 2023. https://www.ers.usda.gov/data-products/adoption-of-genetically-engineered-crops-in-the-u-s/recent-trends-in-ge-adoption/.

U.S. Department of Agriculture. "Regional Integrated Pest Management (IPM) Centers." USDA, Department of Agriculture, National Institute of Food and Agriculture. https://www.nifa.usda.gov/regional-integrated-pest-management-ipm-centers.

U.S. Department of Commerce. "Netherlands—Country Commercial Guide. Agriculture." International Trade Administration. January 17, 2024. https://www.trade.gov/country-commercial-guides/netherlands-agriculture.

U.S. Department of Energy, Energy Saver. "Lighting Choices to Save You Money." https://www.energy.gov/energysaver/lighting-choices-save-you-money.

U.S. Department of Energy, Office of Energy Efficiency & Renewable Energy. "Alternative Fuels Data Center. Hydrogen Benefits and Considerations." https://afdc.energy.gov/fuels/hydrogen-benefits.

U.S. Department of Health and Human Services. "QuickStats: Deaths Involving Exposure to Excessive Heat, by Sex—National Vital Statistics System, United States, 1999–2020." *Morbidity and Mortality Weekly Report* 71, no. 34 (August 26, 2022): 1097. https://doi.org/10.15585/mmwr.mm7134a5.

U.S. Energy Information Administration. "Biomass Explained. Waste-to-Energy (Municipal Solid Waste)." November 6, 2023. https://www.eia.gov/energyexplained/biomass/-waste-to-energy.php.

U.S. Energy Information Administration. "Combined Heat and Power Technology Fills an Important Energy Niche." October 4, 2012. https://www.eia.gov/todayinenergy/detail.php?id=8250.

U.S. Energy Information Administration. "Electricity Explained. Electricity in the United States." https://www.eia.gov/energyexplained/electricity/electricity-in-the-us.php

U.S. Energy Information Administration. "Energy and the Environment Explained. Recycling and Energy." August 17, 2022. https://www.eia.gov/energyexplained/energy-and-the-environment/recycling-and-energy.php.

U.S. Energy Information Administration. "Hydropower Explained. Ocean Thermal Energy Conversion." https://www.eia.gov/energyexplained/hydropower/ocean-thermal-energy-conversion.php.

U.S. Energy Information Administration. "Hydropower Explained. Tidal Power." https://www.eia.gov/energyexplained/hydropower/tidal-power.php.

U.S. Energy Information Administration. "Texas: State Profile and Energy Estimates." Accessed February 9, 2024. https://www.eia.gov/state/?sid=TX#tabs-4.

U.S. Energy Information Administration. "What Is the Efficiency of Different Types of Power Plants?" May 15, 2024. https://www.eia.gov/tools/faqs/faq.php?id=107&t=3.

U.S. Food and Drug Administration. "Bisphenol A (BPA): Use in Food Contact Application." April 20, 2023. https://www.fda.gov/food/food-packaging-other-substances-come-contact-food-information-consumers/bisphenol-bpa-use-food-contact-application.

U.S. Food and Drug Administration. "Science and History of GMOs and Other Food Modification Processes." May 3, 2024. https://www.fda.gov/food/agricultural-biotechnology/science-and-history-gmos-and-other-food-modification-processes.

U.S. Geological Survey. "What Is the Role of Native Bees in the United States?" https://www.usgs.gov/faqs/what-role-native-bees-united-states.

U.S. Green Building Council. "Hunter's Point Residential Community in Florida Pursues Net Positive Power." October 24, 2023. https://www.usgbc.org/articles/hunter-s-point-residential-community-florida-pursues-net-positive-power.

U.S. National Park Service. "Sky Island Fire Ecology." https://www.nps.gov/articles/sky-island-fire-ecology.htm.

U.S. National Park Service. "What Happened to the Bison?" https://www.nps.gov/articles/000/what-happened-to-the-bison.htm.

USAID Bangladesh. "Cold Chain Bangladesh Alliance. USAID's Assets Amplify Local Partner Investments." U.S. Global Development Lab's Global Partnerships Team. November 2015. https://2017-2020.usaid.gov/sites/default/files/documents/15396/ccba-draft_edited.pdf.

Utah Division of Wildlife Resources. "Great Salt Lake Water Levels." Great Salt Lake Ecosystem Program. Accessed June 21, 2024. https://wildlife.utah.gov/gslep/about/water-levels.html.

Utah Senate. "Protect, Conserve and Invest in Statewide Water Resources." February 16, 2024. https://senate.utah.gov/utah-legislature-continues-to-protect-conserve-and-invest-in-statewide-water-resources/.

van de Water, Antoinette, Michelle Henley, Lucy Bates, and Rob Slotow. "The Value of Elephants: A Pluralist Approach." *Ecosystem Services* 58 (December 1, 2022): 101488. https://doi.org/10.1016/j.ecoser.2022.101488.

van den Bosch, Marie. "Saudi Arabia's 60-Year Battle for Food Security." Arab Gulf States Institute in Washington. May 13, 2024. https://agsiw.org/saudi-arabias-60-year-battle-for-food-security.

van Deynze, Braeden, Scott M. Swinton, David A. Hennessy, Nick M. Haddad, and Leslie Ries. "Insecticides, More than Herbicides, Land Use, and Climate, Are Associated with Declines in Butterfly Species Richness and Abundance in the American Midwest." *PloS One* 19, no. 6 (June 20, 2024): e0304319. https://doi.org/10.1371/journal.pone.0304319.

van Dijk, Michiel, Tom Morley, Marie Luise Rau, and Yashar Saghai. "A Meta-Analysis of Projected Global Food Demand and Population at Risk of Hunger for the Period 2010–2050." *Nature Food* 2 (July 21, 2021): 494–501. https://doi.org/10.1038/s43016-021-00322-9.

Vatistas, Christos, Dafni Despoina Avgoustaki, and Thomas Bartzana. "A Systematic Literature Review on Controlled-Environment Agriculture: How Vertical Farms and Greenhouses Can Influence the Sustainability and Footprint of Urban Microclimate with Local Food Production." *Atmosphere* 13, no. 8 (August 8, 2022): 1258. https://doi.org/10.3390/atmos13081258.

Vecellio, Daniel J., Qinqin Kong, W. Larry Kenney, and Matthew Huber. "Greatly Enhanced Risk to Humans as a Consequence of Empirically Determined Lower Moist Heat Stress Tolerance." *Proceedings of the National Academy of Sciences of the United States of America* 120, no. 42 (October 9, 2023): e2305427120. https://doi.org/10.1073/pnas.2305427120.

Velasco, Emily. "History's Mysteries: Caltech Professor Helps Solve Hindenburg Disaster." California Institute of Technology. May 17, 2021. https://www.caltech.edu/about/news/historys-mysteries-caltech-professor-helps-solve-hindenburg-disaster.

Vereckey, Betsy. "How to Choose Carbon Offsets that Actually Cut Emissions." *MIT Sloan School of Management.* November 2, 2022. https://mitsloan.mit.edu/ideas-made-to-matter/how-to-choose-carbon-offsets-actually-cut-emissions.

Verma, Anand, Bharatesh K. Shetty, Vasudeva Guddattu, Mehul K. Chourasia, and Prachi Pundir. "High Prevalence of Dental Fluorosis Among Adolescents Is a Growing Concern: A School Based Cross-Sectional Study from Southern India." *Environmental Health and Preventive Medicine* 22 (April 4, 2017): 17. https://doi.org/10.1186/s12199-017-0624-9.

Vethaak, A. Dick, and Juliette Legler. "Microplastics and Human Health. Knowledge Gaps Should Be Addressed to Ascertain the Health Risks of Microplastics." *Science* 371, no. 6530 (February 12, 2021): 672–74. https://doi.org/10.1126/science.abe5041.

Vicente, Ana, Célia Alves, Ana I. Calvo, Ana P. Fernandes, Teresa Nunes, Cristina

Monteiro, Susana Marta Almeida, and Casimiro Pio. "Emission Factors and Detailed Chemical Composition of Smoke Particles from the 2010 Wildfire Season." *Atmospheric Environment* 71 (June 1, 2013): 295–303. https://doi.org/10.1016/j.atmosenv.2013.01.062.

Vines, Brian. "Ugly Food Fight: Misfits Market, Imperfect Foods, and the Battle Against Food Waste." *Consumer Reports*. January 12, 2022. https://www.consumerreports.org/health/food-shopping/ugly-food-fight-misfits-market-imperfect-foods-food-waste-a6326488257/.

Voiland, Adam. "America's Sinking East Coast." NASA Earth Observatory. https://earthobservatory.nasa.gov/images/152452/americas-sinking-east-coast.

Voiland, Adam. "Making Sense of Amazon Deforestation Patterns." NASA Earth Observatory. November 22, 2019. https://earthobservatory.nasa.gov/images/145888/making-sense-of-amazon-deforestation-patterns.

vom Saal, Frederick S., Michael Antoniou, Scott M. Belcher, Ake Bergman, Ramji K. Bhandari, Linda S. Birnbaum, Aly Cohen, et al. "The Conflict Between Regulatory Agencies over the 20,000-Fold Lowering of the Tolerable Daily Intake (TDI) for Bisphenol A (BPA) by the European Food Safety Authority (EFSA)." *Environmental Health Perspectives* 132, no. 4 (April 9, 2024). https://doi.org/10.1289/ehp13812.

Vyawahare, Malavika, and ClimateWire. "Hawaii First to Harness Deep-Ocean Temperatures for Power." *Scientific American*. August 27, 2015. https://www.scientificamerican.com/article/hawaii-first-to-harness-deep-ocean-temperatures-for-power/.

Wagner, David L., Eliza M. Grames, Matthew L. Forister, May R. Berenbaum, and David Stopak. "Insect Decline in the Anthropocene: Death by a Thousand Cuts." *Proceedings of the National Academy of Sciences of the United States of America* 118, no. 2 (January 11, 2021): e2023989118. https://doi.org/10.1073/pnas.2023989118.

Walsh, Niall Patrick. "How the Dutch Use Architecture to Feed the World." *ArchDaily*. January 24, 2020. https://www.archdaily.com/932301/how-the-dutch-use-architecture-to-feed-the-world.

Walton, Daniel. "Micro Solar Leases: A New Income Stream for Black Farmers in the South?" *Civil Eats*. February 14, 2024. https://civileats.com/2024/02/14/micro-solar-leases-a-new-income-stream-for-black-farmers-in-the-south/.

Wang, Tong, Peter Berrill, Julie B. Zimmerman, and Edgar G. Hertwich. "Copper Recycling Flow Model for the United States Economy: Impact of Scrap Quality on Potential Energy Benefit." *Environmental Science & Technology* 55, no. 8 (March 30, 2021): 5485–95. https://doi.org/10.1021/acs.est.0c08227.

Wang, Xiaolei, Junze Zhang, Shuai Wang, Yongxiao Ge, Zihao Duan, Lin Sun, Michael E. Meadows, Yi Luo, Bojie Fu, Xi Chen, Yue Huang, Xiaoting Ma, and Jilili Abuduwaili. "Reviving the Aral Sea: A Hydro-Eco-Social Perspective." *Earth's Future* 11, no. 11 (November 22, 2023): e2023EF003657. https://doi.org/10.1029/2023EF003657.

Wang, Zhanyun, Jamie C. DeWitt, Christopher P. Higgins, and Ian T. Cousins. "A Never-Ending Story of Per- and Polyfluoroalkyl Substances (PFASs)?" *Environmental Science & Technology* 51, no. 5 (February 22, 2017): 2508–18. https://doi.org/10.1021/acs.est.6b04806.

Wanner, Brent, and Ryota Taniguchi. "Nuclear Power." *IEA: International Energy Agency*. July 11, 2023. https://www.iea.org/energy-system/electricity/nuclear-power.

Waste No Food. "Diverting Excess Food to Hungry People." https://wastenofood.org/about/.

Welsh Government. "The Well-Being of Future Generations." https://www.gov.wales/well-being-of-future-generations-wales.

Wen, Xin. "Vertical Farming Reaches New Heights in China." *Asia News Network*. April 14, 2023. https://asianews.network/vertical-farming-reaches-new-heights-in-china/.

Wheeler, Perry, and Glen Spain. "U.S. Fishing Groups Sue Tire Manufacturers over 6PPD Impacts on Salmon, Steelhead." *Earthjustice*. November 8, 2023. https://earthjustice.org/press/2023/u-s-fishing-groups-sue-tire-manufacturers-over-6ppd-impacts-on-salmon-steelhead.

White, Helen K., Pen-Yuan Hsing, Walter Cho, Timothy M. Shank, Erik E. Cordes, Andrea M. Quattrini, Robert K. Nelson, Richard Camilli, Amanda W.J. Demopoulos,

Christopher R. German, et al. "Impact of the Deepwater Horizon Oil Spill on a Deep-Water Coral Community in the Gulf of Mexico." *Proceedings of the National Academy of Sciences of the United States of America* 109, no. 50 (March 27, 2012): 20303–8. https://doi.org/10.1073/pnas.1118029109.

Wiggins, Steve, and Sharada Keats. "Leaping and Learning: Linking Smallholders to Markets." ODI. May 29, 2013. https://odi.org/en/publications/leaping-and-learning-linking-smallholders-to-markets/.

Wilcox, Chris, Erik Van Sebille, and Britta Denise Hardesty. "Threat of Plastic Pollution to Seabirds Is Global, Pervasive, and Increasing." *Proceedings of the National Academy of Sciences of the United States of America* 112, no. 38 (August 31, 2015): 11899–904. https://doi.org/10.1073/pnas.1502108112.

Wildlife Conservation Society Newsroom. "Bronx Zoo Bison Join Osage Nation Herd in Oklahoma." May 13, 2022. https://newsroom.wcs.org/News-Releases/articleType/ArticleView/articleId/17527/Bronx-Zoo-Bison-Join-Osage-Nation-Herd-in-Oklahoma.aspx.

Willett, Walter, Johan Rockström, Brent Loken, Marco Springmann, Tim Lang, Sonja Vermeulen, Tara Garnett, et al. "Food in the Anthropocene: The EAT–Lancet Commission on Healthy Diets from Sustainable Food Systems." *Lancet Commissions* 393, no. 10170 (February 2, 2019): 447–92. https://doi.org/10.1016/S0140-6736(18)31788-4.

Williams, Carter. "Dust Hot Spots: Where Is Great Salt Lake's Toxic Dust Most Likely to Originate?" University of Utah, College of Science. Accessed June 21, 2024. https://science.utah.edu/news/toxic-dust-hot-spots/.

Winn, Zach. "Reducing Methane Emissions at Landfills." *MIT News.* February 2, 2022. https://news.mit.edu/2022/loci-methane-emissions-landfills-0202.

Wirawan, Soni S., Maharani D. Solikhah, Hari Setiapraja, and Agus Sugiyono. "Biodiesel Implementation in Indonesia: Experiences and Future Perspectives." *Renewable & Sustainable Energy Reviews* 189 (January 1, 2024): 113911. https://doi.org/10.1016/j.rser.2023.113911.

Woinarski, John C.Z., Andrew A. Burbidge, and Peter L. Harrison. "Ongoing Unraveling of a Continental Fauna: Decline and Extinction of Australian Mammals Since European Settlement." *Proceedings of the National Academy of Sciences of the United States of America* 112, no. 15 (February 9, 2015): 4531–40. https://doi.org/10.1073/pnas.1417301112.

Wolf, Jennyfer, Richard B. Johnston, Argaw Ambelu, Benjamin F. Arnold, Robert Bain, Michael Brauer, Joe Brown, et al. "Burden of Disease Attributable to Unsafe Drinking Water, Sanitation, and Hygiene in Domestic Settings: A Global Analysis for Selected Adverse Health Outcomes." *Lancet* 401, no. 10393 (June 5, 2023): 2060–71. https://doi.org/10.1016/s0140-6736(23)00458-0.

Woodcock, Ben A., Nicholas J.B. Isaac, James M. Bullock, David B. Roy, David G. Garthwaite, Andrew Crowe, and Richard F. Pywell. "Impacts of Neonicotinoid Use on Long-Term Population Changes in Wild Bees in England." *Nature Communications* 7 (August 16, 2016): 12459. https://doi.org/10.1038/ncomms12459.

World Agroforestry. "Niger's Re-Greening Revolution." July 16, 2013. https://www.worldagroforestry.org/news/niger's-re-greening-revolution.

World Bank. "Pakistan: Flood Damages and Economic Losses over USD 30 Billion and Reconstruction Needs over USD 16 Billion—New Assessment." Press Release No: SAR/2022. October 28, 2022. https://www.worldbank.org/en/news/press-release/2022/10/28/-pakistan-flood-damages-and-economic-losses-over-usd-30-billion-and-reconstruction-needs-over-usd-16-billion-new-assessme.

World Bank. "Trends in Solid Waste Management." Accessed October 28, 2023. https://datatopics.worldbank.org/what-a-waste/trends_in_solid_waste_management.html.

World Bank. "Water Security is Critical for Poverty Reduction, But Billions Will Remain Without Water Access Unless Urgent Action is Taken." May 20, 2024. https://www.worldbank.org/en/news/press-release/2024/05/19/water-security-is-critical-for-poverty-reduction.

World Commission on Environment and Development. "Report of the World Commission on Environment and Development: Our Common Future." 1987. http://www.un-documents.net/our-common-future.pdf.

World Counts. "Tons of Steel Recycled." Accessed March 8, 2024. https://www.theworld counts.com/challenges/planet-earth/mining/advantages-of-recycling-steel.

World Economic Forum. "This Chart Shows Which Countries Consume the Most or Least Fish." November 29, 2022. https://www.weforum.org/agenda/2022/11/chart-shows-countries-consume-fish-food-security/.

World Food Program USA. "8 Facts to Know About Food Waste and Hunger." March 22, 2022. https://www.wfpusa.org/articles/8-facts-to-know-about-food-waste-and-hunger.

World Health Organization. "Dioxins." November 29, 2023. https://www.who.int/news-room/fact-sheets/detail/dioxins-and-their-effects-on-human-health.

World Health Organization. "Household Air Pollution." December 15, 2023. https://www.who.int/news-room/fact-sheets/detail/household-air-pollution-and-health.

World Health Organization. "Human Biomonitoring: Facts and Figures." Copenhagen: Regional Office for Europe, 2015. https://iris.who.int/handle/10665/164588.

World Health Organization. "Lead Poisoning." August 11, 2023. https://www.who.int/news-room/fact-sheets/detail/lead-poisoning-and-health.

World Health Organization. "Legionellosis." September 6, 2022. https://www.who.int/news-room/fact-sheets/detail/legionellosis.

World Health Organization. "Malaria." December 4, 2023, https://www.who.int/news-room/fact-sheets/detail/malaria.

World Health Organization. "Natural Toxins in Food." March 10, 2023. https://www.who.int/news-room/fact-sheets/detail/natural-toxins-in-food.

World Health Organization. "Vitamin A Deficiency." Accessed July 20, 2024. https://www.who.int/data/nutrition/nlis/info/vitamin-a-deficiency.

World Health Organization. "WHO Global Air Quality Guidelines: Particulate Matter (PM2.5 and PM10), Ozone, Nitrogen Dioxide, Sulfur Dioxide and Carbon Monoxide." September 22, 2021. https://www.who.int/publications/i/item/9789240034228.

World Meteorological Organization. "Scientific Assessment of Ozone Depletion: 1994." Global Ozone Research and Monitoring Project—Report No. 37, Geneva, 1995. https://csl.noaa.gov/assessments/ozone/1994/copies.html.

World Nuclear Association. "Chernobyl Accident 1986." Accessed February 12, 2024. https://world-nuclear.org/information-library/safety-and-security/safety-of-plants/-chernobyl-accident.aspx.

World Nuclear Association. "Fukushima Daiichi Accident." Accessed February 9, 2024, https://world-nuclear.org/information-library/safety-and-security/safety-of-plants/-fukushima-daiichi-accident.aspx.

World Nuclear Association. "Nuclear Power in the World Today." Accessed February 9, 2024. https://world-nuclear.org/information-library/current-and-future-generation/-nuclear-power-in-the-world-today.aspx.

World Nuclear Association. "Safety of Nuclear Power Reactors." March 2, 2022. https://-world-nuclear.org/information-library/safety-and-security/safety-of-plants/safety-of-nuclear-power-reactors.

World Wildlife Fund. "Bycatch—A Sad Topic." https://www.fishforward.eu/en/project/by-catch/.

World Wildlife Fund. "World Wildlife Fund: History." https://www.worldwildlife.org/about/history.

World Wildlife Fund-UK. "8 Things to Know About Palm Oil." https://www.wwf.org.uk/updates/8-things-know-about-palm-oil.

Wright, John Paul, Bruce P. Lanphear, Kim N. Dietrich, Michelle Bolger, Lisa Tully, Kim M. Cecil, and Catherine Sacarellos. "Developmental Lead Exposure and Adult Criminal Behavior: A 30-Year Prospective Birth Cohort Study." *Neurotoxicology and Teratology* 85 (May 1, 2021): 106960. https://doi.org/10.1016/j.ntt.2021.106960.

Wright, Stephanie, and Paul J.A. Borm. "Applying Existing Particle Paradigms to Inhaled Microplastic Particles." *Frontiers in Public Health* 10 (May 30, 2022): 868822. https://doi.org/10.3389/fpubh.2022.868822.

Wu, Xiao, Erik Sverdrup, Michael D. Mastrandrea, Michael W. Wara, and Stefan Wager. "Low-Intensity Fires Mitigate the Risk of High-Intensity Wildfires in California's Forests."

Science Advances 9, no. 45 (November 10, 2023): eadi4123. https://doi.org/10.1126/sciadv. adi4123.

WWF Australia. "Plastic in Our Oceans Is Killing Marine Mammals." June 26, 2023. https://wwf.org.au/blogs/plastic-in-our-oceans-is-killing-marine-mammals/.

WWF International. "Plastic Ingestion by People Could Be Equating to a Credit Card a Week." June 13, 2019. https://www.wwf.eu/?348458/Plastic-ingestion-by-people-could-be-equating-to-a-credit-card-a-week.

Wyer, Katie E., David B. Kelleghan, Victoria Blanes-Vidal, Günther Schauberger, and Thomas P. Curran. "Ammonia Emissions from Agriculture and Their Contribution to Fine Particulate Matter: A Review of Implications for Human Health." *Journal of Environmental Management* 323 (December 1, 2022): 116285. https://doi.org/10.1016/j. jenvman.2022.116285.

Xu, Hui, Longwen Ou, Yuan Li, Troy R. Hawkins, and Michael Wang. "Life Cycle Greenhouse Gas Emissions of Biodiesel and Renewable Diesel Production in the United States." *Environmental Science & Technology* 56, no. 12 (May 16, 2022): 7512–21. https:// doi.org/10.1021/acs.est.2c00289.

Xu, Jia, Zhao Hong, Yujuan Zhang, Wen Yang, Xinhua Wang, Chunmei Geng, Yan Li, et al. "Reducing Indoor Particulate Air Pollution Improves Student Test Scores: A Randomized Double-Blind Crossover Study." *Environmental Science & Technology* (April 22, 2024). https://doi.org/10.1021/acs.est.3c10372.

Xu, Xiaoming, Prateek Sharma, Shijie Shu, Tzu-Shun Lin, Philippe Ciais, Francesco N. Tubiello, Pete Smith, Nelson Campbell, and Atul K. Jain. "Global Greenhouse Gas Emissions from Animal-Based Foods Are Twice Those of Plant-Based Foods." *Nature Food* 2 (September 3, 2021): 724–32. https://doi.org/10.1038/s43016-021-00358-x.

Yang, Xiaolin, Jinran Xiong, Taisheng Du, Xiaotang Ju, Yantai Gan, Sien Li, Longlong Xia, et al. "Diversifying Crop Rotation Increases Food Production, Reduces Net Greenhouse Gas Emissions and Improves Soil Health." *Nature Communications* 15 (January 3, 2024): 198. https://doi.org/10.1038/s41467-023-44464-9.

You, Yujia, Mingfang Ting, and Michela Biasutti. "Climate Warming Contributes to the Record-Shattering 2022 Pakistan Rainfall." *npj Climate and Atmospheric Science* 7 (April 13, 2024): 89. https://doi.org/10.1038/s41612-024-00630-4.

Young, Michael T., Karen Jansen, Kristen E. Cosselman, Timothy R. Gould, James A. Stewart, Timothy Larson, Coralynn Sack, Sverre Vedal, Adam A. Szpiro, and Joel D. Kaufman. "Blood Pressure Effect of Traffic-Related Air Pollution: A Crossover Trial of In-Vehicle Filtration." *Annals of Internal Medicine* 176, no. 12 (November 28, 2023): 1586–94. https://doi.org/10.7326/m23-1309.

Zagema, Bertram, Jan Kowalzig, Lyndsay Walsh, Andrew Hattle, Christopher Roy, and Peter Hans Dejgaard. "Climate Finance Shadow Report 2023. Assessing the Delivery of the $100 Billion Commitment." *Oxfam International.* June 5, 2023. https://doi. org/10.21201/2023.621500.

Zhang, Boya, Jennifer Weuve, Kenneth M. Langa, Jennifer D'Souza, Adam A. Szpiro, Jessica Faul, Carlos Mendes De Leon, et al. "Comparison of Particulate Air Pollution from Different Emission Sources and Incident Dementia in the US." *JAMA Internal Medicine* 183, no. 10 (October 1, 2023): 1080–89. https://doi.org/10.1001/jamainternmed.2023.3300.

Zhang, X., and X. Peng. "How Long for Plastics to Decompose in the Deep Sea?" *Geochemical Perspectives Letters* 22 (June 27, 2022): 20–25. https://doi.org/10.7185/ geochemlet.2222.

Zhang, Xin, Tan Zou, Luis Lassaletta, Nathaniel D. Mueller, Francesco N. Tubiello, Matthew D. Lisk, Chaoqun Lu, et al. "Quantification of Global and National Nitrogen Budgets for Crop Production." *Nature Food* 2, no. 7 (July 15, 2021): 529–40. https://doi.org/1 0.1038/s43016-021-00318-5.

Zhao, Chuang, Bing Liu, Shilong Piao, Xuhui Wang, David B. Lobell, Yao Huang, Mengtian Huang, Yitong Yao, et al. "Temperature Increase Reduces Global Yields of Major Crops in Four Independent Estimates." *Proceedings of the National Academy of Sciences of the United States of America* 114, no. 35 (August 15, 2017): 9326–31. https://doi. org/10.1073/pnas.1701762114.

Zhao, Xiaoying, Katrina Cornish, and Yael Vodovotz. "Narrowing the Gap for Bioplastic Use in Food Packaging: An Update." *Environmental Science & Technology* 54, no. 8 (March 23, 2020): 4712–32. https://doi.org/10.1021/acs.est.9b03755.

Zibold Reiss, Louise. "Strontium-90 Absorption by Deciduous Teeth." *Science* 134, no. 3491 (November 24, 1961): 1669–73. https://doi.org/10.1126/science.134.3491.1669.

Zientara, Ben. "Solar Panel Payback Period and ROI: How Long Does It Take for Solar Panels to Pay for Themselves?" *SolarReviews*. https://www.solarreviews.com/blog/how-to-calculate-your-solar-payback-period.

Zu Ermgassen, Erasmus K.H.J., Melquesedek Pereira de Alcântara, Andrew Balmford, Luis Barioni, Francisco Beduschi Neto, Murilo M.F. Bettarello, Genivaldo De Brito, et al. "Results from On-the-Ground Efforts to Promote Sustainable Cattle Ranching in the Brazilian Amazon." *Sustainability* 10, no. 4 (April 23, 2018): 1301. https://doi.org/10.3390/su10041301.

Zurub, Rewa E., Yusmaris Cariaco, Michael G. Wade, and Shannon A. Bainbridge. "Microplastics Exposure: Implications for Human Fertility, Pregnancy and Child Health." *Frontiers in Endocrinology* 14 (January 3, 2024): 1330396. https://doi.org/10.3389/fendo.2023.1330396.

Index